EXECUTIONER

*For Rodney Dale – who provided
the inspiration for this book*

EXECUTIONER

The Chronicles of a
Victorian
Hangman

STEWART P. EVANS

The History Press

This book was first published in 2004 by
Sutton Publishing Limited

This revised paperback edition first published in 2005

Reprinted in 2009 by
The History Press
The Mill, Brimscombe Port,
Stroud, Gloucestershire, GL5 2QG
www.thehistorypress.co.uk

British Library Cataloguing in Publication Data
A catalogue record for this book is available from the British
Library

ISBN 978 0 7509 3408 4

Typeset in 10.5/12pt Goudy.
Typesetting and origination by
Sutton Publishing Limited.
Printed and bound in Great Britain.

Contents

A Note to the New Edition

Information that came to hand after this book had been printed shows that Berry's last execution was not that of Edward Fawcett at Winchester in August in 1891, but that of Frederick Storey at Greenock in January 1892. Both *The Scots Black Kalendar* and *The Hangman's Record* give the wrong year, 1891, for Storey's execution, which is how the mistake arose, though Berry's own account of the execution does not date it, nor does he show it as his last execution. (see pp 374–6 for the account of this execution.) For this new edition, the list of Berry's executions has been corrected. Other minor corrections have been made to the text and some new material added. The ultimate fate of John 'Babbacombe' Lee has also been corrected as the author had previously been given incorrect information on this point.

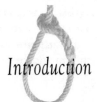

Introduction

The subject of capital punishment is emotive. However, this is not a book intended to argue the rights or wrongs of the 'ultimate penalty of the law', nor to moralise on the subject, nor to persuade the reader one way or the other concerning this vexed issue, although the stories told will no doubt influence the reader upon this question. It is more a biographical portrait of the life and times of one of the most notable and controversial figures thrown into prominence in the late Victorian era, and is intended both as a reference work and as an insight into the life of a 'hangman of England' and his grim work. It touches on many notable and infamous murder cases of the day and some of the notorious characters associated with these. Executions now seem part of the distant past, and are considered barbaric by most modern people. Yet the last executions in England were conducted as recently as August 1964, well within living memory and still using methods partly developed by Berry.

James Berry – a central figure in 'the man they couldn't hang' drama and, so he claims, the man who hanged Jack the Ripper – has remained something of a mystery, and past accounts of his life have been somewhat inaccurate and lacking in detail. In this book, then, I examine his life to a degree never before attempted, from his inauspicious early years, through his controversial adult years as policeman and executioner, and on to his quiet later years with their evangelical overtones.

Berry took a genuine interest in his 'victims' and the crimes they had committed. As a self-styled amateur criminologist he built his own 'black museum' and kept scrapbooks relating to his cases. He was also something of a showman, not averse to press publicity. As such he became an embarrassment to the government of the day to the degree that his activities were discussed in the House of Commons. It will be seen that his actions even resulted in new regulations with regard to capital punishment. His age was one of great change and development and he witnessed the end of the reign of Victoria and the beginning of the twentieth century. Prone to sometimes 'gilding the lily' or showing himself in a more favourable light, this fascinating and somewhat bizarre character was a man to whom great public curiosity and dread attached. Aware of this intense public fascination the press was always keen to recount the adventures of the public hangman and his 'dread offices', and this has resulted in an immense amount of source material on this public 'official', the like of whom will never be seen again. It has sometimes, though, been difficult to separate fact from fancy.

A staunch family man and a Yorkshireman born and bred, Berry was a 'no nonsense' character yet also full of contradictions. Capable of the cold, maybe even callous detachment that his work required, he could equally be sensitive and humane, not above being genuinely upset on occasions by the task he was called to do. He regarded his work as something of an exact science, and always aspired to be efficient and merciful. He worked to a 'table of drops' and on several occasions clashed with the prison authorities over details of an execution. This did not prevent a few horrific incidents on the gallows and, beyond doubt, the despatching of over 130 souls to eternity significantly affected him. He knew, though, that his job was necessary and believed he could carry it out with the skill and efficiency required. So he travelled throughout England, Wales, Scotland and Ireland, to act as the law's ultimate enforcer. The experiences of those years were etched on his mind with vivid clarity. As well as writing about them or issuing reports to the press, he toured the country talking of his career and showing flickering lantern slides of grim prison scenes. Chap-books with lurid titles such as *Cries of the Condemned* and *Groans of the Gallows* were still popular and Berry inspired awe in his audiences. He continues to fascinate to this day.

Notes on Sources

The reader will note that there is a large amount of conversation in the text. This is not invented by the author but is reproduced verbatim from the sources indicated. On his retirement Berry published a book, *My Experiences as an Executioner*, edited and written for him by H. Snowden Ward and henceforward referred to simply as *Experiences*. He also had another, smaller book, *Thoughts Above the Gallows*, published in 1905. Besides these, he left an unpublished manuscript, 'A Hangman's Wages' (henceforward referred to as *Wages*), which was written for him by a Mr Paterson, as well as notebooks, collections of press cuttings, and diaries that were quoted at length in two major newspaper serialisations of his career. All the sources I have used are noted in the text, I having deliberately decided to avoid lengthy footnotes that would detract from the narrative quality of the text and spoil the flow for the reader.

Where Berry's own texts are quoted, the grammar, spelling and punctuation are shown as in the original form. The 1888 government report on capital punishment, compiled by Lord Aberdare, is referred to simply as 'Aberdare'.

Previous books on Berry, such as his own *My Experiences as an Executioner* and Justin Atholl's study *The Reluctant Hangman: The Public and Private Life of a Hangman*, do not relate incidents in chronological order nor generally include dates. Furthermore, neither records all of Berry's executions. Steve Fielding's excellent touchstone work, *The Hangman's Record: Volume One 1868–1899*, offers such a list, together with brief details of each execution, but is not a specific study of Berry. This book aims to fill the gap.

1

Beginning of the odyssey

'What manner of man is this ex-hangman?'

It was an age when the news lacked the immediacy afforded by today's modern media. Newspapers were at the forefront of bringing stories of national interest to the attention of the public, and crime was always a subject of great fascination for Victorian readers. This was also an age when the ultimate penalty, death, was exacted by the law for the crime of murder – though no longer for theft or dishonesty – and the executioner was a national celebrity whose name was known to all; indeed, later in life Berry was to have his effigy made for display at Madame Tussaud's.

The Victorian era was a time of transition in the history of capital punishment. The death penalty was contentious even in those days and there was a strong abolitionist contingency, represented by the Howard Association. Abolitionists may have been in the minority, but governments did not like to be too closely linked with executions, so it fell to the High Sheriffs of the land to ensure, as best they could, that the sentence was carried out. In time, the barbarous public spectacles of slow strangulation that had typified the reign of William Calcraft as executioner were replaced by the private more technical affairs conducted by his successors, William Marwood and James Berry. These men conducted their hangings more carefully, using methods refined by experience, but 'accidents' still occurred.

Details of Berry's early years are confined to *Wages*, the manuscript put together by Mr Paterson from Berry's own recollections, but before turning to this Paterson looks back on the celebrated hangman's life:

. . . the curiosity that drew folk to see and hear the late hangman seemed to me morbid and illegitimate. On one matter my mind was, as I believed, finally made up. I had settled it that I was not going to join the company of those that went to hear Berry. Such was my honest conviction.

And James Berry has been in White Memorial pulpit! And he was there on my invitation! And I am now, by means of the pen, trying to open for him the doors of other pulpits! What has wrought the change in my attitude? Will my readers bear with me if I answer that question with considerable fullness?

Having thus embarked upon his short biography, injecting into the narrative as he does so many of his Presbyterian beliefs, he proceeded to explain the rationale behind the book:

I want James Berry to be seen. What manner of man is this ex-hangman? As he speaks he is seen . . . After knowing Berry there is astonishment at the fact that such a man was for ten years our Public Executioner. We want to know how it came about. He makes answer as follows.

Yes Sir, I am the late Public Executioner. . . . Standing now as I do with my hands free of this terrible business. I confess that I feel my position very keenly.

When I took the office I never imagined for one moment that I should be looked on as being different from other men . . .

There follows an account of how Berry became a hangman, and of the latter's apparent (we must question whether it was genuine) abhorrence of his late career. No doubt his feelings were ambivalent. The first part of the account is out of chronological sequence, clearly aimed at grabbing the reader's attention prior to what the writer presumably felt was the less interesting part of his biography. A new chapter initially entitled 'Early Life', but deleted and substituted with the more sensational 'The Black Sheep', tells of Berry's early years.

Berry was born on the morning of Sunday 8 February 1852 at Heckmondwike, in the Spen Valley of Yorkshire. His father was Daniel Berry, a wool-stapler, and his mother Mary Ann, formerly

Kelley. Daniel Berry seems to have enjoyed a fairly comfortable status, possessing his own wool warehouse. Both parents were Wesleyan Methodists, and his brothers and sisters became members of the Chapel, one brother going on to become a Christian worker and Temperance Advocate. James also had to attend Chapel, but, he tells us, 'I did it unwillingly'. It would appear that young Berry was a recalcitrant child in other ways too:

> Even when very young I was a trouble to my parents. One Sunday when I was about nine years of age I played truant from the Saltbath school and went down to the recreation grounds where some horses were feeding. I made an attempt to catch one of them – a chestnut blood horse. It allowed me to get quite near, then it wheeled round and struck out and caught me on my right cheek laying it open and nearly knocking out my right eye. I was stunned by the blow. By and by I was able to pick myself up but I hardly knew where I was till assistance came. I was led home with my cheek open and blood running down my clothes. I was accompanied by an ever growing crowd. My father and mother were visiting a relation. They rushed home as soon as they heard, and were greatly troubled to see me in such a state. The doctor was sent for. He sewed up the wounds in my cheek and ear and ordered that I at once be put to bed and kept very quiet as it was a case of life or death in twenty four hours. He was not sure that he would be able to stop the hemorage [sic] or keep down the inflamation [sic]. I was thus in a dangerous state. But the doctor was successful.

After a week the wound had to be opened to release the poison that could have caused mortification and death, and it was washed with friar's balsam. While convalescing he was taken in his father's phaeton to Harrogate to recover, but although the wound eventually healed he was left with a scar on his cheek that he carried for the rest of his life.

The result of this episode was that Berry was 'sent to a school to which ladies' daughters were sent'. He was there for just over a year but became so mischievous and caused so much trouble, that the principal, Madame Armitage, eventually lost patience and Berry was asked to stay away. Daniel Berry then sent his problem son to Heckmondwike Day School to be taught with the other boys of the town. However, young James had not been there long before, egged on by another boy who, Berry tells us 'was as bad if not worse than myself', he 'took it into his head' to abscond.

Every Monday morning I was given the school money to pay to the master for my education. Instead of giving it to the master I spent it on tops and sweets, and unknown to my parents, was absent from school for six weeks. The schoolmaster happened to meet my father in the market place and said 'James has not been at school for six weeks'. It was the first inkling my father had of it, as I had been sent off regularly to go to school. On that day I went home to dinner as usual. As I sat at the table my father asked me if I had been to school that morning. I said 'Yes.'

'Did you pay your school money to the master?'

'Yes.'

Then he told me to leave the table. He would teach me to speak the truth and go regularly to school. I was ordered to the front room. I at once left the table. After dinner my father came in with an ashplant and gave me a right good thrashing. I promised to give the money regularly to the master and never again play truant. For a time I kept my promise.

Berry was subsequently 'led away by another wicked boy'. He successfully played truant for two months before his father again detected his transgression. This time the schoolmaster told Daniel that he would prefer it if James could be sent to another school since he was setting the other boys a bad example. However, after a long conversation, Daniel managed to persuade the schoolmaster to give James another chance. The two of them took the boy home, where Daniel administered a thrashing 'until he was tired out', upon which the flogging was then taken up by the schoolmaster 'until both were satisfied'. James was then led to the school 'more like a prisoner than a scholar'. Further punishment followed, including Berry having to carry a pole with a large jar at each end to the schoolmaster's house a mile distant. There he was locked in an inner room for two hours, before being marched back to the school for his lessons. The school closed at four o'clock but Berry was locked in until eight at night, and then imprisoned in similar fashion the next day during the dinner hour. Berry, however, resolved to escape. Putting the master's desk up to the door, he climbed out through a sliding window above, went home, ate his dinner, and returned to the school. There he persuaded two boys to stand against the door while he scrambled up and got back into the classroom the same way he had escaped. Having replaced the desk in its usual position, he was sitting doing his lessons when the master returned to unlock the door. 'Flogging seems to do you no good', the latter remarked; 'I'll try what keeping you without meals will do.' At four o'clock that afternoon Berry was again locked in, having this time been set some work that the master reckoned would take until eight to complete. James was out in less than ten minutes through the window above the door. Taking his slate with him, he got his brother to show him how to do the work, had his tea, then enlisted the help of two boys to get back into the school. Just after eight the schoolmaster returned to let him out. Whether he was surprised to find the work done correctly we are not told, but he extracted a promise from Berry never to run away from school again, pledging in return to do his utmost to advance the lad's education provided he paid proper attention to his lessons.

Bearing in mind that these were the days of stringent Victorian schooling and discipline, it would seem that Berry's master was doing his best to put the boy on the right track. Though we might question the efficacy of meting out floggings, Berry certainly seemed to behave himself afterwards for a time. But one day he witnessed the master giving a similar thrashing to another young boy, and all because the lad 'could not say his lessons'. Feeling this to be unwarranted, young Berry protested, whereupon the master responded by striking him across the hand with a ruler, causing blood to ooze out of his hand. At this Berry was seized by 'an angry passion' and, without thinking, he hurled a heavy ruler at the master's head. The master staggered and fell, and Berry ran from the school. This time it was too much for the master to accept and he contacted Daniel Berry telling him that his son would not be allowed to return.

Daniel put James into his wool warehouse to make himself generally useful there, while alternative arrangements were made for his education. Shortly afterwards, James was sent away to a boarding school, Mr Hinchcliffe's Wren Green Academy, and it would appear that this time he made more of a success of his schooling, staying at Wren Green for three years and winning many prizes for writing, drawing and Indian-ink sketches.

Further incidents from Berry's schooldays give a fascinating insight not only into the life of the young Yorkshire schoolboy but also into those long gone days when children were required to amuse themselves to a degree unknown in modern times:

> While getting oat nuts in the Drill field one Saturday afternoon I noticed that two little boys were playing on the banks of the brook. At the place where they were playing the water was deep. While one of them was attempting to get some wild bluebells he overbalanced and fell into the water. The other boy began to scream. I ran to see what was the matter. I was just in time to see the child come up from the bottom. I jumped in and caught him and brought him to the bank and laid his face downward and allowed the water to run out of his body. I thought he was dead, but after a while he began to breathe and became sick. I carried him home to his mother. When she heard I had jumped into six feet of water and caught her child when he was coming up the third time she said: 'I am thankful Jimmie thou hast saved my child. Thou art a grand lad.'

There can be little doubt that Berry had saved the child's life, and it says much for his personal courage that he effected this timely rescue.

Another anecdote Berry relates concerns an adventure with his kite:

> While still very young I was fond of kite flying. On one occasion I made a monster kite with two plasterers laths and a calico front. It was six feet high and three feet broad. It had a tail about four yards long. At the end of the tail was a huge Chinese Lantern which I had purchased at a chapel Bazaar. I put a wax candle into the socket and along with another boy set out about eight o'clock at night to have a fly. The night was

dark but the stars were shining very bright. I ran out about 500 yards of twine that I had taken out of my father's warehouse. When it got up a great height some one brought another large ball of twine and I allowed the kite to run that out also. It was at a tremendous height and the lamp shone beautifully.

The inhabitants began to turn out to look at what was taken for a strange planet that had never been seen before. Hundreds of people were out to see what this great star was that was hovering above our town and gradually drawing nearer the earth. I had begun to wind in the twine. We noticed crowds of people looking up into the sky watching it. One of the boys went to see what the people were looking at. They said it was a new planet and that if it struck the earth we should all be burnt up with fire. The boy said: 'Why; it's only James Berry's kite with a Chinese Lantern tied to the end of its tail.' We could hear the people as they returned within their homes, laughing heartily at the way they had been taken in. One had said:– 'It's a planet.' Another, 'Nay it's a new star.' While another cried out 'It's a ball of fire denoting that the world's coming to an end.'

As we have already seen, not all Berry's adventures were without hazard. Another incident occurred one Sunday afternoon when he was strolling in fields with a friend. A large brewery was under construction nearby, and as the lads approached it they saw a bucket suspended on a rope from the top of the unfinished chimney, this being used to raise the mortar and bricks to the top. The bucket was at ground level so Berry asked his friend to haul him up so that he could survey the surrounding area. The boy did so and Berry was soon enjoying 'a grand view' of the village and surrounding countryside. Berry then began to unloose the rope with the intention of descending, but unfortunately the iron hook on the bucket snagged on the ironwork of the chimney fittings. Unable to release it, Berry was forced to slide down the rope, a painful exercise during which he found it necessary to keep resting on projecting stones 'or I would have fallen in a faint' and both hurt his hands and burnt his trousers. According to Berry, he was in such a state when he got to the bottom that he had to be carried home. On the following Monday the contractor discovered the bucket was at the top of the chimney and, learning that young Berry was the culprit, went to inform Daniel of his son's misdemeanour. Having been suitably reprimanded, Berry sought out the contractor, who told him that he was 'sorry to have me summoned for damages' and offered to give him two shillings and sixpence if he would reascend the rope and come down with the bucket. Berry explained that it was stuck fast, but the contractor provided instructions on how to release it, a hammer to strike the bolt, and the half-crown in advance. James removed his jacket and climbed the rope inside the chimney. It proved easier going up than coming down, and he reached the top in 20 minutes, whereupon he released the bucket, adjusted the rope in the pulley, and shouted to the men below that all was ready for the bucket to be lowered. Safely back at ground level, he was met by his father, who thrashed him for not doing what he was told and 'also gave the contractor a bit of his mind'.

The land on which the brewery in question was built had originally belonged to his mother's family, indicating that they were not poor. Berry notes that a well on the land gave a good supply of clean water, it being the quality of this that had led to the brewery acquiring the land.

These early adventures reveal that Berry was a headstrong lad with steady nerves and a spirit of adventure, but also somewhat footloose, unpredictable and stubborn. Those traits, perhaps, gave early indications that his future career would be anything but ordinary; the mundane did not appeal to James Berry.

2

Running away from home and early careers

'We left home when all was still a little after midnight . . . '

The year 1868 saw James Berry reach sixteen years of age, his schooldays behind him. It also saw the last public execution to take place in Britain; that of Michael Barrett, a Glasgow Fenian, hanged on 26 May by the public executioner, William Calcraft, in front of Newgate Prison. From then on, as a result of new legislation, executions were conducted within prison walls out of public view, both to reduce the tasteless and disorderly scenes such events frequently resulted in and, to some degree, to appease the abolitionists.

For Berry it was fortunate that his father owned a warehouse, for it gave him the opportunity to work there until he decided upon a career. Another of his tales dates from this period:

Take another incident. When I was a youth of sixteen I was going on an errand for my father to a place some 4½ miles from the warehouse. There was a short cut across some fields. It was heavy walking. The drifts of snow made it almost impossible for me to accomplish the journey. The short cut led past a farm steading and thereon by a footpath from field to field. I had got onto the footpath and through one field and had reached the steps by which the climb was made into the next field. I sat down on the bottom step to have a rest. When I rose, without any reason for doing so, I went along the hedge for about ten yards. All the explanation that I can give is that I was led to do it. By the time I had gone these ten yards I heard a kind of moan. My attention was drawn to the surface of the snow.

There were cracks in the snow at the place where the moan seemed to come from. I began to remove the snowdrift. It was very deep by the hedge bottom. Underneath I found a woman with a beautiful lambswool shawl round her head and shoulders. I unwrapped her to see her face and her eyes were half open. I asked her how she came there but she gave no answer. I touched her cheek. It was cold. I saw that she had become unconscious. I hastened to the police station and told what I had seen. The sergeant sent a police officer with me and I led him to where the woman was lying. The officer went to the farm house and got the loan of a door and the woman was laid on it. Another officer came to our assistance and the woman, who was well known, was carried to her home. She was a woman in good circumstances. She had the best of medical attention and of nursing but some of her toes were frost bitten and had to be amputated. She lived for some time afterwards but never fully recovered her natural healthy state. Nor was that to be wondered at. She had been out a night and nearly a day in a night of wild freezing snowstorms.

Another experience that Berry recalls occurred when he was just 16. He and a friend shared a strong desire to go to sea, so, in mid-November, the two lads secretly left home after midnight and for two days worked their way to Goole. After spending their second night away there, they made their way in the morning to the docks to seek a ship needing a cabin boy. A captain eyed Berry suspiciously and asked for his details, warning him that a seafaring life was a hard one, but Berry was undeterred, defiantly declaring his resolve to go to sea in the hope of one day working his way up to become captain of his own ship. Privately convinced the boy had run away from a respectable home, the captain nonetheless took him on, with the words, 'However our voyage will tell a tale on you.' Berry was set to work cleaning the captain's boots, and polishing swords and cutlasses.

While Berry was thus engaged, his friend was trying to secure employment on other ships. However, the boy's father had communicated with the police and arrived in Goole to find his son, whom, once located, he took home to Heckmondwike the same evening. Berry slept onboard ship that night, but when the crew went ashore the next day – the ship being due to sail at midnight – he asked the captain for an allowance to buy some clothes and leave to go ashore. Equipped with a 5 shillings subsidy he wandered around the town, bought some veal pies and a glass of wine, and then, having decided that a seaman's life was not for him, went to the station to enquire about a train back home. He bought a ticket to Wakefield and after arriving there at 8 p.m., he walked the rest of the way home, arriving at midnight.

According to Berry, the ship he had been on – an old three-masted, fully-rigged, wooden vessel – was towed to the mouth of the Humber at midnight and set sail just as a fierce storm moved in from the north-east. Neither she nor her captain and twenty-two men were ever seen again. Some time later the captain of a steamer reported from the Baltic that he had seen floating wreckage that he believed to be part of a three-masted vessel that had traded between Goole and the Baltic ports.

Back in charge of the books in his father's warehouse, Berry was allowed to keep some pigeons in a loft that he had constructed in the top storey of the warehouse. He noticed one night that one of these had not gone into the cote with the others, so, true to form, he climbed the down-pipe to reach the offending bird. Having reached the top of the pipe, three storeys up, he crept along the edge of the spouting, before, unsurprisingly, he fell. It was to prove a narrow escape from death, his fall being broken by a covered archway that led from the house to the building. Even so, he suffered a broken leg and severe shock, and was confined to his room for some weeks afterwards, his mother and sister in constant attendance. As soon as he was fit enough to be moved he was taken to Matlock to convalesce, after which he returned home to resume work at the warehouse. As for the pigeons, his exasperated father had the unfortunate creatures' necks twisted.

The unsettled Berry did not appear to have much of a future before him, and his mother was understandably anxious for him to learn a trade, believing that he would be too old to do so unless he acted quickly. Berry expressed interest in becoming a joiner and cabinet-maker and was accordingly found a position within that trade. Unfortunately his employer dabbled in shares and lost his money, his financial ruin such that he had to auction off his business to meet his debts, subsequently setting sail for a new life in New Zealand. So, after six months of apprenticeship, Berry's new career was brought to an unhappy end. He returned to his father's warehouse but was again told by his mother that he needed to learn a trade since the business could not provide a living for all the family.

Berry this time decided to be an engineer and was placed as an apprentice to Messrs Sands and Walker, a firm of machine-makers, engineers and iron-founders in Heckmondwike. Initially he was put to work on a screwing machine – a job that he so 'gave his mind' to that he was soon able to put a screw on a bolt and make a corresponding nut to fit. Having served nine months on the machine, he advanced to the next stage of his new career. The foreman, impressed by the way he had taken to the work, gave him charge of an upright drilling machine, warning him always to fasten the ironwork he was to drill before setting the machine in motion, and never to hold any article he was drilling unless he wanted to risk losing an arm. Berry operated the drill without mishap for four months, but one day the blacksmith brought a handle through which he wanted a hole drilled. Asked to do the job before lunchtime that day, Berry allowed his usual standards to drop, not only failing to fasten the handle but also attempting to hold it while the drill was in action. As the drill began to bite he found himself unable to retain his grip – 'the tension was too strong' – and moments later, having held on as long as he could, he was thrown onto his back. Thankfully a fellow worker had seen what was happening and immediately stopped the machine, probably saving Berry's arm. So shocked was Berry by this incident that he refused to return to the works and gave up all idea of being an engineer.

His next apprenticeship was with a man who was 'at once butcher, grocer, draper and keeper of General Post Office', the tasks allotted to Berry being similarly varied. On Monday mornings he had to wash out the butcher's shop, scrub the logo, and clean the weights and scales. In the afternoon he had to weigh up currants, raisins and sugar until five o'clock, after which he was required to walk 2 miles to Starmingley Station for the mail. Kindly allowed by the stationmaster to open the bag and sort the mail inside the booking office, he delivered the mail on the way back before being provided with tea. After that he had to dress the grocery window.

On Tuesdays he had to be up by 5.00 a.m. in order to collect the mail, delivery of which took two hours and was undertaken before breakfast. After breakfast he had to weigh soda and other items of stock. Wednesday was 'killing day', Berry being required to attend the slaughterhouse, where he learned the art of butchering.

Berry found the Post Office work demanding and considered the other tasks alone were sufficient fully to occupy his time. In addition, his 'bedroom' was uncomfortable, doubling up as storeroom with sacks of flour and other items kept in stock there. His health began to suffer, and eventually, after three months of this, he asked his 'master' to allow a small extra wage for his Post Office duties. When this was refused he lost heart. The following Sunday, he tells us, 'instead of going to church I ran away home to Heckmondwike'. Berry's attentive mother appealed to the employer to continue the apprenticeship without the Post Office work, but this was flatly refused, the latter being regarded by the employer as a sort of payment in kind. As a result, Berry was once more unemployed.

After a few weeks at home he was apprenticed to his uncle Clegg, of the Britannia Printing Works. Once more he put his mind to the work, swiftly grasping the skills involved, and he advanced quickly, overtaking some who had been there years before him. After three and a half years at the works it looked as though he had at last found his niche, but, perhaps inevitably, his progress caused resentment, the foreman being particularly jealous. Faced with an ultimatum – to submit to the foreman or abandon his apprenticeship – Berry, true to form, 'left at once and went home'.

More of the same was to follow. His father came across an advertisement in the *Leeds Mercury* for a turn-over apprentice at a printing works in Leeds, and James agreed to apply. A horse was harnessed to the gig and, recalls Berry, 'my dear father himself drove me over to Leeds'. Accepted for the post, he was engaged for eighteen months in order to complete his apprenticeship, but just nine months later, he tells us, 'a disturbance arose that caused my dismissal'. No further elaboration of this incident is given.

He again returned to the warehouse where he began to weave blankets by loom, but soon afterwards he 'took it into his head' to go into the Lancashire and Yorkshire Railway service, where he commenced duties as a porter at Thornhill Station near Dewsbury. After a few months he transferred to Wakefield as a parcel porter, and not long afterwards he was made night superintendent at Low Moor Station. While acting in that capacity he caught some engine cleaners stealing oil from the cups of the Manchester Express that was standing in a covered siding at the station, and on another occasion he caught a man attempting to break into the booking office. Perhaps experiences such as these helped pave the way for his next career move. Work in law enforcement beckoned.

3

Police service and a wife

'I was sent out as Police Officer . . .'

Getting tired of the railway service', Berry applied for appointment as a police officer with the Wakefield West Riding Depot. The Victorian provincial police forces were by this time well organised and offered an able young man the chance of a career with good promotion and pay prospects. His 'credentials being considered very satisfactory', Berry was duly appointed and given six weeks' training, during which, he tells us, 'I had the good fortune to meet the young lady who is now my wife.' The young lady was Sarah Ann Ackroyd, a year younger than Berry and daughter of John Ackroyd, a wool-comber of 112 Tumbling Hill, Horton.

Sarah was on a visit to her aunt and uncle who catered for the depot and provided lodgings for the young recruits. Seeing her standing at the private entrance to her uncle's house, one Saturday afternoon, Berry 'mustered courage' to speak to her, it being the first time that he had 'ventured to address her'. He was clearly smitten:

It was also the first time that I had ever felt my heart in a flicker. I had never been in love before. I asked her if she would do some sewing for me. After some little hesitation she consented. I journeyed into Wakefield; bought the material; took it to her as I got it from the draper, told her what I wanted done with it and said that I would pay whatever she charged.

During the week I again had the honour of having a few words with her. Before her visit to her aunt and uncle had come to an end I had pleaded to be accepted as her future husband. She refused to consent without consulting her

15

mother. I got her address from her aunt. I wrote to her that I would visit her in her own home and get her answer there. I went to her home and was introduced to her mother. Before I left the daughter consented to an engagement. I came on my way rejoicing.

For originality of 'chat-up lines', Berry's sewing request was a winner. No one could criticise him either for being slow off the mark in terms of courtship: he had spotted the love of his life and there was no way he was going to let the grass grow under his feet.

His six weeks of training complete, Berry 'was sent out as Police Officer to Keighley', and soon found himself busy.

My first case was one of fowl stealing. I had also several other cases. My success brought my name before the public. I was there for ten months. I was corresponding with my sweetheart in Bradford and I began to desire a home of my own. My sweetheart wished to live in Bradford so I resigned my appointment in Keighley and came to Bradford with the purpose of getting an appointment there. I made application to the Chief Constable and got the promise of an appointment when a vacancy occurred. While waiting for the coming of the vacancy I secured temporary employment as a grocer-warehouseman without having to leave Bradford. I kept that appointment until there was an opening for me in the Bradford Borough Police Force. By and by that opening occurred and I became one of the Bradford Police Officers. Soon after that I got married.

The wedding, a Wesleyan Methodist service, took place at the Richmond Terrace Chapel, Horton, Bradford on 6 April 1874, and Berry's address at that time was given as 11 Blythe Street, Horton. James was aged 22 at the time, and Sarah 21. Oddly, Berry says very little about his marriage, but, never slow in singing his own praises, he had much to say about his time in the police service:

I was credited by my brother constables with being an effective officer. That was due to the fact that I was fortunate in bringing to justice several notorious criminals. One of these was a man who was wanted for breaking into a Pawn-broker's shop. Detectives had been out day and night looking for this man but had not been able to find any trace of him. I had seen his photo in the detective office. I had the good fortune when on duty in Manningham Lane to see the man himself. I at once apprehended him and took him to the Town Hall and locked him up. He was tried and sentenced to six months imprisonment.

A great many soldier deserters came under my notice; also sailors absenting themselves without leave of absence. This happened with such frequency that I was credited with being a very smart and intelligent officer.

Among the cases given unto me to deal with was a case of arson. On a Sunday afternoon the letters in a pillar box had been maliciously set on fire. I was able to secure reliable information and apprehended three youths. They were defended by the best solicitor in the town. They ought to have been arrested on a warrant taken out by the Postal authorities. That had not been done. On the ground of that technical omission they were acquitted.

On one occasion I noticed two men in the middle of the day making plans of a jeweller's shop at the corner of Thornton Road. My suspicions were aroused. I called in the assistance of another officer. We arrested them on the charge of loitering with intent to commit a felony. They turned out to be two dangerous thieves and burglars from Manchester. They got twelve months imprisonment with hard labour.

I also arrested two men who were dressed like gentlemen and were carrying a little mahogany case with brass fittings. They were going from shop to shop representing that they were Inspectors from the Town Hall sent to test the weights and measures. They were receiving money under false pretences. I followed them into a grocer's shop in Little Horton and caught them in the act of adjusting the scales. I locked the shop door and handcuffed them together in the shop, and marched them to the Town Hall and charged them with the offence. They pleaded guilty before the magistrates next morning and were sentenced to the Sessions and there were given eighteen months with hard labour.

On the street one day I faced a mad dog from which everybody was fleeing. I was fortunate in being able to fell it with my truncheon. I put a string round its neck and took it to the Town Hall where it was ordered to be destroyed.

One night I was on Market St beat. It was twelve o'clock midnight. The Town Hall bells were chiming:– 'A few more years shall roll'. The snow was falling in large flakes. The last train from Leeds had just come in. A woman cut into Market Street and walked right up to the Exchange. I had been standing under the portico. I stepped out and asked her where she was going. She wanted to know the way to Manchester. I turned up lamp on her face. She tried to hide her features. Withdrawing her shawl I at once recognised her as a woman whose photo I had seen in the Town Hall as the photo of a woman who was wanted for a series of burglaries. I took her into custody. On the way to the Town Hall she dropped a bundle of pawn tickets. These shewed where she had deposited the stolen goods. Next morning she was brought up and handed over to the West Riding Police.

During the time that I was in the Bradford Borough Police Force I was twice over complimented by the magistrates. After serving nine months the Chief Constable had me taken before the Watch Committee and given a rise of salary, advancing me into the Second class. After serving eighteen months I was advanced into the First class. It was evident that if a policeman was obedient to his superior officers and willing to give himself to his work there was no necessity why he should not rise to a higher position in the calling he was following.

After serving some years I resigned the Bradford Borough Police appointment.

Berry's explanation for his sudden resignation was that he didn't get the credit for the work he did, and that the powers that be wouldn't make him a detective 'when it suited me'. Having arrested a burglar, he continues, whom a number of detectives had been seeking for some time 'to my disappointment, they handed him over to an officer in another town. And nobody heard about me, and no credit came my way!' This, according to Berry, was but one of several similar cases, and in frustration he complained to the Chief Constable, at that time James Withers. Withers attempted to placate him, but on being told that, despite being 'a good man', he could not be considered for promotion by the Watch Committee as they felt he had not served long enough, Berry's patience snapped, such that, he tells us, 'in a fit of pique I threw off my uniform and went to serve in a boot shop'.

In a complete turnaround, he decided to start a business as an egg and butter merchant. Perhaps he saw a chance to build up his own business and become wealthy; money was certainly a big consideration for Berry. Whatever, the business was soon thriving to the point that he was obliged to buy a pony and cart to transport his wares. Then, however, he characteristically made a blunder, being 'foolish enough to begin to let his customers have credit'. His catchment area had a 10-mile radius and he claimed to have a weekly turnover upwards of 100 boxes of fresh butter, each containing 30lb, besides a very good egg trade. Before long he was allowing more on trust than he could afford, many of the shops he was supplying exploiting his little capital. Unable to pay bills to his own suppliers, his debts grew, and he was eventually forced to sell up and pay off his creditors as best he was able.

By this point he and Sarah had four children, so he was desperate to find alternative employment (the couple had six children in all but dates of birth and death are not given). It would appear that three died either as babies or in their infancy. Passing a machine shop, Berry went in, asked for work, and was taken on, but after working there for upwards of twelve months, trade slackened and men were laid off, Berry among them.

With police experience to his credit he applied to the Chief Constable of Nottingham Borough Police Force for a post. He was sent for, passed his medical examination and appointed to that Force, but he remained there for only twelve months, his reason for leaving given as follows:

> One night when on duty I was called into a jeweller's shop. The master had been drinking and was in the grip of delerium tremens. He was threatening to kill his wife who had her sister with her for protection. I had a very rough time of it with him.

At last I had him safely tied down in bed. When I went out I had to pass by the back of a licensed house to get into my beat. I met my sergeant. He asked me if I had a report to make. I told him what had just occurred. Without making the investigation that he could easily have made he accused me with oaths of telling an untruth. In my indignation I told him that he was a sample of men who were put into positions before they were fit for the place;- looking after other people when they could not control themselves. I was taken before the Chief Constable for speaking to a superior officer in the way I had spoken. He had the whole matter investigated. He found that the Sergeant had been the aggressor and that he was to blame; and the Sergeant was reprimanded. But the incident had taken away all feeling of security in the Service. I felt that no one was safe under such an officer. I resigned my appointment and returned to Bradford. I might mention that when serving in the Nottingham Boro Force I had the honour of being on duty when the Prince of Wales our present King opened the Technical College there. When a photo was taken of the opening ceremony I was at the entrance and appeared in that photo.

Disillusioned, Berry returned to Bradford, seeking orders for coal on salary and commission. He kept his agency for a time but 'a slight error about some accounts that were not collected led to a misunderstanding' and he 'gave up the situation'. Enterprising as always, Berry then secured his own orders and for a time did 'nicely', but soon he again began to run short of capital. Owing a large sum of money to one coal merchant in particular – his main supplier – he made arrangements to manage one of the latter's branches at a weekly wage, a portion of which he paid back until his debt was cleared. However, when the merchant subsequently sold off that branch, he found himself unemployed once more.

Scanning advertisements in the *Bradford Observer*, Berry noticed one for a boot-salesman's post and successfully applied. His new 'master' was very pleased with his work, considering him 'a clever salesman', and before long he had learnt the 'secrets of the trade' and become 'an expert in the business', boasting 'My master often said that I could not have done better even if I had been brought up to the business.' There was, however, a downside:

> The only drawback was the little money at the week-end. When Saturday night came at eleven o'clock my weekly wage, twenty shillings, was given to me. I used to think;- 'If I cannot make more than that a week I will not settle in the Bootsale trade.' I had a wife and four children to keep. I had such a thirst for more money that I would at that time have done anything to secure greater comfort for those dependent on me. I used to think of trying a foreign country.
>
> While I was in that mood a young man came in accompanied by a soldier of the 17th Lancers. I began to ask the soldier about his calling. He told me that if I thought of enlisting in the cavalry I should join the Scots Greys. He said that was the best regiment in the British service. After a long conversation he left. I began to ponder over what he had told me.
>
> But it was not to soldiering I was to turn . . .

By 1881 the British census showed that Berry and Sarah, both 29 years of age, were living with Sarah's mother, Hannah Ackroyd, a 58-year-old widow and worsted weaver, at 58 Thorp Street, Horton, in Bradford. They had two children, Herbert aged 5 and Luther aged 6. It would appear that two infants had already died.

4

The office of public executioner

'Altogether, Mr. Marwood never encouraged me . . . '

In 1861 treason and murder became the only statutory capital crimes. Indeed, since 1841 only murderers had been hanged in this country (except in 1861, when a man was hanged for a nasty attempted murder). Between 1837 and 1868 a total of 347 murderers were executed, the majority by William Calcraft. While the plea of insanity had been recognised as a legitimate defence since the seventeenth century, in 1843 Judges' Rules, set out as a result of the McNaughton case (McNaughton had murdered Mr Edward Drummond, the secretary of Sir Robert Peel), legally defined insanity, such that for the plea to succeed it had to be established that:

> . . . at the time of committing the act, the party accused was labouring under such defect of reason, from disease of the mind, as not to know the nature and quality of the act he was doing, or, if he did know it, that he did not know what he was doing was wrong.

The government line on the controversial subject of capital punishment in general was that it had to be carried out by the local authorities: the High Sheriffs for the area in which the sentence had been passed. Thus the executioner was employed locally rather than by the government itself. The official public executioner from 1829 to 1874 – making him the longest serving hangman – was William Calcraft. Paid a yearly retainer by the London Sheriffs of £20 for his duties as executioner for the City of London and Middlesex, he was 'number one', his services also being used throughout the kingdom. His successor, William Marwood, served from 1874 to 1883, and was seen by Berry as a sort of mentor from whom he gained most knowledge relating to his grim occupation.

Over the years, death by hanging evolved from a primitive public spectacle to a private and technical process. Although the 'drop' style gallows, with a trapdoor in the platform, was already in use before Calcraft's time, the drop used was very short and usually resulted in death by strangulation. Calcraft was often required to descend below the gallows and hold on to his victim, adding his own weight to expedite death. He thus gained something of a reputation as a bungler and a 'butcher'. Many harrowing and unseemly acts were witnessed on the scaffold at public executions, and it was popularly believed that the executioner must be a brutal and degraded being. Calcraft was once asked if he was ever agitated or upset by his task.

'No, not a bit. Why should I be? I am only doing my duty,' replied the hangman.
'Still it is a very dreadful duty; and even as a matter of duty, few persons could kill a man without . . .'
'Kill a man!' broke in the elderly executioner, 'Who kills a man? I never killed a man.'

There was a momentary embarrassment for his questioner, and then Calcraft proceeded to explain, 'They kills themselves. I merely put the rope round their necks and knock away the platform beneath them.'

He then remarked emphatically, 'I don't kill 'em; it's their own weight as does it.' (*Cassell's Saturday Journal*, 23 January 1892)

Unlike Calcraft, Marwood was not officially retained by the City of London and Middlesex authorities on a yearly payment. Born in Horncastle in 1818, and, like Calcraft before him, a shoemaker by trade until he began his new profession, he carried out his first execution in April 1872 at Lincoln Castle, where he had been employed by the local authorities. He was the first English executioner to refine the 'long drop', a more humane method, already used in Ireland, that usually resulted in an instant death. From August 1868 all executions were conducted in private behind the prison walls, public executions having been abolished by the Capital Punishment Amendment Act. By the time Calcraft retired in May 1874, Marwood, by then aged 56, had a reputation for proficiency. He was accepted as the new 'number one' and also conducted executions in London. A popular riddle was often repeated in homes across the country around that time:

'If Pa killed Ma who'd kill Pa?'
'Marwood'

'Marwood died.' With these two words Berry introduced the calling he decided to follow. It was 4 September 1883, and the great public official had died quietly during the afternoon in his little house in Horncastle, Lincolnshire. The executioner's craft had been improved greatly by Marwood with his more technical approach and his favoured long drop that resulted in the dislocation of the vertebrae and a quick death. He had even formulated a 'table of drops', giving the varying lengths of drop required in relation to the weight of the subject. The heavier the subject, the shorter the drop. Marwood was disdainful of Calcraft, calling him 'the short drop man', and adding, 'He choked his prisoners to death!' 'He *hanged* them,' Marwood would boast, 'I *execute* them.' Proud of his grim calling, Marwood had a sign, 'Crown Office', displayed on his Horncastle cobbler's shop. He also displayed the coiled ropes of his calling in his shop, including one of Calcraft's, 'a rope that terminated in a clumsy slip-knot of most unworkmanlike appearance'. In those days the hangman supplied and used his own ropes, and the one used by Marwood was described as 'a fearsome object which made one's blood run cold, a contraption of his own invention with a running noose fitted with a ring of metal, fashioned to his order at a Government workshop'. Major Arthur Griffiths, a writer on prisons and crime who served with the prison service for many years, and who from 1878 to 1896 was Inspector of Prisons, met Marwood when the latter was visiting the Home Office to discuss methods of inflicting capital punishment:

He was a connoisseur in rope, and greatly preferred to use that of his own selection, as he told us one day when he tried his 'noose' on some of us. I shall not easily forget the feeling of the awful cravat around my neck, the horror of it greatly emphasised by the gruesome touch of his twisted, knotty, extraordinarily powerful hands. 'It's a first rate article,' he wished to impress on us, when we would have no more of his experiments; 'I always use the purest hemp; it's what I supply the Colonies when they ask for it' (he did quite a trade in 'rope'); 'quite silky to the touch; none of your rough Manila, which has no grip.' (*Fifty Years of Public Service*)

When he died Marwood had been public executioner for over eleven years and had amassed a fair amount of wealth, owning several cottages and other investments. Although he had initially been highly regarded it was noted 'during the latter part of his career [that he] was frequently drunk' (Aberdare report). A vague rumour circulated that his death was somehow connected with the Irish Invincibles, as a result of him hanging Irish Nationalists, but the coroner at his inquest scotched that story, giving details of his final illness during which a doctor had attended Marwood regularly from 30 August until the day of his death and pronouncing the cause of death as acute pneumonia. A sale of Marwood's effects took place by auction at Horncastle on 6 November, with brokers from London and elsewhere present. A rope realised 90 shillings and a Gladstone bag 60 shillings.

Berry tells of how he decided to follow in Marwood's footsteps and enter the dread calling of public executioner. The principal attraction was the good money a hangman could earn, but he claimed also to have been influenced by Marwood directly, having both met him and witnessed executions he conducted, including that of the infamous burglar/murderer Charles Peace, although this has not been confirmed. Berry puts it thus (extracted from *Wages*):

Marwood died. The executioner's post was vacant. I knew that in the line in which I was then working there was no prospect of a material improvement in my position. I was troubled at the poverty-stricken condition of my family whom I could not keep in reasonable comfort. I knew that I was a man of no extraordinary ability so that my chances of rising were few. The vacancy in the executioner's post seemed to me my only chance in life, my 'tide in the affairs of life.' The work was distasteful but I had to weigh my family's wants against my personal inclination. It seemed to me at that time that my duty was clear so I made application for the vacant position.

Besides the edge had for me been taken off the horror of such a grim calling by having met Marwood one day while still in the Police Force. I had called at a friend's house. Marwood was staying there and I was introduced to him. I met him again a few days later and spent an evening in his company. He was a quiet unassuming man, kindly and almost benevolent in his manners and was in no way ashamed of his calling though reticent in speaking about it, excepting to those whom he knew well. He keenly felt the odium with which his office was regarded by the public; and aimed by performing his duties in a satisfactory manner, and by conducting his private life respectably, at removing the stigma which he felt was undeserved. At times the attitude of the public towards him was keenly felt and I well remember one time when this subject was the topic of conversation at the supper table that he remarked to a gentleman present:– 'My position is not a pleasant one' and turning to me repeated with emphasis 'No! it is not a pleasant one.' The words seemed to come from the depths of a full heart and I shall never forget their pathos and feeling. Altogether, Mr. Marwood never encouraged me in any way to think of his calling with feelings of envy; and though he did give me all particulars of his methods and apparatus it was merely because I asked all sorts of questions from natural curiosity.

It was only when in company with Mr. Marwood, with whom I became quite friendly, that I ever contemplated the question of capital punishment. At other times it was far from my thoughts. My application for the post, which was left vacant at his death, was, therefore, in no way the result of a personal desire for the work or of a pre-conceived plan. I was simply driven to it by the poverty-stricken condition of my family, which I was unable to keep in reasonable comfort upon my earnings . . .

Berry's memoirs, from his old diaries and notebooks, were serialised in *The Saturday Post* (hereafter referred to as *The Post*) in 1914 and in *Thomson's Weekly News* (hereafter referred to as *Thomson's*) in 1927. In the account of Berry's relationship with Marwood that appeared in *Thomson's* on 29 January 1927, there is some interesting additional detail, and wording, to the above:

> It was only when in company with him that I ever thought of the question of capital punishment, and I even refused his offer to go with him as his assistant.
>
> In time he passed out of my thoughts altogether, though I had bought a rope from him. But one day I was aroused in the streets of Bradford by the shouts of the newsboys, 'Death of Marwood, the hangman!'
>
> They were shouting out the news at the pitch of their voices, and I remember that as I bought a paper I wondered who would carry out the work which he had so skilfully performed.
>
> 'Why not yourself?'
>
> I started at what seemed the voice of the tempter in my ear, and then came the thought that I was poor and my family ill-provided for at the moment.
>
> It almost seemed as if Fate had kept me poor to drive me into the position. It seemed that I was predestined from birth to become the follower of Marwood, for, extraordinary though it may seem, the Chief Constable of Bradford was setting out to ask me to take the job at the very moment I was setting out to ask him to use his influence with the people of London.
>
> He knew that I had been friendly with the dead man; he knew my character as well as I did myself, and from that moment there was never any doubt about it.

The account in *Wages* states:

> Thus it came to pass that I made application to the Sheriffs of London and Middlesex in September 1883. There were some 1400 applicants for the post. After waiting some time I received the following letter

London

The Sheriffs of London and Middlesex will be at the Old Bailey on Monday next, the 24th instant, at 2 o'clock p.m. for the purpose of seeing the selected applicants for the post of executioner.

If you (as one of those selected for consideration) are disposed to attend at the above time and place you are at liberty at your own expense to do so.

19th September 1883

To Mr. J. Berry

Of course I kept the appointment and was duly examined amongst some nineteen others and was told that the chosen executioner would be communicated with.

The Times of Tuesday 25 September reported on the selection for the post of public executioner:

THE PUBLIC EXECUTIONER. – A telegram was received at Bradford yesterday afternoon from James Berry, who was in London, stating that he had been appointed public executioner for the Corporation of the City of London only, and that he was going to the Home Office, as he stated, to 'receive and sign.' Berry is about 30 years of age, is at present employed as a messenger by Mr. Joseph Wilson, boot and shoe dealer, Ivegate, Bradford, and was some time ago for a short time a member of the Bradford Borough police force. He was a friend of Marwood, and had frequent discussions with him on the best and most effective modes of 'despatching' criminals.

It would seem that an enthusiastic Berry had assumed that he had successfully passed all the interviews and was to be the new hangman and, as a result, had sent a telegram to his family to that effect. *The Times* of the following day corrected the news they had carried of Berry's appointment:

THE POST OF HANGMAN. – It is understood that no definite selection has yet been arrived at by the authorities of a fit and proper person to fill the position of common hangman. Mr. Alderman and Sheriff De Keyser, Mr. Alderman and Sheriff Savory, and the High Sheriff of Essex examined a number of candidates for the office at the Sessions-house, Old Bailey, on Monday, and the number was reduced to two – James Berry of Bradford, and Taylor of Lincoln, but Berry's statement that he had been selected for the post is incorrect. The authorities have the matter still under consideration.

Alderman Polydore De Keyser of the City of London later gave evidence before the Aberdare Committee and stated that Berry 'had come with recommendations, and with letters also, from different gentlemen of position in his own county, and also from London'. Berry was strongly recommended and accepted, but:

On the morning of the selection we had a telegram from Bradford, where Berry came from, stating that he was subject to epileptic fits; but on asking him whether that was the case he answered no; but that he had had one some years ago, we thought it was quite sufficient not to run the risk of having a man who was subject to fits, which might be brought on again at any moment, so we selected Binns who had no family, who had been for years employed as foreman of a gang of platelayers on the railway at Dewsbury, and who had a very good character from the station-master and also from the company. (Aberdare report of 1888)

The new hangman, Bartholomew Binns, was thus officially selected by the London authorities and was to receive the yearly retainer of £20. Berry bemoaned his failure to be selected:

My action in applying for the post was a great sorrow to my relations. They did everything they possibly could to prevent me getting the appointment. Some of my friends wrote either personally or through solicitors to the Sheriffs. Certain members of my own family petitioned the Home Secretary to dismiss the application on the ground that if the appointment was given to me, a hitherto respectable family would be disgraced. I believe it was mainly on account of these representations that I was passed over and the post given to Mr. Bartholomew Binns.

My wages were now twenty five shillings per week. I had a wife and four children. The expense of that journey to London made the poverty still greater. My poor mother died. Grief on account of the step I had taken probably hastened the end. Upon myself the opposition had an effect that was the very opposite of that intended. It made me devote considerable thought and care to the work of an executioner, and made me determine that if ever the opportunity again occurred I should do my best to secure the appointment. During the four months that Mr. Binns held the office I had consultations with some eminent medical men and when, much earlier than I expected a new executioner was wanted I was very well grounded in the theory of the subject.

For a better understanding of the climate of the times and the nature of the job that Berry was to step into, it is necessary to take a rather detailed look at Binns, whose reign as public executioner was short. Binns was soon recognised as 'a drunken fellow, strong but very clumsy and obviously unintelligent', according to Dr Barr (Aberdare). Leonard Ward, the experienced Chief Warder at Newgate, said of Binns,

The sheriffs appeared to think that he was a strong man; of course he was a tall, strong man, and of good character; they thought he was a brave sort of man who would not flinch at carrying out anything of the sort; else he had not had any experience until he was appointed. (Aberdare)

At his first execution, at Wandsworth on 6 November 1883, it was stated that Binns was tipsy the night before and was exhibiting his ropes and pinioning straps.

A sign of worse to come was witnessed on Monday 26 November 1883 at the execution of Henry Dutton, a 22-year-old iron moulder who had murdered his wife's grandmother, Hannah Henshaw, aged 72, at Liverpool. Two representatives of the press were present at the execution. Binns arrived at Kirkdale prison at a little after 7.00 a.m. with a young man whom he described as his assistant. The prison officials would admit only Binns. At 7.45 a.m. the prison bell began to toll and the prisoner was taken to the reception room where he was introduced to Binns. Binns pinioned his man and the procession was formed to go to the scaffold. Dutton ascended the scaffold steadily but uttered a sigh of relief when he reached the drop. Binns rapidly pinioned his legs and adjusted the rope. Seeing the end was near Dutton repeated the chaplain's prayer, 'Lord Jesus, receive my soul', and Binns withdrew as if to pull the lever. However, instead of drawing the bolt, he moved forward again and looked at Dutton. Binns's explanation for doing this was that the clock had not struck the hour. Immediately upon hearing it strike he activated the drop. The body turned round several times on the end of the rope and the doctor remarked, 'This is poor work. He is not dead yet.' In fact, the body convulsed for a full two minutes and the pulse did not cease beating for eight minutes.

The drop given was 7ft 5½in and the rope was described as 'nearly as thick as a ship's hawser'. Dutton was only 5ft 2in tall and weighed only 128lb. The doctor's opinion was that the rope was far too thick and the unfortunate man had died of simple strangulation instead of fracture to the spinal cord. The body was taken down after hanging for the usual hour.

At the inquest the coroner, Mr Barker, heard the grim details, Dr James Barr, the prison doctor, stating that there was a slight separation of the first and second cervical vertebrae. The rope was too thick, the drop too short, and the noose had been placed in the wrong place, at the nape of the neck instead of under the jaw or under the ear. It was calculated that it took momentum of a ton weight (2,240lb) to dislocate the vertebrae. In this case the momentum would have been only 1,920lb. Similarly, the drop required to produce the momentum of a ton needed to be 9 feet, and a rope about seven-eighths of an inch thick would have sufficed to bear this momentum. It was explained that when the noose was placed at the nape of the neck there was no leverage exerted against the head to assist dislocation, whereas when placed under the jaw this gave a leverage of several inches. The following pointed exchange then took place:

The Coroner. – 'Was the executioner sober?'
The doctor, 'Well I should not like to say.'
The Coroner. – 'Has he left the gaol?'
Major Leggett (the prison Governor), 'Yes.'
The Coroner. – 'I wish he were here.'

The doctor then explained that he had examined the vertebrae and ascertained that strangulation was the cause of death, notwithstanding Binns's assertion that the man's neck was broken. A juryman asked Major Leggett for his opinion of the execution:

'I think it was inefficiently performed. I did not like his general manner of conducting the execution. He seemed, in adjusting the strap on the man, to do it in a very bungling way, which I did not like at all.'

Dr Barr endorsed this opinion, 'I think the execution was performed clumsily.' The coroner summed up by saying that, in carrying out the ultimate sentence of the law, there regrettably seemed to have been an error of judgement, to put it mildly. Noting that the executioner seemed to be a new hand at the work, he agreed with the doctor's statements and added that although the long drop, as used by Marwood, had been ridiculed, it was, after all, the most humane way of 'putting an end to existence'. Far better than the mode used in the present instance, or that employed by Calcraft of going below and holding the culprit's legs until the battle for life was over. He declared himself glad that two gentlemen of the press were present at the execution, this arrangement being for the benefit of the public as well as in the interest of the gaol officials. Members of the jury were satisfied that the cause of death was strangulation.

Dr Barr took a keen interest in the 'science' of hanging; he would later give evidence before the Aberdare Committee of enquiry and become involved in a dispute with Berry (see chapter 31).

The Times of 4 January 1884 carried the following report, adding to the list of transgressions by Binns:

THE HANGMAN FINED. – Bartholomew Binns, the public hangman, and Alfred Archer, his assistant, were brought up yesterday morning at the Dewsbury Court-house and fined 20s. each and costs, for defrauding the London and North-Western Railway Company by travelling on their line without tickets, with intent to escape payment.

Binns was finally dismissed after the execution of Michael McLean, aged 18, a street hooligan who had murdered a Spanish sailor in Liverpool. The execution took place on Monday 10 March 1884, and Binns, not for the first time, arrived at the prison drunk. Despite his inebriated condition he carried out the execution, but McLean's heart did not stop beating for thirteen minutes and Binns was censured for inefficiency. It is unlikely, thankfully, that McLean suffered, as he probably lost consciousness immediately. After leaving the prison, Binns visited two pubs in succession exhibiting his ropes and other 'apparatus', leading the prison governor to make an official complaint. *The Times* of Wednesday 12 March 1884 summed up the unfortunate situation:

> The common hangman is an unsavoury and repulsive subject, which we should be very glad to leave severely alone. But it is, unfortunately, impossible to ignore the scandals which occur with almost unfailing regularity every time the present public executioner has occasion to do his ghastly office. It is equally impossible to doubt that, unless steps are taken to put an end to them and to insure the carrying out of a capital sentence with some degree of decency, the law itself will be discredited by the misconduct which it fails to put down . . .

Not only was Binns seen to be suffering the effects of drink on the scaffold; he was also holding 'receptions' at the inns where he stayed whilst attending a town for an execution. There crowds went to see his 'apparatus' and '. . . to enjoy the felicity of his society having been so great that it was with difficulty that the landlord cleared his house in time to comply with the law'. The unique standing of the public executioner was summed up in *The Times* as follows:

> These scandals are due to the fact that there is no sort of control over the public executioner. He is not, in point of fact,

known to the law, and he holds no official appointment. At the same time, a *quasi*-recognition has, if we mistake not, been accorded to him. Our impression is that, though the Home Office has no power to appoint him, SIR WILLIAM HARCOURT [the Home Secretary] did in some way notify that BINNS might be considered fit for the work after he had conducted an execution in Newgate on the appointment of the Sheriffs of London and Middlesex. The whole arrangement is obviously one of the makeshifts to which this country is addicted. It is legally the duty of the sheriff to carry out the sentence of the Court either personally or by deputy, and no doubt there was a time when the duty seemed considerably less onerous than it is today . . .

So the procedure that existed was that on sentence of death being passed by the court, it was the duty of the High Sheriff to commission someone to carry out the punishment. Normally the recognised hangman, on seeing this sentence passed, would write to the appropriate sheriff offering his services. Obviously it was the practice for nearly all sheriffs to employ the same 'deputy' to carry out this function, hence a single 'number one' hangman was used throughout Britain apart from Yorkshire, which appointed its own hangman. The question was raised in the House on 14 March and the hangman's disgraceful conduct was discussed. His drinking and displaying of his ropes to the public were deplored. It was accepted that a new, more capable, executioner was required and that the fee paid of £10 per execution might not be sufficient.

The Times stated that Marwood had been 'an efficient executioner and behaved with propriety'. However:

It is not to be expected that any man of fine feeling will seek the post, but we may reasonably expect to find a man of sufficient steadiness and self-control to discharge the duty in a decent and serious manner . . .

There was a further piece in *The Times* of Monday 17 March 1884:

THE OFFICE OF HANGMAN. – A committee of the Court of Aldermen was held at the Guildhall on Saturday, the Lord

Mayor, M.P., presiding. Alderman Sir Andrew Lusk, M.P., called the attention of the Court to the subject of the appointment of Bartholomew Binns to the office of hangman, and in view of what had recently taken place with reference to him, moved that the honorarium of 20 guineas annually paid out of the City's cash to Binns should be withdrawn. The subject was discussed with closed doors, but it is understood that upon the Town Clerk's pointing out that notice of motion would have to be given, Sir Andrew Lusk withdrew his resolution, promising to give the necessary notice. The matter consequently stands over, and in the meantime the subject was referred to the Sheriffs of London and Middlesex, with whom the appointment of executioner rests, and who, having been present during the proceedings, promised to take the matter into consideration.

On Thursday 20 March, Binns was called before the sheriffs at the Old Bailey, and gave his explanation for the problems at the Liverpool execution and 'other matters' in which his conduct had been called into question. Binns denied the allegations of drunkenness and blamed the 'animosity and vindictiveness' of the Liverpool officials for his plight. He also denied allegations of attempting to defraud the railway companies by evading payment of his fare, and of making an exhibition at public houses of his 'ropes and other accessories to his vocation as hangman'. Though the sheriffs did not give their decision immediately, they were inundated with applications for the appointment. Dr Barr stated of Binns, 'For his drunkenness he was dismissed, but not before he had given frequent proofs of his utter unfitness for his duties' (Aberdare).

It was clear that a new public executioner was urgently required. Berry's day had come and he was determined to prove himself the right man for the job.

At this time, March 1884, there had been four executions that year, including a double hanging. The previous year had witnessed twenty-five executions, including three double executions. Hangings always excited strong public feeling, especially in Scotland and Ireland, no doubt exacerbated by the fact that it was an Englishman carrying out the sentence. Although in the minority the abolitionists had a loud and strong voice. The example of Binns was fuel for their cause and was the last thing that the officials needed to see. The conduct of Binns, however, had at least led to some improvement in procedure. Regulations as to the housing of the executioner when on duty in county towns, resulting in his being accommodated at the gaols on his arrival and during his stay, had also worked well.

5

Berry's first execution

'. . . the two men were launched into eternity . . .'

Berry entered his new career adopting Marwood's well-tried methods, his 'table of drops', the same type of ropes and a more technical approach to his trade. He was never appointed 'officially' as executioner for the City of London and Middlesex on the £20 retainer, but worked on individual application for commissions as executioner. As a great improvement on Binns he would soon be accepted as 'number one'.

In March 1884 Berry submitted an application to execute two condemned prisoners in Scotland. The magistrates of the City of Edinburgh needed a man to execute Robert Vickers and William Innes, two poachers who had been convicted of murder. The Sheriffs of London and Middlesex recommended Berry and he posted a letter to the magistrates asking to be permitted to conduct the execution:

March 18th 1884
52 Thorpe St
Shearbridge
Bradford
Yorkshire

To the Mayor of Edinburgh
Dear Sir
I beg most respectfully to apply to you, to ask if you will permit me to conduct the execution of the two convicts now lying under sentence of death in Edinboro. I was very intimate with

the late Mr. Marwood and he made me thoroughly acquainted with his system of carrying out his work, and also the information which he learnt from the Doctors of different prisons which he had to visit to carry out the last sentence of the law. I have now one rope of his which I bought from him at Horncastle, and have made two from it. I have also two pinioning straps made from his; also two leg straps. I have seen Mr. Calcraft execute three convicts at Manchester thirteen years ago; and should you think fit to give me the appointment I should endeavour to meet your patronage.

I have served 3½ years in Bradford West Riding Police Force and resigned without a stain on my character and could satisfy you as to my abilities and fitness for the appointment. You can apply to Mr. James Withers, Chief Constable, Bradford; also to the High Sheriff for the City of London, Mr. Clarence Smith, Mansion House Buildings 4 Queen Victoria St London E.C., who will testify as to my character and fitness to carry out the law. Should you require me I could be at your command at twenty four hours notice.

Hoping these few lines will meet with your approval.

> I remain Sir
> Your Most Obedient Servant
> James Berry
> To the Chief Magistrate
> Boro. of Edinburgh
> Scotland

P.S. An answer would greatly oblige as I should take it as a favour.

Berry had seen an opportunity that he wasn't going to miss. *The Times* of Monday 24 March 1884 reported:

THE HANGMAN. – Joseph [*sic*] Berry, of Bradford, has been selected as the public executioner of Inns and Vicars at Glasgow [*sic*] on the 31st inst. These two men have been condemned to death for murder in a poaching affray. Berry was an unsuccessful candidate for the office of public executioner when the vacancy arose by the death of Marwood, and the result of some communication which has recently been made with Mr. James Withers, the chief constable of Bradford, is this appointment of Berry.

On 10 March 1884 Robert Flockart Vickers and William Innes had been charged before the High Court of Justiciary at Edinburgh with the murder of two assistant gamekeepers named John Fortune and John McDiarmid. They were also charged with a serious assault on James Grosset, head gamekeeper, at Rosebery. The killing of gamekeepers by poachers was not unusual in Victorian days and many similar offenders kept appointments with the hangman.

Lord Rosebery employed the gamekeepers on his estate at the foot of the Moorfoot Hills. The two offenders, miners from Gorebridge, had gone poaching on 15 December 1883. Grossett and his two assistants had gone out looking for them. It was a clear, frosty morning and a full moon overlooked the drama being played out below. About 3.00 a.m. the gamekeepers located their quarry, who were armed with guns. The poachers were called upon to give themselves up and one of them was heard to say, 'Take that on the left and I will do for that on the right.' With this the two poachers fired their weapons and the two assistant gamekeepers fell fatally wounded. Before they could reload their guns, Grosset made off and heard the shout, 'Quick, don't let him get away; we'll catch him at the bridge', the bridge being one that spanned the South Esk at this point. Grosset changed his route and reached Edgelaw Farm where he roused the farmer, Mr Simpson.

Mr Simpson drove into Gorebridge and informed Sergeant Adamson. The two wounded gamekeepers were taken to the Edinburgh Royal Infirmary but succumbed to their wounds, Fortune on 18 December and his colleague on 8 January. From information supplied by Grosset, Vickers and Innes, known poachers, were arrested. They duly appeared before Lord Young in the High Court. The prosecution was conducted by the Solicitor-General, Asher, whilst the Dean of Faculty, Macdonald, appeared on behalf of the prisoners. The defence amounted to a simple denial that they had ever left their homes that night. The jury, however, found the case proved and Lord Young concurred. The two were sentenced to death and removed to await their fate at Calton Jail, Edinburgh.

The sentence was to be carried out on 31 March. A week after sentence was passed they admitted their guilt. Despite efforts to effect a reprieve none was granted, although both men, especially Vickers, felt that they would be shown mercy.

As this was his first execution Berry remembered the occasion in great detail. On 21 March 1884 he received a letter from the Magistrates' Clerk, City Chambers, Edinburgh, appointing him to act as executioner. He was to provide all the necessary appliances for carrying out the execution. Berry accepted and on Thursday 27 March 1884 set out from his Bradford home to the Midland Station where he booked a third-class seat for Edinburgh. An assistant, a 36-year-old wagoner who used the pseudonym 'Richard Chester', accompanied him. In his accounts of the execution Berry made no mention of 'Chester'. Over the years he preferred to work alone; 'Chester' was to assist only with the pinioning of the prisoners. They arrived at Waverley Station, Edinburgh at 4.20 p.m. and hired a cab to take them to the jail. They were met at the doors of the prison by 'a good-looking warder', who was very courteous. They were led through the large portal gates and entered their names in the prison book. The governor was called and he came and greeted Berry, the two 'passing the usual conversation'. The governor assured Berry that he would get a good, substantial tea, and as soon as he had washed and combed his hair, his tea was ready. A satisfied Berry summed it up thus, '. . . everything that could be desired. I sat down, and quite enjoyed my first Scotch meal in Bonnie Scotland.'

The governor questioned Berry and examined his equipment, after which Berry made his own inspection of the gallows he was to use. Berry returned to his room, staying in during the daytime. He spent that night smoking and reading. At 10.00 p.m. he was escorted to his bedroom, a roundhouse situated at the rear area of the jail, about 40 yards from the rear entrance. Berry described it as 'a snug little place' that, he was informed, was last occupied by his predecessor, William Marwood, some five years previously (on the occasion of the execution of the infamous Edinburgh wife-poisoner Eugene Marie Chantrelle on 31 May 1878). The chief warder seemed unwilling to discuss the purpose of Berry's visit and said that he 'felt quite upset concerning the two culprits, and that he hoped they would get a reprieve'. Such sympathy for condemned prisoners was often to be found in their custodians. That night, left alone, Berry locked his door and sat down on his bed in a reflective mood. He could hear the trains departing from the station below the prison wall and he looked out of his window at the mail taking its departure for the South. Berry felt as much a prisoner as the two men awaiting their fate. He knelt and 'asked the Almighty to help me in my most painful task, which I had undertaken to carry out'. He passed a disturbed night exacerbated by a smoking chimney.

At 8.00 a.m. the following morning breakfast was brought to Berry's room and he enjoyed a meal of toast, ham and eggs, and coffee. Two hours later he was introduced to the magistrates and those responsible for seeing the execution carried out. Berry exposed his ropes and straps for their inspection, with a long and careful investigation of all points. After that Berry paid another visit to the scaffold where the builders were carrying out final work on the newly erected shed provided to keep the execution private. Berry tested the gallows using bags of cement of the same weight as the prisoners on his ropes. He calculated the length of drop required, its consequences, and other details, before the committee departed, satisfied with their visit. Berry then filled his time with walking around the prison grounds and 'thinking of the poor men who were nearing their end, full of life, and knowing the fatal hour, which made me quite ill to think about'.

Berry's awful responsibility was beginning to play on his mind. His meals seemed to do him no good and his appetite disappeared:

Nothing felt good to me, everything that I put into my mouth felt like sand, and I felt as I wished I had never undertaken such an awful calling. I regretted for a while, and then I thought the public would only think that I had not the pluck, and I would not allow my feelings to overthrow me, so I never gave way to such thoughts again.

At 1.00 p.m. Berry's dinner arrived and he went to his room and sat down to pudding, beef and vegetables, Scotch broth, and Cochrane & Cantrell's ginger ale (at that time he was a total abstainer from alcohol). After tea he chatted with the prison warders going off duty for the day. He soon had a taste of the morbid curiosity he would excite by the nature of his work. As the warders passed through the wicket gate he heard one say, 'He looks a nice fellow for a job like that.' Another seemed more confident of Berry's abilities, noting 'But he has a wicked eye.' Berry chatted for a time with the prison gatekeeper, with whom he seems to have struck up quite a rapport, describing him as 'a straight, honest man . . . like myself'.

The gatekeeper said, 'I'm glad you never began to say anything in the presence of that man, as he would stop until morning.'

Saturday morning, 29 March 1884 dawned, and after his breakfast Berry had another interview with the magistrates and made his final arrangements. Again the scaffold was tested in their presence, with the ropes he was going to use on the Monday morning. Vickers weighed 10 stone and a drop of 8 feet had been calculated for him, while Innes, at 9 stone, was given 10 feet. Again Berry tested the ropes by attaching bags of cement to them on the marks made for the criminals and then letting off the traps. His audience 'looked quite satisfied with the results'. The ropes used were of Italian silk hemp, 'made specially for the work', five-eighths of an inch thick, very pliable and running through a brass thimble. The result was 'dislocation and a painless death if rightly adjusted'.

In the afternoon Berry was granted a drive outside the prison by the magistrates:

> After dining, I had the honour of having a drive in an open carriage (provided by the Governor) for a couple of hours . . . which I enjoyed, after being inside the prison gates since my arrival on Thursday . . .

Berry had a pleasant drive, wrapped in rugs, and spent upwards of two hours in the sunshine seeing the places of special interest: the monument to Burns, Portobello, along the Forth, Princes Street and the castle. Having dismissed his earlier fears, and being satisfied with the proceedings thus far, he was in a better mood. And then . . .

> I gave my friend another night's visit at the lodge gate. We chatted on different topics of the day, and spent a nice, jovial evening together, smoking our weed; when a voice came to the door from a visitor from the offices of the town, that a reprieve

was refused, and the law was to take its course, and I had a paper sent, with the words in full, GOREBRIDGE MURDERERS, NO REPRIEVE, which made me feel as bad as the condemned men for some time. But, what with the jolly gate-keeper, and another of the warders, I drove it out of my mind for a while . . .

Berry retired to bed at 10.00 p.m., after saying his prayers and turning his thoughts to being back home soon with his wife and children. Nevertheless, he was very restless that night and did not feel refreshed when he rose the next morning. His previous thoughts had returned to haunt him. He kept thinking of:

. . . the poor creatures who was [sic] slumbering their hours away, in the prison cell, just beyond where I was laid, thinking of the dreadful fate that awaited them in such a short space of time. Two men, in full bloom, and had to come to such an untimely end, leaving wives and large families. One poor woman, I was informed, her mind was so affected that she was removed to the asylum, she took it so to heart . . .

Again affected by his thoughts, Berry retired to his day room at the front entrance where he 'partook only sparingly of the nice and tempting ham and poached eggs' placed before him. He spent most of the morning looking around the inside of the prison, while the prisoners were at chapel until lunchtime. At four o'clock he had a 'late dinner [lunch], consisting of rice pudding, black currants, chicken, vegetables, potatoes, bread, and the usual teetotal beverages'. He tried to eat as well as he could but, again, his appetite was gone. Later, he managed to eat a little before retiring at 10 p.m. that night, the eve of the execution. It was another restless night, Berry snatching only occasional catnaps, 'one eye shut and the other open, thinking and fancying things that never will be, and which is impossible [sic]'.

Up and dressed at 5.00 a.m. on the fateful Monday, he 'felt more dead than alive', aware that he was to be the central player in the drama that was about to unfold. Fears began to assail his mind. He fancied the ropes breaking; that he would tremble and could not do it; that he would fall sick at the last moment. He was becoming frantic, but was careful not to let others notice his disquiet. The hands of the clock moved to 6.00 a.m. and Berry heard the sound of keys grating in locks, the clattering of doors and the sliding of bolts. Breakfast was taken earlier than usual and none of the other prisoners was to be allowed out of his cell until the execution was over. The public had begun to assemble on Calton Hill, in groups, outside the prison. The final hour had arrived and at 7.00 a.m. Berry made his way to the scaffold securing his 'arrangements' and clearing the scaffold shed. The principal warder then locked the door of the shed so that it could not be opened again until the arrival of the procession with the condemned men.

At 7.45 a.m. those attending the execution made their way to the prison and into the doctor's room ready for the enactment of the final scene in the drama. Vickers and Innes were brought face to face for the first time since their conviction and they kissed each other. Berry described the scene as 'a very painful one, to see mates going to meet their end on the gallows'. They were conducted into a room adjoining that of the doctor, where they spent time in prayer with the two ministers in attendance.

Berry was then called to do his duty. He was handed the warrant that had been made out by the judge who had sentenced them to death, after which he shook hands with the prisoners and pinioned them. Both men appeared to feel their position very much. The procession was formed, headed by the High Bailiff. The chaplains read the litany for the dead and the prisoners walked without assistance to the execution shed, where they were immediately placed under the beam on the 'drop'. Vickers was buoyed up with the hope of a late reprieve, a hope that he clung to until the final moment. It was not until the noose touched his neck that he realised that there was to be no reprieve, and he fainted. Innes had already had the white cap placed over his face and stood unmoved. Unaware of his friend's plight, he was resigned and calm, 'without either hope or fear'. The fainting man was momentarily supported and Berry activated the lever. The support was no longer required. At the 'chime of the clock the two men were launched into eternity without the moving of a muscle or even a quiver of a nerve'. Still making no mention of the activities of his assistant, Chester, Berry recalls: 'everything was done as quick as lightning, and both culprits paid the highest penalty of the law . . .'

The magistrates, doctors, and even the members of the press present admitted that the execution of the two men had been carried out in as humane a manner as possible and that neither had suffered the slightest pain. Indeed, the doctors gave Berry a testimonial as to the skilful way he had carried out the execution. At 9.00 a.m. breakfast arrived, but Berry had again lost his appetite as 'I was so much affected by the sad sight I had witnessed'. He merely drank a cup of coffee but ate no food.

Berry had achieved his goal; he had carried out an efficient and quick execution without a hitch. He now had vital experience and testimonials. Glowing written recommendations were received from the magistrates, George Roberts and Thomas Clark; the prison governor, J.E. Christie; and the doctors: James A. Sidney MD, the prison surgeon, and Henry D. Littlejohn MD, the police surgeon. Berry now felt that he was competent at his chosen task and ready for his new career.

As what may undeniably be termed a professional killer, an executioner was in a unique position among those who could legally take the life of another. Soldiers, for instance, may be called upon to kill in the defence of their country, but such killing is usually done in the heat of battle and usually with a detached remoteness not afforded the executioner. The personal contact with his 'victims', the fixed time of execution, the ritual and the time thus allowed for pondering his actions all took their toll on Berry. He was, undoubtedly, a religious and humane man, with much time to analyse the moral and religious implications of his grim task. Eventually he would become, to some degree, inured to his work, but it would never rest totally at ease with his conscience. The fact was, though, that he needed the money the work provided to keep his family, and thus he rationalised his work, regarding himself as simply an agent of the law, the last in a line of legal professionals all bringing the condemned offender to his final retribution for his crime.

Berry stated that he had gained his knowledge of hanging from Marwood, but there was one important point on which he appears not to have followed his mentor. On 10 December 1875 a meeting of the Surgical Society was held at the Royal College of Surgeons of Ireland to discuss the best method of execution by hanging and the importance of a long drop. Several surgeons with experience of gaol executions attended this meeting, and one of the decisions reached was that the 'knot' should be placed under the chin (the sub-mental position) instead of the back of the neck (the sub-occipital position). This was because the former resulted in a quick snapping of the neck whereas the latter meant that the rope had to press through all the soft parts of the neck before striking the spinal column. It was also believed that this reduced the length of the drop required. Marwood was known to have used the sub-mental position, placing the 'knot' under the left side of the chin, but Berry apparently always placed the knot at the back of the left ear, the sub-aural position.

6

Mary Lefley

'On my approach she threw up her hands and shrieked . . . '

Berry's next 'job' was again to cause him much agonising, leading him, in fact, to question his choice of career. It was, in his own words, 'a very different experience', one that presented him with what must have been the most awful of questions – was he hanging an innocent party? The 'victim' this time was a woman, Mary Lefley, and the hanging took place within two months of the double execution at Edinburgh. Although he had not been officially taken on and accorded a retainer, he was now the accepted successor to Binns as the executioner for the City of London and Middlesex, and the authorities in Lincoln readily accepted him when he applied for the commission to execute Lefley in that town.

Mary Lefley, 49 years of age, was the wife of a Lincolnshire farmer, William Lefley, ten years her senior. William had made a meagre living travelling to and from the village of Wrangle as a country carrier, taking parcels and letters to the town. Once a week his wife had journeyed with him, taking butter, eggs and other produce of their dairy farm. According to Berry, William (who he called John) was a hard-grasping man, not too intelligent but cunning in his business dealings. Others put it less charitably, claiming that Lefley was 'a little short of his change'.

In his account of the Lefley case Berry told the story of a business transaction between Lefley and a neighbouring farmer. They met at the market and the farmer tried to deal to his own advantage. However, the simple-minded Lefley outwitted his neighbour and the man became a laughing-stock in the neighbourhood, for which he never forgave Lefley. In Berry's opinion, the reason for which we

47

shall see shortly, had this been mentioned at Mary's trial it might have saved her. Doing his best to cast her in a good light, Berry records how Mary prepared a rice pudding with eggs and milk and put it into the oven as a treat for her husband on his return. His somewhat glowing account, however, is rather inaccurate and does not tell the full story.

On 6 February 1884 Mary had gone to the market at Boston to sell butter while her husband returned and took his meal from the oven. After the meal he fell asleep but was soon awakened by pains in his stomach. He set out for the home of the local surgeon, Dr Bubb, only to be told that he was out, upon which he began vomiting violently and asked to see the doctor's sister. When Miss Bubb duly came to the door he took a half-full bowl of rice pudding from a basket and claimed to have been poisoned by it. An incoming locum, Dr Faskally, returned at 4.30 p.m. to find Lefley collapsed. Lefley again repeated that he had been poisoned, but after the doctor had attended to him he was taken home and put to bed. Mary returned to the cottage just after 6.00 p.m., went up to the bedroom, and asked what was happening. The parish clerk, Richard Wright, and a villager, Mrs Longden, were present. The dying Lefley said, 'You know all about it, my dear. Go down and don't let me see you any more.' She went downstairs without saying anything else. Wright went down to get a cup of tea for Lefley and Mary said, 'I suppose he says he's been poisoned. We haven't any poison in the house to my knowledge and haven't had any for years. I felt very impressed in the van going to Boston. I thought I must have got out and come back.'

Lefley began vomiting again and called out for Wright. Dr Faskally arrived and Mrs Longden went downstairs. Mary offered the woman some beer but she declined. 'Well, have some tea,' said Mary. 'I've had nothing all day because I felt so queer. I put the sugar and rice together for the pudding and left my husband to put the milk in. He told me I needn't make a pudding, for there was plenty cooked, but I said I always did make a pudding and would do so as usual.'

At 8.00 p.m. the doctor decided that there was nothing more he could do for the dying man. Mary asked if it was true that he had been poisoned and added that she hoped the doctor could save him.

Dr Faskally told her that there was no hope but that he was not yet certain that he had been poisoned.

'If he's been poisoned,' declared Mary, 'I'm innocent. People don't know how he went out the other night and wanted to hang himself. I don't know where he could have got it.'

The doctor left and the village constable's wife, Mrs Curl, arrived. Mary repeated what her husband had said and Mrs Curl observed how strange it was that he should claim Mary had poisoned the pudding but not then have her upstairs.

'It's his badness,' said Mary. 'He's been an old brute since Christmas, and if I go up again I'll tell him a thing or two.'

The Wrangle miller, James Cooper, arrived and Mary told him, 'This is a strange job. I've had a deal of trouble with him lately. He's been very uneasy.' Cooper went upstairs and later came down to tell Mary that her husband was dying fast. She replied, 'Is he?' but did not go up. Cooper returned again shortly to get her but she did not reply; instead she 'seemed rather wild and went into the kitchen'. Lefley died at 9.00 p.m. in the presence of Wright, Cooper and Mrs Longden.

At midnight the police attended and Mary said, 'It seems strange to me. He was well this morning. I made a rice pudding in a basin and put it in the oven for him to cook for himself, as I always do when I go to Boston. If he got any poison, he must have taken it himself, for I know nothing about it. I've not had any poison in the house for years.'

When Mary met Cooper the next day she told him, 'As I was on my way to Boston I felt very queer and asked myself the question, "What am I going to Boston for? I've nothing to go for but to the shop." Every time the van stopped I had a mind to get out and go home.'

That evening Mary visited a local farmer, Mr Saul, to ask for advice. She told him, 'I've not been on very good terms with my husband lately, and a few nights ago he went into the yard intending to hang himself.'

'Did you go after him?' asked Mr Saul.

'No,' she replied. The following day Mary was arrested and charged with poisoning her husband with arsenic. She asked the arresting sergeant 'Where did the arsenic come from?' The police had found a screw of paper containing some white powder. Analysis was made and arsenic was found in the remains of the rice pudding and in the body of the deceased. She protested her innocence, swearing she had no reason to kill him and that he had always been kind to her. There was no other suspect and her case seemed hopeless.

She appeared for trial at Lincoln Assizes on 7 May. Dressed entirely in black she had to be assisted into the dock, since she suffered from rheumatism in her hands and legs. She pleaded 'Not Guilty' in a clear, firm voice. Evidence was given that the remains of the rice pudding had contained the huge amount of 135½ grains of arsenic. It had been cooked in the pudding, and parts of the crust adhering to the bowl were almost solid arsenic. Two grains is normally a fatal dose. The white powder found was analysed and found to be harmless.

A nephew, William Lister, had stayed with the Lefleys for five weeks until 2 February. In his evidence he recalled the couple sometimes 'having words', which would be quite normal with any couple. On 1 February they had quarrelled over a cask of ale that her husband did not want in the house. In the middle of the night William had joined his nephew in bed saying that he had just tried to hang himself. Lister went off to sleep, and when he awoke he found that his uncle had returned to his own room. He informed his aunt of the night's events. Among other evidence adduced, Maidens Smith, a local potato dealer, said that on 2 February Mary had complained that her husband had sold some potatoes to a neighbour, and said she wished he were dead and out of the way. The defence claimed that Lefley had committed suicide, but argued that if he had instead been murdered the possibility that a third party had entered the cottage to poison the pudding could not be excluded. The judge's summing up was not favourable and the jury retired for 35 minutes, after which a guilty verdict was returned, despite Mary protesting 'I'm not guilty, and I never poisoned anyone in my life.'

Lefley was placed in Lincoln Prison to await her execution, which was set for 9.00 a.m. on Monday 26 May 1884. She remained almost prostrate the whole time and never confessed her guilt. A good summary of reasons to question that guilt is made by Patrick Wilson in his book *Murderess*. Certainly in the light of what we know there can be no certainty as to her guilt, and the doubts that can be raised should have resulted in her acquittal. On the other hand, in his book *My Experiences as an Executioner*, Berry pointed out the intriguing fact that some sixteen years earlier another female poisoner, Priscilla Biggadyke, aged 29, had died on the Lincoln gallows. She had poisoned her husband with arsenic, and had been a friend of Mary Lefley!

In view of Mary Lefley's demeanour the prison governor anticipated that there might be problems with the execution. Berry felt that an assistant was advisable and 'Chester' was again used. Typically, however, Berry makes no mention of his assistant as he relates the story of Mary's execution:

> . . . and to the last she protested her innocence; though on the night before she was very restless and constantly exclaimed, 'Lord! Thou knowest all,' and prayed fervently. She would have no breakfast and when I approached her she was in a nervous, agitated state, praying to God for salvation, not as a murderess but as an innocent woman. On my approach she threw up her hands and shrieked, 'Murder! Murder!' and she had to be led to the scaffold by two female warders, shrieking wildly all the time. She died as she had lived, impenitent and untruthful, denying her guilt to the last.

When Berry's account of Mary Lefley was repeated in his serialised experiences related in *The Post* in 1913, just after his death, his thoughts on her guilt had changed. This, apparently, was the result of a later alleged confession to the crime by another. The headline to the story was 'How I Hanged An Innocent Woman'. He related an account of the Lefley case, with some inaccuracies, but his account of the execution contained much more detail, adding many points of interest and elucidation. It is a harrowing story:

> When I reached the gaol I found it in a state of panic.
>
> 'She has never ceased to protest her innocence' said one of the women warders, 'and oh, Mr Berry, I am sure as can be that she never committed the dreadful crime. You have only to talk to the woman to know that, whatever she may have been, she is no murderess.'
>
> The Governor, too, felt that she was innocent, the chaplain said, 'God forbid that she should be hanged,' and there was not

an authority, no, not one, but looked tremblingly into the future.

Imagine my feelings when I went to the condemned cell to prepare her for her doom. I know that my hands trembled as the turnkey held open the door, and my tongue clove to the roof of my mouth as I essayed speech.

Mary Lefley was in bed. She had been too ill to get up that morning, and we had to shake her into consciousness. She looked round with dazed eyes, and shivered as we told her to arise.

'Come along now, Mary, it is time you were getting ready.'

'Don't hang me!' she screamed when she realised that the hand of fate was upon her, and shivered in every limb. We had to drag her out of bed, and as she sat half-dressed in the gloom of the condemned cell I scanned her face, and tried to read her inmost thoughts as I had the thoughts of others.

Imagine if you can a woman in the prime of life, with eyes that had once sparkled with light, and a face that even in grief and terror was not forbidding.

Mary Lefley bore no trace upon that face of a guilty conscience, and I was more than ever convinced that an error of justice had been committed.

'Come along now, Mary, it is time you were dressed,' we said. She understood what we meant, but still she did not move, except in terror.

Then she spoke –

'Don't hang me! If you do you will commit another murder! Oh, don't hang me!'

'Mary,' I said gently, 'I have got to do my duty. You would never have been here to-day if you had not committed that murder.'

I said that because I wanted to be absolutely sure in my own mind about the crime. What a relief it would have been had her answer been otherwise but this –

'I am innocent. God knows I am innocent.'

'But the poison!' I said.

'I know nothing about it,' she replied. 'I never had any arsenic in the house.'

'But it was found in the pudding you made.'

'I know nothing about it,' was her reply, 'I do not know how it got there.'

We told her to dress herself now, but, poor creature, she could not do it, and I and the others had to help her into her clothes.

Think of the scene; think of it well and reflect on it when some poor, wretched woman is condemned to die.

Still protesting her innocence I pinioned her, and gave the signal that everything was in readiness for the last act of all.

The Governor, the chaplain, the Sheriff, and the doctor formed up for the procession to the scaffold, and I turned her round, and with unrelenting fingers pointed to the door.

Ah! never shall I forget the ordeal through which we passed during the next few minutes, which seemed like a lifetime.

Her scream was heartrending.

'Murder!' she cried, and again, 'Murder!' and then she declared her innocence once more and repeated – 'If you hang me you will commit a murder.'

There was neither man nor woman who walked with feet that did not falter, or face that did not blanche.

The chaplain's prayer sounded like a sob, now like a wail, long and drawn out. Our eyes were downcast, our senses numbed, and down the cheeks of some the tears were rolling.

Her cries as she was dragged along the scaffold were piercing. The walls of the very prison seemed nought but space, for at any part of the building her voice was distinctly heard.

Still protesting her innocence on the scaffold I dropped her into eternity.

Death was instantaneous and the usual formal inquest was held afterwards, but reporters were not admitted.

According to Berry, nine years later there was a sequel to the story. A Lincolnshire farmer, on his deathbed, had confessed the crime to his doctor. It was the very same farmer who had been bested by Lefley in the business deal and made a laughing-stock. He had crept into the cottage that day when it was unoccupied and emptied arsenic from a parcel he had carried there into the rice that was simmering on the hob, and stirred it in.

When Berry had been interviewed for the post of executioner of London and Middlesex, by the sheriffs, he had been asked about the possibility of hanging a person whom he felt to be innocent. Berry had stated that he would not hesitate, as the fault would be that of the law and not his. The law put no more responsibility on the executioner than it did on the prison governor whose order was to see the sentence carried out. Despite carrying no legal blame for the execution of an innocent party, if such was the case, Berry certainly did carry a moral one and it weighed upon his conscience. He was neither a brute nor a callous man.

7

Police-killers and wife-murderers

'You'll hear his confession before you swing him.'

Experienced at his work, Berry had gained a reputation for efficiency and humanity. Indeed, his services were required the very day after the Mary Lefley execution. The case was that of Joseph Lowson, a 25-year-old miner, weighing over 16 stone and standing over 6 feet tall. He had been convicted for the murder of Police Sergeant Smith and was awaiting his fate at Durham. Berry travelled by train directly from Lincoln to Durham, changing at Doncaster en route, from the Great Eastern to the Great Northern line. In his book, Berry tells of an incident that occurred on this journey:

> I looked out for a carriage with a vacant corner seat, and got into one containing three rough-looking men. When the train had started they began to talk amongst themselves, and to look at me, and eventually began to chaff me. Of course I pretended not to understand their allusions to the execution that morning, and was indignant at their supposing me to be an executioner, but they were confident that they were right, and began offering to bet amongst themselves as to which of them I should get first. I was glad to get to York, where I parted from their company.

Berry would meet these same three men nearly two years later, as we shall see. He was already being recognised as a high-profile figure, despite his discreet demeanour and short time in the office. The hangman was very newsworthy in those days and a rather celebrated character. The public was aware that he had to travel to various prisons to carry out his work. On the same rail journey, after changing trains, Berry again experienced public curiosity:

> . . . I got into a carriage with a benevolent-looking old gentleman. A little crowd collected round the door, and just as we were starting a porter stuck his head into the window, pointed to my fellow passenger, and with a silly attempt at jocularity said: – 'I hope you'll give him the right tightener.' The old gentleman seemed much mystified, and of course I was quite unable to imagine what it meant. At Darlington there was another little crowd, which collected for a short time about our carriage. Fortunately none of the people knew me, so that when the old gentleman asked them what was the matter they could only tell him that Berry was travelling by that train and that they wanted to have a look at him. The old gentleman seemed anxious to see such an awful man as the executioner, and asked me if I should know him if I saw him. I pointed out a low-looking character as being possibly the man, and my fellow traveller said, 'Yes! very much like him.' I suppose he had seen a so-called portrait of me in one of the newspapers. We got quite friendly, and when we reached Durham, where I was getting out, he asked for my card. The reader can imagine his surprise when I handed it to him.
>
> This little story has been much warped and magnified, and has even been made the subject of a leading article which takes me to task for 'glorying in my gruesome calling,' and shocking respectable people by giving them my cards.

Despite this statement, it appears fairly obvious that Berry did indeed take a delight in surprising people with his identity and enjoyed most of the attention and importance he was thus accorded.

On Saturday 23 February 1884, Joseph Lowson and two of his workmates, Joseph Hodgson aged 20, and William Siddle aged 25, had been to a pigeon-shooting event at Butterknowle, in the county of Durham. Afterwards they repaired to a local pub, the Diamond Inn, where they spent the evening. On leaving the pub the three men saw Sergeant William Smith, said to be a popular and sporting man, watching them from across the road. They walked a short way then turned back and Siddle made an insulting remark to Sergeant Smith. There had been bad blood between the two since the police officer had warned Siddle about his conduct at a gala the previous August, and Siddle had assaulted him. The police officer ignored the remark and walked off. A little later the sergeant returned to Butterknowle Lane to ensure that all was quiet. Smith lived nearby with his wife and seven children. Not long afterwards his battered and bruised body was found at the roadside. He was still breathing, but very heavily, and he soon died. The doctor who attended saw the three miners coming from an old engine house belonging to the disused Diamond Colliery, and he reproached them for the cowardly attack on the officer, at which they threw stones at him before following him back towards where the officer was lying. When the doctor shouted 'Murder!', however, they hurriedly fled, only to be arrested later on suspicion of the murder. The policeman had been attacked with bricks and a large piece of sandstone, and bloodstains were found on Lowson's jacket and shirt.

On 1 May they stood trial at Durham Assizes before Mr Justice Hawkins. Hodgson was acquitted but the other two found guilty, despite the defendants' claims that the prosecution witnesses were swearing away their lives. The sentence of death was passed, but, following local agitation that the evidence was only circumstantial and that Berry should therefore not be called, Siddle was granted a reprieve a few days before the execution date. The Home Office made inquiries and a week's respite was granted. The evidence was considered and the sentence allowed to stand in respect of Lowson, Siddle having made a statement to the effect that Lowson and Hodgson had committed the murder.

Berry's description of the execution of Lowson appeared in the 1913 *Saturday Post* series and was headed, 'The Only Spiritualist I Ever Hanged'. Still suffering anguish over the execution of Mary Lefley the previous day, and worried that Lowson might be innocent, he recalls asking himself whether he could endure the same ordeal again. On arrival at the gaol, therefore, he immediately asked the officials for reassurance that his man was guilty. 'Don't you worry Mr Berry,' they said, 'He did it right enough. You'll hear his confession before you swing him.' 'He is as callous as they make them,' they went on. 'He won't have anything to do with the chaplain. He keeps talking about his friends in the spirit world.'

That night Berry saw Lowson in his cell, but 'did not have the courage to go in and talk with him'. He wrote:

> I went to my room and spent a sleepless night, wishing as I had so often wished that I had never taken on the grim, heartrending, and mind-torturing work of the public executioner.

The next day, 27 May, a dense fog 'hung like a pall' over Durham, 'through which the bold towers of the cathedral were only dimly visible'. As the fatal hour approached the fog dispelled and the temperature rose as the sun appeared. It was not until the hour of eight o'clock approached that a crowd began to form outside the prison and pitmen from the neighbouring villages began to troop into the town.

Lowson – 'a terrible fellow' according to Berry – apparently spent a peaceful night, rising as the bell tolled for six o'clock. Chief Warder Allison entered the cell at this time to oversee the charge of the prisoner being transferred from the night to the day warder, upon which Lowson cheerfully bade the night warder 'good morning' and laughingly remarked that they might meet again (*The Times*, 28 May 1884). Lowson then consumed a good breakfast and listened to the words of the prison chaplain but took little heed of them, declaring that he intended to 'die game'.

Close to eight, Berry entered the cell with the chief warder, who informed the prisoner that 'the moment had arrived when he must meet his doom'. Lowson rose quietly and walked steadily to the clerk's room, where Berry asked, 'Are you ready Lowson?' As Berry pinioned him, Lowson moved to facilitate the hangman's work, and on leaving the room he looked round and wished one or two of the warders 'good morning'. They silently acknowledged.

Walking behind Lowson, Berry kept his hand on the strap in case his man should falter, but he required no assistance. Telling the officiating priest that he preferred the comfort of the spiritualist doctrine, he laughed, cursed at Berry, and said, 'In a minute or two I'll know more about it than any of you.' Berry continued:

Above the words of the chaplain arose his threats and curses, and of the two of us I was the one who trembled most.

As the procession moved into the open air there was a burst of sunshine, contrasting in a strange manner with the melancholy nature of the proceedings that day.

Passing round the angle of the prison brought the scaffold into view. One of the warders was standing with his foot on the lever, while from the black beam dangled the rope. Just at this moment the sound of the Cathedral clock was heard striking the hour of eight, and when it had ceased the bell of the prison began to emit its harsh, metallic message. These were the last sounds of the outer world that Joseph Lowson was to hear.

He walked up the incline, at the top of which the scaffold was erected, and, reaching it, stopped almost mechanically on the drop with his face to the east.

'Not that way, Lowson,' I said in a firm voice.

It was a custom of Marwood's to turn the face of his victim from the east, and I followed it through my career, except on one occasion. I allowed Dr. Cross, the bravest man I ever hanged, to die as a Christian.

On each side of Lowson stood two warders, and as soon as he turned I began to adjust the straps around his ankles. When he felt them tighten he began to speak.

'He is innocent,' he declared, mentioning the name of the man who had been reprieved. 'The other man,' and he mentioned the name of his companion who had been acquitted, 'struck the first blow, and I assisted.'

I was relieved to hear the confession, but still I was trembling violently, and terrified that I would make a mistake.

While I was adjusting the rope with nervous fingers he began to speak in a loud voice concerning the man who was still in prison, and who had escaped the rope by a hair's breadth.

'I hope the country and the Crown will look after him, and see that they get him safe home again.' The next minute he had taken his last view of earthly things.

The chaplain, who had halted temporarily while I was busy, resumed the service, and had uttered a few sentences, when, without any signal, I stepped to the lever. It would not move.

The sweat began to run down my cheeks, and I felt a faintness coming over me.

What was I doing? I could not understand it. Every eye was upon me, and I felt as if I were about to go mad. I glanced up at one of the warders, and saw he was making desperate signals to me. Ah! That was it! I had been tugging the wrong way at the lever, and, of course, it would not move. Pulling it in the other direction, the doors went down with a clang, and, still clinging to the lever, I saw Lawson plunge backwards and then disappear.

Releasing my hold, I dashed towards the wall, and, panting for breath, I leaned against it.

'Is it all right?' I asked, when the warden came up to me.

'Yes, all right, Mr Berry. He died instantaneously.'

'You are sure there was no bungling?'

'Quite sure. You are not feeling quite yourself, Mr Berry.'

'No; I am feeling as if I had been hanged and not him,' I replied. 'This is one of the worst executions I ever carried out.'

Everybody was feeling upset at the behaviour of my victim on the way to his doom, but one and all they agreed that I had done my work mercifully and well.

They were exceedingly kind to me, tried to make me forget my misery by talking of other things, and anon I felt well enough to leave the prison.

Berry stated that he had never dealt before with a man who exhibited so much coolness and nerve in his last moments as Lowson. Berry journeyed home to Bradford from Durham, his mind filled with 'frightful memories'. He claimed he was looking 'a shadow of his former self' when he arrived home. His wife gave him strength:

God knows what would have happened to me but for the blessing of a good and faithful wife, who gave me the comfort I needed so badly, and by her loving assurances helped me to regain my health and strength.

Siddle, who was Lowson's brother-in-law, was subsequently released from prison but was later certified insane and committed to an asylum, where he eventually died. The locals regarded Hodgson as a killer for the rest of his days.

Berry now enjoyed what he must have seen as a welcome break from his unpleasant experiences. His next execution, at Liverpool, did not take place until mid-August. In the meantime it was reported in *The Times* of 22 June 1884 that a Bill had been introduced in Parliament by Sir Edmund Lechmere, MP, proposing the appointment of a public executioner by the Home Secretary, together with 'assistant officers as may be thought necessary'. It was advocated that the hangman's duties could thus be regulated and the cases and manner in which the duties were to be exercised. They would also be subject to removal by the Home Secretary and would receive a certificate of appointment. Parliament would provide remuneration and the Bill prohibited the appointment of the executioner by the sheriff. Anyone else employed would have to be sanctioned by the Home Secretary.

Peter Cassidy, aged 54, was a tinsmith who lived with his wife at Bootle on Merseyside. On 25 June he had been out on a drunken binge and returned home to find his wife in a similar state. An argument ensued and the normally placid Cassidy erupted in a drink-fuelled rage. He grabbed a cleaver and a wooden mallet and beat in his wife's head. He was tried at Liverpool Assizes on 31 July 1884 before Mr Justice Day. Found guilty he was duly sentenced to death, the execution fixed for 19 August.

Berry thought Cassidy's to be a 'difficult' case, one 'in which it is difficult to know whether the man should be most pitied or blamed, whether he was not more sinned against than sinning'. At least this time he could feel certain of the man's guilt for the crime; Cassidy had not denied it. Cassidy paid great attention to the ministrations of the Reverend Father Bonté, the Roman Catholic Chaplain, and seemed peaceful and resigned to his fate. Berry described the moving experience of this execution:

He walked to the scaffold with a free, firm stride. The morning was dark and gloomy, but just as we passed across the prison yard a thin bright gleam of sunlight pierced the leaden clouds and rested for a moment upon the little procession. In that moment of sunshine Cassidy breathed convulsively, but the sky clouded over almost instantly and he regained his composure. On the scaffold he entered into the Roman Catholic service, which Father Bonté was reading, repeating the responses firmly and fervently, in fact, he was so engrossed in the service that I do not think he knew that I pinioned his legs. He continued his prayers as I adjusted the white cap over his eyes, but when the rope touched his neck he blushed crimson to the roots of his hair, and his lips twitched. Intense shame and sorrow were never more plainly expressed by any man.

The hanging was completed without a problem.

Berry's next execution was only five days later and involved a trip to Wexford, in Ireland, where James Tobin awaited the death penalty for murder. On 19 May 1884 an elderly farmer by the name of Moore returned to his farm at Rathlow after an hour's absence on business. His 80-year-old wife Elizabeth was missing and, after a search, he found her beaten to death in a field, the murder weapon, a broken shovel, lying beside her. There were items missing from the house and the motive was presumed to be robbery. Tobin, a tramp, was seen nearby and was arrested later in the day when he sold some of the stolen property. No problem with the execution, on 24 August 1884, was recorded.

On 26 August 1884, this time at Armley Gaol, Leeds, another execution took place: that of Joseph Laycock, aged 34, for the murder of his wife and four children, all of whose throats he had cut. However, Berry was not employed, this being the first execution undertaken by James Billington, a barber from Farnworth, executioner for the county of Yorkshire. He had applied to be 'number one hangman' for London at the same time as Berry, and, having failed in that, had secured the Yorkshire post.

On 6 October 1884, Berry conducted a double execution at Newgate Prison. It was his first double execution since the case of Vickers and Innes at Edinburgh, and the first of a succession of three such executions. One of his 'victims' at Newgate was the notorious Thomas Henry Orrock, 21 years of age and the son of a respectable chapel-going Dalston family. Orrock, a cabinet-maker by trade, had drifted into the criminal fraternity and acquired a revolver, armed with which he set out on the foggy night of 1

December 1882, equipped also with housebreaking tools. He was caught while in the act of breaking into a Baptist chapel in Ashwin Street, Dalston. Police Constable George Cole, a young and newly married man, detained him, but while taking him to the police station a struggle took place, during which Orrock drew his gun and fired four shots at the officer. PC Cole fell dying and Orrock disappeared into the all-encompassing fog. Two chisels, a small wooden wedge, and a low-crowned, black felt, wideawake hat were found at the scene. One of the chisels, a cabinet-maker's, had a wooden handle and 1¼in-wide blade with scratches on it. On examination the scratches were found to contain the partial word 'r-o-c-k'; later determined to be part of Orrock's name, of course.

Two women had witnessed the struggle and ran to the police station to raise the alarm. The only description they could give was that the offender was wearing a wide-brimmed hat. Sergeant Cobb knew most of the local youths and recalled seeing Orrock earlier that evening in such a hat. Orrock was arrested but an identification parade failed and he went to ground. It was over a year later that Sergeant Cobb discovered that a group of local youths, including Orrock, had gone to Tottenham marshes, where he practised target shooting at a tree with his gun. The diligent Cobb went to the marshes and located the tree, retrieving bullets embedded in it. These were found to have been fired from the same weapon that had been used on PC Cole.

Orrock was eventually located in Coldbath Fields Prison where he was serving a sentence for burglary. Tried for murder, he was found guilty on 19 September 1884, having first confessed to the crime.

The second Newgate convict was Thomas Harris, aged 48, a market gardener with eleven children. He was sentenced to death for the murder of his wife, by cutting her throat with a razor, at Kilburn on 9 August. Despite a plea of insanity – he claimed non-recollection of the murder stating his mind was a blank – he was found guilty.

The prison chaplain, Revd Mr Duffield, attended both condemned men in their cells. They retired on the Sunday night at ten o'clock and rose at 6.00 a.m., after which they were again attended by the chaplain. Both appeared resigned to their fate, Harris remaining particularly stolid. At twenty minutes to eight Mr Sheriff Phillips, one of the sheriffs of London and Middlesex, and the under-sheriffs, Mr H. Homewood Crawford and Mr F. Kynaston Metcalfe, arrived at the prison and were received by the governor, Captain Sutton Kirkpatrick. The officials went to the condemned cell, where Berry was pinioning the prisoners. The procession was formed and moved into the yard with the chaplain reading part of the Burial Service of the Church of England. The bell of nearby St Sepulchre's Church had begun to toll. First Orrock was placed on the drop and Berry quickly pulled the white cap over his face and adjusted the rope around his neck, with the knot on the left side, in the usual manner. Harris, who had been looking on, was then also placed on the drop, Berry quickly placing the cap over his face and adjusting the knot in the same way he had with Orrock. Both prisoners appeared calm and, everything being ready, the signal was given as the hour of eight o'clock struck. Berry pulled the lever and both men fell through the trap, the large crowd outside the prison watching eagerly as the black flag was hoisted over the prison. However, although Dr Gilbert, the prison surgeon, was of the opinion that death in each case must have been instantaneous, all had not gone as smoothly as planned. According to Mr Kynaston Metcalfe, Berry was very quick at his work but 'he very nearly had a man's head off [Harris] . . . it was a terrible sight altogether, it did not get in the papers. I was on the scaffold and would not let any of the press representatives come up; I told the warders to put the shutters up while I talked to the press to keep them away' (Aberdare).

The City Coroner, Mr S.F. Langham, held an inquest into the death of the condemned men at the Sessions House in the Old Bailey, at which Metcalfe stated that Harris was given a 7ft 6in drop (Berry had in fact allowed a drop of 7ft 5in), but, given that Harris was a heavy man weighing over 14 stone, Berry's miscalculation in giving too great a drop 'showed a want of common sense'. Challenging Berry concerning this, he had received the answer 'there must have been something the matter with the man's neck'. Mr Metcalfe suggested that a shorter drop would have been in order and that the rope, 'not a Home Office rope' but one of Berry's own, may have been too thin. Chief Warder Ward stated, '. . . the man Harris was a heavy man, and the drop no doubt was excessive because the whole front of his throat tore right away; he was hanged by the back of the neck'.

Two weeks later Berry and 'Chester' travelled to Manchester to carry out another double execution, this time at Strangeways Prison. The first prisoner was Kay Howarth, 25 years old and a well-known Bolton ne'er-do-well. Richard Dugdale, aged 37, a commercial traveller from Wakefield employed by Austin Brothers maltsters, had arrived in Bolton on 3 October on business at the local pubs. He had been in a bar with a friend, Robert Hall, when Howarth joined them. Hall knew Howarth to be a thief and tried to get rid of him, but Howarth followed them to various local bars as Dugdale conducted his business and collected a quantity of money from his various deals. Hall was obliged to leave during the evening, and since by then Dugdale was the worse for drink, Hall had asked Howarth to escort his friend back to his hotel. Later Dugdale's body was discovered on some waste ground off a street with horrific throat wounds. A faked suicide note was found beside the body. The police spoke to Robert Hall and then located Howarth, finding some of the deceased's possessions and money in his room. Howarth also had blood on his clothing. He was found guilty at Manchester Assizes and sentenced to death by Mr Justice Smith.

The second prisoner was Harry Hammond Swindells, aged 51, a bookkeeper who worked for his wife, Suzannah, in a successful yeast business that she had been left from a previous marriage. Swindells was constantly pestering her for money and spent most of it on drink and womanising. When a woman became pregnant things came to a head and Suzannah threw him out. He emigrated to America but his money soon ran out, and he returned to try and win back his wife – and her money. Supported by her children, she rejected him. Then, in July 1884, he again turned up at the house causing trouble. His stepdaughter immediately went to fetch her uncle, James Wild, 59, who lived nearby. On his arrival a fierce dispute erupted and Swindells shot Wild dead. Swindells fled and was not located until a few weeks later, in August, when he was arrested, dressed as a tramp, near Oldham. He was sentenced to death at Manchester Assizes. Immediately before he was executed he confessed that he had gone to the home of his wife 'with the intention to kill'.

Berry and his assistant arrived at the prison on Saturday 22 November. At 6.00 a.m. on Monday 24 November 1884 the two condemned men breakfasted and were then visited by the prison chaplain, Mr Cox, an Oldham missionary. They bore themselves firmly during pinioning and walked steadily to the gallows without assistance. Swindells made the responses to the service being read by the chaplain and seemed calm, but Howarth seemed agitated and sobbed aloud. A drop of 8 feet was given and in each case death was instantaneous.

There had been some confusion prior to this execution concerning the granting of orders of admission to witness the event. The High Sheriff had maintained that discretion rested with the visiting justices and had declined to issue further orders, but the clerk to the visiting justices, the prison governor and other authorities all held that the power of admitting witnesses to the execution rested entirely with the High Sheriff. In this instance, he finally granted admission for the press to attend.

Berry's tally of 'victims' now stood at ten; he was becoming practised at his calling.

The third double execution was scheduled for 8 December at Kirkdale Gaol, Liverpool. The first prisoner was a Russian sailor named Ernest Ewerstadt, aged 23, who had murdered Elizabeth Hamblin, a married woman. The couple had lived together for several months until she left him in the summer of 1884 after he withheld housekeeping money from her. Despite the parting they remained on good terms, and on 19 September he asked a friend to request Elizabeth to meet him that evening. She sent the message back that she did not wish to see him. On learning from his friend that she was in the company of two black sailors, with whom she was drinking, Ewerstadt then declared that on getting his wages he would buy a gun and shoot her. The following day he in fact purchased a dagger and, finding Elizabeth in a bar, he told her that unless she came back with him there would be 'a bloody deed done that night'. Apparently ignoring this threat, the two of them visited a friend's house together, but when he threatened to kill her she left. He followed her home, and after a dispute on the doorstep, fatally stabbed her. Having initially fled, he later confessed to a friend, 'Me kill my Lizzie, me die too!' He was arrested and tried at Liverpool Assizes where Mr Justice Day sentenced him to death on 22 November.

The second prisoner was Arthur Shaw, a 31-year-old tailor in Collyhurst, Manchester. A police constable found the body of Ellen Shaw on the floor at her home on 3 November 1884. Ellen, who had a history of drinking problems, had been chatting to a neighbour when her young daughter came out stating that Shaw wanted to see her. Soon after that Arthur Shaw went out and told the neighbour that his wife had fallen and hurt herself, and the police were called. Shaw pleaded innocence but it was found that his wife had, in fact, been strangled.

A new man named Speight – brought by Berry rather than appointed by the authorities – assisted Berry on this occasion, and, according to Dr Barr (recorded in Aberdare), Berry executed one man and his assistant the other. A drop of 7 feet was set for Ewerstadt, but Shaw, being lighter at 142lb, was given 7ft 8in. The additional 8 inches was apparently not enough as it was noted that Shaw took over 2 minutes to die and 'struggled slightly'. Further investigation revealed that the trapdoor had swung back and displaced the noose and its 'thimble', resulting in strangulation instead of the desired dislocation of the vertebrae. Ironically, therefore, Shaw had died in a similar manner to his wife. Ewerstadt's death was also put down to asphyxiation rather than dislocation of the vertebrae. In each case the drop given had been too short, but it was nonetheless stated that Berry appeared to do his work well.

Christmas 1884 arrived, and Berry was now well established as the country's 'number one' hangman. However, within two months a momentous event was to occur on the gallows that would ensure him immortal fame in the annals of crime and capital punishment. It would forever remain on his mind.

8

The man they could not hang

'. . . there are exceptional incidents . . . which stand out on the tablet of one's memory . . . '

1885 began uneventfully enough. On Tuesday 13 January, at Wandsworth, Berry executed 23-year-old Horace Robert Jay who had murdered his young sweetheart on 15 November 1884. It was a tragic case. The girl was Florence Kemp, only 17 years old when the couple met the previous Christmas. They had lived together until mid-1884, when she left him to return to her parents. He invited her to tea at his lodgings on the fatal day but she refused to move back in with him saying that she now had another man friend. In a jealous rage he cut her throat and attempted to cut his own. He was tried at the Central Criminal Court before Mr Justice Hawkins on 22 December. Found guilty, he was sentenced and hanged by Berry without incident.

Just two days later Berry made a second trip to Ireland, this time for two separate executions. 'Richard Chester' accompanied him. The first was at Galway and involved Michael Downey who had been sentenced to death in December for the murder of a farmer, John Moylan. Moylan, recently returned from America and a tenant farmer at Clonbooland near Galway, had been having an affair with Downey's wife, and when Downey discovered the two of them walking together he shot him. He was tried three times, first in the Summer Assizes, then twice at the Winter Assizes, the verdict of the jury being split in the first two trials. Before the execution, on Friday 16 January, he left a note admitting his guilt.

The second execution, on Tuesday 20 January, was that of

Thomas Parry, aged 26, again at Galway. Having been jilted by his fiancée, Miss Burns, Parry, a steward from Kings County, had travelled over 100 miles to the hotel where she was staying to ask if the relationship was really at an end. When she indicated that it was he produced a gun and shot her, following which he then turned the gun on himself, but suffered only a minor wound. Despite the jury's recommendation to show mercy Mr Justice Lawson sentenced him to death. Inquiries were made concerning his sanity but Lord Spencer decided that justice must take its course. Parry walked firmly to the scaffold and refused to accept the aid of a warder who offered it. He stood motionless on the drop and said nothing apart from responding to the words of the chaplain. Using the same trusty rope that had despatched Downey a few days before, Berry activated the bolt and Parry died instantly. The subsequent inquest revealed that death had been caused by dislocation of the neck.

The most memorable and infamous event of Berry's career occurred on Monday 23 February 1885, after he had accepted what seemed another routine commission at Exeter. The Babbacombe murder had received extensive press coverage. John Henry George Lee, a 19-year-old footman of Abbotskerswell, had been employed by Miss Emma Keyse, a 68-year-old spinster who lived at the Glen (formerly 'Beach House'), at Babbacombe, near Torquay, South Devon, a picturesque cottage on the seafront at the bottom of a steep hill, overlooking the bay. Early on Saturday 15 November 1884, Miss Keyse, a deeply religious lady who had required her servants to attend daily prayers, was found brutally murdered in the dining room, her throat cut and head battered, and the room having been set on fire. It was thought that Lee, who had already served a prison sentence for theft, was angered by his employer's mean-spiritedness, she having reduced his already small wage because of some trivial offence. Arrested on suspicion of her murder and tried on 2–4 February 1885 at Exeter Assizes, he was convicted and received the death sentence. Initially, Reginald Gwynne Templer, a young solicitor and acquaintance of Miss Keyse, represented Lee, but he became ill and was replaced by his brother. As Lee never confessed to the murder, much controversy has attached itself to his conviction and the full facts of what happened that fateful night are far from certain. Elizabeth Harris, the cook, was Lee's half-sister and was pregnant, so it is possible that a wealthy adulterer may have been involved.

On the day sentence was passed the Under-Sheriff of Devon, Henry M. James, telegraphed Berry at Bradford,

'. . . who I believed to be fully up to his work as an executioner, asking him to perform that office on Lee on Monday 23rd February. On receiving his reply I immediately informed the Governor of the prison that the execution would take place on that day at 800am' (letter dated 10 March 1885 Ref. National Archives HO 144/148/A438492 XC12399).

Berry travelled from Bradford to Bristol and then on to Exeter on the morning of Friday 20 February. He arrived at Exeter station at 11.50 a.m., walked to the prison, and was shown to the governor's office, where he conferred with Mr Edwin Cowtan. Having left to get his lunch, he returned at 1.50 p.m. and was shown his bedroom, an officer's room in the new hospital ward, after which he went to the prison coach house, where the prison van was normally kept and where the scaffold had been erected. Berry described the machinery of execution:

In the coach house I found a beam, about four inches thick and about a foot in depth, was placed across the top of the coach house, the ends being fixed in the walls on each side. Through this beam an iron bolt was fastened with an iron nut on the upper side, and to this bolt a wrought iron rod was fixed, about three quarters of a yard long, with a hole at the lower end, to which the rope was to be attached. Two trap-doors were placed in the floor of the coach house, which is flagged with stone, and these doors cover a pit about 2 yards by 1½ yards across and about 11 feet deep. On inspecting these doors I found they were only about an inch thick, but to have been constructed properly should have been three or four inches thick. The ironwork of the doors was of a frail kind, and much too weak for the purpose.

There was a lever to these doors, and it was placed near the top of them. I pulled the lever, and the doors dropped, the catches acting all right. I had the doors raised, and tried the lever a second time, when the catches again acted all right. The Governor was watching me through the window of his office, and saw me try the doors. After the examination I went to him, explained how I found the doors, and suggested to him that for future executions new trap-doors should be made about three times as thick as those then fixed. I also suggested that a spring should be fixed in the wall to hold the doors back when they fell, so that no rebounding occurred, and that the iron work of the doors should be stronger. The Governor said that he would see to these matters in the future.

The platform was flush with the floor and consisted of two wooden doors, each having two hinges. The hinges on one of the doors were extended so that they stretched across the width of the other door, supporting it, and resting on the draw bolt. The draw bolt had two 'U' shaped bends (or cranks) in it, and as it was drawn by pressure on the lever the bolt slid along until the supporting ends of the extended hinges dropped through the 'U' bends and the doors fell. The equipment was overhauled, cleaned and tested on the Saturday preceding the execution by the Artizan Warder, Charles Edwards, and Assistant Warder A.J. Titford. Berry also checked and tested it and passed the comment that he felt the trapdoors were not thick enough. It was tested five times on the Saturday but no weight had been used on the doors, these being allowed to drop by their own weight only. On the Sunday the van-house was closed and locked throughout the day and Berry remained in the prison all day, retiring at 9.45 p.m. It had rained heavily on both the Saturday and Sunday nights.

On the morning of Monday 23 February the van-house was cleared and prepared. At 7.15 a.m. Mr Cowtan went with Berry to see the rope fixed to the beam. At 7.55 a.m. he accompanied Berry to the condemned cell and Lee was pinioned. Outside the cell the chaplain, John Pitkin, began to read the burial service and walked in front of Lee as the governor, followed by the chief warder, led the procession to the place of execution. Lee was placed under the beam and Berry, 'with considerable skill and rapidity', strapped the prisoner's legs above the ankles, placed the hood over his head and adjusted the noose about his neck, stepped back and pulled the lever. The bolt drew but the trapdoors moved about a quarter of an inch only and failed to fall. They appeared to be tightly jammed. The Chief Constable of Devon, C. de Courcy Hamilton, was present and thought that, as it was 'a very wet and damp morning', the 'footboards' had become swollen and jammed when 'their top edges came in contact'.

Lee was moved back from the drop, still pinioned, with the white cap over his face and the rope still around his neck, while Berry and the warders tested the trapdoors and stamped on them. The doors then worked. Lee was replaced on the doors and the lever again pulled, but the doors again failed to drop.

Again Lee was removed and Berry unloosed the leg strap, removed the white cap and took the rope from his neck. This time Lee was taken from the shed, and the equipment was checked. According to the Chief Constable, 'A prison warder was made to stand on them, holding on by both hands to the rope; the trigger was pulled, and the boards fell.'

Lee was replaced and prepared, the noose readjusted. For the third time Berry pulled the lever in an attempt to activate the drop, 'and in trying to force it, the lever was slightly strained'. Again it failed. It was suggested that the wood fitted too tightly, and an axe and plane were fetched. A piece of wood was sawn off one of the doors close to where the iron catches were, and with the aid of an iron crowbar the catches were knocked off and the doors fell. The chaplain appealed to the governor to stop the proceedings and the medical officer, T. Wilson Gaird, ordered Lee's removal to a nearby cell. The medical officer said, 'You may experiment as much as you like on a sack of flour, but you shall not experiment on this man any longer.'

The chaplain later reported:

More than 30 minutes had elapsed since I first began the service at the condemned cell. Then, when I saw the helpless confusion that prevailed, the great mental suffering through which the culprit had passed, and the improbability of the scaffold working, I joined with the medical officer in an appeal to the Under Sheriff to postpone the execution for that day. Great cruelty would have characterized further effort to carry out the sentence that day. Lee suffered much and seemed to be almost unconscious of what was going on. He would rather have died, I verily believe, and the first words he uttered after he had been led back to his cell, and recovered from his state of apparent semi-consciousness, were, 'Why am I not to die?' On looking back on the events as they happened, one cannot help deploring them; and one is driven to the conclusion that if only thoughtful care and supervision had been exercised in the erection of the drop, and in its examination prior to the attempted execution, all this public scandal would have been avoided.

The under-sheriff travelled to London that very afternoon to consult with the Home Secretary Sir William Harcourt. On being told the story Harcourt decided: '. . . I thought it would shock the feelings of anyone if a man had to twice incur the pangs of imminent death. I therefore signed a respite in the case to continue during Her Majesty's pleasure' (Hansard, February 23 1885).

The Home Office immediately requested the Governor of Exeter Prison to report on the failure of the scaffold equipment. The scaffold had been originally fixed in 1879 in the old hospital, which was afterwards demolished. This was for the execution of Annie Tooke, a 'baby farmer', who had murdered a child. Marwood executed her on 11 August 1879 and the equipment had not been used since. The scaffold was re-erected in 1882 in the prison van-house, where the pit was about 2ft 6in shallower than the old one. The clerks of works, Messrs Libby and Cuthbert, were requested to examine and report on the equipment. On attending the van-house two days after the attempted execution of Lee, they found the execution apparatus was under cover and dry. They descended into the pit and examined the mechanism from below. The draw bolt was examined from above and they found signs of friction on the inner surface of one of the cranks. They believed that the bearing end of the extended hinge at this point was the cause of the failure of the drop to operate. They placed a 168lb weight on the platform and found that it would not fall. They then discovered that the end of one of the long hinges was resting on a mere one eighth of an inch overlap on the draw bolt at the 'U' bend or crank. They again tested the drop without a weight and found it would operate when the lever was pulled quickly. When the lever was pulled slowly the drop remained stuck on one test but fell on another, but seemed to bind or grate at the end of the long hinge in question. Thus the failure of the gallows machinery to work was fixed as 'due to the fact that one of the long hinges rested on the draw-bolt one eight of an inch too much'. That one eighth of an inch overlap had saved Lee's life.

It is probable that when the scaffold machinery was fixed over the pit in the van-house the two sides were placed one eighth of an inch nearer than they had been when previously assembled. Or, possibly, the long hinge had been very slightly bent in some way at that time. The Home Office Prison Department engineer, George Cuthbert, who had travelled to Exeter to discover the cause of the failure and examined the apparatus early on the morning of 24 February, drew up a report with diagrams, illustrating the defect.

The scaffold had been erected by the prison authorities and not by the sheriff's arrangement. The equipment was deemed faulty and the bearing bars (extended hinges) were too light. The Home Office Secretary stated that the sheriff rather than the prison authorities should be responsible for ensuring that proper equipment was used. Berry was asked for his account of the incident and wrote a long letter to the under-sheriff dated 4 March 1885. The fact that there was no known repurcussion for Berry indicates that the blame for the failed execution had rightly been ascribed to the faulty gallows and not Berry's expertise. Unfortunately for him, however, history seems to have accorded the incident to him as another 'bungled execution'.

Long regarded as a great mystery, various reasons for the failure of the execution were advanced over the years, from divine intervention to interference with the trapdoors by a fellow convict. None of these is correct, and the matter was never a mystery in official circles.

Lee's sentence was commuted to life imprisonment and he soon rejoiced in the sobriquet 'The Man They Could Not Hang'. Finally released from Portland Prison on 17 December 1907, he had continued to protest his innocence throughout twenty-two years' imprisonment. His fate, for years shrouded in mystery, is now known, his case having been extensively researched by authors Mike Holgate and Ian Waugh. Lee emigrated to America where he lived with his wife Adelina. He died in 1945 at the age of 80 at home in Milwaukee, and he had outlived his hangman by many years.

9

The case of James Lee and a near decapitation

'. . . nodding to signify he was ready, awaited the adjusting of the noose.'

Berry had just over three weeks to recover from his unnerving experience at Exeter. His next 'victim', Henry Kimberley, awaited execution at Birmingham Prison. On Saturday 27 December 1884, Kimberley had shot his ex-partner of seventeen years, Harriet Stewart, and her friend Mrs Emma Palmer, the wife of a local publican. Mrs Palmer died but Harriet was only wounded. It was the common domestic scenario: he wanted her back, but she refused. Kimberley fired a third time, but was then restrained by a barman and customers until the arrival of the police.

A petition asking for reprieve was forwarded to the Home Secretary but the latter ruled that there were no grounds to warrant such a move. For the purpose of the execution a small brick building had been erected adjoining the outer walls of the storeroom of the gaol. In its essential features it was described as resembling the scaffold 'lately employed at Exeter'. A massive oak beam ran across the shed, which was about 15 feet square. The ends of this beam were fixed in the walls at a height of 8 feet. Beneath the platform was a pit allowing a drop of upwards of 10 feet. The platform itself consisted of two wooden doors constructed like an ordinary cellar-flap with hinges, falling inwards. The doors were supported on two horizontal iron bars hinged at one end and at the other resting upon a crossbar. The latter was arranged so that it could slide along at the pull of a lever. When drawn, the horizontal bars fell and the doors gave way so that the culprit dropped into the pit, out of view.

Shortly before eight o'clock Kimberley took his place under the beam, saying in a low, sobbing tone, 'Lord have mercy upon me' in response to the chaplain's words. Berry 'performed his task with despatch' and Kimberley died instantly. A crowd that had assembled outside the prison, estimated at around 15,000 to 20,000 people, saw the black flag immediately hoisted. The execution was followed by the customary inquest, before the local deputy coroner Mr B. Weekes. A small group of official witnesses and representatives of the press had witnessed the execution, the first at the Birmingham Borough gaol since Birmingham was created an assize town.

On Tuesday 20 January 1885, Inspector Thomas Simmons of the Essex County Police was driving the police trap at South Hornchurch accompanied by PC 107 Alfred Marden. Near Rainham railway station they were met by PC Wilderspoon of the Metropolitan Police who told them that he had just seen three men getting off the London train, one of whom he recognised as a well-known criminal named David Dredge. The two Essex officers made a search and at about 4.00 p.m. saw Dredge and the other two men near Blewitts Farm on the lower road towards Rainham walking towards Hornchurch. Simmons instructed Marden to keep watch on them while he drove to Rainham to procure back-up. Marden followed the men but lost sight of them at Ford Lane, so he waited in the Hornchurch Road for the return of the inspector. Simmons arrived with another constable and the officers set out in search of the men. They located Dredge and his friends in the Romford Road, about a hundred yards ahead of them. The men heard the approach of the police trap and, on seeing the officers, made off. Dredge scrambled through a hedge but was detained by Marden in a field. Inspector Simmons stopped the other two. Asked by Marden what he was doing in the area, Dredge produced a revolver from his pocket and pointed it at the policeman's head, threatening to 'blow his brains out'.

Marden then heard a shot, turned and saw the taller of Dredge's companions standing with a smoking revolver in his hand, aimed at the inspector, who was staggering back clutching at his stomach. PC Marden ran towards the men, but they fled down the road. Simmons, though still standing, was obviously in great pain, but he assured Marden that he could be left, so the PC pursued the fleeing men across a nearby field. The taller man, who had fired the shot, took off and discarded his overcoat, clearly finding it an encumbrance. Marden took the coat up and, still in pursuit, checked the pockets. The two men disappeared behind a haystack but then reappeared, armed with revolvers and facing Marden. They fired, and Marden tripped and fell to the ground, at which the two continued to flee, the unarmed policeman once more in pursuit. Reaching a river the men turned to face Marden, guns raised, but instead of firing they took to the river and made their way across. It was beginning to get dark and Marden lost the men in the gathering shadows, so he headed back, meeting the inspector on his way. He assisted the latter, who was evidently still in great pain, back to the trap and they went to the nearest police station, at Dagenham.

The alarm was raised and the description of the three offenders circulated. The wounded inspector was taken to his home in South Street, Romford, where he lingered for four days before dying on Saturday 24 January. A subsequent post-mortem revealed that the bullet had entered his abdomen, travelled through his body and lodged at the base of his spine. A native of Weeley near Colchester, he was 38 years old when he died.

Extensive press coverage was given to the incident and Superintendent Dobson of Brentwood led an intensive manhunt. The pockets of the discarded overcoat had been found to contain seven ball cartridges matching the bullet found in Simmons's body, one cartridge case, a selection of skeleton keys and a spectacle case. The search was extended to London's East End, with officers of the Metropolitan Police's H or Whitechapel Division now involved, and on 3 February Detective Sergeant Rolf spotted Dredge in Burdett Road, Stepney. The fugitive surrendered quietly and was taken to the local police station. The Essex Police were informed and Sergeant Rolf was ordered to convey his man by train to Romford.

Dredge was initially charged only with threatening to shoot PC Marden and was remanded in custody to Chelmsford Prison. He subsequently appeared before the Romford magistrates again on 19 February, when he was charged with the murder of Inspector Simmons. Though he claimed to have been nowhere near the inspector when he was shot, the charge included the fact that he was engaged in a common enterprise to commit an unlawful act with the other two men and was thus culpable. He pleaded 'not guilty', and in view of local antagonism to the accused the trial was scheduled for hearing at the Hertford Assizes.

Meanwhile the hunt continued for the other two men. On 10 March a pawnbroker in Euston Square, London, sent an employee to report to the police that a man fitting the description of one of the wanted men was in the shop offering a revolver for sale. The police attended and there found James Lee, aged 45. On seeing the two constables, Lee attempted to flee and a frantic struggle ensued, but, with the assistance of members of the public, the two officers overpowered him and took him to Platt Street Police Station.

Due to the confusion caused by the struggle at his arrest, Lee had not been searched, and while in the interview room he took a handful of cartridges from his pocket and threw them into an open fire. The cartridges exploded and Lee again attempted to escape. He was restrained and then conveyed to Romford Police Station, where, despite protesting his innocence, he was charged with the wilful murder of Inspector Simmons. Lee claimed that he had been nowhere near the location at the time of the shooting and that he had been falsely identified, but PC Wilderspoon positively identified him as one of Dredge's companions. Throughout the ensuing proceedings, Lee proved so belligerent that it was necessary to handcuff him to an officer on either side when escorting him to and from the hearings.

As with Dredge, application was also made to try Lee elsewhere, and he was committed for trial at the Central Criminal Court at the Old Bailey. Application was further made for the two men to be tried together, so Dredge was also committed to the Old Bailey. On Monday 27 April the two men stood together in the dock before Mr Justice Hawkins. Various witnesses were called including witnesses to the shooting. Dredge's defence was that he had not fired the fatal shot, while Lee continued to deny even being at the scene. Dredge was acquitted but then rearrested over his threats to shoot PC Marden. Lee was found guilty. Asked if he had anything to say, he denied his guilt and became involved in an argument with the judge. He was sentenced to death and his execution set for 8.00 a.m. on Monday 18 May. Dredge was later found guilty of the lesser offence and sentenced to twelve months hard labour. The third man could not be found.

Lee, an Irishman, had in fact been born James Menson in 1844 at Cork. He had drifted into crime at an early age, having served three prison sentences in Ireland before moving over to London and settling in Somerstown. He joined a gang of thieves and burglars, a leading member of which was one Jack Martin. The two teamed up, carrying firearms at all times. Lee's first conviction came in England in 1871 under the alias Adams. The police were in no doubt that 'the third man' was Jack Martin, who by now had disappeared into the underworld.

Shortly after Menson's arrival in London he had read newspaper accounts of the John 'Babbacombe' Lee case and the celebrated failure of the gallows (detailed in the last chapter). Apparently, on reading this, he immediately changed his surname to Lee, declaring that 'They couldn't hang him, no more can they hang me' (see *From Constable to Commissioner* by Lt Col Sir Henry Smith, K.C.B., London, Chatto & Windus, 1910, which contains a fascinating account of Menson/Lee). His claim that he could not be hanged was proved wrong by the same executioner who had failed to hang John Lee. What was not previously known is the incredible fact that he died on the end of the same rope that John Lee had worn around his neck just under three months earlier.

Later events were to convince Berry that in hanging James Lee an innocent man had died. Indeed, such an impression did Lee make that he went on to state that he had 'never hanged a braver man'.

Berry had left Bradford on the Saturday morning, arriving in Chelmsford at 3.30 in the afternoon. *The Essex Herald* described him as

> a man of medium height, with a fresh complexion and a sleek and perfectly contented appearance. Like Marwood, he is communicative, but, unlike Marwood, he seems to be an abstemious and very quiet man.

At Springfield Prison he took a 'peep' at Lee and tested the gallows, describing them as 'an antiquated affair', upon which he superintended alterations, no doubt with the Exeter affair in mind. The scaffold had been erected in the prison yard at the Springfield end, over a pit 12 feet deep with stone steps leading down to the bottom. At the last two executions at the gaol, both performed by Marwood, the feet of the hanged men touched the ground in each case, so the pit had since been deepened. Berry tried the drop using a dummy that corresponded with Lee's weight and height. As he had no assistant with him, he rehearsed the execution with one of the warders, writing afterwards:

> Unfortunately, the head of the dummy came off, so I had to work some time before I could be sure of my calculations, but at last I was satisfied, and decided to go out for a walk.

One of the warders took Berry around the town, following which he returned to the Three Cups Inn, where he was staying, and had a cup of tea. During the afternoon he saw Lee's wife and her sister enter the prison for a last visit with the doomed man. Mrs Lee was carrying an infant child and her head was bowed. Both women were weeping. Lee, a Roman Catholic who wanted his children brought up in that faith, was attended by a Roman Catholic priest, Father Butt.

Berry, meanwhile, was experiencing some anxiety:

> I was a little bit frightened at having to hang a fellow like Lee. He had threatened Justice Hawkins to such an extent that he had six or seven officers with him in the dock, and he had told one of the warders that there was no scaffold in England strong enough to hang him.

On the Sunday he went to the prison, where he was given a room. Taking another look at Lee through the cell door, he asked one of the warders if he thought that Lee had 'done the job', to which the warder replied that he wasn't so sure.

On the morning of the execution, Berry went to get Lee but did not pinion him in the cell. Lee apparently 'had plenty to say for himself', chiefly concerning what he would do to Mr Justice Hawkins if he could get his hands on him; he went on 'cursing him with his dying breath'. Berry, waiting in the corridor for him to be brought, heard his shouts before he came into view, and confessed to being afraid, having formed the notion that Lee 'was going to use his hands'. The prisoner did not seem afraid of his approaching fate and the warders stayed close to him, wary of trouble. Berry readied his straps with the words, 'Don't give me any more trouble than you can help, I am only doing my duty', but Lee ignored him and began to curse the Home Office officials, complaining that he had not been allowed even to shake hands with his wife. He again cursed Mr Justice Hawkins and protested his innocence. Several Essex magistrates were present; according to Berry, 'A sense of justice brought one or two of them – others came out of morbid curiosity.' The High Sheriff of the county, Mr Lescher, was also present, doing his duty, but could not face witnessing the execution and went to the governor's room. Also present was the under-sheriff, Mr Walter Gepp. The scaffold had been erected in one of the exercise yards. Berry described the final scene:

He was resolute and undaunted, and his feet did not slouch as he walked along in the centre of a group of warders. On every side there was a murmur of admiration for his coolness and courage.

He met his death with great fortitude, and never once flinched or trembled, but bore himself with determined firmness.

When we reached the scaffold he glanced up at the black beam, and then his eyes travelled to the noose which was dangling from it. I have seen men faint at the sight, but Lee remained unmoved, and while I was pinioning his legs he bent and motioned to one of the officials of the prison.

Major Lane [the prison governor] approached, and Lee whispered something in his ear. The Governor nodded, but what he had been told I was not able to find out.

I was not long in completing my work, but while I was busy with it Lee continued to curse the English laws.

When I had finished he looked round, and with a look of recognition here and there he said –

'I have to thank you all, gentlemen, for the kindness I have received in this prison.'

I put the rope round his neck immediately he had made what I took to be his last speech and as I did so he spoke in a voice that was charged with emotion – 'My poor wife! My poor children!'

I could see that resolute as he was the man was suffering terrible mental agony, and I determined to put him out of his misery at once.

He was following my movements, however, and just as I went to pull the lever he shouted – 'I die an innocent man; remember that!'

He had scarcely spoken the words before he was dead.

As Lee was a light man, a drop of 8ft 6in had been allowed, and death appeared to be instantaneous, although it was reported that the rope vibrated for a minute or two and there was a perceptible twitching of the hands. The body was allowed to hang for an hour before being taken down. Immediately after the inquest the body was interred in the prison yard near the east wall, where the bodies of several executed murderers also rested. The general consensus afterwards, according to Berry, was that while Lee was possibly not guilty of the crime in question, he was 'well out of the way'. Berry followed this, in an account for *The Post*, with the rather resentful words:

I thought so myself at the time, but I altered my opinion after I had seen something more of the justice of England, and discovered how cheap human life and liberty are.

That article in *The Post* was headed 'INNOCENT, YET SENT TO THE SCAFFOLD', and began:

'I don't think that anybody would dispute that James Lee was innocent of the murder of Inspector Symmons [*sic*]. The confession afterwards made in my presence by another man removed all doubts, but like another one or two I have in mind it was supposed by the authorities.'

The alleged confession was also heard by one of the Essex magistrates witnessing the execution, the sporting baronet Sir Claude Champion de Crespigny of Maldon. A veteran of steeplechasing and ballooning, among other activities, Sir Claude took this opportunity of chatting with Berry (they were later to work together in a sequel to these events; see chapter 13). *The Essex Herald* reported that 'After the execution he [Berry] returned to London, where he had interviews with officials at the Home Office and the Sheriff's Office in regard to another execution.'

Berry's next execution was scheduled for a week later, on 25 May 1885, at Worcester. The case involved another police murderer, Moses Shrimpton, a 65-year-old dyed-in-the-wool poacher who had served his first prison sentence for poaching in 1848. On the night of 27/28 February 1885, Shrimpton had been out on his nefarious calling at Beoley, near Birmingham. That night a local police officer, PC Davies, had been on duty and had failed to rendezvous with his sergeant at 4.00 a.m. He was found dead in a field later that morning, having suffered over forty stab wounds to his upper body. From bloody footprints at the scene the police obtained a pattern of the offender's boots. Also that night some chickens had been stolen from a farm, an offence that Shrimpton was known for, so he was tracked to lodgings in Birmingham on 4 March and arrested by detectives, who broke down the door. Bloodstained clothing was found in his room, together with a knife of the kind used to kill PC Davies and boots bearing the pattern found at the crime scene. He had sold the policeman's watch and chain to another occupant of the lodgings. Tried at Worcester Assizes on 6 May before Baron Huddlestone, he was found guilty.

Berry was impressed with Shrimpton, as he was with many others he executed. In this case it was the criminal's long career of wrongdoing stretching 'almost from the cradle to the grave' that he noted, describing him as 'a man of strong character and much determination of purpose, a leader amongst the ruffians of his district'. Shrimpton awaited his fate in Worcester gaol where he was already well known as a frequent inmate. He expressed no apparent surprise or sentiment at the death sentence, but became extremely repentant, paying great attention to the chaplain on his visits and constantly reading the Bible. He walked to the gallows, in the prison treadmill house, with a firm stride and stepped onto the drop. Berry wrote:

The drop was similar to the one on which John Lee, of Babbicome [*sic*], had stood, and I was not a little afraid that a hitch might take place . . . he composedly glanced down to see that his feet were in proper position while I fastened the strap around his legs. He was standing with his face towards the treadmill, and the contrast was a strange one. How often in the past had he worked out punishment inflicted for poaching, and now, as the result of a poaching affray, he was about to pay the highest penalty known to the law.

Most of those present could only see his back, but while I was pinioning his feet Moses Shrimpton turned his eyes round towards two or three of the gentlemen who were within his view.

The next moment he motioned to the Sheriff, who came forward. Moses Shrimpton whispered something in his ear, and I distinctly heard him say – 'Remember.' He used the same word that Charles I used at his execution, and I have reason to believe he spoke about certain property he wished conveyed to his relatives. 'All right, I'll see to it,' said the Sheriff.

When all was in readiness I screened the world from his eyes, and, going to the lever, nodded my head to let the chaplain know I was ready. He began to read the burial for the dead – 'In the midst of life we are in death.' Scarcely had the words left the lips of the clergyman than I pulled the lever, and above the tolling of the prison bells the thud of the doors was heard, and Moses Shrimpton disappeared from view.

There was an instant rush by some of those present to look down into the pit, and I shouted to the warders to keep everyone back. I was too late. The spectators were beside me before anything could be done to prevent them reaching the trap door, and peering into the depths they were horrified at what they saw.

Moses Shrimpton had died a painless and instantaneous death, but, an old man, his weight had been difficult to judge, and the warders had not given me the correct information. I had given him what I considered the proper drop, but evidently it had been too much, and the execution had not been so successful as most of the others. I was glad it was over, and left the prison as soon as my work was finished.

What Berry failed to describe was that the long drop given to Shrimpton had caused his head to be almost severed from his body. The walls of the pit were splashed with blood, which was also running down his body. Reports of the bloody death appeared in the press, but since death had been instantaneous, painless, and the result of legal hanging, there appears to have been no real criticism at the inquest.

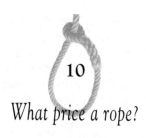

10

What price a rope?

'I tell you this rope is most remarkable . . . '

After the unfortunate incident at Shrimpton's execution Berry had another lengthy break before his next execution; this time a full seven weeks. Undoubtedly distressed by recent experiences, he probably needed time to regain his composure and to re-examine his methods of calculating the required 'drop'. As an avid reader of the newspapers, he would have been all too aware of the problems encountered by his predecessors, as these had always received wide press coverage, but despite his attempts to avoid them, mishaps were still rather too frequent.

His next execution was to be that of Henry Alt, a 31-year-old German national and journeyman baker. Alt had been found guilty of the murder of one Charles Howard, a jealous-lover scenario again the motive. Apparently he had stabbed Howard while drinking in a pub after a dispute over the affections of a woman, the woman having chosen the latter over the former. After stabbing Howard, Alt had then turned the knife on the woman and himself, both sustaining knife wounds. The German Consulate intervened on Alt's part but the idea of a reprieve was rejected.

Mr Kynaston Metcalfe was again present at the execution, held on 13 July 1885, and in view of the previous accident with Harris he had 'made' Berry buy a government rope:

I said, for one thing, I must insist upon a Government rope being employed, as after what took place at Harris's execution I was afraid that something might happen again. He came up to my office and saw me, and I had a talk with him for about a quarter of an hour on the point, and he went to the Governor of the prison, and got one of the ropes.

The execution appears to have gone off without incident, although Mr Kynaston Metcalfe noticed afterwards that Alt had a bruise on his face:

> It appears that the shutters [trapdoors] as they go down rebound, and they came back and hit the man on his face. I saw this man when he was cut down and put in his coffin, and though they have an arrangement that works very well, that thing struck me at the time as wanting alteration.

The 'Government' pattern execution ropes were made by contractors, Messrs Edgington & Co., 48 Long Lane, London, E.C. and were approved by the Home Office authorities. The official ropes were made of white Italian hemp, four strand, and 2½ inches in circumference. Although Berry liked to use his own ropes, usually bringing two or more to an execution, he was now well aware that the officials preferred him to use those supplied to the prison service. The official ropes could be bought by application to the Governor of Newgate, but they were kept at Clerkenwell. The sheriffs sometimes applied for them in different parts of the country and others were sent abroad to the Colonies. According to Chief Warder Ward,

> 'The rope which Berry has bought himself is not the Government regulation rope; it is a smaller rope than that, but it is a harder and harsher rope, and a rope, I should imagine, more likely to cut the culprit's neck than the regulation rope.'

Up to the year 1878 the practice had been for the executioner to provide his own ropes, but that year a failure took place in Yorkshire when a rope broke. As a result the Secretary of State ordered an inquiry and directed that a pattern rope should be made that might safely be used for executions, this subsequently being produced by Edgington & Co. This ruling, however, did not stop Marwood, Binns and Berry from using ropes they had obtained from their own sources.

On Monday 3 August 1885, a Bank Holiday, Berry, having arrived the previous Saturday, was scheduled to execute Joseph Tucker at Nottingham. Tucker, a 37-year-old shoe finisher from the Mapperley district, who worked for Mr Hooley, a Nottingham boot manufacturer, had murdered the woman with whom he had been living for almost nine years, Elizabeth Williamson, aged 32. Both were heavy drinkers and had frequently engaged in altercations. The murder occurred on the evening of Saturday 9 May 1885 at 38 Trumpet Street, Nottingham, where they were living at the time. On returning home from the Horse and Trumpet Inn Tucker had found her collapsed and drunk, whereupon he threw paraffin over her and set her alight with a match. Her screams roused the neighbours and she was taken to hospital, but she succumbed to her severe burns the following Thursday. Tucker was sentenced to death at Nottingham Assizes on 18 July.

Awaiting his fate in prison Tucker turned to the church for solace. Canon Monahan and the Sisters of Mercy prepared him and he was received into the Roman Catholic faith by rite of baptism the day before his execution at Bagthorpe gaol. Like Shrimpton, Tucker was a small man, weighing only 7 stone 12 pounds.

As Berry pinioned him, the only words Tucker uttered were, 'That's rather tight.' Berry assured him it was all right. The scaffold was situated in a secluded area of the prison's outer yard and had been in use for some years. According to Berry, it was old-fashioned, the door of the drop being in one piece rather than opening in halves at the centre as he preferred. There was also no way down into the whitewashed pit should it be necessary to gain access. Fortunately that was not to be the case. Standing on the drop Tucker pressed his hands together in the attitude of prayer and repeated over and over again, 'Lord have mercy upon us.' Berry drew the white cap over his head and adjusted the rope round his neck. An 'indiarubber and leather contrivance' at the 'knot' of the noose was placed exactly under his left ear. The leather washer used to stop the noose slipping was an invention of Marwood's. At 8.00 a.m. the trap opened, Berry having again calculated a drop of 9 feet, and this time there was no bungling. The rope – the same one that he had used in the execution of Henry Alt – remained motionless, and the indiarubber and leather was kept perpendicular in its place.

A crowd of hundreds had gathered outside the gaol for the execution and a large contingent of police was present. The *Nottingham Evening News* commented:

> . . . when the black flag was hoisted at five minutes past eight o'clock there was a subdued murmur and a hush, which lasted for half a minute. The officers of the Church Army, who had taken advantage of the occasion, distributed tracts, but the only thing the people seemed to think of was to catch a glimpse of Berry, the executioner. They lingered about in order to gratify this vulgar curiosity, but so far as we know their desire was not met, as Berry remained in the gaol for some time.

The usual inquest was held and the jury viewed the body of Tucker. It had been laid on a board in the basement of the gaol. He was dressed in the clothes in which he had been hanged, a black jacket and corduroy trousers. The only indication that he had met his end by hanging was a slight discolouration around the throat, and his face appeared placid indicating that he had died quickly and without a struggle.

Berry was familiar with Nottingham, having patrolled its streets for a year as a police constable in the Borough Force in the 1870s. While there to execute Tucker he visited a pub in the vicinity, The Golden Fleece at 41 Mansfield Road, the landlord of which was Daniel Dominic, aged 35 years. Having taken over the pub in 1885, Dominic – who lived there with his wife, Eliza, 34, and their 11-year-old son, George – was to be its longest serving landlord, remaining for forty years until his son George took over for seven years in 1925.

Having the hangman in a pub was a great bonus for the landlord as it attracted customers curious to see this 'public official', and it was not unknown for the hangman to hold levees to recount his tales to an enthralled and drink-buying audience. Hangmen were always keen to supplement their income in those days and this was one way to do it. We can only guess at the incentives that an appreciative publican put in the way of the executioner to encourage his patronage.

Another long-established 'perk' for a hangman was to sell his used ropes, either as pieces or complete. Tales were told that Foxon, the executioner of William Corder for the murder of Maria Martin (traditionally but incorrectly rendered as Marten) in the famous 'Red Barn' case of 1828, sold one-inch sections of the execution rope for a guinea each. But that was a celebrated case, the executions were then in public, and the rich scrambled to obtain such gallows relics, oddly considering them to be very lucky. In Berry's day things were different, but he still owned the ropes he used and disposed of them as he wished, his practice being to use one rope for up to a dozen executions.

In *Experiences*, Berry sheds important light on this crucial piece of equipment (see Appendix II). The rope was made of the finest Italian hemp, ¾in thick, 13 feet long, pliable and with the noose formed by the rope running through a brass ring woven into one end of it.

Berry's technical discourse on the main tool of his trade showed the amount of thought put into what may be regarded as a rather mundane object – a length of rope. It should be noted that the execution rope was nothing like the popular image often depicted in illustrations showing the American-type noose, with a huge knot consisting of many winds of the rope forming the knot.

The rope Berry used to execute Shrimpton had previously been used on Peter Cassidy, James Tobin, Thomas Orrock, Kay Howarth, Ernest Ewerstadt, Michael Downey, Thomas Parry, John Lee at Exeter (failed hanging), and James Lee. Having become bloodstained in the Shrimpton execution it could not be used again, but Dan Dominic felt that such an item displayed in his pub would attract customers and make an interesting conversation piece. While at the Golden Fleece, Berry evidently discussed this with Dominic, and on Thursday 6 August 1885, three days after his Nottingham visit, he wrote the following letter to the publican:

1

Bilton Place City Rd

Bradford 6th. 1885
Dear Friend
I will come on Saturday and bring you my Favourite Rope which has Hanged 12 persons with all respect to you I tell you this rope is most remarkable for it is not a pin worse for been

used but it is rather stained at the noose. I will take 25/- for it and bring it if I hear from you by return. Hoping you and the family is all well.

I remain Yours Truly
James Berry,
Executioner
These are the Persons names
Henry Orrocks   Newgate   London
Kay Howarth   Strangeways   Manchester
Peter Cassidy   Kirkdale   Liverpool
Ernest Ewerstadt   do   do
James Tobin   Wexford   Ireland
Michael Downey   Galway   Ireland
Thomas Parry   do   do
James Lee   Exeter   Devonshire   XXX
John Lee   Chelmsford   Essex
Moses Shrimpton   Worcester   Worcestershire

To the left of the list of names Berry added 'Executed by the rope I mention above' and with three arrows he indicated that the 'James' and the 'John' next to the two Lees should be juxtaposed. The three crosses next to Lee's name indicate the three failures, and they, with the nine others actually executed, add up to twelve uses of the rope. Of course only nine of the twelve men indicated by Berry were actually executed.

The Saturday trip to Nottingham took place and the deal on the rope was successfully negotiated. The publican must have asked a couple of questions, for on Monday 10 August Berry wrote from Bradford:

Dear Friend,
I have been looking at my private books for the dates and I cannot find them I should just put on a card, this Rope who belonged to Mr. Berry was purchased by me. and it has executed 12 persons in England Ireland & Scotland. I have been to the likeness shop and ordered him to strike some Cabinets off the negitive and the will be ready in the course of a week. I will send you the first. I got pretty well full before I

left. I hope you will do as you say as regards the Owl. I should just like to hear of somebody giving him a good sluging. Excuse more at present as I am verry badly. Remember to family.

To Dan Dominic   Yours Truly

Golden Fleece   James Berry

   Notts.   Executioner

This letter indicates that Dominic wanted to make a display of the rope to include a list of the rope's 'victims' and a cabinet photograph of the redoubtable executioner. The second part of the letter is rather cryptic, but seems to indicate that while at the Golden Fleece Berry had been upset by a local ne'er-do-well rejoicing in the sobriquet 'The Owl'. Possibly this man had been aggressive towards the executioner, who clearly felt the man should be subjected to a beating. It would seem that Dominic had assured Berry that he would do something with regard to the man, perhaps banning him from the pub.

Monday 17 August 1885 saw Berry at Stafford for the execution of Thomas Boulton a 47-year-old labourer who had been convicted for the murder of his 15-year-old niece, Elizabeth Bunting, at Handsworth, Birmingham. Boulton was in receipt of an army pension and had been working as a gardener while staying with his married sister and her family. On 20 April he had been out drinking, but he returned home at 9.45 p.m. and his niece read to him. Mr Bunting was at work and Mrs Bunting retired to bed at ten o'clock, leaving the girl with her uncle. The mother was soon alerted by a piercing scream and went down to find her brother standing over her daughter's body. He had beaten her to death with a hammer, which he immediately dropped and fled. His only excuse for the crime was that he didn't like the girl's boyfriend, so some sort of sexual motive may be conjectured. The defence pleaded insanity, citing the fact that Boulton had suffered from sunstroke whilst serving in India, but he was found guilty and duly hanged by Berry.

Dan Dominic again wrote to Berry around this time, for a further letter from Berry, sent on Thursday 27 August, mentions Boulton's recent execution:

Augt. 27th 1885

Bilton Place
City Road
Bradford

Dear Dan,

You must excuse me for not writing before now but I have been verry porley and I am nothing to crack on yet. I went to Blackpool but my wife persisted on going with me and so I took her and I have not enjoyed my self a damed bit the boger allways with me would not let me go out by myself and bi god when I went down to have a van to bathe she would wait and what with one thing and rhumatic I am about settled. But we will have a off together yet I was going to Telegram for you but I thought it would be no use making your pleasure as you know you cannot enjoy yourself with a women allways stuck at your heels. I am sure I shall never set off again with a woman let the devils go together and men same. I shall pop over before long all been well. I am getting Turkish Baths twice a week did you read my last do at Stafford. it went off like lightning hoping you and family his well remember me to Harry Barker I expect he will be dry before this a can of ale please Tell him I am just drawing cork out of ½ pint Bottle stout for my forenoon lunch. I often think about old Hal, well good day

I remain Yours Truly
James Berry
Executioner

Dan Dominic
Golden Fleece
Mansfield Road
Nottingham

The surviving envelope for this letter shows that it was posted on 31 August. The letter gives a wonderful insight into Berry's character. His sense of humour and the close friendship he obviously shared with the publican are clear. He had apparently befriended one of the regulars at the pub 'old Hal', Harry Barker, who obviously enjoyed his tipple. It also indicates that at this time Berry similarly enjoyed his drink. In fact, it was noted by Leonard Ward, the Chief Warder at Newgate, in March 1886, that Berry 'was a teetotaller at first for a year or so, but I do not think he is now' (Aberdare). The other important aspect is the glimpse revealed of Berry's relationship with his wife. There can be little doubt that they were dedicated to each other but, as with most marriages, things did not always run smoothly. She was obviously very attentive to him but, it would seem, he preferred to be with other men, and not the womenfolk. He was also clearly not averse to commenting on his ailments.

Berry's activities while at different locations to conduct executions had come to the notice of the Home Office, and it was considered undesirable that he should stay at a local hostelry at such times. The following letter was sent to the Chairman of the Prison Commissioners and circulated to interested parties, such as the prison governors and county sheriffs:

Whitehall, 7th October, 1885.

Sir,

I am directed by the Secretary of State to acquaint you that on several recent occasions his attention has been called to the proceedings, before and after an execution, of the person employed as executioner, which appear to have given rise to grave public scandal.

The Secretary of State thinks that the danger of the repetition of such occurrences would be much diminished if it could be arranged that, on the occasion of every execution, the executioner should reside in the prison while he is in the place where the execution takes place. The Secretary of State has, of course, no authority to control the movements of the executioner, who is engaged and paid solely by the Sheriff, as the officer solely responsible for the carrying out of the execution; but the Secretary of State has, as you are aware, already given instructions that quarters should be provided for the executioner in the prison, whenever the Sheriff wishes him to reside there, and he thinks that it is desirable that in future, when it is known that an execution is about to take place in any prison, the Governor should be instructed at once to communicate with the Sheriff and inform him that, if he so desires, the executioner will be provided with lodging and maintenance in the prison, and that, in the opinion of the Secretary of State, he should, in engaging the executioner, make it compulsory that he should sleep there so long as he may remain in the place where the sentence is to be executed, and certainly on the night preceding the execution.

The Sheriff should, of course, understand that this matter is one entirely for his discretion, but that the Secretary of State, while not wishing to interfere with his responsibility, desires him to be informed of his opinion that grave public scandals may be avoided by insisting on this as a condition in the engagement of the executioner.

I am, &c.

(Signed) GODFREY LUSHINGTON.

The Chairman of
The Prison Commissioners,
&c. &c. &c.

This letter indicates the gravity with which the Home Office regarded the executioner's activities and consequent public image. Little wonder that they always tried to distance themselves from this recalcitrant public official. It was better for them to have the Prison Commissioners and High Sheriffs address the problem. However, it did not bode well for Berry at this early stage in his career. He may not have been any worse than his predecessors – indeed, it would have been difficult to sink lower than Binns – but he was still attracting unwanted publicity, and his growing notoriety was a gift for the vociferous abolitionists. Eventually steps would be taken to exercise control.

11

Eventful autumn – the 'Goodale Mess'

'We were horrified . . . to see that the rope jerked upwards . . . '

Berry had been public executioner for eighteen months and after the execution of Boulton, a 'copybook job', he must have felt that he was now getting things exactly right. His next commission, scheduled for Monday 5 October 1885, was another execution at the famous Newgate Prison in the City of London, and the convict was Henry Norman, a 31-year-old painter, sentenced for the murder of his wife. Incensed by her adultery, he had stabbed her as she slept, claiming that she had indulged in numerous liaisons, it finally becoming too much when he discovered she had been conducting an affair with the landlord of their lodgings. Mr Justice Hawkins, who had a reputation as a 'hanging judge', presided at the Old Bailey trial and Norman was duly sentenced, Berry carrying out the execution in the shed set aside for this purpose in the prison yard at Newgate.

A trip to Hereford was next on his books. It was another double execution, and the date set was Monday 23 November. The two men, John Hill and John Williams, had been convicted for the same murder, 'Irish Jack' and 'Sailor Jack' having together murdered Anne Dickinson at Weobley.

On a late-September night a group of hop-pickers had gathered in the Lion Inn at Weobley. They were joined by Hill, an ex-soldier, and Williams a sailor. Both out of work, they decided they could get money by joining the hop-pickers and, according to Hill, also find a woman. They met two girls in the pub and at closing time Hill proposed they should see the girls home to their hut. Anne Dickinson agreed but the other girl was reluctant, not liking the look of Williams. She finally agreed, however, and the four set off, but the girl became increasingly apprehensive and finally decided to leave. Williams threatened her with violence but she roused a shepherd in a nearby cottage and Williams fled. He approached Hill and Dickinson and a dispute began between the drunken men over who should accompany her. What actually happened next is unclear, as the two men tried to put the blame on each other, but it seems that, seeing the opportunity to flee, the girl tried to escape, upon which one of the men seized a large stick and struck her. Many more blows were rained on her as she was lying on the ground. Two labourers found the girl's body the following day. The descriptions of the two offenders were circulated and they were arrested. Tried at Gloucester Assizes, both were found guilty and sentenced to death. Williams tried to gain a reprieve, and failed, but Hill made no plea.

Berry arrived at Hereford, from Bradford, on the evening of Saturday 21 November and went straight to the gaol. Tea was brought to him from a hotel and while he was eating this one of the warders went to see him. The warder told Berry he would have no trouble, claiming that he would willingly hang them himself, as they were both brutes. Berry commented, 'You seem to have taken a great dislike to them!' The warder replied, 'And you will, too, when you see them. Would you believe it, they are glorying in their crime. They are making fun of what they have done. See that you make the noose right, so that you don't let them slip through your fingers.'

Berry assured the warder that he would carry out his duty. On the Sunday evening he went to see the two offenders, first visiting Hill, 'the worst of the two', whom he described as '. . . an evil fellow with a hangdog look and a bulging brow'. When Berry entered his cell the man assumed an air of bravado, and, according to Berry, after an initial exchange of pleasantries, the following incredible conversation took place. Of course Berry could not possibly have remembered it word for word, so the accuracy must be doubtful.

'Are you prepared to meet your doom in the morning at eight o'clock?'

'Oh, yes, I suppose I am going at eight. There is no getting out of it?'

'No. You can be assured there isn't.'

'Well, what sort of a drop are you going to give me?'

The cool way in which he asked the question surprised and angered me. Here was a man on the verge of death, who ought to be preparing himself to meet his Maker, pretending to take an interest in the arrangements of the hangman. I believe that he asked the question merely to show me how little he cared for James Berry, the hangman.

'You will alter your tune before I am done with you, my man,' I said to myself.

'What do you want to know about the drop for?'

He laughed at my question. 'It concerns me mostly, doesn't it? I'd like to know.'

'Very well, I'll tell you, but, first of all, you must tell me your weight.'

'I'm sure I don't know. They don't give you much information in this building. Have a guess. You ought to be good at that sort of thing.'

Berry was amazed at his impudence and a long exchange followed. Hill continued in the same vein and the warder gave the man's weight. 'Oh, six or seven feet ought to kill you,' said Berry. 'At least we will try you with that first.' He clearly felt that he had identified a weakness in Hill, a fear of physical pain. He realised what he was saying was cruel, but justified it with the argument that the man deserved it. However Hill, apparently, 'laughed in his face', prompting Berry to retort, 'Well, wait until morning, when you stand on the edge of doom with the hempen rope about your neck. We'll see if you laugh then.'

If the account is reasonably accurate then Berry obviously had no excuse for such treatment of the doomed man. He was goading him, inexcusable behaviour whatever the failings of the prisoner might be.

The warder then took Berry to see Williams, whom he found to be a totally different character, looking so dazed and pathetic that Berry felt sorry for him. As they talked Williams, who had been in prison before for offences of burglary and theft, was reduced to tears, and Berry elicited the story of the murder from him. Berry gives a heartrending account of how he persuaded the prisoner to pray for forgiveness, following which Berry concluded, 'In the morning I will come for you about five minutes to eight, and I hope you will cause me no trouble. I think it would be better if you did not have any breakfast.' He continues:

> I went straight to my room and closed the door. I took out a cigar and lit it, but I could not enjoy it one bit. Had I seen Hill only I would not have felt a bit out of the ordinary, but the interview with his companion the man he had dragged with him to his doom, kept me from peace of mind. I threw the cigar away and began to pace up and down the room.
>
> It was just such a night as I had spent before my first execution after I had seen the wives and children of Vicars [sic] and Innes going to bid farewell in the prison of Edinburgh.
>
> I felt ill and overburdened, and longing to get away from my duty to Bradford, where I knew rest and peace of mind awaited me.
>
> The hours wore on, and I still could find no rest. When I tried to lie down something seemed to be throbbing within my head, and I rose up and began to walk about again.

Berry says he then prayed and was able to sleep. Early in the morning he rose and went to the scaffold. He could hear the murmur of the voices of the crowd that had, as usual on such an occasion, gathered in front of the prison. The warder of the previous night came and told him that the prisoners were now acting differently. Hill was 'trembling like a child' with his teeth chattering. Berry soon saw this for himself, describing Hill as 'a wretched specimen of humanity', his face 'livid and his eyes staring out of his head'. As Berry approached him, Hill shrank back and shivered, whereupon the hangman told him to pull himself together and pinioned him. He then attended to Williams, who was brought from his cell showing a brave face. He had followed Berry's advice and taken no breakfast. Asked if he would like anything he asked for a glass of nut brown ale, which Berry duly fetched for him. He appeared better for the drink and bade an emotional farewell to the two warders who had been looking after him.

The gallows was situated near the north-western extremity of the prison confines, just within the inner wall. Two block uprights, about 7 feet high, supported a black cross-beam with two iron rings secured to it by iron bands, and this structure was all that was visible above the ground level of the yard. The pit was below ground level under the twin trapdoors of the drop. The two convicts were taken together to the scaffold, at the sight of which they almost fainted. Berry hurried them onto the drop, the white caps were drawn over their faces and he fastened the straps round their legs. He described the final moment:

> My hand was on the lever, and I was just about to do my duty when one of the clergymen held up his hand. He was the Catholic priest, and he addressed me in a tremulous voice.
>
> 'One moment Mr. Berry. May I be allowed to have another word?'
>
> I did not know what he wanted to say, and I do not know why I acted as I did.
>
> 'No, you are too late,' said I, as I pulled the lever and dropped them into the abyss of death. 'You are too late.'
>
> The wonder is that I did not follow the two into the pit below.
>
> The warders had to run for brandy to keep me from fainting, so terribly was I overcome by the ordeal through which I had gone.

The gaol surgeon, Dr Vevers, noted that the bodies jerked at the end of the drop and those present could hear the breaking of the bones of the prisoners' necks. Those of the crowd outside the prison who had assembled in the area of the workhouse-walk, in the vicinity of the gallows, were able to hear a harsh grating sound, no doubt the withdrawal of the bolt, followed by the dull thud of the falling of the trapdoors. The black flag was hoisted and the bell of the Parish of St Peter tolled. The usual inquest was held and it was noted that the 'knot' of the rope had broken the skin under Hill's left ear. The only other sign of violent death on either body was a livid line round their necks and a livid colouration of their faces and hands. Hill, the heavier of the two men, had been allowed an 8-foot drop, while that given to Williams was 6 inches more. Berry expressed himself well satisfied with his work, remarking that it would be impossible to improve on it (*The Hereford Journal*, 28 November 1885).

Berry described Hill, in an account in the 1914 *The Post* series, as 'The Worst Man I Ever Hanged'. *The Hereford Journal* of 28 November 1885 commented on the fact that the execution had been carried out in 'secrecy' with no reporters present. This was due to the action of the High Sheriff of the county, Sir Robert Lighton. Despite the efforts of the press to gain admission to witness the executions 'on behalf of the public', he had denied access. The paper carried a long discourse on the moral rights of the press to attend such events and criticised the High Sheriff.

Just a week later Berry was to suffer more agonies at his next execution. Robert Goodale appeared at the Norfolk Assizes in Norwich before Mr Justice Stephen on 13 November 1885. Goodale was a 45-year-old market gardener who had been indicted for the wilful murder of his wife, Bathsheba, at Walsoken Marsh, near their home at Wisbech, on 15 September. They had a history of quarrelling and she had apparently been unfaithful to him. Goodale struck her several times on the head with a hatchet and then put her down a well, where she drowned. It was reported in the local press as 'The Walsoken Tragedy'. He was duly found guilty and sentenced to death, the execution set for Monday 30 November.

Professing the beliefs of the Baptist Church, Goodale was attended by the Revd T.A. Wheeler, the Baptist minister, to whom the prisoner paid great attention. On the Friday before the execution he then received a last visit by his sister and two sons.

Berry attended Norwich Castle, then in use as a prison, to carry out the sentence. 'At that time', he writes, 'I was using my original table of lengths of drop, which I had based on Mr Marwood's system.' Goodale weighed 15 stone and was 5ft 11in tall, and according to this table the drop 'for a man of that weight' should have been 7ft 8in, but Berry reduced it to, as closely as he could measure it, 5ft 9in. The rope on this occasion was one made and supplied by the government, and had been used in the execution of Williams a week before. The drop itself was built in accordance with a government plan and had also been used before. Everything appeared to be 'in perfect working order'. The prison governor, Mr A.E. Dent, was anxious that everything should go without a hitch, and to this end he had tested the drop on the Thursday and Saturday before the execution, in company with the engineer. In fact it would seem that the governor was not too keen to see the execution take place at all. Goodale had spoken to him and the chief warder on the Friday night and had pleaded extreme provocation, stating that he had struck his wife with a piece of iron as a result of her saying that she liked other men better. The governor at once sent a document containing the confession to the Home Secretary. Mr Wheeler and the ex-Sheriff of Norwich, Mr W.H. Dakin, went to London for an interview with the Under-Secretary of State, but their efforts were to no avail and the execution order stayed in force.

Berry's account in *The Post*, unlike that in his book, contains the claim that one of the officials at the prison had told him, on his arrival, that he had had a dream that an 'accident' would take place. Berry was further told that Goodale was 'an awful coward' and that there was sure to be a 'scene'. According to Berry 'the whole place was in a panic' over the impending execution. Berry visited Goodale in his cell on the eve of the execution and spoke with the condemned man, without telling him who he was. The scaffold and rope were tested by Berry at 7.30 a.m. using a 16-stone weight, in accordance with Home Office regulations, in the presence of the acting under-sheriff, Mr J.B.T. Hales. At five minutes to eight the great bell of St Peter's was heard to toll, and then, shortly before the hour, the acting under-sheriff, the surgeon of the gaol Mr H.S. Robinson, and the governor went to the condemned man and saw him pinioned by Berry. Berry's account of the execution was considerably more dramatic and detailed than the report that appeared in *The Eastern Daily Press*. It continued:

The man was a physical wreck, and while I stood waiting for him I could hear his pitiful cries in the condemned cell.

Outside a dense crowd awaited the hoisting of the black flag. Robert Goodale had been known in most of the market towns, and in contrast to the usual crowds which await the signal that the sentence of the law has been duly carried out, there was a goodly number of farmers and market gardeners outside the prison.

Peeping from the opening in the doorway the warder on duty could see that consternation had seized the crowd when they realised that it was long past the time for the execution. They thought that the man must have committed suicide in his cell over night or that a reprieve had arrived at the last minute. Eagerly they gazed at the halyards of the flag-post wondering if they would see the black flag fluttering in the breeze.

The victim of the law was to be pinioned in the bathroom of the prison and thence led through a small doorway into the execution shed. I had previously tested the scaffold and found it to be in perfect order.

When the warders began to lead him down the passage he screamed out and his cries could be heard all over the prison. The convicts in their narrow cells heard them and terror entered their hearts. They shouted and bellowed and beat on the doors in protest against the scene which was about to be enacted.

The wail of the prisoner sounded louder and louder as he approached, and then it sank into a sob. When I went forward to pinion him he was crying like a little child.

Approaching him from behind I slipped the strap around his body. He wriggled to prevent me buckling it, and I had to tell him in a firm tone to be a man.

'You won't do yourself any good by doing that sort of thing. You'll only prolong the agony.'

'Oh, don't do it! Don't do it!' he whined. 'Have mercy upon me.'

I buckled the two straps and exerted my strength to bring the other two together.

'Be gentle,' he cried. 'Please be gentle, I am so old. Have mercy upon me.'

I was trembling myself and wishing it were all over, and it unnerved me not a little to find I could not get the straps to meet.

'Here some of you. Get me a piece of wire or string.'

A warder hurried off and brought me some wire and a bit of tin, and I succeeded in completing the pinioning, while all the time he was pleading for mercy.

'I will have mercy upon you,' said I. 'Do not be afraid.'

The signal was now given that all was in readiness, and the procession moved along to the scaffold.

Robert Goodale refused to budge, however, and still screaming he had to be dragged along. It took three or four warders to get him to the door, and when he saw the scaffold his terror was turned to madness. It was clear to me that a scene unparalleled in the annals of prison life was about to be enacted. His eyes were staring wildly, his face was ashen with terror, and his huge body was quivering and rocking to and fro.

The scene was too much for one of the high officials. With a gasp he walked away and remained out of sight until the execution was over. As for me big beads of sweat were standing on my forehead, and my limbs were trembling. I wondered if I would be able to go on with my duty.

Pulling myself together, I shouted to the warders to bring a rope. A scream came from the lips of the condemned man when he heard the order. He saw one rope dangling from the beam, and he knew why I wanted the other. The warder who had hurried off at my bidding handed me the rope and I passed the ends to his comrades.

'There is nothing else for it,' I shouted. 'You must help me to do my duty. Pull him along.'

Robert Goodale exerted all his weight the other way, but the warders pulled at the word of command, and after a long struggle they succeeded in dragging him on to the scaffold.

They held him there while I pinioned him hurriedly, but before I had the rope adjusted round his neck he gave one last cry and collapsed. 'Oh, my God, forgive me!' he ejaculated, and tumbled on [sic] a heap on the ground.

The misery of the moment was awful, but there was more to be endured.

'Get him to his feet,' I screamed. 'One of you help me to lift him.'

A warder came to my assistance and we raised him up.

'Keep your hands round him. Don't leave go or we will bungle it,' I shouted. 'Are you ready?' The white-faced trembling warder nodded. Stepping aside, I pulled the lever and quick as lightning Robert Goodale disappeared from sight.

'Thank heaven!' I murmured, but a cry of horror caused me to look up quickly, and when I saw what had happened my legs nearly collapsed.

The warder who had been assisting me had been standing too near the trap door, and the weight of the victim had pulled him over. He was clutching the sides of the opening, and it was only by the mercy of providence that he did not crash down to the foot of the well.

It was the first accident of the kind that I had ever had, and I was unable to go to his assistance. Hand and brain refused to move. I stood there as if rooted to the spot, and others had to finish it for me. When I recovered I went to the edge of the well, and to my horror I saw that the rope hung limply, that the body of my victim was at the bottom of the pit.

Mr Charles Mackie of the *Norfolk Chronicle* represented the local press at the execution, and the witnesses were horrified to see the rope jerk upwards as Goodale disappeared from sight and it appeared for a moment that the noose had slipped from his head, or had broken. However, the rope had severed the head entirely from the body, and both had fallen together to the bottom of the pit. The prison governor was distraught. Berry went down with the prison doctor into the pit, upon which he collapsed and had to be assisted to ascend from the pit by warders. The doctor attended to Berry and assured him that he was not to blame. As soon as the execution had been carried out the black flag was hoisted on a flagstaff erected over the right-hand entrance to the gaol.

The usual inquest was held in the magistrates' room at the castle before the coroner, Mr Bignold, the jury having viewed the body, laid in a coffin, before entering the room. The governor and prison surgeon gave evidence of the great care that had been shown in the arrangements for the execution, emphasising that the drop used was one built by the governor himself in accordance with plans supplied by the Home Office, the distance from the floor of the drop to the bottom of the pit having been 11ft 5in. In giving his evidence, Berry, who described himself as a boot salesman at Bradford, stated that he had hanged one heavier man previously, Joseph Lowson, who weighed 16 stone 8 pounds and to whom he gave a drop of 8 feet. In that case there 'was not even abrasion of the skin of the neck'. In Goodale's case, he did not think the drop to be too much at 5ft 9½in or 5ft 10in. He had purposely kept it short of 6 feet because of the weight of the prisoner, but the head had come off as though severed from the body with a knife. The coroner consoled Berry stating, 'I am bound to say, before you leave the room, that as far as the evidence has gone there seems to be nothing to throw any blame upon you, either from want of skill or being in an improper condition.'

The jury found that death was caused by hanging and 'they imputed no blame to anyone for what had occurred'. This must have been an immense relief to Berry but he was greatly unnerved. The incident became known as 'the Goodale Mess', and full reports appeared in the contemporary press. The editorial in *The Eastern Daily Press* of Tuesday 1 December 1885 wrote that the 'catastrophe . . . so far as we know, is unparalleled in the history of executions'. It stated:

> . . . we are persuaded that capital punishment is useless to prevent murders, and that it is an offence to society. It shocks human nature. Every cultured sense revolts at the spectacle of a man legally done to death. We hope that never again shall we be called upon to record so awful and disgusting an occurrence as that which this day sullies our pages. There will doubtless be an official inquiry. We trust that attention being thus awakened to the revolting formalities which take place in our prisons a strong public opinion will be formed, and that before it this remnant of barbarism and savagery will disappear.

Berry wrote (*The Post*, 6 December 1913):

> After I had executed Robert Goodale at Norwich I resolved to hand in my resignation.
>   The agony of mind which followed the futile attempt to hang John Lee of Babbicome [*sic*], was bad enough, but multiply it a thousandfold and you could not estimate the

mental torture through which I passed as I journeyed homeward to Bradford . . .

All the way home I was dreadfully ill, and I vowed that if I recovered – and I did not expect ever to get over the effects – I would give up the business and go back to the old life.

Unfortunately for my resolution, I had gone too far, and there was to be no drawing back for me. The hand of every man was against me. The neighbours, who knew all about my calling, had forced me to buy the adjoining houses from the landlord rather than be turned outside my own home, and I had had to bear the expense of sending my children away to be educated. It meant that either I had to go on with the work or go abroad to begin a new life.

My poor wife was heartbroken at my misery, and she would have been glad if I had stuck to my resolution. She would have gone with me wherever I desired to take her, but as time went on my spirit became hardened, and I resolved to fight. Why should my wife and children be martyred simply because James Berry had done the duty of the State which other men were afraid to do? My own people were still bitter against me, and there was no hope of ever gaining their forgiveness.

How wrong I was to misjudge them! All the time they appeared to be bitter, they were never ceasing to pray for my redemption, and I am glad to say that before my dear sister passed away she gave me her full forgiveness.

Berry carried out two more executions before the end of the year. The first was another trip to Newgate in the case of Daniel Minahan, a 28-year-old labourer who had beaten his wife to death with a hammer on 28 October at Bromley. The couple had two children and had apparently enjoyed a happy married life until the day of the murder, when she had woken him up late for work. In a rage he inflicted over a dozen blows to her head and others to her chest. Tried on 17 November, before Mr Justice Smith at the Old Bailey, he claimed provocation but was found guilty and sentenced to death. Berry executed him on Monday 7 December, Chief Warder Ward noting that on this occasion Berry had two government ropes with him, one of which he had used in the unfortunate decapitation of Goodale. Berry apparently said to him at the time, 'There, that was the rope I used in Norwich' (Aberdare).

Berry's last execution of 1885 was at Liverpool on 9 December. George Thomas, a black sailor, had returned from sea on 7 September to find that his common law wife of eight years, a former prostitute named Mary Askins, did not wish to live with him any more. Two days later they went to a pub together and Thomas pulled out a gun and shot her in the head. She fell dead and he turned the gun on himself in an effort to commit suicide. However, he suffered only slight injury. He had obtained the gun the day before the shooting, indicating that he had planned his actions. He was sentenced at Liverpool Assizes. These last two executions were uneventful, which must have been a relief to Berry.

By 1885 the Secretary of State had issued a memorandum of instruction on the subject of executions, clearly defining responsibilities. The sheriff was solely responsible for carrying into effect the sentence of death, and it was the duty of the prison governor to inform the sheriff whenever he received into custody a person so sentenced. The governor at that time also had to inform the sheriff what means were at his disposal for carrying out the sentence. In order to improve this facility the memorandum required that the governor should inquire of the sheriff whether he desired any work to be done in the prison, either to improve the apparatus or to facilitate the carrying out of the execution. If the sheriff identified such work then it was incumbent on the governor to inform the sheriff that the responsibility rested with him and it was for him to select the proper workmen and direct them in carrying out the necessary work. However, the Prison Commissioners had to offer all facilities required and, if requested in due time, place at the sheriff's disposal all such labour and materials as they had at their command, free of cost, unless otherwise notified.

The Conservative Home Secretary in 1886, Sir Richard Cross, realised that capital punishment was again suffering 'bad press', not least through publicity given to such events as the 'Goodale Mess'. Accordingly the confidential Departmental Committee, chaired by Lord Aberdare, himself a former Home Secretary (albeit for the Liberals), was appointed to enquire into the propriety of executions.

The Committee would make their report two years later. Improvements would come, but it was to be a long and drawn-out process. Other members of the Committee were Sir Henry Selwin Ibbetson, Baronet, MP; Sir Frederick Joseph Bramwell, FRS; the Revd Professor Haughton, MD, FRS; and Robert Mundy Gover Esq., MD. They were required to:

> . . . inquire into, and report to me upon, the existing practice as to carrying out of sentence of death, and the causes which in several recent cases have led either to failure or to unseemly occurrences, and to consider and report what arrangements may be adopted (without altering the existing law) to ensure that all executions may be carried out in a becoming manner without risk of failure or miscarriage in any respect.

The Committee was aware of stories of:

> . . . the executioners both before and after executions frequenting public-houses and entertaining the guests there with stories of their performances, and of selling portions of the rope which had been used in the previous executions, and of selling portraits of the culprits, and so forth . . .

However, there would be more unpleasant incidents, more bad press and many more executions by James Berry. And the Committee's report would not be published until 1888.

12

A New Year trip to Ireland

'My journey to Ireland was not a pleasant one . . . '

Berry disliked making trips to Ireland, always feeling unsafe whenever he crossed the water. As an Englishman travelling to execute an Irishman, there was little liking for him among the public, prison officials or police. And Berry's first two jobs of the new year were in Ireland.

The first scheduled was the execution of John Cronin at Mullingar gaol. He had been convicted on 12 December, at the Sligo Winter Assizes, for the murder of his father Thomas, at Longford, during a family dispute. Several memorials for commutation of the sentence were presented but to no avail. Berry carried out the sentence on Tuesday 12 January 1886 and death was seen to be instantaneous. It was the first execution at Mullingar for nearly forty years and a large crowd had assembled outside the gaol to see the black flag hoisted.

The second case was that of William Sheehan who had murdered his brother, sister and widowed mother at Castletown Roche, six miles from Ballyhooly, County Cork, in 1877. His family had objected to his pending marriage and at the time of the murder were about to move away from the farm where they lived. Mrs Sheehan was a tenant of the farm, which consisted of 83 acres. The daughter of a neighbouring farmer was to marry William, and her father had entered into negotiations with Mrs Sheehan, being prepared to give Mrs Sheehan, together with William's brother and sister, a dowry of £170 on condition that they would leave the farm for William and his daughter to run. Mrs Sheehan wanted the figure increased to £300 but the old farmer was unwilling to pay so much. Negotiations were broken off, much to the disappointment of William and his sweetheart, but despite this setback the couple stayed together. William, however, became resentful, claiming that his own family was trying to ruin his life. One night he sent Mary Reilly, a servant girl who worked on the farm, to water the cattle, and then went to the stable where his brother, Thomas, was working. An altercation developed during which he struck Thomas with a griffann (a sort of spade), and he fell dead. He then killed his sister and mother, and threw their bodies down a well some distance away. When the servant returned Sheehan told her that the others had gone. No alarm was raised as the family had been about to move away, so Sheehan married his girl and the two of them settled at the farm for some months as man and wife before emigrating to New Zealand later that year.

It was not until 1885 that bones and clothing remnants were discovered in the well by a new tenant farmer. Sheehan, who had farmed in Australia for the past two years, was immediately traced and arrested. He was tried and found guilty. His brother-in-law was also arrested after an old farmhand claimed he had been involved in the murders, but Sheehan stepped in to defend him, declaring 'The other man is innocent, my Lord.' The brother-in-law was tried but acquitted.

Sheehan was held at Cork gaol for execution, scheduled for Wednesday 20 January 1886. Berry recalled his arrival there:

My journey to Ireland was not a pleasant one, as the folks of Cork had made up their minds to give me an unpleasant reception.

The people of Ireland hated me like poison and every time I left the country I vowed that I would never return. Even the officials of the gaol, from the governor and priest down to the turnkey at the gate, showed their abhorrence of me and my calling, and generally made me feel that I would rather have left the job to someone else.

Sheehan appeared repentant and resigned to his fate. He was visited by his wife while awaiting execution, 'a most affecting interview' taking place between them, after which he 'devoted himself to spiritual matters' and was earnestly engaged in prayer. As for Berry, he claims to have received little co-operation in his preparations for the execution, even his request to see the prisoner before the execution being refused.

The execution shed was a small place in the main building, the scaffold permanently fixed there. Berry, feeling very nervous and lonely, examined it on the morning of the execution. He waited for the warders to take him to the condemned cell but was instead conducted into the yard where the governor, so he was told, had instructed he should wait for the prisoner. Sheehan, described by Berry as one of the strangest-looking men he had ever seen, was brought out. He was about 5ft 4in tall, his head perfectly bald, and, according to Berry, he looked 'cunning and deceitful'.

Berry introduced himself and the prisoner replied, 'Well, don't give me any more pain than is necessary. I will try and be brave.'

The prisoner requested a long drop and Berry agreed. On the way to the shed Sheehan was in constant conversation with the priest, who then turned to Berry:

'Mr. Berry, he wants you to oblige him by giving him eight feet of a drop.'

'Yes, if he wants it. I will be better pleased. It will make things easier for me.'

The priest nodded to me.

'There is one thing however. I will have to alter the rope.'

'You can do it quickly?'

While Sheehan waited on the drop, I lengthened it, and then I put the noose round his neck. The rest was soon over, and I am glad to say that my victim died without a struggle.

An armed escort took me out of Cork, and I was so grateful for the protection that I offered to give them all refreshment. One and all refused to accept it from me – I was the hangman of England.

The account of the execution in *The Times* of 21 January stated that a drop of 6½ feet had been given and that medical evidence given at the inquest showed that death was the result of strangulation.

To illustrate why he felt so unsafe in Ireland, Berry told the tale of an incident there during which he felt his life was definitely threatened. The date and exact details are impossible to ascertain; all we have is Berry's account, given in *The Post* series, 16 May 1914:

It is not often that I feel frightened, for I am pretty well able to take care of myself, but I once had a little adventure in the train coming from Galway to Dublin that gave me one or two cold shudders. On that occasion I believe that a plot was formed to take my life by shooting me.

It was at a time when Ireland was much disturbed by agrarian outrages, and I knew that amongst some of the lower classes there was a feeling of hatred against myself on account of my occupation.

My journey to Galway was undertaken for the purpose of hanging four men who were condemned to death for moonlighting.

The four men who were condemned to death were reprieved, one after the other, as the days fixed for their executions drew near, so that I was not required to carry out my painful duty after all.

I was heartily glad when the last reprieve arrived, and I was free to return home. To avoid observation as much as possible, I took the midnight train, and as there were very few passengers I secured a compartment to myself, and made all snug for a sleep. I was not disturbed until we reached Mullingar, when I noticed a man who looked into my compartment, then walked the whole length of the train, and finally came into my compartment, although there were others in the train quite empty.

He at once began to talk to me in a friendly sort of style, with a strong American twang, but I did not like his looks at all, so pretended to want to go to sleep.

As I sized him up from my half-shut lids I set him down as a 'heavy swell' Yankee. He wore a big slouch hat and cape coat, carried an elaborately silver-mounted handbag, and his coat pocket showed the unmistakable outline of a revolver. He plied me with all sorts of questions on Irish politics, asked me where I lived, what was my business, where I was going to stay in Dublin, and a host of other questions, which I evaded as far as I decently could.

I did tell him, amongst other things, that my name was Aykroyd, that I lived in the North of England, but not very much beyond this. After a while he pulled out his revolver, and commenced examining it in a careless sort of fashion.

As I did not like this turn of affairs, I pulled out my own weapon, which was built for business, and twice the size of the one carried by the stranger, and made a pretence of looking it over very carefully.

The stranger asked me to let him examine my 'gun,' but I told him that it was a weapon that I did not like to hand about for fear of accidents, and after a final look at the charges I put it back into my coat pocket in such a position that it covered the stranger, and kept my finger on the trigger until we reached Dublin.

The American tried to keep up a conversation all the way, but I was not very encouraging, and I thought that by the time we reached Dublin he would be heartily sick of my company. But when I got out of the station and was driving off to my hotel I was surprised to find that he jumped on to the same car, and said he would go to the same hotel as I did.

After having a wash I came down into the breakfast-room, and heard the American asking the waitress if she knew Mr. Berry, to which she replied that she did, and then if Mr. Berry was there that morning, to which she replied that she had not seen him.

As a matter of fact, she had not, and I slipped along the passage to tell her, as she went to the kitchen, that my name for the time being was Aykroyd.

I found in the coffee-room that there was a letter addressed to me on the mantel-piece. The stranger was examining this, and asked me if I knew the hangman by sight. When it was nearly time to catch my boat the stranger still stuck to me, and at the last moment he suggested that we should have a drink together. We went to Mooney's, where I was known to the bar-tender, to whom I tipped a vigorous wink as we went in, which showed him there was something in the wind.

After ordering our drinks the American asked him if he knew Berry, the hangman, to which he truthfully replied that he did.

The American then asked if he knew whether Berry had come from Galway by the night mail, adding, 'He was expected to travel by that train, but Mr. Aykroyd and myself came by it, and we saw nobody like him, though I carefully looked along the whole train.'

The bar-tender, of course, knew nothing, so we drank up, and I went out to my car, the American shaking hands with me and wishing me a pleasant voyage.

I had run it rather close, and quick driving only just brought us to the quay in time for me to get aboard. As the ship swung out from the quayside, a car, driven at red-hot speed, came dashing along, and the passenger, whom I recognised as my American, gesticulated wildly, as if he wanted the vessel to stop.

The next time I was at Mooney's I heard some further particulars. The stranger had gone back for another drink, and after chatting for a few minutes the bar-tender told him that his friend Mr. Aykroyd was the very Berry for whom he had been inquiring.

I have never seen him since, nor has the bar-tender, and I never knew what were the motives for his particular conduct.

Berry was on friendlier ground for his next execution, which entailed a trip to Devizes in Wiltshire. The condemned man this time was 36-year-old John Horton, convicted for a double murder he had committed on 21 November 1885. Horton lived in a large house of his own in the village of Westwood, on the lane leading to Bradford-on-Avon, only a mile and a half distant. His father lived with a grandson in a small cottage in the village street, about a quarter of a mile away. Berry said that he had often seen the house occupied by Horton while travelling past on the train on his various excursions.

Horton and his father had not been on good terms for some years but were drinking together one night at an inn on the outskirts of Bradford-on-Avon. They had a dispute about a money matter, and then Horton accused his father of being on too friendly terms with their shared housekeeper, Charlotte Lindsay. The exchange became so heated that a passing police inspector called in and cautioned them. Later that night Horton beat his father to death and then walked two miles or so to the house on the other side of Bradford-on-Avon, where he attacked Charlotte Lindsay, who later died of her injuries. Horton returned home, took off his bloodstained clothing, and went to bed as if nothing had happened. He went to work the next day and was arrested. He appeared at Wiltshire Assizes on 13 January, was found guilty of the murder of his father and sentenced to death, the execution being fixed for Monday 1 February 1886.

Berry arrived at Devizes prison to be told that Horton had shown 'utter callousness' since he had arrived there. Horton, who had been visited by some of his eleven children, had hoped for an effort to obtain a reprieve, but was told that if that were successful he would then be tried for the murder of Charlotte Lindsay, whereupon he gave up all hope. He ate and slept well, however, joking with prison officials about the stone he had put on in weight. Berry told an official that he had never dealt with a man whose muscles were 'more largely developed'.

A new scaffold had been erected at the prison, and after testing it Berry was satisfied that it was all in order. He subsequently went to see Horton again and found that he had retained his composure, exhibiting no sign of discomfort whatsoever at his impending fate.

Horton went to bed at 8.10 p.m. on the Sunday evening and slept soundly through the night. At 6.00 a.m. a warder went to him and shook him by the shoulder, upon which he rose and dressed, then ate a full breakfast including 'skilly', bread and butter and a pint of tea. After this, however, he became uncommunicative and solemn, replying to questions only in monosyllables. The governor asked him if he was satisfied with the treatment he had been accorded while in the prison, and he nodded.

Aware of past problems, Berry was nervous when he went into the cell to pinion him. He asked Horton to stand still as soon as the rope was placed around his neck, but Horton stared at him and made no reply. Berry explained that it was important not to disturb the 'knot' but Horton again took no notice.

'I would advise you to stand perfectly upright and not move your head while the rope is being adjusted,' said Berry, 'and if you do that you will feel no more pain than from the prick of a pin.'

Much to Berry's relief, Horton gave a very slight nod to indicate that he understood. The two then chatted, Berry seeking to elicit some sign of penitence, but there was no response:

While I was pinioning my victim the chaplain stood in the doorway, and in a tremulous voice he read a passage from the Litany.

He commenced the burial service when I brought my man out, and then started to walk to the scaffold, a distance of only six or seven yards. The door at the end of the corridor was open, and Horton, the two warders, and myself stepped out on the drop.

Not a word escaped from the lips of the man who was about to die. He looked straight in front of him as he walked, except for an instant when his eye caught sight of one of his attendants, to whom he gave a glance of recognition.

I was feeling dreadfully nervous, and all the time I kept saying to myself, 'Now, James, pull yourself together or there will be another bungle.' I knew that if I failed to hang John Horton I would never hang another man, and in my heart of hearts I felt sure that there was going to be a bungle.

Walking very unsteadily, I fear, I placed the broad pinioning strap around Horton's legs and then I pulled the white cap over his face and slipped the noose of the rope down over his neck at the same time. I pressed down the brass-eye in which the noose ran and placed the knot close behind the left ear of my victim and all was in readiness.

I signalled to the warders and they stood clear of the drop, taking hold of the slab on either side. Glancing up I saw that Horton was standing bolt upright as firm as a rock, and I pulled my lever, which drew three bolts and released from its bearings the floor upon which the culprit stood, and the unhappy man reached the end of the five-foot drop.

Horton had died within three minutes of his leaving the condemned cell.

What Berry had feared would be another bungle had gone off as a very speedy and uncomplicated execution. It is interesting to note that he routinely engaged in conversation with the condemned, usually to ascertain that they were guilty and looking for signs of penitence. This may have helped Berry's feelings, but such conversations must have been excruciating for some of those about to die.

His tally of 'victims' now stood at thirty-one, and with his next job, only one week later, this was to rise to thirty-four with one pull of the lever.

13

The Netherby Hall burglary

'All the three men walked firmly to the scaffold . . . '

In chapter 9 I told the story of the arrest, trial and execution of James Lee for the murder of Essex policeman Inspector Simmons. That story, however, was incomplete, for, you may recall, the third alleged offender, Jack Martin, had disappeared without trace.

The sequel to that tale began on 27 October 1885, when a burglary occurred at Netherby Hall, the seat of Sir Frederick Graham, in Cumberland. A large quantity of jewellery was stolen, and a manhunt was started for four men who had been seen that night near the location of the crime.

With road checks in place it was not long before four men, all members of a London gang, walked into a police checkpoint manned by Police Sergeant Roche and Constables Johnstone and Fortune on the road near Kingstown at about 11 p.m. One of these men was the fugitive, John 'Jack' Martin (alias John White), who immediately pulled a revolver from his pocket and shot the sergeant, wounding him in the arm. Another of the four, Anthony Benjamin Rudge (alias William Fennell, alias William Walsh), shot and wounded PC Johnstone in the chest. Further along the road the gang came upon PC Fortune, and left him for dead with serious face and head injuries. The other two gang members were James 'One Armed Jimmy' Smith and James Baker. Smith decided to separate from the others in an attempt to make his way back to London, and headed south. Martin, Rudge and Baker decided to make for Carlisle, which was about eight miles away.

Near Penrith the fleeing men asked about a train for London, but the suspicious stationmaster called for the local policeman, PC

Byrnes. The courageous officer intercepted and tackled the three men, who had been to a local pub for some food and drink, at Plumpton. He was shot in the head and thrown into a dyke. Though still alive when he was found about 30 minutes later, he soon died. His assailants were desperate men. They made their way to the London and North Western Railway siding at Penrith but were seen by the guard concealing themselves under a tarpaulin on a goods train. At Tebay the train stopped and, alerted by the guard, a number of railway employees hauled the men out by their legs. A furious struggle ensued, during which the fugitives attempted to use their revolvers, but Martin and Rudge were finally restrained. Baker, however, escaped by leaping onto the goods train that was leaving the station, but his attempt to escape was futile, for when his train arrived at Lancaster the police were waiting to arrest him.

The three men were incarcerated in Carlisle gaol. Detective Sergeant Rolf, the Metropolitan Police officer who had originally been hunting Martin, travelled from London to interview him. Questioned on the murder of Inspector Simmons in Essex the previous January, Martin refused to admit involvement, but Rolf was certain of his complicity, convinced it was he who had fired the shot that killed Simmons. Martin, Rudge and Baker were convicted of murder and their joint execution set for Monday 8 February 1886. The fourth man, 'One Armed Jimmy' Smith, made it back to London.

Berry had his first, and only, triple execution to carry out. He had an assistant this time, called 'Charles Maldon'; in reality, none other than the sporting baronet and magistrate who had met Berry at the execution of James Lee: Sir Claude Champion de Crespigny, of Champion Lodge, Heybridge, near Maldon in Essex. Sir Claude was a well-known character in his day. A strong man, tales were told of his horse-whipping members of the Salvation Army, and boxing with his servants. He had even made an epic balloon flight, with a well-known balloonist, Mr Simmons from Maldon, across the Channel to Oudekerk near Flushing on 1 August 1883; a distance of 140 miles covered in 6 hours. Indeed, it was said that he excelled in a variety of sports, and remained in later life 'one of the hardest and pluckiest men in England . . . ready to box, ride, walk, run, shoot, fence, sail or swim and [one who] enjoyed a cold tub before breakfast'. In sporting circles he was a legend in his time. A fellow club member and imperialist, Alfred Pease, observed that, in assisting in this hanging he was showing that 'he would not care to ask a man to do what he himself was afraid of doing'. De Crespigny argued that aristocratic sporting pleasures and military duty went hand in hand, and that every able-bodied Briton had an obligation to defend his country and could not be considered a 'man' until he had done so.

Major Arthur Griffiths, in *Mysteries of Police and Crime* (London, Cassell & Company, 1898), observed:

> Some interest attaches to the execution, which subsequently took place within the gaol at Carlisle, from the fact that Berry, the hangman, was assisted by an amateur, an eccentric Baronet, Sir Claude de Crespigny.

In the descriptive account of the triple execution, from Berry's notebooks, in *Thomson's* of 5 February 1927, Berry has much to say of his illustrious assistant, but does not name him:

Who was Charles Maldon?

It is rather a direct question to answer, and I do not know that I am justified in so doing.

He was only assistant hangman of England for one day, and I do not know but what he has regretted by this time the part he played in the execution of Rudge, Martin and Baker, whatever his motive may have been.

I think it will be sufficient to say that he is one of the best-known men in England – a real, live Baronet . . .

. . . as soon as he heard that I was journeying to Carlisle he wrote asking if I would allow him to accompany me as the assistant executioner under the name of Charles Maldon.

He stated in the letter that he had had the whole of the gang before him at one time or another in his capacity of Magistrate and he was anxious to see the end of them.

He told me that he intended to put up in a hotel near the station, invited me to come and stay there also, and said that if I agreed to take him with me as assistant he would pay me ten pounds.

Of course, I accepted the offer. I wrote and told him, however, that I could not stay in the hotel with him, as the authorities insisted on me staying in the prison.

When Berry arrived at the prison, he mentioned to the governor that his assistant was staying in the hotel, and hinted that he would like to entertain him or go and see him. The governor was amenable and invited the assistant to tea. Sir Claude accepted the invitation and, after tea, the two hangmen stayed on for dinner in the governor's room. The odd pair – the dour Yorkshireman with his broad accent and the polished member of the aristocracy – must have presented a stark contrast. The three enjoyed a pleasant evening telling stories of their experiences, and the governor found Berry's assistant to be a very charming man. Hardly surprisingly, he entertained suspicions that his guest was rather more than a mere assistant executioner. As Berry put it:

The Baronet does not have the bearing of an ordinary man, nor the manners, either, and it was clear to the Governor that he had been entertaining a gentleman.

'Who is he, Berry?' he asked when he had gone.

'He is my assistant,' I thought it well to reply, and, of course, the matter was in nobody's hands but my own. I could employ just whoever I pleased.

In the morning, when Sir Claude entered the prison his appearance caused a great deal of suspicion in the minds of the local pressmen in attendance. They afterwards commented on the unusual assistant, who they described as 'sprucely dressed' and someone who 'bore himself with singular nonchalance'. Commenting on the fact that he was obviously no ordinary person they said:

We respect his pseudonym, but whether he was animated by the spirit of an enthusiastic amateur in the dreadful craft, or what, we cannot say.

Berry claimed that he had previously met the three condemned men on the train to Durham on 26 May 1884, and that they had 'chaffed' him (see chapter 7). He went on:

These men, when once their sentence was passed, had no further interest in life; and I believe that if the choice could have been offered to them they would have preferred to walk straight from the dock to the scaffold, rather than to have had the three weeks' grace which is given to condemned men. In the case of almost all habitual criminals I believe this is so – they do not fear death and they do not repent their crime. So long as there is a ghost of a chance of acquittal or reprieve, they cling to life, but as soon as the death sentence is passed they become indifferent, and would like to 'get it over' as soon as possible, mainly because the prison life bores them.

Of the three men . . . Rudge was the only one who seemed to care to take any interest in life.

According to Berry, Rudge spent a good deal of time in writing his views on the penal system for the information of the Home Office. Having served two long sentences in the past, he knew his subject. He talked freely with his attendants about himself and other matters, insisting that there was something wrong with his head and, although he did not seek a reprieve on this premise, suggesting to the chaplain that his brain should be examined after his execution.

The other two were quiet while awaiting execution and spent most of their time in bed. Rudge and Martin were Roman Catholics, but did not seem to care for the ministrations of the priest or gaol chaplain. Baker, however, had received Protestant teaching and appeared to listen to the chaplain, partaking of Holy Communion an hour before the execution. He was concerned about his sweetheart, Nellie, and wrote a long letter to her the night before his execution, assuring her of his love and urging her to 'keep to the path of the right'.

Close upon eight o'clock, Berry and 'Maldon' went to pinion the prisoners. Sir Claude dealt with Baker, a thin, wiry man who, when he entered, was pacing his cell in the company of the chaplain, and who submitted placidly to the application of the straps, saying only 'I wish it was all over'. Berry pinioned the other two men, describing Martin afterwards as one of the bravest men he had walked to the scaffold. The doomed man acknowledged that he was getting his just deserts, but claimed to be innocent of the crime he was being hanged for:

'I ought to have been hanged before . . . though I am being hanged for a murder I did not commit. Innocent men have been put to death for murders I committed.'

'Who are they?' asked the sheriff.

'Never mind,' replied Martin calmly 'I will tell you one and one only. You hanged Lee at Chelmsford for shooting Inspector Symons [*sic*] at Romford. He was innocent. That crime was committed by me.'

More than that he would not say, although it was afterwards stated in the press that previous to my seeing him he had confessed to shooting Constable Byrnes.

The platform from the hall to the old treadmill shed was only about 8–10 yards across and they crossed it quickly to the scaffold. The gallows had been constructed in the old treadmill shed to prevent people on buildings outside the prison witnessing the proceedings. Present at the execution were the High Sheriff of Cumberland, Mr L.F.B. Dykes; the under-sheriff, Mr E.L. Waugh; three visiting justices; two reporters; and the prison officials.

A pit 10 feet deep had been dug to give the required drop, and the trapdoors were on a level with the floor of the shed. The procession turned to the right, and before the three realised it they were on the drop beneath the strong beam from which dangled three nooses. All three men walked firmly to the scaffold, where they shook hands all round, saying, 'Good-bye, old pal, good-bye' – nothing more. The drop had been chalked with their names – Martin in the centre, with Rudge on the right and Baker on the left. The men stepped to their places and gave all the assistance they could in the final pinioning. 'Maldon' pulled the white cap over Baker's eyes as Berry busied himself with the other two. According to Berry, as the clergymen were giving their ministrations Rudge and Martin cried, 'Lord Jesus, receive my soul', Martin continuing, 'Into Thy hands I commit my spirit', after which Baker called out, 'Lord Jesus have mercy upon me, I die innocent. I forgive everybody.' Berry rapidly fastened the nooses round the necks of the white-capped men and signalled the priests to stand clear. Just before the drop fell Baker cried, 'Keep straight, Nellie!' and then the three men died together, with a brave demeanour. Death appeared to be almost instantaneous. A drop of 4 feet had been given to Rudge, who was the heaviest. Martin was given 6 feet and Baker 6½ feet. Afterwards Berry observed, 'the youth and manly bearing of Baker, and the strong affection of which he was capable, as shown by the way his Nellie was always uppermost in his thoughts, affected me very much. His execution was one of the saddest of my many experiences.'

He also later enlarged on the claim that he had hanged an innocent man in the shape of James Lee at Chelmsford, mentioning that he had discussed this with Sir Claude (*The Post*, 17 January 1914):

We talked about the confession afterwards, and at the time were both agreed that Martin was undoubtedly the man who shot the police inspector, and on his own confession committed other murders for which innocent men had been hanged.

. . . The authorities know that to own up would be to endanger their own position, and so they remain silent.

. . . The officials told me that he had committed more murders than Charles Peace, but what I maintain is that in the absence of sworn evidence in a Court of Law that he was a murderer he ought to have been given the benefit of the doubt for at least a week. Had the Home Secretary given him the time he told me that he could have proved his innocence up to the hilt.

I am half inclined to think that, while his was certainly not the hand that fired the fatal shot, he was near the scene of the crime. He belonged to the same gang as the man who undoubtedly did murder Police Inspector Symmons [*sic*], but there was another man who ought to have figured in the notorious case.

One of the Essex Magistrates, a Baronet by the way, did all in his power to get this man brought into it, but even his powerful influence was not sufficient. It would have got one or two prominent people into trouble, and so James was made the scapegoat.

. . . It was Jack Martin, one of the Netherby Hall burglars, who confessed to the murder when I hanged him in Carlisle Gaol. The confession was made in my presence to the Sheriff, and was heard by more than one of the officials. I notified the authorities myself about it, and I take it that the Sheriff did the same, but the information was never given to the public.

Jack Martin certainly answered the description of the man wanted for the Romford murder, and whether he fired the fatal shot or not I cannot see what he hoped to gain by confessing to a crime for which he had never been put in the dock. James Lee was dead and, and he could do him no good beyond clearing his name, at the same time making his own memory blacker.

Berry did not consider the possibility that a hardened criminal such as Martin revelled in his own notoriety and might have made such a confession just to vex the authorities he hated, knowing he had nothing to lose by adding another crime to his black tally. It is difficult to know the exact truth in view of the lack of corroborative evidence. There can be little doubt, however, that Lee was a hardened criminal who used a gun and was involved with the London gang. Furthermore, we need to remember that some of Berry's later writings seem coloured by his obvious resentment at losing his post and his disputes with officialdom. Detective Sergeant Rolf of the Metropolitan Police had failed to secure a confession from Martin despite being convinced of his guilt. Major Griffiths, in his account of the case, wrote, '. . . Martin was soon identified as the man who had murdered Police-Inspector Symmonds [sic], near Romford, for which another of the gang had been hanged'. Lt Col Sir Henry Smith, of the City of London Police, described the Netherby Hall burglary in his book *From Constable to Commissioner*, and said that he knew 'Jack' Martin, the latter having lived in the East End throughout his time in London:

When the men were safely in Carlisle Gaol, Rolf, a detective-sergeant of the H Division, was sent down to see if he could identify any or all of them; and in the first cell he was taken to was Jack, in no way put about, but cool and collected, as usual. 'Well,' he said, 'what's the chance this time Rolf?' 'Chance!' replied Rolf, 'you haven't the ghost of a chance if what I hear is true.' 'That's it, is it?' said Martin, shaking him warmly by the hand. 'You never did me no dirty tricks; you always tried to take me fair. I won't give you no more trouble. Good-bye.'

Besides the two men hanged with him at Carlisle, Martin had other pals, notably Jimmy Smith, alias 'One-armed Jimmy,' and Menson, alias Lee, hanged at Chelmsford for shooting Inspector Simmonds [sic], of the Essex Constabulary. Lee and Martin always carried six-shooters, and from information received after the former's execution, I knew that the latter was concerned with him in the murder of Simmonds between Romford and Rainham, and told Rolf to try and get hold of him.

Smith said that Martin and Rudge had tried to make out that the fourth man, who had escaped, was not a member of the gang but had joined them on the road from Longtown. He also maintained that Baker claimed to die an innocent man – having previously admitted his guilt – freely forgiving all that had given false evidence against him. Smith summed up by saying:

It has often astonished me that notice should be taken, either by the Press or public, or credence given to statements made by such men, who even with the rope round their necks lie pertinaciously to the end.

According to Sir Henry, 'One-armed Jimmy Smith' was traced by the City Police to the Regent Street area about ten days after the execution. The police in Carlisle were contacted but stated that three men had been hanged and one of the injured constables was in a 'precarious condition' and should not be troubled with an attempted identification. Amazingly Smith was released without charge. This brought Sir Henry to add an interesting postscript to the story:

The July following, Sergeant Rolf was at Wood Green Races, and, meeting Jimmy, asked him to have a drink. Adjourning to a booth, they were having a talk of old times over a glass of gin-and-water, when they were joined by a third man, whom Rolf introduced as a 'friend of mine.' Presently Rolf's friend, having finished his drink, left. 'Who's that?' said Jimmy. 'He seems a decent sort of chap.' 'Oh, he's decent enough,' replied Rolf. 'That's Berry, the hangman.' Jimmy's feelings were sorely hurt, and in very forcible language he intimated that, had he known the profession of the gentleman to whom he had been introduced he would have declined to partake of refreshment in his company.

Jimmy shortly afterwards mysteriously disappeared, and what became of him I never could discover.

The full story of this desperate London gang and the Romford and Netherby Hall murders deserves fuller examination than is possible here.

Sir Claude returned to his hotel to find he was not the only well-known person staying there. The then renowned war correspondent Archibald Forbes spotted him in the smoking-room and, having heard the stories of the gentlemanly assistant executioner, was naturally curious. After initially being unable to place Sir Claude he finally remembered who he was, but, as a gentleman himself, he did not reveal the secret. Sir Claude had been ready, however, for such an eventuality, having decided that should his identity be revealed he would highlight the very real possibility that he would become a sheriff for the county of Essex, in which capacity he would have to order the execution of anyone so sentenced. He would not order someone else to do anything that he was not prepared to do himself, hence his involvement at Carlisle.

After the execution Berry dined with Sir Claude at the hotel. Being 'extremely nervous after the grim business', he upset his cup of coffee on the tablecloth, upon which one of the waiters went over to him and, seeing his consternation, said, 'Don't trouble, Mr. Berry!' At an opposite table sat a military-looking man with his wife and son. The man looked up in evident agitation and called the waiter over, asking whom Berry was. Then, furious to learn that he was sharing the room with the hangman, he stormed out of the room with his family, collared the hotel manager and asked that

Berry be removed, threatening to leave the hotel when the manager refused to do anything.

'All right,' said the manager, 'do you want your boxes down? His money is as good as yours.'

Berry recalls the incident:

He was dumbfounded, and at that moment I happened to be coming out of the dining room. He turned on me at once.

'Mr. Berry?' he asked.

'I am!'

'What right have you to be here?'

'As much right as you,' I said.

At that he began to call me every name he could bring to mind. He told me I ought to keep to my own society, and ended by saying – 'I have seen a better man than you flogged with the cat.'

'And I have hanged many a better man than you,' said I.

Then the storm broke with a vengeance. His wife and son began to assail me, and if my English Baronet friend had not taken up the cudgels on my behalf I would have been unable, I believe, to go on to Lancaster to do another job there.

Berry recorded a strange sequel to this incident. A month or two afterwards a stranger drove up to his house in Bradford, the man turning out to be the son of the angry man from the hotel. Berry was not in, so he spoke with Mrs Berry and asked if he could wait. Mrs Berry invited him in and left him in her husband's room. When she returned later, he was smoking a cigar and going over Berry's private papers, being particularly interested in the death warrants that Berry had kept as part of his collection of execution-related ephemera (Berry retained the warrants of all his victims). When Mrs Berry reprimanded him, he merely replied, 'Oh, that's all right.'

Berry returned and was surprised to see his uninvited visitor.

'Hullo! What brings you here?'

'Oh, I just came in to tell you to keep your own society in life,' said the unabashed stranger. 'You will do yourself no good if you try to get into high society.'

'And you came to tell me that?'

'Oh, more than that. I came to tell you that you did yourself no good insulting my father. Do you know he has influence at the Home Office?'

'What do I care about that?'

'Oh, well, I just thought a hint would do you no harm. My father could give you a lift up if he liked. Will you come to my hotel with me?'

Berry was perplexed and went with the man, staying until it was time for the latter to catch the train back to London. The stranger departed, as much a mystery to Berry as he had been when he arrived. Three weeks later he called again to ask Berry if he could have a death warrant. Berry declined to let him have one, and was puzzled by the man's motives in coming all the way from London to make such a request. Subsequently, all Berry's death warrants disappeared in a burglary one night. He and Mrs Berry had noticed a man watching the house for some weeks before but had thought he looked more like a detective than a burglar. He never heard of the missing warrants again.

This is a mysterious episode but the answer may be quite prosaic. The hangman of the period excited much public curiosity and fascination, his relics and ephemera being highly desirable collectables. The stranger may have been merely fascinated with Berry and his trade. Whether the theft of the warrants was connected to him or instigated by some other wealthy collector will never be known.

14

Sad cases of 1886

'The worst woman I ever hanged'

The day after the triple execution at Carlisle, Berry travelled south to Lancaster for the execution of John Bains, a Barrow fish hawker whose wife had left him after months of domestic disputes that had culminated in a threat to kill her. A final quarrel took place on Christmas Day 1885, Bains having followed her to her friend's house where he stabbed her four times with a butcher's knife. The execution was successfully carried out on Tuesday 9 February 1886.

A third execution in as many days was scheduled at Norwich, John Thurston, a labourer aged 30, awaiting Berry's attentions there in Norwich Castle. Thurston, a nephew of one Henry Webster, who was hanged in the same prison on 1 May 1876 for the murder of his wife at Cranworth (*Norfolk Annals*), had appeared on 22 January 1886 at the Norfolk Assizes before Mr Justice Hawkins, indicted for the wilful murder of an old man, Henry Springall, at Hingham on 5 December 1885. The motive for the attack was robbery, Thurston having battered in the victim's head with a large stone. Informing the Under-Sheriff of Norwich, Clement Taylor, of his plans, Berry wrote:

Sir,
I received your telegram stating that you accepted my services on Wednesday Feb 10th all been well I shall arrive all about the same time I arrived before. I shall go straight to the Prison on my arrival in Norwich. You can depend on me been there.
I remain
Your Most Humble & Obedt. Servant
James Berry   Executioner

This time Berry's visit to Norwich was not so harrowing as his last. Thurston was executed without incident on Wednesday 10 February.

Berry's next execution was also in East Anglia. George Saunders, aged 29, awaited execution at Ipswich on Tuesday 16 February 1886. A Lowestoft fisherman, he had murdered his wife during a drunken quarrel on Christmas Eve 1885, cutting her throat with a razor as she sat in a chair. Having gone straight to the police to report it, he was arrested and subsequently found guilty at Ipswich Assizes on 29 January. While awaiting execution he showed great contrition, listening intently to the ministrations of the chaplain, and as he walked to the scaffold he showed great composure, quietly submitting to Berry's operations. Asked if he had anything to say, he replied, 'Yes, may the Lord Jesus receive my poor soul and have mercy on my poor children.' Death appeared to be instantaneous (*The Times*, 17 February 1886).

Owen McGill, a 39-year-old Irishman and farm labourer, was another wife-murderer. On 31 October 1885 he and his wife Mary had been out delivering corn in Birkenhead and had called at a couple of pubs for a drink on the way back. Later in the afternoon Mrs McGill prevented Owen from getting into a fight with a couple of farm workers. That evening a neighbour saw her run screaming from the couple's house in Lincarton. Another neighbour saw her lying on the ground, with Owen standing over her telling her to get up. McGill visited his cousin the next morning, asking him to return home with him, as his wife was ill. On arriving at the house the woman was found battered and beaten to death. McGill claimed she had fallen from the cart the previous day but the evidence of the neighbours told against this. It was obvious to the police that she had been murdered. Owen was found guilty before Lord Chief Justice Coleridge on 3 February and sentenced to death, Berry hanging him at Knutsford Prison, Cheshire, the first execution to be conducted there, on Monday 22 February 1886.

Berry's next job was a sad case indeed, for it involved the murder of a child. The offender, Thomas Nash, a labourer employed by Swansea Corporation, had murdered his 6-year-old daughter by throwing her off a pier into the sea at Swansea. Described by Berry as a 'friendless being for whom a great many were filled with the greatest pity. A strange, uncouth man', his case was heard before the Cardiff Assizes on 9 February. The grim tale that unfolded was appalling. Just after dusk on the day in question, a number of pilots standing near the boathouse of the extension pier at Swansea had spotted a man leading a small poorly clad girl by the hand in the direction of the pier. Despite it being an odd time and location for the two to be out, and even though it was both windy and pouring with rain, they had taken little notice, but a short while later an assistant pilot saw the man jump from the pier to the sands and run away. Of the little girl there was no sign. Some of the pilots pursued the fleeing figure and stopped him, discovering him to be Thomas Nash, of Graham Street, Hafod. Trembling with fear, he offered no resistance as he was seized, and when asked where the little girl was he answered that she was on top of the extension pier, changing this to the bottom of the pier when the men commented that it was an odd place to leave a child alone on a bleak night such as that. He attempted to walk away in the direction of the pier but the men detained him, by which time an angry crowd had gathered, convinced that his intention had been to sexually abuse the child. Eventually he was taken to the boathouse and handed over to a dock policeman. He refused at first to say where the child was; then claimed that he had been carrying her on his back near the rails, and that she had somehow slipped and been blown over the side of the pier. He was taken to the police station and there accused of the murder of his daughter.

With the aid of lanterns a search was conducted of all parts of the pier and the sands, and after a couple of hours a constable discovered the body of the child on a heap of rubbish left by the receding tide, about thirty yards from the high water mark and some distance from the pier. Enquiries revealed that Nash, a widower for five years, together with his daughter Martha Ann aged about 6 (the deceased) and another daughter aged 16, had lodged with a widow in the town. A month before the tragedy he had left his daughters at the lodgings and, unknown to them, had remarried. Owed two weeks' rent and understandably unwilling to support the children herself, the widow had approached him for the money and given him an ultimatum: the children would either have to leave or go to the workhouse. When Nash subsequently failed to act, she took the youngest child to him as he collected his wages from the Town Hall, and left her with him. He collected his wages and immediately left for the pier, apparently having decided to get rid of the child. Despite sticking to his story of an accident, it was evident from the fact that the child's body was uninjured that she had been thrown off the pier, for only thus could she have cleared the extending beams below. Nash was found guilty as charged.

Berry travelled to Swansea gaol by hansom cab, in cold but fine weather. When he arose the next morning he found that snow had fallen heavily during the night shrouding everything in a thick blanket of white. There was a very cold wind and the town looked bleak and miserable. Despite his hopeless plight the prisoner had been eating heartily, and, seeing he was particularly fond of eggs, the governor had promised him a couple of eggs on the morning of his execution to supplement his ordinary breakfast of a large mutton chop, potatoes, bread and butter and a pint of tea. The eggs were delayed, and noticing they were not there, Nash rang for them, subsequently eating the whole meal apart from a small piece of bread and butter.

Berry had read the story of the crime in the newspapers and was satisfied that the condemned man was guilty, but he was nonetheless relieved to hear on his arrival that Nash had confessed to the crime. Having been attended by the chaplain, Nash had confessed everything to him and written a long confessional letter to ensure that the papers got the story correct. According to this, he had since spent his time in prayer, asking God for mercy and forgiveness, and, he claimed, God had taken his sins from him such that he was departing life assured of forgiveness and of being forever in peace with Jesus and Martha Ann. Making strong religious protestations he said that he would rather 'die in the Lord' than have a reprieve and live in misery. He wrote another letter to the chaplain thanking him for attending him and for pointing him to the way of Jesus Christ.

Early that morning of Monday 1 March 1886 Berry trudged through the snow to the execution shed and examined the apparatus, which he found to be 'in perfect order'. The doomed man was in his cell listening intently to the chaplain's ministrations, while in the snow outside the prison a large crowd had gathered.

The prison surgeon arrived and spoke with Berry. About 10 minutes prior to the execution the High Sheriff and the under-sheriff arrived and were received by the prison governor. A minute or two before the hour they all met in the corridor and went with Berry to the condemned cell. There were two clergymen with the prisoner, one of whom was weeping. Berry pinioned Nash in the presence of the officials, the prisoner remaining silent, after which, accompanied by the chief warder, he led him out of the cell and down some steps to the courtyard. The snow lay like a white pall, but Nash stepped out with a firm stride, bracing his shoulders and heading for the wheelhouse, where he took up his position on the drop, those in the procession forming on either side. Only the tolling of the minute bell and the soft murmuring of the burial service could be heard. An indistinct murmur was heard from the lips of the unfortunate victim as Berry pinioned his feet and put the white cap over his head. Then, at the words of the burial service 'We therefore commit his body to the ground', Berry took hold of the lever, and as Nash uttered the words 'Lord have mercy upon my soul' the floor fell from beneath his feet and he disappeared from view. He died instantly. The clock in the house had struck eight as the bolt was drawn.

The black flag was hoisted over the entrance gates of the prison and a cheer went up from the expectant crowd. As a breeze caught the flag the crowd shuddered and they began to disperse. The warder on the tower gazed down on a few that had remained. They had commenced a snowball fight!

Berry stayed on in Wales for another execution, at Cardiff, scheduled for the following day: that of David Roberts, a labourer aged about 30 years, who had been convicted at Cardiff Assizes. On 30 October 1885 a travelling cattle dealer, David Thomas, aged 48, had left the Duke of Wellington Inn, Cowbridge in the company of two men: David Roberts, and his father Edward, aged 60. Thomas had rashly boasted of the money he was carrying round, having about £78 on him at that time. After a wild night marked by strong winds and heavy rain, Thomas was found dead in the early hours of the following morning, halfway between where he had left David and Edward Roberts – a stile at Town Mill – and his farm. He had been beaten and his money was gone. Acting on information received, the police arrested David, who denied any knowledge of what had happened. Later that day his father and another man were arrested in the same hotel that they had drunk at the day before.

It emerged that the three had been out for a drink, and at closing time David Roberts had started off for home in Llanblethian with his father, Thomas heading for his own home, Stall Court Farm. Roberts junior, however, had doubled back and followed Thomas, subsequently robbing and killing him. Some of the dead man's papers were found in the Roberts's fireplace, and a bloody handkerchief containing nearly £70 and a sovereign with a hole in it, known to have been in the possession of Thomas, was found in a cupboard. At the trial before Lord Chief Justice Coleridge, the father was acquitted but David, who had led a rather dissolute life and had been drummed out of the army a few months previously, pleaded guilty and was duly sentenced to death. He stated emphatically that his father – who visited him in prison for an emotional farewell the afternoon before the execution – had nothing to do with the crime. Writing of that visit, Berry observed, 'David was considerably upset, but not too upset to partake of a good meal of sausages.' Roberts wrote to his friends to say goodbye and to ask them not to visit him. He also wrote to his victim's wife asking for forgiveness. He handed another letter to Berry just before the execution. Addressed to a Cardiff newspaper, this expressed his thanks to the prison staff for the kindness they had shown him, and again exonerated his father from the crime. The governor, who Berry considered one of the most kind-hearted men he had ever met, had spent a good deal of time with the condemned man on the eve of his execution.

As to the execution itself, Berry claims to have suffered considerable mental agonising over it, describing Roberts as a strong man who was determined to fight for his life. He wrote:

> I used to think that Roberts had determined in his mind that he would not die at my hands, and brought a powerful mental effort to bear during the last few minutes on the scaffold. He was a man of iron nerve, and remarkable in many ways.

By 7.00 a.m. a crowd had gathered in front of the gaol, and the police took up position in front of the massive prison doors. Snow had fallen heavily from a leaden sky and the spacious prison yard was covered as Berry entered it. He found the prison governor and chief warder pacing and engrossed in earnest conversation. The gallows had been erected in a small courtyard near the male prison, about 20 yards in length by 12 feet wide. The crossbeam of the gallows was of pitch-pine wood and one end of the framework was fixed to the wall, the opposite end supported by a pine upright. The drop was on a level with the yard, the pit being about 10 feet deep with a 'manhole' should it be necessary to enter it. The gallows was overlooked by the small windows of the male quarters, but these were designed in such a way that the inmates could not see through them. It was so bitterly cold that Berry wore a long tweed overcoat and a Scotch cap of the same material. However, he took this off when he saw the reporters and the High Sheriff.

Roberts took no breakfast but drank a cup of tea and awaited the arrival of Berry, who met him in the corridor surrounded by four warders. Berry immediately began to pinion him in the presence of the High Sheriff and the others, Roberts submitting quietly with barely a glance at anyone. As soon as Berry had finished, the chaplain approached and the procession started for the scaffold. On the drop Roberts did not flinch, once again taking no notice of anyone around him as Berry pinioned his legs. According to Berry, he looked pale and haggard but showed no unsteadiness as he quietly repeated responses after the chaplain. Strapping Roberts's ankles together, Berry removed the hat Roberts was wearing, put the rope around his neck and drew the white cap over his head. He then immediately stepped aside and pulled the lever, launching Roberts into the pit:

It was then that I noticed the struggle for life, and my experience told me plainly that an accident had taken place. The reporters were eagerly waiting, and as I did not wish for the papers filled with the story of a bungle I kept my head, and after a minute and a half had elapsed I turned to one of the warders, and in a tone loud enough for the reporters to hear I said – 'He is dead now.'

The movements continued, however, for some considerable time, and it was then that I signalled to the chief warder, and he in turn spoke to the Governor, and the press were conducted out of the gaol.

The drop in this case had been too short, the whole length for the stretching of the rope being only four feet. It had been decided to make the rope so unusually slack because of the weight of my victim, and the danger thereby of having a worse accident. The result was that the jerk of the rope was too slight, and sometime after he had been hanging there Roberts began to heave violently for breath. The doctor was sure that his neck had been dislocated, and that death had been instantaneous, the movements, he said, having merely been caused by muscular contraction.

I did not share his opinion, however, although I must admit that when I left the city I told everyone that the execution was the cleverest job I had yet done. I had to talk like that in such cases, otherwise I might never have got safely out of the place.

Unfortunately for Berry, local reporters subsequently wrote about the problems with the execution. According to one of them, he had entered the waiting room of the gaol where Berry was having his breakfast, and when Berry commented that it had been a 'clever' execution he demurred, stating that it had taken some time for the man to die. An enraged Berry had threatened to bring an action against anyone circulating such a report, but when the body was viewed it was seen that the face had turned purple.

Berry returned to Bradford pondering over this latest mistake. His next job was not to take place until the end of the month. Scheduled for Monday 31 May 1886 at Winchester, it was to be another double execution, the victims this time being Albert Edward Brown and James Whelan. Brown was a sailor who had embarked on an around the coast voyage from Millwall to Southampton on 8 April. He had been in the company of one James Stanley Parker, and when the two arrived at Southampton they had set off on foot for Winchester. The next morning Parker was found dead in a field, his throat cut. Brown was soon detained by the police and found to have blood on his clothing. Convicted at Winchester Assizes, he later admitted that he had killed his companion by hitting him with a hammer and cutting his throat in order to steal four shillings.

Whelan, also a seaman, had worked out of Nova Scotia on a brigantine called the *Emma J Shore*. It was a British-registered vessel with a mixed, mostly Scandinavian, crew. On a voyage from New York to the River Plate the second mate, George Richardson, had warned Whelan about his work and threatened him, to which Whelan had retorted that if he saw Richardson again on the trip he would kill him. Several days later, on 15 March, Whelan attacked Richardson, beating him about the head and throwing him overboard. He was lost at sea. Detained by the crew and secured in irons, Whelan was later shipped back to England to stand trial, appearing on 8 May before Mr Justice Day at Winchester Assizes. Despite pleading self-defence he was found guilty – a note was found in his cell after his execution in which he admitted to murdering two other men.

Present at the two men's execution was John J. De Zouche-Marshall, LRCSI, (whose proposal for a 'chin trough', a device that would cause the head to snap backwards during execution, was rejected by the Aberdare Committee), a medical man interested in the 'increased certainty and humanity of the operation' of judicial execution. He was there under the authority of the Home Office to observe the procedure in order to gain 'additional experience' and to report his findings to the Aberdare Committee. In that report he states that Whelan weighed about 13st and was given a drop of about 4ft, while Brown, being lighter at a little over 10st, was given 6ft 6in. The only movement from Whelan on falling, he notes, was of the diaphragm, and when the cap was removed from the culprit's face there were no signs of suffering, even though his pulse beat for 10 minutes and his diaphragm moved for three.

In the case of Brown, he 'made very violent efforts at inspiration, much more so than Whelan, and for a longer time, nearly four minutes, and his pulse beat for 12½ minutes', the face afterwards being congested. Despite this, the press reported that death was instantaneous. Dr Marshall reported to the Committee, 'I may say that I make it a point never to tell the newspaper men anything.' Asked for his general observations he replied:

> Berry said, that in the case of Whelan, the 13-stone man, another foot would have decapitated him. I am certain that in Whelan's case he did not suffer an atom; although his pulse beat for ten minutes he had not the slightest sign of suffering,

so far as I can give an opinion. Brown must have suffered very little, if anything. His face was congested, but there was no sign of his suffering much.

It would seem that having erred on the side of the drops being too long, Berry had now readjusted the opposite way.

Edward Hewitt was a 34-year-old itinerant worker who held no regular employment. His wife Sarah Ann was eleven years his senior and they lived in Wells Court, Gloucester in some privation. After securing employment for a week in Sharpness, a seaport on the Severn, he returned home with his wages. He gave his wife a sovereign as housekeeping money but asked for 6 shillings back for himself for drink. He went out on the Sunday morning and returned home later demanding some money back from his wife. An argument ensued during which he lost his temper and kicked her to death. Found guilty, he was sentenced to death and the execution date set for Tuesday 15 June. Berry wrote his standard letter offering his services:

> Bradford
> Yorks May 26th. 86.
>
> Dear Sir:
> I beg to offer my services
> In the case where the Convict was Sentenced to Death at Worcester & Gloucester Assizes.
> Should my services be required I am at your command either by letter or Telegram.
>
> I am Sir
> Yours most obdt. Servant
> James Berry
> The High Sheriff
> Assize Courts
> Worcester

Berry was duly commissioned and travelled to Gloucester County Prison to carry out the execution. The local press carried a description of the hangman:

He is a thickset young man with a pleasant expression of the eyes, light brown hair, whiskers, moustache and beard. He also has a scar on one cheek.

The gallows was also described:

The apparatus of death stands before us; it is a cross beam supported by two upright struts about six feet high, between which is a platform level with the courtyard. The platform consists of two trap doors, the edges of which rest on a cross bar secured by a bolt; beneath these is a brick-lined pit nine feet deep.

The press representatives present saw a door in the corner open and the chaplain emerge, reading the service of the dead. Hewitt followed, his arms pinioned down to his elbows. He was dressed in his best suit and had grown a beard since his first appearance before the magistrate, had a ghastly pale face, and wore a dazed look. On the drop Berry put a white cap over his head, strapped his hands and his feet, then adjusted and tightened the rope around his neck. A leather washer on the rope was pushed over the covered 'iron ring' of the noose. Hewitt was heard to murmur, 'Oh dear.' Berry stooped, unscrewed a nut and jerked the lever at the side, releasing the bolt. The two doors dropped and fell on their hinges against the padded sides of the pit. Hewitt disappeared from view.

Unfortunately it was yet another 'accident'. Immediately after the trap had fallen the doctor hurriedly made his way down into the pit. The pressmen advanced a few paces, suspecting a bungle, and they were right. Hewitt's body was distinctly seen to be quivering, and though the doctor said at the time that it was only muscular contractions he stated afterwards at the inquest that he found the heart still beating. On lifting the white cap, he had further found Hewitt's face to be distorted, apparently as a result of extreme agony, his eyes bulging, his tongue bitten through and protruding. As *The Gloucester Chronicle* afterwards reported, these are all signs of death by strangulation as opposed to instant death by dislocation of the vertebrae; Berry had apparently made the drop too short.

Again observing on behalf of the Home Office, Dr Marshall

reported that Hewitt, a lightweight man of around 10st 4lb, had been given a drop of about 6 feet. On taking the cap off Hewitt's face he saw 'unmistakeable evidence of intense suffering . . . His eyes were open and starting out of his head, and his tongue was protruding.' Marshall also noted that Hewitt had 'made distinct efforts to free his hand or, instinctive efforts, one might say, to get hold of the rope'. In his view, the suffering had lasted about 2¼ minutes, but, despite this, he offered no criticism of the manner in which the execution had been performed. Medical men subsequently examined the body, cutting down to the spine to discover that there had, indeed, been no dislocation of the vertebrae. A full post-mortem examination was not conducted.

Shortly afterwards, in July 1886, the Conservative Government under the premiership of Lord Salisbury was elected for a second term, and a new Home Secretary, a Roman Catholic barrister named Henry Matthews QC, was chosen. He would remain in this office until 1895 and would eventually witness the retirement of James Berry from the position of public executioner. From this point on, the Aberdare Committee would be reporting to him.

Berry's next execution was scheduled for Tuesday 27 July 1886. On 9 July at Newton Assizes, North Wales, William Samuels, a grocer's assistant, had been found guilty before Mr Justice Groves of the murder of William Mabbots at Welshpool. Mabbots had died after drinking beer poisoned with strychnine. Although admitting he had offered the beer to the victim, Samuels initially denied knowledge of the poison, but he later left a confession in the condemned cell. The execution appears to have been successfully carried out, no hitch being noted.

Poison was a common weapon for the nineteenth-century murderer, and was the preferred choice of many female offenders. It was far more difficult to detect in those days, death often being attributed to some stomach ailment or other.

Mary Ann Britland, a 39-year-old factory worker, lived with her barman husband Thomas, aged 44, and two daughters at 92 Turner Lane, Ashton-under-Lyne. Their neighbours were Thomas Dixon and his 29-year-old wife, and it was rumoured that Mrs Britland and Thomas were having an affair. On Tuesday 9 March Mary Ann bought a threepenny packet of Harrison's Vermin Powder, containing a mixture of arsenic and strychnine, and, that night, the Britlands' eldest daughter, Elizabeth Hannah aged 19 and engaged to be married, died after vomiting all night, having first suffered, according to Mary Ann, a fit and convulsions. On the death of Elizabeth, Mary Ann collected £10 insurance money. On 30 April Mrs Britland visited the wife of her insurance agent to pay the money due on the insurances of her husband and her daughter, Susannah. That same day she bought some vermin powder, this time containing strychnine but no arsenic. On 1 May her husband, Thomas, fell ill with symptoms similar to those experienced by his deceased daughter. He was still alive, however, two days later when Mrs Britland bought three more packets of Harrison's Vermin Powder, but he subsequently died that evening. Shortly afterwards Mary Ann collected £19 insurance money on him. She then went with her daughter Susannah to stay with the Dixons, and nine days later Mrs Dixon fell ill with by now all too familiar symptoms, dying the following day, 13 May. This time Thomas Dixon, husband of the deceased, collected £19 insurance money. Suspicions were aroused over the deaths, an autopsy was ordered and traces of poison were found. Mrs Britland and Mr Dixon were arrested, though the latter was later cleared and released. Exhumation orders were issued in respect of the bodies of Mary Ann's daughter and husband, and when poison was again found Britland confessed to the triple killing, giving the fact that she wished to marry Mr Dixon as her motive. The trial took place at Leeds on 21 and 22 July. Britland was found guilty, and as Mr Justice Cave sentenced her to death she broke down, crying in the dock for mercy and pleading her innocence, her cries being heard from the cells below.

There is no doubting Britland's guilt but it is uncertain whether Thomas Dixon played any part in the crime. There is no evidence that he did, but Mrs Britland stated, 'He's no right to get off, and he wouldn't if I could tell my mind. He ought to be locked up all the time, the same as me. It was him that led me into it, and he wanted me to go away before I was locked up, and said he would go away with me when the bother was over.'

In writing of this case Berry described Mrs Britland as 'the worst woman I ever hanged'. He dramatically stated:

I never hanged a woman without going through all the torture of the condemned myself. Even when I sent Mary Britland to her doom, I felt as if I were about to die. Her pitiful cries ring in my ears to this day.

Despite this Berry described the woman as unworthy of any pity:

. . . a demon who inhabited the body of a human being. Mad she must have been, and bad as she was mad. Lucrezia Borgia was a saint compared to her, for, although both employed the same methods, the Italian woman did not poison her own child.

Mrs Britland was described as a woman of 'prepossessing appearance' who sang in the choir of the Zion Chapel and enjoyed universal respect. Apparently her daughter had returned home from work unexpectedly one day and found her in the arms of her lover. She had threatened to tell her father, after which she fell ill and died. The poison Mary Ann used was arsenic, as its symptoms imitated certain stomach ailments.

The execution had been set for Monday 9 August at Strangeways Prison, Manchester. Friends and her two other daughters visited her in prison, and she swore to them that she was innocent. Berry described his fraught time at Strangeways while preparing to execute the woman:

The worst night I ever spent in an English gaol was the one on the eve of Mary Ann Britland's death, and I shiver even yet when I recall it to my mind. I went to the cell door early in the night and had a good look at her. She was sitting on the bed moaning and rocking her body to and fro, and, bad as she was, I felt sorry for her.

After all, she was a woman!

When, later on that night, she realised that there could be no hope of a reprieve, she began to wail so loudly that her cries penetrated the walls of the prison. The agonising sounds awakened everyone, and as a woman had never yet been executed in Strangeways Gaol, one can well imagine what the officers felt like.

There was a concentration of pitiful helplessness and terror in her outcries which penetrated the heart with distressful emotions, and never a wink of sleep did I get that night. In the morning she was awakened, but she was unable to get out of bed. When I went to the condemned cell the governor pushed the door open, and I saw a sight I am never likely to forget so long as life lasts.

Mary Ann Britland, with pale, sunken cheeks and staring eyes, reclined in her bed, her head supported by two female warders. On his knees at the bedside was the chaplain, praying fervently for the soul of the woman, and the breath of death hung like a funeral pall over all.

I tapped the clergyman on the shoulder to let him know that all was in readiness. Outside the passing bell was awaking the echoes, but he could not hear of it. His thoughts were of the other world.

'Come along now, Mary. Time is up.'

A shriek left her lips, and she shivered in terror.

The others stepped back. They did not like their task, and so I had to put my arm around her and drag her to her feet.

'Come now, Mary, I have to do my duty, and it is a disagreeable one. Don't make it worse for both of us by going out of the world with your sin unconfessed. Why did you do it?'

She remained silent while I was putting the straps around her.

'Why did you do it, Mary?'

'I must have been mad! Oh, God forgive me, I must have been mad,' she sobbed.

The procession started at a signal from me.

It was headed by the chaplain, then came the woman herself, and she was supported by two women warders, with two male warders walking behind.

Along with the Governor and the Sheriff was one of the Aldermen of Ashton, who had been admitted by the authority of the High Sheriff.

Mary Ann Britland's terror grew greater with every step she took from the condemned cell.

'Oh! oh! oh!' she wailed, as half walking, half stumbling, sometimes being dragged along, she progressed to her doom.

Her wail rising in volume and intensity as the dread procession neared the fatal spot, punctuated every sentence of the chaplain as he went on – 'I know that my Redeemer liveth and that He will stand at the latter day upon earth.'

In response the enfeebled woman shrieked forth in distressing crescendo, 'Oh, oh, oh,' the last coming as if from a breaking heart.

And then she varied it with – 'Oh dear me! Oh dear me!' It was pitiful to hear her.

The look on the poor woman's face was terrible. She was worn and thin, and showed signs of the extreme suffering she had undergone, and when she came in sight of the gallows, she was unable to keep her feet.

The warders had to run up and take hold of her by the arms, otherwise she would have fallen on to her face.

By this time, wretched woman as she was, there was not one in the prison that did not feel heartbroken to think of the fate that awaited her.

Personally, I felt as if I were about to drop. Her pitiful screams went through my heart like the stab of a knife, and I was afraid lest I should bungle the business.

The last few yards' walk to the scaffold were the most terrible, and when we got to the drop we had to lift her upon it.

'God save me!' she cried. 'Oh, forgive me, forgive me!'

The terrible instrument of destruction at Strangeways juts out at a level of about eight feet from a blank wall, and the condemned woman had no prospect before her but a high stone wall. Underneath, about two feet of earth had been excavated at my order to allow a little extra for the drop.

When I put the rope round her neck a dreadful scream left her bloodless lips.

'Oh, Lord save me! Have mercy upon me!' she cried.

The faces of the onlookers were pale, and everyone shivered at the sight of the woman as she stood supported by the two wardresses. One or two put their hands over their ears and some closed their eyes so that the dread spectacle might be blotted out.

She continued to wail and cry for mercy, and as she felt the white cap passing over her head the most heartrending of her cries were uttered – such as one might expect at the actual separation of body and spirit through mortal terror. The worst was now over with her.

The governor of the prison had arranged that as soon as the white cap was on the female warders should be relieved of their dreadful task.

At the signal they stepped back shuddering, and as I went to the lever two officers sprang forward and took their places – one on each side of Mary Britland.

They held her up, and when I heard the words – 'Redeemer of the world, have mercy upon her,' – I turned my face away and released the bolts of death.

Instantly the doors flew open, the poor woman dropped through the pit to instant death. Every man in the crowd around the scaffold bared his head, and stood for a few minutes looking at the vacant spot where Mary Ann Britland had stood, and then there was a rush to get away from the scene.

Berry had given her a drop of 7 feet and death appeared to be instantaneous. Britland made no formal confession. Berry's description of her last moments paints an evocative picture of the terror that execution held for the condemned. A plea to God for mercy was the only consolation left open to them; their situation was utterly hopeless. Whether the prospect of such punishment would have deterred Britland from her fatal course, had she stopped to think about it, is another matter.

15

A busy end to the year

'There are three men on the roof Mr. Berry . . . '

Whatever the state of Berry's mind and nerves was after the excruciating execution of Mrs Britland he at least had three months to recover before his next job. The execution of Patrick Judge had been scheduled for Tuesday 16 November 1886 at Newcastle. Judge, a former soldier aged 47 years, had been found guilty at Newcastle Assizes of the murder of his wife, Jane. The couple, who had lived at Walker-on-Tyne, had been unhappily married. Then, while working as a labourer at Byker, Judge lost a leg in an accident, which, coupled with the demon drink that exacerbated his already aggressive nature, did nothing to enhance his disposition. His wife had decided to set herself up with a business, but he objected, and, after a dispute concerning the matter, he shot her twice in the head using a revolver he had purchased only two days prior to the shooting.

Berry, as an established celebrity of his day, was well aware that he would be the object of public curiosity and that his arrival would attract a crowd. In view of this, when he left Bradford for Newcastle he decided to get off the train at Durham and change to a slower train. He alighted at Gateshead, walked across the low-level bridge, and then, en route to Newcastle, took a look at the cathedral which, he writes, '. . . filled me with solemn thoughts, and when I left it I was feeling much better than when I set out from Bradford'.

On reaching Newcastle Berry found that his plan had been anticipated and there were a good many people waiting for him. However, they did not molest him and he 'passed inside the gloomy gates to see that everything was in readiness for the execution'. He went to the cell to take a look at Judge, and was impressed with the 'stalwart bearing' of the prisoner, noting that he must have cut an impressive figure in uniform in his soldiering days. Described by the warder accompanying him as 'a nice sort of chap' who gave no trouble, he had a handsome face and a good physique apart from the wooden leg he was obliged to use. 'The fellow is so strong and powerful', remarked Berry. 'He looks to me like a six foot drop.' He then subjected the scaffold to close scrutiny, and finding it to be in good working order was satisfied with the arrangements.

Judge said farewell to his friends on the Monday afternoon, the scene apparently of such an affecting nature that Berry was 'bitterly cast down'. In most prisons the condemned man was not allowed to come close to his relatives, not even to kiss his wife, for fear of poison being passed across that might confound the legal process, but, says Berry, 'They had a different way with the condemned in the north – the human way.' Allowed by kind-hearted officials to kiss his beloved sister, Judge had sobbed as he clutched her in his arms, other relatives present also sobbing and clinging to him. It was a distressing scene for those who witnessed it. After the relatives left, the Roman Catholic priest spent the afternoon with Judge, comforting him. Judge bore up 'wonderfully well' and that night ate a hearty supper consisting of mutton chops and potatoes washed down with a glass of beer. At seven o'clock he expressed the wish to go to bed and the clergyman bade him goodnight. About an hour later Berry peeped through the door, and was surprised to see the attentive figure of the priest by the bedside, and the man asleep in his bed. Berry observed of the priest:

> He sat there in the silence of the condemned cell face to face with death which seemed to brood over the prison, so that should sleep refuse to remain with the murderer, he would be there to comfort him.

In the event Judge slept soundly for nearly eleven hours and was woken by a warder at six o'clock. He rose immediately and washed and dressed with evident care. He had a breakfast of bread, a beefsteak and coffee. After this he dictated a letter to his sister, a copy of which was given to Berry. It read:

My dear sister, – I wish to say a few words to you for the last time, and to return my sincere thanks to the people of Walker and neighbourhood for the kind manner and interest in my case which they took. I hope you will keep up your heart yourself, and not grieve for me, for you know that your poor brother was only lent to you by the Almighty God, and that you will not begrudge the Almighty God to get his loan back again.

My dear sister, I must conclude with sincere thanks to all during my imprisonment, and with my kind love to you and family. I only wish to say a few words on behalf of my treatment in Newcastle prison. I wish to thank the Governor and all the officials for the kind manner in which they have treated me during the time I have been in their charge.

And as for myself, I will face my doom with a good heart, and like a good soldier, as Father Wood has given me a good heart to meet my doom.

I have no more to say, but I forgive the whole world. I hope I have no enemy, and I hope the Lord will have mercy upon me. The last words of Patrick Judge.

His X. mark.

It was a bright and calm morning. From dawn people had begun to assemble in the thoroughfares adjoining the prison. Worswich Street was impassable as it gave an unobstructed view of the roof of the prison and the flagstaff where the black flag would be hoisted at eight o'clock after the sentence was carried out. The crowd included women and children, and was estimated to number between 1,500 and 2,000.

A warder came into the corridor in a state of excitement and said, 'There are three men on the roof Mr. Berry. They will see the procession.'

Berry said, 'You had better go and order them away. How did they get into the prison?'

'They are not in the prison. They are on the roof of a building opposite, and we cannot interfere with them because it is private property,' he replied.

Berry was concerned that they might be relatives of Judge and said that he would take a look. On going out into the yard he saw three men perched on the roof of a high building. The men saw Berry and the warder and waved. Berry decided that if the procession closely followed the wall of the prison it would be hidden from their view. As the prison bell tolled, the under-sheriff entered the cell where Judge was praying with Father Wood, followed by Berry. Judge glanced at him anxiously but said nothing, and when Berry brought out the straps from behind his back he squared his shoulders and calmly submitted to Berry pinioning him

The under-sheriff headed the procession to the scaffold, followed by the governor and then Judge, who was holding a crucifix. The priest followed, carrying a cross and reciting prayers of the Church for the dying. A number of warders walked either side of the prisoner. Before entering the yard Judge handed his rosary to the priest. They then went out into the morning air and Judge gazed thoughtfully at the blue sky for a moment, before marching on across the yard. The distance from the cell to the scaffold was some fifty yards. Judge walked as firmly as he could, impeded somewhat by his wooden leg, and stayed as close to the prison wall as possible.

To hide the drop from the doomed man the entire floor of the room had been sprinkled with soil. This was a new idea and it made it impossible to see the folding doors of the trap. The door of the execution shed faced southwards, and as soon as Judge was in the centre of the room Berry went up to him and turned him to face north. The poor man continued to respond feebly to the prayers of the priest, and as Berry placed the rope around his neck he braced himself for the final moment, but did not falter. Berry quickly and efficiently adjusted the rope and cap, bent down to strap the man's legs together, then stepped off the drop, leaving Judge standing alone. A quick glance around told him that all was in order and he pulled the lever. The door fell with a loud crash and 'the poor fellow shot down into the pit beneath'. He died instantly.

The fact that he had hanged 'a poor cripple' vexed Berry 'not a little' and during the morning he took a walk up Grainger Street to see the shops and try to cheer himself. He went into one of the hotels in the Bigg market to get some refreshment and there met an acquaintance, who told him of an amusing incident.

Apparently, shortly after eight o'clock on the Saturday night a man had arrived at the Duke of Wellington Inn, opposite Newcastle gaol, and immediately attracted the attention of the patrons. He was aged about 30, had a dark complexion and spoke with a slight Irish brogue. After a drink or two a tailor in the bar had asked him if he was 'one of us'. The stranger answered that he was not 'a Knight of the Cloth', but of the rope – in fact, he was Berry the executioner. News that the hangman was in the bar quickly spread and 'the executioner' was soon holding a levee. At first he appeared rather nervous, saying that he had wanted to keep his arrival quiet, but after being pressed he began to relate stories of the men he had hanged, describing his style as superior to Marwood and stating that he would hang Judge without a blunder. He said his next job was at York, where he had to hang Murphy the Barnsley murderer, indicating that he was familiar with the hangman's schedule. On being asked to show his rope and straps he said that he had left them at the hotel.

'When I hang a man I do it in a genteel manner. I do not do it ruffianly, and behave cowardly to him,' he declared.

He was liberally treated and one of those present invited him to have dinner at his house in Gateshead on Sunday. To the man's delight 'Berry' accepted and the levee went on until eleven o'clock. He was pressed to accompany another man home, which he did, remaining until one o'clock on the Sunday morning. He then took leave of his new friends, who were delighted at having spent the time with 'Berry'. The hoax was finally revealed when the dinner invitation was not taken up and it was found that Berry had not in fact arrived on the Saturday.

Berry managed to leave Newcastle without anyone recognising him, and as he travelled south on the train he espied the towers of York standing out against the evening sky. This caused him to wonder how he would fare in the pending execution of 'the Barnsley murderer' who was lying there under sentence of death. Berry had heard it said that he would never be able to hang the man, and that the people of Barnsley were so incensed at the sentence that they were talking of storming the gates of the gaol. It would prove to be a trying ordeal.

James Murphy was a murderer but, according to Berry, he was also a brave man, one of the bravest he ever knew. A collier from

Lambert Fold, Dudsworth, near Barnsley, Murphy was also a poacher, having had twenty-five convictions for this offence as well as serving a prison sentence for housebreaking at Batley. PC Alfred Austwick, who had cautioned him previously for various other minor offences, arrested him for drunkenness in March 1886. As a result Murphy held a grudge against the arresting officer, convinced that he was out to trap him. Having been served a summons by Austwick, he told some friends that the officer would never serve him with 'another bit of blue paper'. Then, on 31 July, he left home carrying a gun, accosted PC Austwick, shot him and fled. The policeman was very popular in the area and a hue and cry was raised. It was known that the fugitive was still in the area but he kept well hidden, six weeks elapsing before he was spotted in the house of his brother-in-law. Three officers attended to arrest him, but on seeing their approach Murphy ran upstairs and appeared at a window with a gun. Being unarmed, the officers withdrew, and Murphy fled over a back wall into the fields. He took refuge in a house in Kingstone Place, Barnsley, but was arrested two days later in a police 'swoop', though not before offering violent resistance during which he fired his gun at Detective Sergeant Lodge. Thankfully, he missed, and other officers charged at him and overpowered him.

He was tried, found guilty and sentenced to death at York Assizes, the execution date set for Monday 29 November 1886. Despite visits from friends and family, he remained cool and resigned, facing up to his fate with fortitude. His wife, daughter and brother were stricken with grief at their last meeting, but Murphy remained firm and showed no regret.

Berry was aware that the death sentence passed on Murphy had not been received well by the local populace, his crime deemed to have been an act committed in the heat of passion. There had been public anger at the refusal of the Home Secretary to grant a reprieve and Berry claimed that he risked being hanged himself from a lamp-post in York if he ventured there to carry out the execution. He had heard rumours of lynch law but travelled to York 'with an easy mind' and without misgivings.

He arrived at York Castle on the Saturday, only a few people seeing him enter the gaol. On the Sunday he tested the scaffold and then asked one of the warders if he could see the prisoner. He had been told that Murphy – 'one of the finest chaps we have ever had in the gaol' – would not be afraid of him, but he suspected it would be a different story when he confronted the doomed man. Following the prison governor and a warder to the condemned man's cell, he found Murphy eating his dinner; the latter looking up questioningly when told that he had a visitor. According to Berry the following conversation took place:

'A gentleman from Bradford just dropped in to see you, Jim.'

Murphy was gnawing a bone of a mutton chop.

'Bradford, Bradford,' he exclaimed, 'I know nobody in Bradford.'

'You have heard of Mr. Berry?'

'Do you mean Berry, the hangman?'

'Yes that's him.'

Murphy did not desist from his efforts upon the bone, but with the utmost nonchalance exclaimed, 'Bring him in. I am ready for him at any time.'

The warders nodded, and I came into the room.

'Are you Mr. Berry?' he asked.

'I am Mr. Berry.'

'Well, you know the business. You won't make any mistake?'

'No, you can rest assured I will not. I hope you will forgive me for what I am to do. I have to do my duty.'

'That's all right,' he replied, taking my hand. 'It is an unpleasant job, but I bear you no malice.'

'I am glad of that, Murphy.'

He held out his hand and I took it.

'We are chums, Mr. Berry, for you come from Bradford, and I come from Barnsley. We are not far from one another.'

'I hope you won't give any trouble when the time comes.'

He looked at me and smiled.

'I won't give you any trouble. I am not afraid to die. A lot of people have been making a fuss over this business, and I'm hanged if I can see what there is to make a fuss about.'

I was [so] surprised at his joke, that I could say nothing, and so I left him and did not see him again until I went to pinion him.

On the Sunday night Murphy wrote letters to his family. To his brother he wrote about meeting the hangman:

I received your letter and was glad to hear of you being well, as it leaves me at present. I am in good spirits. The Governor brought your letter to me at dinner time, and the hangman with him.

I shook hands with the hangman, and he asked me to forgive him, and I did so. But I ate my dinner none the worse of that. My dear brother. I don't seem to fear death, so do not be uneasy. Dear Jesus died for us all, so I am only taking a part with him. I shall stand as good a chance as the best. There, you must cheer up. We shall meet again in the next world, I hope.

This is my writing, dear brother, and you will see that my hand does not tremble, so I give my kind and last love in this world to you all. Jesus Deus Pacis –

James Murphy his last writing

Murphy also wrote to his wife:

Dear Wife, I write you these lines hoping to find you all well, as it leaves me at present, but on Monday I shall meet my death, then I shall know the great secret. There is no mercy for me, so I must die. I hope you will altogether give me a prayer, and I will meet my fate as brave as I can.

Dear wife, you will think of the next world and our next meeting, for you will not be here for ever. So farewell, dear wife, and farewell dear children, too. Farewell dear brothers, and relations for this life. We all must part. May the Lord have mercy on you all. – James Murphy.

Murphy chatted with the warders who were keeping him company and slept soundly that night. He woke about 6.30 in the morning and his last meal was brought to him, which he ate with relish and then asked for 'a pipe of bacca'. This, however, was refused. Shortly before eight o'clock the under-sheriff arrived at the castle and produced his precept to the governor for possession of the body of the murderer. Berry received his warrant and went to the condemned cell, whereupon Murphy rose to meet him with a smile on his face and a demeanour bearing no trace of fear:

'Well! here you are, Mr Berry,' he said. 'How do you feel this morning?'

'Oh! I don't feel very well,' I said. 'I shall be better when it is all over.'

'Pull yourself together. Look at me. I am not afraid of the business,' he answered in tones that surprised me.

'I am glad of that,' I replied. 'Would you like something to drink?'

'I should have liked a smoke,' he said, 'but seeing they haven't given it to me I don't mind having a last drink.'

'Very well, you shall have it,' was my reply.

I sent for a glass of brandy and milk, and he took it from me with a nod of the head.

'Good health, Mr. Berry,' he said.

He gulped down the beverage, and then he held up the glass to me. 'And when I get to the other side, Mr. Berry, I will begin afresh.'

'That's right,' said I.

'I feel like a schoolboy again,' he went on. 'I am not going to funk when it has come at last. I am not afraid of being hanged.'

He submitted himself with the utmost coolness while I put the straps around him, and just as I was taking him out he made a last request.

'You will do it as painlessly as you can Mr. Berry? Not that I am frightened, but you got no call to hurt me.'

'You will never feel it,' I replied. 'Once we are out of here it will be all over before you know what is happening.'

'All right then, Mr. Berry, and good luck to you,' he said.

The procession was waiting for us outside the cell. The Sheriff stood there with his wand of office, the warders, the priest, and the Governor. With his head erect Murphy walked out into the yard and when I saw what lay before us, I ran forward to place the white cap over his eyes.

In my hurry I had forgotten that the murderer had to pass by his own grave. The morning sun gleamed on the brown earth of the yawning pit and spoke of the nameless fate that awaited the man in our midst.

A shudder ran through the little crowd and from the lips of one of the spectators there burst a heart-rending sob. It was a barbarous ordeal that no man should have been asked to pass through, and I trembled as we came in sight of that open grave, which in an hour's time would be filled with the body of my victim.

James Murphy saw it, but never a look of fear came over his face.

He looked at the grave, and turned to me and said: -

'Yon's where I'm going to sleep tonight.'

I shuddered at his words.

He stepped upon the scaffold and placed his feet together. Hurriedly I adjusted the straps, and then I began to place the rope about his neck. The man had less fear than a baby, and his bearing in the face of death unnerved me. My hands were trembling as I placed the rope about his neck.

'Now, then,' he said, 'You're trembling, don't be nervous.'

It was true I was nervous, and his words only made me worse, but somehow or other I managed to get the rope adjusted, and then, still trembling, I stepped back and pulled the lever. James Murphy was dead.

It would seem that James Murphy was a man of contrasts. Despite having cold-bloodedly murdered a police officer he was still liked by all, including his custodians. He exhibited a bravery borne of his deep faith that he was going on to something better, and this obviously had a profound effect on the deeply religious Berry.

Apropos of the threat Berry felt he was under as a result of executing Murphy, he stated:

I hanged James Murphy in spite of threats, and then I heard that I would never dare to put my foot in Barnsley, the town whence the victim hailed.

People said that the Barnsley miners would murder me, but in spite of that threat I visited the town on many occasions.

When I gave up my post as hangman I turned auctioneer,

and I often stood in the market place of the town selling my wares – remnants of cloth, odds and ends, anything I could buy cheaply – to the very people who had sworn to have their revenge on me.

They did not know me, nor did they have the slightest suspicion that I was the retired executioner. If they had, things might have been different.

Berry was scheduled to hang James Barton at Leicester the following day. Barton, 27 years old, was a labourer who dabbled in poaching. In August 1886 he had been caught poaching with a friend by a police officer, who confiscated their nets. The two then went drinking and made the fateful decision to go to the police station and retrieve their equipment. On leaving the pub they saw PC Barrett, whom they abused, attempting to pick a fight. Barton grappled with the officer and they both fell down an embankment, whereupon Barton beat his opponent to death with a stick, which he later brandished in the street while shouting he had killed a policeman. The body was found the next day and Barton was arrested. Berry hanged him.

Berry's last execution of the year took place at Norwich Castle on Monday 13 December. George Harmer, a plasterer aged 28, was a petty thief who had just been released from gaol. He had then visited a friend, to whom he revealed that he intended to rob a wealthy recluse, Henry Last, aged about 66, a master carpenter who lived in a cottage at Old Post Office Yard, Norwich. On 14 August, Harmer made an approach to his victim on the pretext of having a model made from a drawing. Later the old man was found battered to death in his bed. Harmer – who was seen to have come into some money, redeeming some clothing he had previously pawned – was finally arrested in London on 19 August and confessed. Tried at Norwich Assizes before Mr Justice Field on 22 November, he was found guilty and sentenced to death. One can only imagine how Berry must have felt on finding himself again within the walls of the historic castle, his thoughts surely going back to the appalling execution of Goodale there a year earlier. Harmer's execution turned out to be the last conducted at Norwich Castle, and appears to have been carried out uneventfully.

16

A busy month for the executioner

'. . . he was one of the few murderers for whom I felt sorry'.

With the Aberdare Committee holding its hearings, Berry was keen to put the executioner's point of view, feeling that the office he held should be a government appointment with a fixed salary instead of an 'uncertain commission'. He wrote the following letter to Lord Aberdare:

> 1, Bilton Place
> City Road, Bradford.
> February, 1887

My Lord,

I have been for some time past in correspondence with Mr. Howard Vincent, M.P. for Sheffield, with reference to alteration in the mode of remunerating my services, in carrying into effect the Sentence of the Law upon Criminals convicted of Capital Crimes. Mr. Howard Vincent has suggested that I should address myself to the Honourable Committee on Capital Punishment, through your Lordship as their President.

I would therefore respectfully point out to your Lordship and your Honourable Committee that the present mode of payment for my services is unsatisfactory and undesirable, and that a change is needed.

As your Lordship is doubtless aware, under the existing arrangements I am paid the sum of £10 together with travelling and other incidental expenses for each Execution conducted by me. There are, on an average, roughly speaking, 25 Executions yearly. What I would respectfully suggest is, that, instead of this payment by Commission, I should receive a Fixed Salary from the Government of £350 per annum. I may say that since accepting the appointment I have never received less than £270 in any one year. I am informed that in determining a Fixed Salary, or Compensation in lieu of a payment by Commission, the average annual amount received is made the basis for the calculation.

It will be apparent to your Lordship that an offer of a *less* sum than the former average would not be sufficiently advantageous to induce me to exchange the old system for the new. I may further, with your Lordship's permission, draw attention to the peculiar Social position in which I am placed by reason of holding the office above referred to. I am to a great extent alone in the world, as a certain social ostracism is attendant upon such office, and extends, not to myself alone, but also includes the members of my family. It therefore becomes extremely desirable that my children should, for their own sakes, be sent to a school away from this town. To do this of course would entail serious expenditure, only to be incurred in the event of my being able to rely on a fixed source of income, less liable to variation than the present remuneration by Commission alone. I am also unable for obvious reasons to obtain any other employment. My situation as boot salesman held by me previous to my acceptance of the Office of Executioner, had to be given up on that account alone, my employer having no fault to find with me, but giving that as the sole reason for dispensing with my services.

My late Employer will give me a good reference as to General character, and the Governors of Gaols in which I have conducted Executions will be ready to speak as to my steadiness and also my ability and skill on performing the duties devolving upon me.

In conclusion I should be ready to give and call Evidence on the points hereinbefore referred to (if it should seem fit to your Lordship and your Honourable Committee), on receiving a notification to that effect.

Under these circumstances I trust that your Lordship will be able to see the way clear to embody in your Honourable

Committee's report a recommendation to the effect that a fixed annual sum of £350 should be paid for my services rendered in the Office of Executioner.

I have the honour to be
Your Lordship's Obedient humble servant,
JAMES BERRY.

To the Right Honourable Lord Aberdare.

President,

Capital Punishment Committee,

Whitehall, London, S.W.

P.S. If your Honourable Committee has an alternative to the foregoing proposal I would respectfully suggest that I am permanently retained by the Home Office at a nominal sum of £100 a year, exclusive of fees at present paid to me by Sheriffs of different Counties and the usual Expenses.

Berry pointed out, in his book, that Calcraft had enjoyed such status, being a permanently established and recognised official until his retirement in 1874. The sheriffs of the City of London had retained Calcraft with a weekly fee of £1 1s 0d, plus a retainer from Horsemonger Lane Gaol. In addition, he carried out executions all over the country for which he was paid at a rate similar to Berry's. When he retired he was allowed a pension of 25 shillings a week for life.

Marwood had no official status and had to depend on his fees for individual executions and reprieves, like Berry. An odd perk for Marwood was the fact that the clothing and personal property of the executed criminal became the property of the hangman. These relics were often sold for high prices and became a substantial source of additional income, but the government finally ended this distasteful practice, ordering that personal property left by criminals should be burned.

Berry had no call to carry out his grim duties in January 1887, but February witnessed five executions. The first took him to Leicester on Monday 14 February, where he executed Thomas Bloxham, aged 62. Bloxham, a framework knitter, had murdered his wife in November 1886, stabbing her five times in the chest and cutting her throat. Sentenced to death at Leicester Assizes, he appeared utterly callous while awaiting his fate, but eventually placed himself calmly in Berry's hands.

After hanging Bloxham, Berry travelled directly to Manchester where he was engaged to execute Thomas Leatherbarrow the following day. Leatherbarrow, aged 47, had, prior to Christmas 1886, been living in part of a small cottage at Pendleton with Mrs Kate Quinn, the latter having separated from her husband. Being unemployed they had little money and were constantly arguing, and in another drunken row on New Year's Eve 1886 he was heard to shout threats at her. The New Year saw Leatherbarrow briefly in work, but, returning home on Saturday 8 January, he became embroiled in another domestic dispute during which he kicked Quinn to death. He then went off to drink in a pub, where the police arrested him. He was found guilty at Manchester Assizes, before Mr Justice Smith, and was hanged by Berry on 15 February 1887.

Just two days later Berry's services were again required at Gloucester. Edward 'Ned' Pritchard, a 20-year-old living in Stroud, had a long history of criminal activity. As early as 12 years of age he had been convicted as an 'associate of thieves', subsequently spending two years in a reformatory. After leaving that establishment he had managed to steer clear of a custodial sentence for three years, but at the age of 17 was sentenced to four months imprisonment for shop-breaking, after which he was in and out of gaol. By the age of 19 he appeared to be somewhat reformed, attending Sunday school and chapel, but his final crime was an atrocious case of robbery and murder.

On Friday 31 December 1886 Henry James Allen, a 14-year-old messenger boy employed at Lightfield Mills, about a mile from Stroud, was sent to the town to cash the fortnightly wages cheque. Pritchard and an associate named Noyes had watched the boy carry out this task on previous occasions. Young Allen called at the Capital and Counties Bank, as usual, and received the money, the amount involved being the then considerable sum of £120 in gold, £61 4s 7d in silver and bronze, and four £5 notes. He also purchased a pair of skates for a fellow workman at the mill, and then set out on the return journey. About an hour later he was found lying at the side of a lane leading off the main road, his bag and the skates stolen. Badly beaten, he had suffered terrible head wounds, from which he expired on 4 January in Stroud Hospital.

The police began their inquiries and ascertained that on the day of the murder Edward Pritchard, apparently in a hurry and a state of excitement, had hired a horse and trap from a baker. A witness had seen him pull up and overtake the lad a short distance from the bank, lifting him on board. Others saw him driving along the Cainscross Road with the boy, and then along Lodgemore Lane, where the body was found. Pritchard was seen to emerge from the other end of the lane in the trap but without the boy and driving at a furious pace. Reckless in his actions, it seems he took no steps to cover his crime, returning the horse and trap about two hours after robbing his victim, and paying seven shillings for the hire, three shillings above the actual cost. Bloodstains were found in the trap.

The police discovered that he had driven straight from the scene of the attack to a house at Pitchcombe occupied by another young man, where, stating that he had been carrying meat in it, he washed out the trap with a flannel and water. He met Noyes, his accomplice, who got into the trap with various purchases amounting to several shillings, and they had driven back to Stroud, calling at pubs on the way and spending money freely. Pritchard then left his friend in a pub while he returned the trap, after which the two men walked back to Pitchcombe, about 2 miles away, Pritchard giving odd shillings away to acquaintances they met on the way. They went to the Eagle Inn, where Pritchard handed the bag stolen from his victim to the land-lady for safe keeping until the next day, telling her it contained money and belonged to a jewellery traveller into whose service he was entering. He also said that he was meeting the man in Gloucester the next day, before going to Nottingham and then New Zealand. Aware of the robbery, the landlady alerted the police.

Pritchard had arranged with a fly-man to take him to Gloucester the next morning at seven o'clock, but Superintendent Philpott arrested the two men that very evening. The four £5 notes and £120 in a canvas bag were recovered, and the bank identified the notes as those issued to the beaten boy. All the silver taken was found, except for a few missing shillings. About two weeks later a billhook was found behind a hedge on the road from Stroud to Pitchcombe.

It belonged to Pritchard's mother and was undoubtedly the murder weapon; clearly then the crime had been premeditated. Both men were tried, Pritchard for murder and Noyes for being an accessory. Noyes was acquitted but Pritchard's guilt was clear, his crime so heinous that there could be no question of a reprieve once Mr Justice Manisty had passed the sentence of death.

Despite the appalling nature of the crime, Berry later stated that he felt sorry for the offender:

> To me he was a typical instance of 'evil communications corrupting good manners,' and a striking example of the unfortunate uselessness of our reformatory system.

Pritchard wrote to one of his Sunday school teachers stating that he had seen the error of his ways and urging all his companions to shun bad company, drinking and smoking. He spoke of his pleasure in recalling some of the Sunday school hymns, claiming that he looked forward to singing them 'up there', and it would seem this religious enthusiasm was his redeeming feature in the eyes of Berry. Pritchard said little after his conviction and made no formal confession, but he wrote the following letter to the parents of the murdered boy, subsequently printed in *The Post* (11 July 1914; the name of his alleged accomplice, Noyes, was censored out, no doubt because he had been acquitted):

> I write these lines to you to express my deep sorrow for the dreadful crime I have done to you and your master. I write to ask you if you and your wife will forgive me for killing your boy, and please ask the master if he will forgive me for taking his money from him. It would not have happened if I had not been incited to do it. It was no other person than ——. He was a witness against me. He persuaded me to do it, and said he might do it himself if I did not, so I done the unhappy affair.
>
> I am very sorry I ever met with —— at all, but it cannot be called back now. I have cried to God for mercy; I must still cry and hope I shall gain a better home. I have asked Him to forgive me and blot out all my sins and wash me in my Saviour's precious blood, and I think I feel He will do it. I am

going to receive the Holy Communion on Wednesday before I go to be partaker of that Holy feast. If you will forgive me I shall be more at peace. I am very, very sorry indeed for what I have done. There is nothing that can save me from my doom, but I can ask God to have mercy upon my poor soul.

I have no more to say at present, only that I was a great friend of poor Harry, and I went nearly mad about it. The first few nights I could not sleep, but now I find comfort in Jesus. Goodbye, sir. Please send me an answer by return of post, and I hope we shall meet in Heaven. – From EDWARD PRITCHARD.

Mr Allen was obviously a compassionate man and Pritchard's letter moved him. For some unknown reason the reply was delayed but Allen journeyed to Gloucester to convey his forgiveness in person and to pray for the doomed convict. Prison regulations did not allow him to see Pritchard but the fact that he had made the effort was a great consolation to the convict.

Berry arrived at the prison just after Allen's visit, at about 4.30 on the afternoon of Wednesday 16 February, the eve of the execution. Normally this would have been carried out on a Monday but a three-day respite had been obtained as a result of Berry's busy schedule. Berry commented:

At this stage of my career as hangman the desire of people to see me was simply overwhelming, and I was always more or less dubious as to the feelings of the people whom I was about to go amongst. My visit to Gloucester was no exception to the rule. At the station I was met by one of the prison authorities. We drove straight to our destination by cab, followed by a large crowd of people.

I at once went to examine the scaffold which I found to be in good working order. Directly afterwards I went to size up my man. At the time he was praying fervently for forgiveness along with the chaplain, but I was able to gather all the information I wanted by peeping through the bars of the cell.

'Poor fellow!' I thought. 'He looks barely out of his teens.' It seemed such a pity that I should have to send to eternity one so young and one so penitent of the crime he had committed.

There was always the consolation, though, that if I did not do the job someone else would, and I believe I could carry out the work as quickly and as painlessly as anyone else.

The week had been a particularly busy one for me. On the Monday I hanged a man at Leicester, another was sent to his doom at Manchester on the Tuesday, and on the Wednesday I was engaged at Durham, but I was very thankful to hear that the condemned man had got a reprieve.

As the evening wore on I ventured outside the gaol. A large crowd of people was assembled there, and each one of the number was gazing intently at a window where lights were burning. It was the window of the cell where young Pritchard was on his bended knees asking his Maker for forgiveness.

I was unable to pass unrecognised, and the deep note of sympathy on the lips of every man, woman, and child made the dreadful business that I had to do the next morning all the more sorrowful. Children exchanged a whisper as they hurried past. Men and women would come as if for a last look. Such expressions as 'Sad job!' 'So young!' 'Only about twenty!' caught my ear. It was at this moment, perhaps more than at any other time, that the horror of my calling was driven home to me.

Berry was glad to return to his quarters but had his usual restless night. The next morning he felt the return of his old feeling that something untoward was going to happen. He saw the prison governor, Major Knox, and asked how the condemned man had slept, being told in reply that Pritchard had gone to sleep at eleven o'clock, and had had to be shaken, to awaken him, that morning. The governor assured Berry that no trouble was anticipated. Having been visited again by the chaplain, the prisoner had eaten a hearty breakfast, but there is no doubt that the gravity of his crime was playing on his mind.

It was a cold, raw morning, but the thick fog that had enveloped the town had cleared quickly, having fully dispersed when the time for the execution arrived. A crowd had begun to gather in the square as early as a quarter past seven and shortly afterwards about half a dozen reporters gathered at the entrance to the prison. They were not admitted until a quarter to eight, at which time the prison bell began to toll. Berry readied himself and entered the cell five minutes before the hour to find Pritchard talking with the chaplain. He felt he discerned the man shudder thus confronted by his executioner.

'Are you Mr. Berry?' he asked.

'Yes. You are not going to give me any trouble, I hope, Edward. It will be all over in a few minutes now, and you won't feel anything if you will do as I tell you,' answered Berry.

'Oh, I'm not afraid to die. I'm more concerned about the people I have wronged. I shouldn't have done it had I not been urged on by someone else,' he calmly replied.

Berry said, 'You know I feel somehow very sorry for you, lad.'

'Yes, everyone seems sorry for me, Mr. Berry. The people whom I have wronged have forgiven me. Even they are sorry. That's why I don't feel unhappy now,' he replied.

During this conversation Pritchard stood still while Berry pinioned his arms and hands. Unusually, this was carried out in the corridor instead of the cell, and the chaplain, reading the burial service, perhaps unaware of what was happening, proceeded alone down the stairs leading from the cells and into the yard, upon which the under-sheriff called to him and asked him to wait. This caused some of those assembled to fear there had been a hitch, and a whisper went round that Pritchard had swooned. The prisoner, however, subsequently appeared and walked firmly to the scaffold without assistance. Berry's mind was by now at ease and the young man stood as bravely below the raised beam of the black gallows as any man Berry had yet seen.

'Put your feet together,' Berry whispered to him as he bent to strap his legs. Silently the doomed man obeyed and on facing him again Berry noted that his eyes were looking around the prison yard. He seemed to be taking everything in, including the officials and the open grave in the corner where his body was to be interred. He gave a long look in the direction of the group of reporters, as if to show he was being brave, then looked at Berry and said, half-smiling, 'I'm quite happy and prepared. Goodbye, Mr. Berry.'

'Keep quite still,' Berry instructed as he lowered the white cap over the young man's eyes:

I stepped towards the drop, motioned the warders to one side, and the next moment the Stroud murderer was hanging dead at the end of the rope as the chaplain read, 'Man hath but a short time to live.'

The black flag was run up on the flag post and the crowd outside, estimated to number about 800, began to disperse. A drop of 4ft 6in had been given to Pritchard, who weighed 10st 7lb. The *Gloucester Chronicle* commented, erroneously, that Berry was on a retaining fee of £100 a year, paid by the sheriffs of London and Middlesex, claiming also that he was paid a fee of £10 per execution plus travelling and hotel expenses.

On Monday 21 February 1887, Berry was in Lincoln to carry out the execution of Richard Insole, a 24-year-old Grimsby fisherman who had murdered his wife, apparently out of jealousy after she had left him, shooting her five times with a revolver, the final rounds being fired as she was lying on the ground. He had been found guilty at Nottingham Assizes before Mr Justice Field on 1 February.

The final execution in that busy month took place the very next day at Nottingham, where Berry hanged Benjamin Terry, aged 29; sentenced to death for the murder of his wife on 29 December 1886. Having constantly, though it seems mistakenly, suspected his wife of having affairs, he had beaten her to death with a poker in their bedroom, after which, having put the children in the care of some neighbours, he had given himself up to the police. He stated that he had intended to kill her the night before but had fallen into a gin-induced sleep. A plea of insanity was rejected, as was a request for a reprieve, and Berry executed him in accordance with his sentence.

Berry's next job was only three weeks away, and was to present him with a strange coincidence.

17

Mr Berry executes Mrs Berry

'I did not know you are going to hang an old flame, Berry.'

Elizabeth Berry, aged 31, was a widow and worked as a nurse in Oldham workhouse. She earned £25 a year, of which she paid £12 to her sister-in-law, who looked after her 11-year-old daughter Edith Annie. On 29 December 1886 Edith and a school friend went to stay with Mrs Berry at the workhouse. The children played happily in the wards and corridors of the building. The following Saturday, New Year's Day 1887, Mrs Berry was in the kitchen preparing sago when Edith was violently sick, and Mrs Berry was seen shortly afterwards trying to get her daughter to drink a milky liquid in a glass. At midday Mrs Berry asked Dr Patterson, who was in daily attendance at the workhouse, to look at her daughter who, she said, had eaten something at breakfast that had made her ill. He prescribed a mixture of iron and quinine but the child's symptoms persisted into the evening. By midday Sunday the doctor felt that the girl was looking a little better and informed her mother that he thought she would recover. Mrs Berry then showed him a towel bearing blood and vomit stains, and he also noticed an acidic smell. Since Mrs Berry held the only key to the workhouse dispensary, he asked for the key in order to prepare a bicarbonate mixture, and, finding the bottle of creosote in the dispensary to be empty, he wrote an order for a fresh supply, telling Mrs Berry to obtain a fresh supply and mix a few drops in water for her daughter to take. On Sunday evening the girl was again violently ill and the doctor noticed red marks around her mouth. He consulted a second doctor and the two decided that the girl had taken a corrosive poison. She vomited out all the medicine given and weakened rapidly. By the next day her pulse could hardly be felt and she had blisters around her mouth. She died at five o'clock on the Tuesday morning.

Dr Patterson suspected that Mrs Berry had given her daughter the contents of the bottle of creosote on the Saturday and another huge dose, after he had prescribed it, on the Sunday. He refused to issue a death certificate and an autopsy was carried out, soon after which Mrs Berry was arrested for the murder of her daughter. She was tried at Liverpool Assizes over four days, beginning on 21 February. The medical experts all agreed that the cause of death was a corrosive poison, namely the acid content of the creosote. Having received £10 from a burial society, in April 1886 Mrs Berry had tried to insure her life and that of her daughter for £100, this amount to go to the survivor when the first died. Though she had failed to pay the premium on this, many believed she still expected the insurance to be paid. She was found guilty and sentenced to death. It was also suspected that she had previously disposed of her husband and mother by a similar means, again for the insurance money. Her husband had died five years previously and a son fourteen months afterwards, the very time that Mrs Berry had placed her daughter with her sister-in-law. The execution date was fixed for Monday 14 March 1887.

When Berry arrived at Walton gaol he was received by the governor, who gave him a peculiar smile.

'I did not know you are going to hang an old flame, Berry?'

'What do you mean?' asked Berry, who thought that the man must be joking on account of the condemned woman's name being the same as his.

'She says she knows you very well,' he replied. 'You had better go and have a look at her tonight. I will make the necessary arrangements.'

Later, Berry gazed curiously through the narrow slit in the cell door and recognised the woman inside as someone he had met in the past. Describing her as 'a woman of not unpleasant appearance' whose 'chief charm about her was her beautiful chestnut tresses', he went on to relate how he had once met her in a crowded ballroom while having some refreshment. She had approached him, asking if he was alone, and then, with a coy glance and a smile, enquired if he would dance with her. With his arm around the waist of 'a young woman of charm and vivacity, who chatted gaily' to him about herself and her work (she told him that she was a nurse working in Oldham Hospital), he had trodden 'the mazy dance'. Then, after sharing refreshments together and another dance or two, they had discovered they were travelling home in the same direction, so he had invited her to join him in his cab, the two also travelling together subsequently for part of the train journey. Berry finished this tale:

> The story goes to show something of the romance of my life, and I may say that Mrs. Berry was not the only acquaintance I was to have to send out of the world.

During the early part of her imprisonment, after sentence had been passed, she was confined in a cell in the female debtors' wing, but since the windows of this cell were near to the coach house where 'the implement of death' was being constructed it was felt advisable to move her to a different part of the building – only, however, after she had heard the joiners hammering at the construction of the scaffold and asked what was going on. After the scaffold was finished she was moved back to the condemned cell, where Berry went to see her on the night before her execution. She passed a restless night punctuated by periods of praying.

The following morning, we read, Berry

> . . . was early at her cell. I never liked to hang a woman. It always made me shiver like a leaf, but it was sometimes a consolation in these days to believe that I was carrying out the last dread sentence of the law on one who was not worthy to be allowed to live.
>
> When I opened the door of her cell she looked up and nodded to me.
>
> 'Good morning Mrs. Berry,' I said.
>
> She came forward instantly and held out her hand. 'Good morning Mr. Berry. You and I have met before.'
>
> 'Where was that now?' I asked, pretending to have forgotten.
>
> 'Oh, at the ball in Manchester, given by the police,' she said. 'Surely you can't have forgotten.'

'Oh, yes, I remember,' said I. 'It is a long time ago, and I did not realise that I was to officiate at the execution of a friend of mine.'

'No, I suppose you didn't,' she said.

'Well, I'm very sorry to have to do it,' I said.

She looked at me, and with a toss of her head said – 'You've no doubt heard a lot of dreadful things about me, but it isn't all true what people say about one.'

'Well, I've heard a great deal about you,' said I. 'But you must pull yourself together and die bravely.'

'Oh, I'll go bravely enough,' she said with a shudder. 'You need not be a bit afraid of me, Mr. Berry. You don't suppose I'd want to give you any trouble, do you.'

'I hope you won't give me any trouble.'

'You'll be easy with me. You won't give me any pain. You'll be gentle with an old friend, won't you?'

'I shall not prolong your life a single minute,' said I. 'Have you made your peace with God?'

She made no reply, and I besought her to make the most of what time remained to her.

I went outside and caught hold of the arm of one of the warders. 'That woman is one of the biggest cowards in the world,' said I.

By this time the street in front of the gaol was 'black with people'. They were mainly women, but none was related to the prisoner. Shortly before eight o'clock Berry returned to the cell to pinion her:

'Now, Mrs. Berry, I've come back again,' said I. 'Is there anything I can do for you before you leave the condemned cell?'

She shivered and shrank back.

'Would you like a drink of water?' I asked. She shook her head again.

'All right, then. Time is getting on. Don't be afraid – I am not going to hurt you.'

After I had pinioned her, the governor of the gaol led the way, followed by the chaplain, reading the prayers for the dying, and the rear was brought up by three doctors.

The distance from the cell to the scaffold was not more than sixty yards, and along the roadway sand had been sprinkled freely. It was in the depth of winter, snow had fallen on the ground, and I was afraid that she would slip and fall.

The condemned woman walked firmly until she turned the angle of the building and saw the gallows. I never liked my victims to see that, and whenever I could I drew the cap so that the fear-bringing sight should be blotted from their eyes. A cry of terror left her lips when she saw it.

'Oh, dear!' she wailed, and then she reeled over and was just about to faint when I rushed up.

'Now, look here, Mrs. Berry,' said I, 'you remember what you promised me in the cell.'

Her only reply was a deep groan.

'You promised me that you would give me no trouble. What do you call this?'

I had caught hold of her arms to keep her from falling, and she begged me to unhand her. 'Let me go, Mr. Berry,' she said; 'let me go, and I will go bravely.'

'All right,' I replied.

She staggered along supported by two warders, and as she looked at the scaffold again a wave of terror came over her, and she shouted – 'Oh, God forbid! God forbid!'

The warders helped her along, and she repeated the responses to the prayers in a faint voice, but at last the ordeal was too much for her and she fainted. They lifted her on to the scaffold, and held her up while I completed my arrangements. She recovered consciousness while I was busy, and continued her responses, and at intervals she called upon her Maker to have mercy upon her.

Just as I was about to pull the cap over her face she exclaimed – 'May God forgive me!' and she repeated the words just as I allowed her to go down.

No sooner was the fatal act over than one of the wardresses came over, and, in bitter tones, spoke thus – 'There goes one of the coldest-blooded murderers – the worst species of womankind to carry out the deeds she has carried out.'

She walked away, and as we were going round the corner she said – 'That shows what a woman can really do in cold blood.'

The two doctors of the prison descended the pit by means of a ladder to make the official examination, and I came back and joined them. We found that she had had a merciful death.

After the execution, at which he had allowed a drop of 6ft 6in, Berry said that he was glad to get out of the prison as he was feeling far from well. He recorded:

. . . I may say that on no occasion did I ever execute a woman without suffering as severe mental and bodily pains as my victim. It may seem a bold thing to say, but, nevertheless, it is true, and when I have been setting out from my house to carry out my duties I have broken down and turned back. My wife and mother on these occasions used to comfort me as best they could.

An odd aside to the story of Mrs Berry's execution, and Berry's agonising, is the fact that he took a 'relic' from the woman. He maintained a sort of 'Black Museum' at his home in relation to the persons he had despatched. This included voluminous scrapbooks of relevant press cuttings about the cases and himself, and after this execution he cut two locks from the woman's 'beautiful chestnut tresses' to keep and take home for his collection. He said:

I used to keep these relics, but they made me uneasy after a time, and one day I decided to sell them, though I had many of them from the day I started the business of public hangman.

And believe me or believe me not, it was a different house, was ours, when they were gone. I found I could sleep. There was no more weary tossing about in bed at night, and the uncanny feeling I used to have when I entered the room in which they were kept, disappeared. It was strange, but it may be that some of the evil influence of my victims clung to these relics.

This was not the only time that a suggestion of the supernatural entered Berry's writings; he was obviously a superstitious, as well as religious man. However, his mercenary nature got the better of him, for instead of merely throwing the items away, he sold them, as he did his ropes.

Berry's next execution was scheduled for Monday 21 March at Newgate, the condemned prisoner this time being one Joseph King, a 41-year-old bricklayer. King lived in a lodging house with several other people, among them a woman named Annie Sutton and her young son Henry. Both King and the woman were unmarried, but on the several occasions he had asked her out she had refused. On 20 January he discovered that she had accepted a similar invitation from another male lodger and, greatly angered, he confronted her, cutting the throats of both the woman and her son such that he almost severed their heads. He was tried at the Old Bailey before Mr Justice Hawkins and found guilty, despite a plea of insanity that he claimed had been brought on by a serious head injury suffered many years earlier. In finding him guilty the jury recommended mercy, but to no avail. King had to be supported on the gallows. Berry quickly adjusted the rope, and at eight o'clock the signal was given and the drop fell, death being instantaneous. A large crowd outside the walls of Newgate witnessed the hoisting of the black flag (*The Times*, 17 May 1887).

Newgate was again the venue for Berry's next execution, scheduled for Monday 18 April. For many years Thomas William Currell, aged 31, had been courting a woman named Lydia Green, who was the same age as himself. Despite their long-standing relationship, they lived apart, she occupying a room in a boarding house in Hoxton, a floor above her mother's. Currell was in the habit of calling at Lydia's room and leaving in the small hours. On the morning of Saturday 5 February the girl's mother discovered her daughter shot dead and lying in a pool of blood. The police were called and Inspector Peel was placed in charge of inquiries. A search began for Currell, who was known to the police but had never been connected with anything serious until his name had cropped up the previous week in connection with a burglary, but he had disappeared. He had, in fact, fled across London to a guesthouse, where he booked in using a false name, but he then made a cardinal error, stealing the coat of a fellow lodger, for which he was arrested. His true identity was discovered and he was charged with murder, tried at the Old Bailey and found guilty. A plea of insanity was ventured, in light of which Currell was examined by Dr Savage of Bethlehem Hospital (Bedlam), accompanied by Dr Gilbert of Newgate. Both men, however, declared him to be sane and Berry made the trip to Newgate Prison.

Berry described the Hoxton murder as 'one of the greatest mysteries of London', but the strange feature of the case related to his assistant at the execution. 'To this day', claimed Berry, 'I have no idea who he was or why he wanted to see Thomas Currell hanged.' In a story reminiscent of that of Sir Claude Champion de Crespigny, he went on to speculate that the mysterious stranger might have known Currell at some time or other, although he thought it unlikely.

The course of events ran as follows. After Berry had reported at Newgate he decided to have a healthy walk and take some refreshment. He called in at a public house near to the prison, one that he habitually visited whenever he was in London. No sooner had he entered than Berry heard his name mentioned.

'Hullo, Mr. Berry!'

'Hullo, inspector,' Berry replied. It was an old acquaintance of his, and Berry asked him how he was getting on.

'Oh, all right. Come and have one with me, Berry. And, by the way, allow me to introduce you to a friend of mine.' Berry turned to see a gentlemanly fellow in a smartly cut suit, who was looking at him with obvious interest.

'Pleased to meet you,' said Berry.

'The pleasure is mine, Mr. Berry,' the stranger replied in a refined voice, 'What will you have?'

The three men conversed for a while and the inspector then said, 'Now, Jim, this gentleman is a very great friend of mine, and I want you to let him go and help you some day. He will do the right thing by you.' The young man nodded in agreement, and Berry, never one to refuse the opportunity of securing extra cash, was happy to oblige.

'Well, I have no objection,' he replied; 'we have this execution coming along on Monday. You can come and see that if you like.'

'I should like to come very much.'

Berry warned, 'The only stipulation is that you must keep your mouth shut. You must not mention who you are to a soul.'

'I don't intend to do so,' was the reply.

'Good! You can come in as my assistant. Can you meet me tomorrow night?'

'Yes, if you like.'

On the Sunday evening Berry took another stroll outside the prison and met his friend the inspector and his companion in one of the hotels near to the Old Bailey.

'What are you going to have?' asked the young 'assistant'.

'I'll have a brandy and soda,' said Berry, 'and you'll better have one, too, if you are coming along with me.'

The man by now appeared very nervous and Berry thought that the drink would help to pull him together.

'Are we going to go in tonight?' he asked.

'Yes, of course. It is time we were in now.'

The stranger hesitated and ran his finger round and round his glass. 'Have you told them about me?' he said.

'Yes, I have told them. It will be all right,' Berry assured him.

They took leave of the inspector and entered the Old Bailey. To Berry's surprise the prison governor appeared, and after looking his guest up and down refused to allow him to stay in the prison overnight.

'Why not, sir?' demanded Berry.

The governor paused for a moment and turned to the stranger, 'You can come in the morning and help him,' he said.

'But why can't he remain?' asked Berry. 'There may be trouble in getting in tomorrow.'

'We'll risk that. Can't you manage without him Berry? I will let you have a warder to help you.'

'No, I can't manage without him. He is a smart man and knows his business. That is why I want him,' Berry persisted.

'Very well then. He can come at seven o'clock in the morning. If he is not at the gate at that hour he won't get in,' said the governor.

The stranger left and the governor took Berry to one side. 'Look here, Berry, I want to speak to you. We want no Baronets here, you know.' The episode involving Sir Claude Champion de Crespigny was obviously well known, and the governor's allusion was clear; he was evidently aware that Berry was attempting to smuggle someone into the prison who had no execution experience, but Berry feigned ignorance.

'What do you mean, sir?' he responded.

'We don't want any one in here who only wants to satisfy his curiosity,' said the governor.

'No, I agree with you there, sir,' replied Berry.

'And so far as this assistant business is concerned I would make it a rule that you would be bound to bring in a man appointed by the Home Office,' the governor continued.

'It would be a good idea, sir,' agreed Berry.

'And would save some people from making fools of themselves and running risks,' the governor concluded. 'Still I am to a certain extent in your hands and you can think over it.'

Berry, however, by his own admission, was 'a stubborn chap in these days, and resented interference', so the more he thought it over the more he was resolved to have his own way.

Currell, meanwhile, had behaved well while in the condemned cell and was paying great attention to the ministrations of the chaplain. On the Sunday he wrote a full confession to the crime, which he passed to the chaplain, who in turn passed it on to the governor, who then forwarded it to the Home Secretary. Giving jealousy as his motive for the murder, Currell indicated that he accepted the justice of his sentence. He stated he had purchased the revolver and cartridges used in the crime for six shillings and sixpence shortly before the murder, and had entered the room and shot his victim without a word being spoken. Afterwards, he had made his way in the direction of his father's residence, throwing the weapon into a canal on the way.

On the morning of the execution, before going to meet his 'assistant', Berry took a look at the usual large crowd that had gathered outside Newgate Prison. He received word that the man had arrived, and on seeing him said, 'Come along, it's about time we were getting to work.'

The man shook hands without saying a word.

'Let me feel your pulse,' said Berry, 'so that I can see if you will stand it.'

The man was trembling and his face was white. 'Oh, you are all right, but you had better have a pick me up. Have a tot of this brandy,' Berry reassured him.

The man was grateful for the stimulant and it appeared to do him good. Berry then took him to see the governor, who merely nodded, apparently indignant that Berry had brought him along. The sheriff and other officials were also present, and it was obvious to all that the young man was a gentleman of some refinement. Accompanied by the governor Berry hurriedly took him out to fetch the prisoner from his cell, where Currell was subsequently pinioned and taken out to his place in the procession. The sheriff came up to the convicted man and asked if he wished to say anything before the sentence was carried out.

'No thank you, sir,' he replied, and the signal was given to move off for the scaffold. As Berry had anticipated, the prisoner gave him no problems. He wheeled round sharply and set off for the gallows with a firm step, remaining silent the whole time.

The Home Office observer, Dr Marshall, was present, and noted that Currell was a light man of about 10st 7lb, being around 5ft 5in in height. A drop of 5 feet had been allowed, but Berry said he would give him an extra 6 inches. One of the warders approached Dr Marshall, exclaiming, 'He is going to give him about 7 feet.' The medical man looked and saw that the warder was right, for there was about 2 foot of rope dangling down below the board that stood over the mouth of the pit. Berry worked fast and after the trap fell there was no movement of the culprit's body, though the pulse continued to beat for 10 minutes. On examining the body afterwards a great deal of bleeding from the mouth was found to have occurred, caused by the rupture of blood vessels and tissue. The skin of the neck, however, was not broken. Dr Marshall also noted that Berry had tightened the knot with extra severity around Currell's neck, after putting the cap over his head. The retaining washer on the rope, at the noose, had risen only 3 inches, as opposed to the usual six, indicating this extra tightening of the noose round the neck before the drop. Marshall stated that:

I always myself, before that, thought that Berry used a great deal of power from the way he drew out his arm, and I have noticed it in my reports on other executions. But in this case I noted that he used more muscular power on the man's neck than usual. He had previously told me that that was his improved system, and that drew my attention to it to a great extent.

No post-mortem examination was conducted, but Dr Marshall immediately confirmed dislocation, by manipulation of the neck, observing that he 'took the spine itself, where it is connected with the head, and pulled it laterally away from the head'.

No sooner had the trap fallen than Berry felt a touch on his arm and his 'assistant' said, 'Can I get out of here now, Mr. Berry? I want to be away as soon as I can.'

Berry could see that the man's face was 'whiter than a sheet' and that he appeared to be on the verge of collapse.

'You had better have a drink first,' said Berry.

'No, thanks. I would rather get out of here. Try to get me out quickly, Mr. Berry.'

'All right then,' said Berry, 'come and I'll see what I can do.'

On the way to the gate the man put something into Berry's hand that clinked, and on looking at it Berry saw that he had been given two sovereigns 'for the service I had done him'.

After the man left, Berry saw the sheriff and the others out of the prison and decided that he would go for a drink himself, in one of the hotels near the prison. On entering the bar, the first person he saw was his 'assistant'. He was seated at a table with half a bottle of champagne in front of him. He had nearly finished the bottle.

On seeing Berry he rose and said, 'Here, Berry, you had better have one of these.'

'Thank you very much. I could do with it,' replied Berry.

The man walked over to the bar, procured the drink, returned, and poured a glass for Berry. He then made an excuse and left. Berry never saw him again. Unfortunately it has been impossible to identify him.

Berry described the Open Brasenose murder as a tragedy of vagrant life. Charles Smith was 63 years old and living a gypsy life with his wife and two children, sometimes sleeping in the open and sometimes under a roof. In February 1887 the poverty-stricken family was living in a tent on common land, swampy and partially covered with furze bushes, known as Open Brasenose, situated near Cowley. They were strangers to the area and were actually trespassers, although they had been left undisturbed. Smith was of low intellect and had mistreated his wife for years.

On the night of Saturday 19 February they retired into the tent, but at about 2.00 a.m. Smith attacked his wife with a hammer as the children slept, her screams awaking the children. She managed to crawl out of the tent, bruised and bleeding, and, ignoring his shouts to come back, crawled as far as a stream, where she collapsed and died. With the help of his daughter, Smith carried her lifeless body back to the tent and covered it with rags, and then sent his two children to tell a neighbour that the woman was dead. Eventually the police were informed and they attended and arrested Smith. He denied beating her to death but was taken to Cowley, where a conveyance was arranged to take him to the County Police Station at Oxford. He was tried before Baron Huddlestone and found guilty of murder after a plea of manslaughter was rejected. He was sentenced to die at Oxford gaol on Monday 9 May.

On his arrival, the first thing Berry went to see was the new scaffold. He writes:

When I went to hang Smith I was glad to find that my directions had been carried out and the new scaffold had been erected. The one which had formerly stood in the deputy governor's garden consisted of a raised platform, reached by a flight of wooden steps, the mounting of which was a needless act of cruelty to the wretched criminal. The ghastly apparatus, moreover, was in full view of the condemned cell at a distance of forty or fifty yards, and on the way he had to pass his freshly-dug grave. Humanity demanded that such horrors should cease, and within a fortnight the scaffold had been erected within the walls of the gaol, not far from the condemned cell, and was situated so that the condemned man would not be aware of its vicinity until he was on the drop.

Well satisfied with it, he then informed the governor and the High Sheriff that all was in order. In the condemned cell, apart from occasional pleas to be spared, Smith displayed a stolid demeanour but Berry doubted he realised either the gravity of his offence or of the punishment that awaited him. He considered Smith a low type of humanity, stating that he hanged him on a day 'when all nature seemed to rejoice'. His account of the execution, published in *The Post* (July 25, 1914), reveals dark thoughts and misgivings about his 'trade':

> I was up early in the morning, and as I took my walk round the courtyard of the Castle it was impossible to suppress the thoughts that forced themselves to the surface as I walked along. Everywhere were the sense and sight of re-invigorated nature, and yet through all and in all 'the inward eye' saw the dark shadow and persons and things within it.
>
> The sun now and again flashed from a spring sky, the south-west wind blew softly and feebly from that balmy quarter, patches of garden in front of this house and that house were gay with the first floral tributes of the year.
>
> The early leafing trees began to don that tender green, the hope rather than the realisation of full vitality, the birds chirped under the eaves, the rooks flew from nest to nest in quest of food for their callow young, and humanity had awakened from sleep, the twin sister of death, to a new life and new duties.
>
> The outward eye saw all this, and the outward ear heard, but the 'inward eye' beheld the frowning walls of the Castle, its heavily grated windows, the implement of death in one of the open spaces, and even the interior of the condemned cell, a life worth less than an hour's purchase, and the last minister of the law ready to do his duty.

There can be little doubt that some of these evocative words were the work of an unknown author 'ghosting' for Berry, but they at least reflect what he must have said and felt, and paint a truly graphic picture of the stark contrasts of his grim calling.

Outside the Castle, New Road appeared quite normal until about 7.30, with folk going about their daily business. That it was not a normal day, however, soon became evident when a small crowd began to gather against the wall of the canal wharf. There was nothing to see but the flagstaff, the prison walls and two policemen standing on watch at the wicket-gate, but the crowd began to increase in numbers, many of them being boys and girls. The usual murmurings of 'Poor soul', 'I wonder what he is doing now' and

'Will he die game?' were to be heard. At ten minutes to eight the prison bell began to toll.

The selfless chaplain had spent the night in the prison, and at 3.00 a.m. Smith had awoken and sent for him. The rest of the night was spent with the clergyman praying for the doomed man, who sang snatches of hymns he had been taught since his incarceration.

Breakfast was taken in to him but he merely drank a cup of tea. Thirty minutes before Berry arrived at the cell, Smith was taken to the prison chapel, where he received Communion before being returned to his cell. When Berry arrived with his straps Smith looked at him in 'a haunted way' and then shrank away.

'You have no need to put these things on me. I will give you no trouble,' said Smith.

'I am not afraid that you will give me trouble. I am putting them on for your own sake. It will be easier for you to die if you have these things on. Come along, now, like a good chap,' reassured Berry.

Smith submitted to the pinioning without another word and the chaplain led the way to the execution shed, followed by the prison officials with their heads uncovered. Berry described the final minutes:

The condemned man, whose face wore a death-like pallor, walked with a firm step to the scaffold, where he was placed under the beam, and supported by two warders. The chaplain immediately knelt down in front of the drop and prayed:– 'O God the Son, Redeemer of the world, have mercy upon this man's soul.' While he was doing so I bent to pinion the culprit's feet, and he lifted one of them, or I thought he did, to prevent me.

'Put your feet down,' I said.

'I can't,' he replied quite coolly, and then I saw that one of his legs was longer than the other.

After that I put the rope round his neck, and while I was doing so he cried – 'Oh, dear,' and immediately fainted away.

When I saw what had happened I shouted to the warders to get ready, and flew to the lever.

Charles Smith shot through the drop to his doom, and I am certain that he had the most peaceful death of any of my victims.

Berry's next execution was scheduled for just a week later and was to take him south to Dorchester, the county town of Dorset. Awaiting execution there was Henry William Young, a 27-year-old one-legged shoemaker who had murdered his wife's one-month-old illegitimate child. The couple lived at Poole and after she gave birth to the child, Percival John, it was obvious that Young had no affection for him, despite being told that he was the father.

On 8 February the baby was taken ill with a stomach upset, and remained under doctor's orders for four days until he appeared to be well again. The following day he was taken ill again while in the care of Young, his wife being out. The child died and the doctor issued a death certificate, but after Young was heard boasting that he had tried to poison the baby with caustic soda, an autopsy revealed that the baby had died from strangulation and chest injuries.

Young confessed to the crime, claiming that his wife had been unfaithful and that the child was not his. He was found guilty at Dorset Assizes and sentenced to death by Mr Justice Denman on 28 April. The date of the execution was set for Monday 16 May 1887.

In connection with this execution Berry related an amusing anecdote (*Experiences*):

In 1887 when I had to go to Dorchester, to hang Henry William Young for the Poole murder, I stayed at Bournemouth, and took a room in a Temperance Hotel. During the evening I got into conversation with the landlady, who was much interested in the subject of executions, and who appeared to like to discuss it. She was decidedly 'down on' Berry, 'the hangman,' and expressed herself very freely as to his character and disposition; amongst other pleasant things, saying that he was a man without a soul, and not fit to have intercourse with respectable people. Of course, I smilingly agreed with everything that she had to say, and chuckled quietly to myself about a little surprise that I had in store for her. The surprise came off at bed-time, when she handed me my bedroom candle, and in return I handed her my card. The good lady nearly fainted.

There is another story that would appear to originate from Berry's visit to Dorchester. In his introduction to *Experiences*, H. Snowden Ward relates another tale gleaned from checking through Berry's manuscript and cuttings. He gave it as another example of Berry's 'tender-heartedness', of which he had no doubt:

I came across a copy of a poem 'For one under Sentence of Death,' and made some enquiry about it. I found that the lines were some which Mr. Berry had copied from a Dorchester newspaper, and that for a long time it had been his habit to make a copy of them, to send to the chaplain in every case where a prisoner was sentenced to death, with a request that they should be read to the prisoner. This was continued until the governor of one of the gaols resented the sending of such a poem to the chaplain, and intimated that in all cases the chaplain was best able to judge of what was necessary for the condemned man, and did not need outside interference. After this Mr. Berry sent no more poems, but he kept one or two copies by him, and I think that it may interest the reader.

LINES FOR ONE UNDER SENTENCE OF DEATH.

My brother, – Sit and think,
While yet some hours on earth are left to thee
Kneel to thy God, who does not from thee shrink,
And lay thy sins on Christ, who died for thee.

He rests His wounded hand
With loving kindness, on thy sin-stained brow,
And says – 'Here at thy side I ready stand,
To make thy scarlet sins as white as snow.

'I did not shed My blood
For sinless angels, good and pure and true;
For hopeless sinners flowed that crimson flood,
My heart's blood ran for you, my son, for you.

'Though thou hast grieved me sore,
My arms of mercy still are open wide,
I still hold open Heaven's shining door,
Come then – take refuge in My wounded side.

'Men shun thee – but not I,
Come close to me – I love my erring sheep,
My blood can cleanse thy sins of blackest dye,
I understand, if thou canst only weep.'

Words fail thee – never mind,
Thy Saviour can read e'en a sigh, or tear;
I came, sin-stricken heart, to heal and bind,
And died to save thee – to My heart thou'rt dear.

Come now – the time is short,
Longing to pardon and to bless, I wait;
Look up to Me, My sheep so dearly bought,
And say, 'forgive me, e'er it is too late'.

E.B.C.

His use of this poem undoubtedly provides another interesting insight into Berry's complex character.

18

Berry hangs a boyhood friend

'I had taken the life of a friend of my youth.'

Berry's next appointment took him to Manchester for the execution of Walter Wood on 30 May 1887. Wood, aged 35 and a machine fitter, lived happily with his wife Emma at Darwen, Lancashire, until he lost his job, this having an adverse effect on the marriage. She also accused him of seeing another woman. After moving to Bolton they eventually parted, she returning to live with her parents at Bury and taking her furniture with her. After several attempts to win her back Wood finally went to Bury on 17 February to make a last desperate plea, telling her that he had at last obtained another job, but it seems this was unsuccessful for he subsequently suggested they went for a walk, during which, in a field near Huntley Brook Farm, he cut her throat. The couple had been spotted together earlier by the farmer, Mr Emmerson, and the woman was later seen by a little boy with her throat cut. Still alive, she was able to run to the farm, but she collapsed and died on the floor a few minutes later. Wood was arrested two days later at his mother's house in Bolton. He was tried at Manchester Assizes, sentenced to death and awaited his fate at Strangeways gaol.

Berry's recollections of the case were recorded in *The Post* series on 4 April 1914. Describing Wood as one of his closest friends, he says he had last seen him only a few months before, when in Manchester for the execution of Leatherbarrow. The two had met outside the gates of the prison and shared a drink together in an adjacent hotel while reminiscing over childhood days, afterwards going to a music hall together. Wood had subsequently invited

Berry home to meet his wife, but he had declined, leaving instead for Bradford.

On arrival at the prison a warder told Berry that Wood was asking for him and claiming he knew him. Berry, on first hearing the name Wood in connection with the murder, had feared it might be his friend, but had been hoping his guess was wrong. Reluctantly he peeped through the door of the condemned cell and, to his dismay, recognised his boyhood friend. The warder tapped on the door, and Wood's face appeared at the grating in the door.

'Hullo James. So you have come to see me,' said Wood.

'Yes. I am sorry to find that you are my old friend,' replied Berry.

'It is a terrible position to be in,' said Wood.

'Yes. I am very sorry to see you in this plight,' Berry responded.

Wood drew his hand across his brow with a shudder. 'It is all through drink, James. If I had not had a drink that day I would never have done this job. I do not remember doing it. I have only a slight remembrance of something taking place. It is an accursed thing this drink,' he said.

Berry told Wood how he had altered since he had last seen him and the condemned man replied, 'Do you remember when we were boys together?'

The two reminisced and Wood reminded Berry of how bad he had been at school. 'You were one of the worst boys in school, James,' he said.

'I have no doubt I was,' Berry replied.

'I wonder you have not got into this before me, you have such a temper. Let this be a warning to you,' said Wood.

'It will be a warning to every man, I hope. It is a terrible thing to commit murder,' said Berry.

Wood asked at what time Berry was to take him to the scaffold and Berry told him it would be about five minutes to eight.

'Will it take long?' queried Wood.

'No! From the time you leave this cell to be sent into eternity, it will scarcely be three minutes,' Berry assured him.

'That is not very long to suffer.'

'No! It is not, and I will be quicker if I can for old time's sake.'

Wood paused for a moment and then, trying to peep round the

corner of the grate, surprised Berry by asking him where the scaffold was positioned.

'That is it,' said Berry, pointing down the corridor.

Wood said that he would not have far to walk and seemed a little easier in his mind. Berry told him to cheer up and it would soon be all over, but Wood was still very worried.

'Does it hurt, James?'

'No, it does not,' Berry replied firmly.

'You are sure of that?' queried Wood.

'As sure as that you and I are talking here together in Strangeways Prison,' said Berry.

'Is it strangulation, or does it break the neck?' persisted Wood.

Berry asked if he had been reading about it and Wood confirmed that he had, such a thing of interest to him as an engineer.

'Well, if you want to know, it is dislocation,' was Berry's answer.

This seemed to reassure Wood, and he thanked Berry for coming to see him, upon which the hangman again emphasised that he had nothing to fear. Wood then asked what people were saying about him in Heckmondwike, their boyhood home, to which Berry replied that he didn't know. Although he had been there a week before, he said, he had not spoken to anyone about the crime, vainly hoping that they would not realise Wood was the culprit.

'It will kill my mother. She was very fond of me,' Wood murmured.

Berry was too upset to stay at this point and took his leave.

'Well! Remember what I have said, James. Reflect that even you in a moment of temper could be carried away and do what I have done. For God's sake, James, do not touch drink; or perhaps you, too, will die as I am about to die on your own gallows.'

'Good-bye, Walter. I will see you in the morning,' said Berry in a trembling voice.

Wood, we are told, had been a model prisoner while in custody, showing penitence with the chaplain and accepting visits from his family bravely. His aged mother, as he had anticipated, was grief stricken, collapsing on leaving the prison for the last time. She died two weeks after her son.

Wood slept until 6.00 a.m. when the warders aroused him for the last time. The chaplain soon joined him and at 7.00 a.m. he was offered breakfast, but he was only able to drink some tea. At 7.30 Berry went to see him to say farewell. Wood, who was smoking a pipe, rose and held out his hand, upon which the two exchanged 'Good mornings' and Berry asked how he felt. Wood replied that he was feeling better than the night before but wished it was all over, which prompted Berry to ask if he would like a glass of beer to cheer him up.

'It has been the ruin of me. But I don't think it can do me much more harm now, James. I have got a craving for a glass, the old habit to the last, you see. Do you think they would give me one?'

'You shall have it with pleasure,' said Berry and a warder was sent to get it. Wood drank the beer with relish and chatted with Berry.

Again Wood mentioned the old times, but Berry suggested it would be better not to recall them.

'In different circumstances maybe, but not now; it will only upset both of us, and it is better for you that I should not be upset. I want to keep control of myself.'

'You are quite right, James, but there is no reason why you should be upset. You can see that I am not afraid to die. Have you been thinking over what I said last night?'

'I have been thinking about nothing else Walter. I never got a wink of sleep.'

'Let me implore you to keep thinking about it when you go outside the prison. Let my fate be a warning to you, and never touch a drop of drink again. When a man lets it take possession of him he is doomed. I never knew anything about this affair. I loved my wife, and would give anything if she were alive now.'

'You had better forget about me and prepare yourself for eternity, Walter. I will come and see you again later on, and you have nothing to fear,' advised Berry.

Berry then went to the scaffold and conducted the fifth or sixth test that morning. He was very nervous and feared an accident, but, finding the apparatus was working smoothly, he did his best to pull himself together. He could not help thinking, however, of their schooldays together and of Wood's kind-hearted mother. It brought to mind his own mother and how she had been borne down with grief on her sickbed when she knew that her son had taken up the position of hangman against her will.

Dejected, he returned to the condemned cell, where Wood greeted him with a shake of the hand.

'Come along now, Walter. Three minutes and it will be all over. Let me get these things round you, and don't be afraid.'

Berry very quickly pinioned Wood and took him out into the corridor, the prisoner all the while repeating the responses to the prayers conducted by the chaplain. The latter led the procession to the scaffold, reading the burial service as he did so, followed by the warders, with Berry and the doomed man walking between them, one hand kept by Berry on the straps at Wood's back in case he should faint. The scaffold was soon reached and Wood stepped under the beam and stood firmly while Berry completed his preparations. On the stroke of eight o'clock, less than a minute after they had reached the gallows, he uttered in a deep voice, 'Lord have mercy upon me!' Berry pulled the bolt and his old friend Walter Wood was dead. He spoke afterwards of how much he regretted having to perform the deed, expressing hope that Wood had forgiven him for doing so.

Two months were to elapse before Berry's next execution. Before then he was to be a key witness before Lord Aberdare's Committee.

19

Before Lord Aberdare

'You are the executioner appointed by the City of London?'

Berry's big day dawned on Saturday 18 June 1887 – he was in London to appear before Lord Aberdare and his Committee. On taking his place, he was greeted by his Lordship with the words, 'You are the executioner appointed by the City of London?', to which he replied 'Yes', stating that he had been executioner for three years and six months, having previously been a boot salesman in a boot shop.

'Had you ever assisted at any execution before your appointment?' he was asked.

'Never,' replied Berry, thus scotching stories that were later to circulate that he had assisted Marwood.

The interview continued.

'May I ask you what induced you to apply for that office?'

'Mr. Marwood used to come to our house when he came to Bradford,' answered Berry, 'and we put him up at our house for a night or two when they could not do with him at his relations, and he put me into the method of doing it. He pinioned me in my own house, and showed me how the process was performed, and I took it into my head when he died that I would apply for the situation.'

'Did you succeed to him or Binns?'

'I was appointed first by the sheriffs of London, but owing to my parents being well off they engaged some solicitors at Heckmondwike to withdraw me from being executioner, as it got into my family circle.'

'Were they opposed to it?'

'Yes, they were opposed to it; but after my mother died I determined to apply for the post again.'

'But practically you succeeded Binns?'

'Yes.'

'Did you know Binns?'

'No, I did not know him only just to see him. I went to see him when he got the post.'

'Did you ever see him conduct an execution?'

'No, never.'

Berry was asked on what points he wished to be examined. He said that he wanted to 'have a certain stipend from the Home Office, and to be under the regulations of the Home Office, so that I should not have to depend upon a criminal's neck for my livelihood'.

'You wish to be paid by a fixed salary instead of being paid by the job, in fact?'

'Yes.'

Lord Aberdare said that he did not know that that matter came strictly within their business but they could probably make his wishes known. He then asked if Berry had any other points he wished to make.

'The authorities wished me to shorten my drop, and I have done so,' Berry answered.

'What authorities do you allude to?'

'It came to Newgate after that man had been decapitated at Norwich that it would be better if I would shorten the length of my drop.'

'How did you regulate the length of your drop before that?'

'It was by taking the weight and height of the man. Then I worked a scale out from experience of the different weights of falling bodies at different distances, and then I got one made out, and I went on working from experience and improving on it, and then I showed it to the chief warder at Newgate, Mr. Ward, and he worked out a scale and this is what he worked out, and I have always worked from it since.'

Berry handed a copy of the table to the Committee, stating that he had used the scale indicated there for twelve months or more, during which time he had conducted about twenty-five executions, death having been instantaneous in each case. He also made mention of several testimonials he had with him.

Lord Aberdare observed that the Committee had Dr Marshall's report before them on the case of Edward Hewitt at Gloucester, and asked Berry if death had been instantaneous in this case. Berry asserted that it had, whereupon Dr Marshall's report was read over to him, prompting Berry to respond, 'The doctor of the prison gave it in that the death was immediate; and not only that but that the culprit had never even suffered anything at all.' Pressed on the fact that the prison doctor Dr Clarke, who had examined the body with Dr Marshall, had delivered a conflicting report, finding there to be no dislocation of the neck – this being read over to Berry – Berry, always ready with an answer, replied, 'In that case the man's neck was not broken, but, at the same time the arteries were severed inside the neck, which caused instantaneous death just as well.' He went on to claim that Dr Marshall had taken him out to lunch in Gloucester after the execution and observed that 'it was very well done indeed'. Berry continued

> . . . as we came back again he went with the doctor to examine the body, and when he came back he told me that the poor wretch had suffered, but he did not tell me so after he had examined him when he was in the prison. As soon as I dropped the body he ran down the steps and was loosening the pinioning apparatus from his hands, and I said, 'Dr. Marshall, you must not loose that apparatus yet; you have no right to touch the body at all, only to examine his pulse.' He was dead then, and the governor said he was satisfied, and so was the sheriff, that man never moved a limb; there was not even a contraction.

Lord Aberdare then pressed on to the case of Currell at Newgate on 18 April. Dr Marshall's report was again read out, stating that Berry had initially said he intended to give a drop of 5 feet, but had then decided on 5 feet 6 inches instead. The report also made reference to Berry's conversation with Marshall, in which the hangman had mentioned his improved system, reducing the drop but fastening the noose more tightly around the neck before the drop was released. Berry was asked since when he had adopted the system of tightening the noose.

'I always have tightened it,' said Berry, 'but I have never pushed the apparatus well up. I have generally left it to tighten of its own accord. But I was advised by several doctors to tighten it, and it would do a lot better, and I have done so ever since; but still at the same time I am following up my scale of the weights of falling bodies in different positions.'

He was pressed further.

'Dr. Marshall states that on this occasion his attention was drawn by an experienced warder to the fact that you were going to give him 7 feet on the rope, and that thereupon Dr. Marshall said he looked very closely, and he found that 7 feet was accurately the amount given.'

'No,' answered Berry, 'the ropes that I get from Newgate are made very pliable, and they have a very varying elasticity about them, and they always give 12 inches. I have known them give 14 inches.'

'What do you say to the facts stated by Dr. Marshall, that whereas you stated that you intended to give him 5 feet 6 inches you actually did give him a length of 7 feet?'

'I did not do so.'

The warder's words to Dr Marshall were repeated but Berry, insisting that no mention had been made of 7 feet, responded with a complex argument about the rope and its elasticity, ending with the words, '. . . but I have never found such ropes in my life as those I am getting from Newgate just at present'.

Discussion followed on the amount of rope allowed for the girth of the neck and the tightening of the noose around it. Lord Aberdare was obviously concerned about any discomfort or pain inflicted on the culprit when Berry adjusted the rope in this way, but, after an irrelevant digression, Berry responded that, in his view, the culprit experienced no pain.

Berry was then questioned on his activities when visiting various locations for executions, and asked if he went into a public house on such occasions.

'Very seldom,' replied Berry.

'We have been told, I do not know that it has been said of you, but it has been said of an executioner (I think of Marwood) that he was in the habit of exhibiting the ropes with which he had hanged various criminals, and, in fact, of selling portions of those ropes to people who were curious about such things; have you ever done anything of that sort?'

'I gave one to a gentleman of high position in the city, but I have never sold any in my life,' lied Berry. He was obviously not going to admit such trade and was no doubt hoping that the Committee did not know about The Golden Fleece public house and Dan Dominic in Nottingham.

'I suppose people are very curious in talking to you about those things, are they not?'

'Yes, there are some very inquisitive people; but when they begin to talk about the subject of hanging I leave the company at once. I will not introduce it at all.'

After further questions about executions Berry was asked about amateur hangmen and the occasion on which Sir Claude Champion de Crespigny had acted as his assistant. Berry explained exactly how Sir Claude had assisted at the triple execution in Carlisle.

After this, the subject of Marwood was again mentioned.

'You had the advantage of having received some instruction from Marwood?'

'Yes.'

'Supposing you had received no such instruction from Marwood, you would hardly have been so handy as you are now, I presume?'

'No.'

'When you began were you perfectly aware of the sort of work that you had to do?'

'Yes, by talking to him. I used to be frightened at the position at first, but when he came into our house and explained things I got familiar with him and attached to him.'

Berry then described his first execution and stated that he had conducted his last eight or ten double executions on his own, without any assistance whatever. Lord Aberdare was obviously assessing the desirability of having others trained or instructed as executioners so that there were standbys in the event of illness or unavailability of the number-one man. Berry agreed that this would be advantageous, stating that on two occasions he was very ill when he performed them.

A key question was then put to him by Dr Haughton: 'Are ropes always supplied to you, or do you supply all your own ropes?'

Berry replied, 'I write to Newgate for a rope, and then they send a letter to the sheriff to say that I have ordered one, and then he writes back to me, and says he is very glad and thankful because I have done so, and then they forward the rope, not to me, but to the person who applies for it when the culprit is going to be hanged.'

Lord Aberdare said, 'Those ropes, I suppose, have very varied degrees of elasticity, some giving more than others?'

'Yes.'

'Would it be impossible to make ropes of the same amount of stiffness in every case?'

'I do not think they could improve upon what they are making at present, excepting in the brass eyelet hole. The brass eyelet hole was in my opinion the very reason that caused the decapitation in the case of the execution at Norwich, and that was the opinion of the doctor as well, and not only that, but, being a large eyelet hole, in cases where a man has a lot of loose skin round his throat, the elasticity of the rope in descending into the pit causes the loose skin to vibrate, and the rope coming through a big eyelet hole causes the blood to flow in some cases. I think it would be an improvement if the eyelet hole which I had reduced at first, when I took up the position, was made exactly like the one that I am now using, but with smaller dimensions, and with a centre hole, so that it would not allow the flesh to come through.'

'You say that your ropes are everything that can be desired now?'

'Yes, they are.'

The question of elasticity of the ropes was again broached. It was asked if testing first would not result in uniform elasticity. Berry said that 'they will go back again the same as india rubber,' even if weighted the day before use. When the rope was stretched it was a five-eighths rope but was actually a three-quarters rope before weighted.

'Could you, by testing it the day before its being used, reduce it to this condition of five-eighths?'

'No, you could not; if you let it stop there it would go back to what it was before. I tried it myself in this way. I have one rope at home that I have executed 16 persons with, and every time that I have executed a criminal with that rope I have taken very particular notice where the leather washer stopped compressing the neck, and how far the rope has given, and I have taken notice where it has not given, and at the end after I had executed a lot of people, I found that it did not give above 6 inches or 6½ inches, but at first when I started it gave 14 inches.

'Then you do reduce the elasticity by constant use?'

'Yes, by constant use, but it is a risk to do it.'

A discussion followed on reducing elasticity. Berry said, 'I have some ropes in my garret where I put my appliances, and I have large weights to hold them down to try to reduce this stretching process, and I have kept them on until I have had to be called upon for the next execution, and then I have taken the weights off and put them into my bag packed up ready for use, and the next day when I have had to begin again it has given again.'

'Have they given as much as they would have done if you had not weighted them before?'

'No; where it would have given 12 inches at first, or getting up to 14 at the latter end, it only gave about 6½ inches.'

More discussion of stretching and elasticity followed, and Berry warned of the danger of stretching the rope so much that it might break when used. He was then asked, 'What I want to know is this: supposing a culprit is to be executed what becomes of the rope, do you keep it?'

'I keep it.'

'By keeping it, as you say, you have it ready for another execution, but when you are asked to carry out an execution in some county town why do you order a new rope from Newgate; why do you not use the one that you had used before?'

'Some sheriffs will not pay for the rope, and then I have to find one myself. I take one out of my box which I have at home, and when I have agreed about an execution I put some weights on it to stretch it before going away to an execution to see whether the end gets out of repair, and if the end gets out of repair I take the weights off and put them back again.'

'Supposing there was no question about payment, would you rather have a new rope for every execution or one that had been used before?'

'I would rather have one that had been used before.'

Further discussion about elasticity followed and Berry described how he tested his rope on the scaffold with a bag of cement and left it, ready for the execution, attached to the chain that hangs from the beam. He had adjusted the length of the rope by tying the knot at the desired position. He said that he usually took two ropes of different lengths with him. The technicalities of length of rope, drop and weight etc. were discussed, as was the positioning of the 'knot', Berry explaining that he always placed it at the back of the left ear. The various types of scaffold were also discussed, Berry declaring that the one at Newgate was particularly satisfactory. Asked if he had ever experienced any trouble with the sheriffs or those appointed to supervise the executions, he replied, 'I have only had trouble with one; I had to put it into my solicitor's hands.'

'What sort of trouble was it?'

'It was in Kilkenny, in Ireland. I had agreed upon the terms and it was a question of recovery of payment.'

'I mean were you interfered with in your method of conducting the execution?'

'No, they generally leave it all to my charge.'

The discussion moved on to money matters.

'What is the cost of a rope?'

'A guinea. Every rope that is paid for at Newgate is one guinea,' said Berry.

'Is that its real value?'

'No; I could have it made at Woods', one of the largest rope manufactories in Lancashire, for about a quarter of the price, for 5s. or 6s.'

'Who gets the profit?'

'I do not know. A guinea is a long price for a rope 12 feet long.'

Berry then withdrew.

On Monday 1 August 1887, he conducted his next execution at Lancaster Castle. The convicted man was Alfred Sowery, aged 24 and from Preston. Described by Berry as one of the biggest cowards he ever hanged, Sowery had been working as a barman in a hotel and had fallen in love with an Irish girl, Annie Kelly, who had come to live in England, being employed as a laundry maid in the same hotel. One Saturday Kelly left the hotel and failed to return until the following Monday. Reprimanded by the manageress of the hotel, she gave up her position, declaring that she would go back to Ireland. On the evening of the same day, the kitchen maid from the hotel saw her out in the street with Sowery, both appearing to be distressed. She spoke to them and learned that Sowery wanted to emigrate with the girl to America, but the latter was unwilling to go. That night Sowery helped Kelly move her luggage from the hotel to a house in Christchurch Place, where he then left her. The following day, before going to meet her, he went to a pawnbroker's shop and purchased a revolver and cartridges. Then, on the Wednesday, the two visited a temperance hotel in the Fishergate, where they sat down to rest. The daughter of the hotel proprietor showed them into the coffee-room and left to prepare a meal for them. About 5 minutes later she heard a peculiar noise, but assumed that a stone had been thrown at the door. On returning to the room, however, she was confronted by the sight of Sowery, revolver held out straight before him, and Annie slumped in an easy chair with blood flowing from a wound in her right temple. Hearing the girl's scream other occupants of the hotel came running, including her mother, who, on entering the room, saw Sowery holding the muzzle of the gun to his own head. She shouted at him not to pull the trigger, and he lowered his weapon. A doctor was called but the wounded girl was dead within 5 minutes. Sowery afterwards claimed he would successfully have shot himself had not the weapon misfired, but no wound could be found on him and this was dismissed as a lie – although, as we shall see in a moment, Berry came to believe otherwise. Admitting to the shooting, Sowery was arrested and found to have £50 and seven live cartridges in his pockets, together with a letter, supposedly written by Annie to her sisters in America, intimating that she intended sailing to New York on a White Star steamer. The revolver was found to be a five-chambered British Bulldog with four live rounds in it, only one having been discharged. Sowery was tried before Mr Justice Day, found guilty and sentenced to death. Removed from the dock in a dazed state, he was taken to a cell in Lancaster Castle, where, closely watched, he sat in silence except for when visited by family and friends.

Berry visited Sowery on the eve of the execution and had a short chat with him, receiving assurances from the condemned man that he would meet his fate bravely and give no trouble. Berry assured him he would have nothing to fear provided he kept his word.

On the morning of the execution a large crowd assembled in the churchyard, while within the gaol Berry examined the scaffold one last time prior to the execution. In use for many years, it comprised a strong framework of timber encircled by a handrail, from the top of which a sombre drapery of black cloth hung down to the ground. Almost filling the chapel yard (which housed the offices of the chief warder, the storekeeper's room, and the room of the visiting justices), it had been erected immediately in front of the chapel entrance, and was approached from the top of a flight of steps leading to the chapel by two wooden steps.

The warders went to see Berry early to warn him that he was likely to have trouble, Sowery seeming to have 'gone mad' and to have lost his nerve completely. His condition was such that four warders had been stationed in the cell with him.

'That is a bad business, but we must just do our best,' said Berry.

On going to the cell, he found his man trembling 'like a leaf', sitting down to his breakfast but then pushing the food away. In all his life, remarked Berry, he had never seen such a fear-stricken face. It went from a vivid blue, to white and then to flushed and rosy, the colours changing as he watched. According to Berry the doctor present declared, 'That is worse than hanging. That man is going through the process of hanging now. It is Hell!'

Such was the man's terror when Berry entered the cell to pinion him that the latter could only pity him. The warders tried to calm him but he pleaded for his mother's sake not to be hanged. He was like a small child, and Berry had difficulty in putting the straps around him. When requested to 'come along', he refused to move, the warders eventually having to carry him out of the cell. His terrible cries could be heard along the inner corridor and out in the chapel yard, and when the robed chaplain endeavoured to quieten him he refused all consolation, attempting instead to throw himself to the ground. Five warders tried to push him along the corridor, but he thrust a foot forward and threw himself back, resisting their efforts and screaming wildly, his cries drowning the words of the chaplain and causing great discomfort to all present. Eventually, there being no other way, Berry told the warders to frogmarch him, so they picked him up and carried him as far as the chapel yard, where they put him down.

At the sight of the gallows the condemned man struggled yet more violently, his face livid and eyes bulging. Hurriedly Berry pulled the white cap over his head in order to blot the dread sight from his vision. Sowery pushed back against the warders but they forced him forward to the scaffold, his struggles by then so desperate that they had to carry him forcibly up the chapel steps and onto the scaffold. With great difficulty four of them held him in position while Berry completed the pinioning, the prisoner kicking, plunging and groaning in terror as soon as he felt his legs being straightened. Berry was by now deeply upset, his hands trembling and heart pounding, so afraid he might not be able to complete the job that he had to force himself to continue. Sowery threw his head about violently, still shrieking, as Berry adjusted the rope around his neck, but at last the preparations were complete, and, sweating from his exertions, Berry stepped back to the lever. The condemned man was still struggling, crying out for his mother and imploring Berry not to hang him. It was all too much for those present, and the warders holding him had tears flowing down their cheeks. Berry gave the signal, the trapdoors flew open and Sowery was dead. It was the worst execution Berry had ever had to endure and one that caused him great mental agonising. The pain, though, was not just in the mind, for, Berry tells us, he also received a nasty kick from Sowery during this execution:

As he saw the beam above him a wilder paroxysm of fear seemed to seize the miserable youth, and four warders were required to hold him in position. Even with this assistance I had the greatest possible difficulty in pinioning his legs, and while doing so I received a nasty kick which took a piece of bone out of my shin, and has left a mark visible even to-day.

A curious footnote to the execution concerns Berry's claim that a lead bullet came from Sowery's head during the execution. He found it, apparently, in the white cap when he removed it from the corpse, and kept it as a souvenir, putting it as a relic in the 'Black Museum' that he maintained at his home. 'How the bullet which I found got into the poor fellow's mouth', he mused, 'will be a mystery to me to my dying day.'

Just over two weeks later, on Tuesday 16 August 1887, Berry carried out an execution at Knutsford. Twenty-year-old Thomas Henry Bevan, an apprentice iron moulder of Crewe, had murdered his aunt, Mrs Sarah Griffiths, on 26 March, stealing 17*s* 6*d* from her purse. Seen by his half-sister Mary Jones, aged just 11, he beat her and left her for dead, but she recovered and was able to give evidence against him. He was tried at Chester Assizes before Mr Justice Denman on 28 July and was duly convicted for the murder, subsequently confessing that, having first tried to strangle his victim, he had jumped up and down on her as she lay on the ground, in order to finish her off. The execution went off without a hitch.

Another execution took place on Monday 22 August 1887, this time of Henry Hobson at Leeds for the murder of his ex-employer, a Mrs Ada Stodhart, who had sacked him. The executioner on this occasion was James Billington, hangman for the county of Yorkshire. Berry's next job was to be another notable case and one that would be reported on at length in the press because of its contentious nature.

20

The Lipski case

'. . . I resolved I would never hang another Jew.'

The case of Israel Lipski was something of a Victorian cause célèbre, and it has continued to arouse interest more recently, having been the subject of a modern study, *The Trials of Israel Lipski* by Martin L. Friedland. Many thought Lipski was innocent of the crime for which he was hanged.

Lipski had arrived in England in 1885 as a 20-year-old immigrant Polish Jew from Warsaw. His name at that time was Lobulsk, but he changed it after arriving in London, presumably adopting that of the Lipskis, with whom he lodged at their home in 16 Batty Street, St George's-in-the-East, off Commercial Road. He was, though, unrelated to them. The house was shared with other lodgers, fifteen people in all living at the address, including fellow Pole Isaac Angel, a boot riveter, who shared a room there with his 22-year-old and 6-months-pregnant wife, Miriam, on the second floor of the property. Lipski lived alone in the attic above, and worked as a stick-maker (used in the making of umbrellas).

On the morning of Tuesday 28 June 1887 Isaac Angel left for work just after 6.00 a.m., as was his habit, leaving his wife in bed and the door to the room unlocked. It was Mrs Angel's routine to rise and go to her nearby mother-in-law's for a nine-o'clock breakfast, so when she failed to arrive that morning her mother-in-law went to 16 Batty Street to investigate. In company with the landlady and another tenant she went to the Angels' room, but found the door locked. She hurried up the stairway leading to the attic, where a small side-window opened onto the Angels' room, and saw that the young woman was lying on the bed, crumpled in an unnatural position. Hurriedly, they forced the door, but they were unable to rouse her. A yellow frothy substance could be seen around her mouth. The landlady went for the doctor, who lived at the end of the street, returning with his assistant, who, realising that the death was suspicious, secured the room pending the arrival of his superior. Dr Kay duly arrived and pronounced the woman dead, identifying the substance around her mouth as some kind of corrosive poison. It was, in fact, nitric acid. A search was made of the room and they discovered Israel Lipski secreted under the bed. He, too, had yellow staining around his mouth and appeared to be semi-conscious. On being revived, he claimed that two workmen had assaulted the young woman and then attacked him, but he was not believed. The position of Miriam Angel's body suggested a sexual assault, even necrophilia, and on turning the covers down it was seen that the whole of her genitals and lower abdomen were exposed and her thighs were wide apart. It looked as though Lipski had poisoned her and then taken poison himself on being disturbed.

Lipski was taken to London Hospital for treatment, and a police guard placed at his bedside. His fiancée, Kate Lyons, attended the hospital and stated that she believed in his innocence. The police officers detailed to deal with the case were Inspector Final and Detective Sergeant William Thick (the latter rejoiced in the nickname 'Johnny Upright', and was to enjoy a degree of prominence the following year in the investigation of the Whitechapel 'Jack the Ripper' murders). With the aid of an interpreter they recorded Lipski's story. He claimed that two workmen, named Rosenbloom and Schmuss, had committed the murder and then attacked him, forcing the poison into his mouth. The next day the inquest into the woman's death was opened before the local coroner, Wynne Baxter, at the Vestry Hall, Cable Street, St George's-in-the-East. It was disclosed that the deceased woman had suffered a violent blow to the right eye and temple, and that nitric acid had been poured into her mouth, she apparently having suffocated after swallowing this. Traces of fluid found in her vagina were later microscopically examined by Dr Kay, and at the next hearing he stated that, though he could not find traces of spermatozoa in the sample, he believed it to be seminal fluid.

The workmen accused by Lipski denied his story, and a

shopkeeper subsequently identified the latter as the man to whom he had sold nitric acid. The coroner's jury returned a verdict of wilful murder. He was committed for trial on a coroner's warrant, and, after being released from the hospital, detained in custody at Holloway Prison. On Saturday 23 July he was transferred to Newgate Prison to facilitate his trial at the Old Bailey, and was subsequently tried at the Central Criminal Court, commencing on 29 July 1887, before Mr Justice James Fitzjames Stephen, a noted judge and baronet who authored several legal works, including *General View of the Criminal Law of England*, 1863, 1890 and *History of the Criminal Law*, 1883. Justice Stephen summed up unfavourably against the accused, and, despite the latter's continued protestations of innocence, he was duly sentenced to death, the execution set for Monday 22 August 1887.

The evidence against Lipski was, obviously, circumstantial but very strong. Nonetheless, the case aroused much controversy. The Permanent Under-Secretary, Godfrey Lushington, wrote a twenty-six-page analysis of the case. Discussion in the press centred on the virtues of commutation as opposed to capital punishment in cases where a modicum of doubt existed regarding the verdict. On the streets anti-Semitism was manifest and Jews were taunted over Lipski, the police having to intervene to prevent further trouble. There was even talk of desperate East End gangs intending to attack Newgate to rescue Lipski, though nothing came of it. A respite of a week was granted to Lipski for the defence to make inquiries regarding the ownership of the bottle of poison found in the murdered woman's room, the Home Secretary, Henry Matthews, being censured for making this allowance but later strongly criticised for failing to recommend mercy. Mr Justice Stephen conferred with Matthews throughout, but no reprieve was granted and the execution date was entered into Berry's diary. It is of interest to note that the Sheriff of London, to whom the task of arranging the execution fell, was a Jewish businessman, Alderman Sir Henry Aaron Isaacs, later to become the Lord Mayor.

On Sunday 21 August Lipski learned from Rabbi Simeon Singer, who was attending him in gaol, that a reprieve had been refused. He then dictated a confession to Rabbi Singer, stating that he alone was guilty of the murder of Miriam Angel (up to this point, apparently, the authorities had been relying on Berry to ascertain whether Lipski had been guilty of the murder, so the former tells us). Giving robbery as his motive, he claimed that he entered the unlocked room while she was asleep, with no intention of 'violating' the woman, but she had awoken and cried out, upon which he had struck her on the head, seized her by the neck and placed his hand over her mouth to keep her quiet. He admitted to having bought the bottle of poison that morning, ostensibly with the intention of committing suicide. Finding this in his pocket that fateful morning, he had poured some of the contents down Angel's throat, at which she had fainted. On realising his desperate position, he had then taken the rest himself before, hearing voices outside, he had finally crawled under the bed where he was discovered.

Rabbi Singer left Newgate Prison early on the Sunday evening. A threatening crowd gathered outside the gaol and a van was sent to the Tower of London to get rifles and ammunition to defend it if necessary. James Berry, who was spending the weekend in the prison, was taken to see Lipski in his cell on the Sunday evening, the warders commenting on how quiet their charge had been, giving them no trouble and constantly reading his Jewish Bible. Berry, who described Lipski as 'a tall fellow, twenty-two years of age, and as nice and gentlemanly a man as I have ever met', asked to see a copy of the confession, 'knowing that at times confessions had been withheld from the public, which made it all the harder for me, people pointing the finger of scorn at me and asserting that I had hanged an innocent man'. According to Berry, Lipski also 'wrote a pathetic letter to the woman that he loved, but I did not read it. Like other men, I had a sense of honour, even if I were a hangman, and to my mind that letter was sacred.'

Lipski retired early to bed and had a good night's rest. At 5.00 a.m. he rose and seemed to be in excellent spirits, resigned to his fate. He ate a hearty breakfast of coffee, eggs and toast, after which Rabbi Singer arrived and, on entering the condemned cell, found the prisoner reading his Bible. Lipski appeared thoroughly penitent, conducting himself with 'wonderful composure'. He was wearing the same suit he had worn at his trial and had on a small blue skullcap. Outside the prison a crowd had been gathering since an early hour, this now seeming as large as any ever witnessed since the abolition of public executions, so dense that it resulted in the virtual stoppage of traffic in the thoroughfares converging on the prison. Windows of the houses in the neighbourhood of the Old Bailey were filled with spectators. About ten minutes to eight the bells in the grey tower of the Church of St Sepulchre began to toll mournfully, and, accompanied by warders, Berry made his way to the condemned cell. He began his grim task of pinioning his man, who did not say a word and behaved with 'singular coolness'. The muffled booing of the crowd outside could be heard. Berry noted:

He did not show the least trace of fear, and seemed glad to die. He looked on me with indifference while his limbs were being bound.

The Sheriff and the other officials came to the cell when I was finished and the official interpreter, in their presence, asked Lipski whether he wished to make any further statement or to add anything to the confession that he had already made.

'No, I have nothing more to add to what I have already said; it is all true, and I am guilty,' said he.

He then expressed his thanks to the Sheriffs, the Governor and the other officials for their kindness to him, and made use of a remarkable expression in broken English.

'I have never been so well treated in my life as I have been since I have been in prison.' Poor fellow! I nearly burst into tears at the words.

To the tolling of the bell we brought him out into the courtyard, the procession headed by the Rabbi, who was reading a Jewish prayer for the dying.

Lipski walked between two warders, but he did not require their assistance. His face was pale, but his step was firm and unhesitating, and his form as erect as the thongs would permit.

In all my life I never saw such a man so devoted to his duty as was the Jewish priest. He was so serious as we stood in the execution shed that one and all we were like children in his hands. The solemnity of his words made me tremble. In despair I put my arm around the beam to support myself, or I would have fallen to the boards in a swoon. The prayers of the dying, spoken in a voice that trembled in majestic awe in the presence of death, bit into my soul. There was but one man in the room who was unaffected. Israel Lipski stood there bound with the noose round his neck, and a fearless look on his face.

The Rabbi took a handful of rice and threw it on the head of the prisoner. It was a symbol of forgiveness or purity and innocence, since he had confessed his guilt and prayed for forgiveness. Then he stepped back, and I asked him in a whisper if he were ready.

'All is over, Mr. Berry,' he whispered back.

I pulled the lever with trembling hand, and Israel Lipski was dead.

We were about to leave the scene, but the Rabbi motioned us to stay. Going nearer to where the dead man swayed at the end of the rope he knelt down and touched him on the head.

'Will you all kindly kneel down?' he asked.

There was not a man in the room who dared to deny him his request in the presence of death, and he prayed long and fervently.

It seemed to me that we were hours kneeling by the scaffold, and when I arose I staggered like a drunken man. I was glad it was all over.

The black flag was raised over the prison and the crowd outside was heard to shout. The doctors who had entered the pit to check Lipski's body found that the pulse continued to beat for 13 minutes; this despite the fact that Berry had allowed a drop of 8 feet as opposed to the 6 feet reported in the press. The body was left to hang for the usual hour before being taken down and placed in a shell (a basic coffin with no trimmings used to transport corpses). Lipski would not have suffered, for insensibility would have been instant. Indeed, according to one of the doctors, in a letter published in the *British Medical Journal* of 28 July 1888, the drop had been so long that it had resulted in near decapitation. A severe discolouration, caused by subcutaneous bleeding, had been noticed extending over the left side of the neck and was the subject of comment by the coroner's jury. The body was buried, in quicklime, in a grave dug in the passage between the Old Bailey and the prison. The conduct of the crowd was considered so bad that it caused comment the following week in the House, it being suggested that the black flag should be dispensed with.

According to an old Newgate warder's account in *Life and Death at the Old Bailey* (R. Thurston Hopkins, 1935), Berry was alarmed when he looked out of the prison window and saw the rowdy and threatening crowd outside. Nothing like this mob had been seen for years and a cabman was asked to bring his hansom into the prison yard. Berry was bundled into this and the cabman, informed who his passenger was, instructed to 'drive like hell'. He initially refused to risk his life for the fare, but the gates were swung open and he whipped up his horse, the crowd scattering in the path of the oncoming hansom. However, when Berry was recognised as the passenger, women shrieked abuse, and men pursued the cab as far as Ludgate Hill but failed to halt their quarry.

Writing later of the execution, Berry stated:

The execution of one of Jewish faith is the most solemn and impressive ceremony, if such I may call it, that it has ever been my lot to figure in, and the departure of Israel Lipski from this world marked itself on my memory.

All through the execution I shuddered and trembled fearfully, and when it was all over I felt so ill that I resolved I would never hang another Jew.

Berry's next execution was scheduled for Monday 29 August 1887 at Lewes Prison. The condemned man was William Wilton, who had been convicted of the murder of his wife at Brighton on 9 July. He had cut her throat as she was lying in bed and then fled from the scene. He was arrested after a search and confessed to the crime. The execution was apparently conducted without a hitch.

September and October 1887 saw no executions, but they did not pass entirely without event. An incident involving Berry in the town of Doncaster, West Yorkshire, recorded in *The Times* of Friday 16 September 1887, tells a brief but intriguing story:

ARREST OF THE HANGMAN. – It is stated that on the police going to a disturbance in Doncaster about midnight on Wednesday [14 September] they saw a man pointing a revolver.

He was arrested and taken to the police-office, where he was identified as Berry, the hangman. The revolver had three of its six chambers loaded, and it has been retained by the police, Berry being informed that a communication would be made to the Home Secretary. He claims to carry a revolver, being a Government servant.

The outcome of this incident was not recorded in the press, but it casts another glimmer of light upon Berry's odd personality and seems to reinforce the idea that he considered himself above the law.

Another item of interest appeared in *The Times* of Wednesday 6 October 1887, which reported:

AN EX-HANGMAN'S SHOW.

A correspondent writes: – Binns, the ex-hangman, is travelling with a show in which he reveals his art for the entertainment of the large crowds who collect to see him perform the happy despatch. The subject is a wax figure representing Mrs. Berry, the Oldham poisoner, and the entertainment is now at Stockport, in Cheshire. The showman, a young man, first gives a biographical sketch of Binns, and then the curtain is rung up, revealing a scaffold with the regular cross beam, and the subject standing on the drop strapped hands and feet. A surpliced chaplain stands at one hand, and a uniformed gaol governor on the other; while two reporters, or individuals to represent them, watch the grim proceedings. Binns, black bag in hand, steps forward, extracts the rope, places the noose round the subject's neck, and when the feeling of the spectators has been wrought to an intense pitch, draws the bolt, and the wax figure disappears into the pit beneath. Mr. Binns then holds a levee.

Obviously Binns was something of an entrepreneur who was not going to allow his dismissal from the office to prevent him from making money from it. Such shows illustrate the intense and morbid public curiosity that existed in certain quarters concerning the hangman and his trade. However, many at the time felt them to be in very bad taste

On Monday 14 November Berry was at Carlisle Prison carrying out the execution of 32-year-old William Hunter, a Glaswegian who had been working as a blacksmith in Manchester. Despite being married he had left his wife and two children and set off with a Mary Steele and her daughter Isabella from Wigton to Carlisle. On Thursday 8 September, as they approached their destination, the girl complained she was tired, upon which Hunter grabbed her by the throat and kicked her, causing the mother to intervene. He had then carried the injured child into a field 'to revive her', but instead cut her throat with a pocketknife, which he then used on himself. Tried at Carlisle Assizes before Mr Justice Day, he was sentenced to death and hanged by Berry. To Berry's surprise, the crowd that gathered for this execution 'wore quite a holiday air. There were some 1500 people, most of whom laughed and jested.'

In a busy schedule, Berry immediately travelled down to Oxford, where he was scheduled to hang Joseph Walker, a saddler from Chipping Norton, the following day. Joseph and his wife endured a miserable life, mainly due to his drinking and jealousy, which had caused her on several occasions to threaten him with a knife such that he needed to restrain her until she calmed down. The situation was exacerbated when she drove one of his sons from his previous marriage away from home, the lad subsequently committing suicide. On Friday 23 September Walker went on a lengthy drinking binge, during which he unwisely told a friend that he would 'do' for his wife when he got home. He returned drunk, put his children to bed, and then became embroiled in a noisy altercation with his wife in the bedroom, finally cutting her throat with a knife, the deed witnessed by one of the children. Sobered by what he had done, Walker called a neighbour and gave himself up to the police. Found guilty he was sentenced to death by Mr Justice Hawkins, and though attempts were made to secure a reprieve these proved to no avail. Walker prayed for his children and walked to the gallows in a composed and calm manner, according to Berry appearing to see nothing, his thoughts far away and on his face an expression of sad composure. Berry, who claimed to be haunted later by that 'sorrow-stricken face', recorded that 'Walker was a heavy man, weighing over sixteen stones, and received a drop of 2ft 10in, the shortest I have ever given' (*Experiences*).

Berry's next victim, Joseph Morley, was only 17 years of age. He was convicted on 10 November at Chelmsford Assizes for the murder of a young married woman, Mrs Rogers, with whom he had lodged at Dagenham, having cut her throat with a razor that he found in her bedroom when she had entered the room. He was executed by Berry on Monday 21 November 1887.

A fourth execution in the same month was scheduled for Monday 28 November 1887 at Gloucester Prison. Enoch Wadley, aged 27, was the main actor in what was called 'the dreadful Kempley tragedy' in the local press. Wadley was a recently retired private in the 2nd Gloucestershire Regiment, and had served in India where he had been ordered into an asylum for 'some extraordinary conduct incompatible with soundness of mind'. He was sent home to England and spent some time in Netley Hospital before being discharged as unfit for service. He visited his parents at Kempley and there made the acquaintance of a young girl, Elizabeth Hanna Evans, aged about 18. They worked together on a farm and while in the fields at Bickerton Court Farm he professed great fondness for her. Unfortunately the feelings were not reciprocated and the girl rejected his advances, Wadley complaining to his sister that it was 'hard to love and not be loved'. Despite this the couple were often seen together, and on the evening of Saturday 18 June Wadley accompanied the girl towards her home as the labourers left the fields. He again made overtures to her, but she indignantly rebuffed him. His frustration turned to rage, and, according to *The Gloucester Chronicle*,

> Frustrated, maddened beyond control he stabbed his victim in nearly forty places and then restrained by neither pity or remorse foully completed his villainy in a manner it is undesirable to describe.

His clothes saturated with blood, Wadley left the unfortunate girl bleeding to death by the roadside and fled towards Dymock. Elizabeth's faint cries were heard by her master, Mr Dyer, who was tending sheep in a neighbouring field, and he ran to assist her, arriving in time to hear her utter the damning words, 'Enoch Wadley did it.' Before she died, she asked Dyer to pray for her. He did so, afterwards taking the girl's body home to her parents, who worked on the same farm. In the meantime Wadley had given his purse, containing £10, to a stranger, then thrown his coat and waistcoat into the garden of a cottage and wandered about the streets of Dymock shouting until finally being arrested for his behaviour by the local constable. Investigations revealed his crime and he was taken to Gloucester gaol. The attack had actually occurred in the parish of Much Marcle in Herefordshire, but, since the girl's death was pronounced in Gloucestershire, the prosecution of the case remained in the jurisdiction of the latter county. Wadley was tried at Gloucester Assizes, where it was claimed that he was a discharged lunatic, unaware of what he was doing, and thus unfit to be at large. The jury, however, was unable to agree on a verdict and the case was postponed to the next Assizes, where a similar plea was raised. Despite this being supported by medical evidence, including that of the doctor who had originally declared Wadley as being of unsound mind, he was found guilty. Berry executed him without a hitch.

Berry's last execution in 1887 was on Tuesday 6 December at Warwick: that of Thomas Payne, a labourer, who had pleaded guilty to the murder of his sister-in-law, Charlotte Taylor, at Coventry. The two, who had shared a house with her sister, had become involved in an affair together, but the obsessive Payne then discovered that she was also having a relationship with a Salvation Army officer. Consumed by jealousy he threatened to kill her unless she broke off this other relationship, and when he later saw the couple out together he cut her throat after she returned home, subsequently giving himself up to the police. He was tried at Warwick Assizes before Baron Huddlestone and pleaded guilty before a packed courtroom consisting mainly of women.

21

Another trip to Ireland – 1888 – Year of the Ripper

'Have a little patience with me, I am getting on in years.'

The year of our Lord 1888 was to be a momentous one in the annals of crime. It was to see Berry hang no less than twenty-one victims, and to be remembered forever afterwards as the year of the autumn of terror – the year of 'Jack the Ripper'.

For Berry it began with another trip to Ireland and another controversial execution. Dr Phillip Henry Eustace Cross, MD, a 62-year-old retired army surgeon-major, awaited his fate in Cork Prison. It was another tale of illicit love. Dr Cross, who was of a good family, retired from military service and settled in County Cork at Shandy Hall, Dripsey, a large house on the Coachford Road. He lived there with his wife Laura and their six children, together with Effie Skinner, an attractive 21-year-old whom Mrs Cross had hired as governess to the children. Normally restricting his interest to some hunting and fishing, the erstwhile major soon became more than interested in the young governess. In fact, he became infatuated with the girl and a relationship developed, which resulted in the furious Mrs Cross dismissing Effie. The doctor's feelings were too strong, however, and he continued to see his young paramour in secret.

Shortly afterwards Mrs Cross became ill, suffering from stomach pains. Her condition rapidly worsened and on Thursday 2 June 1887 she died, apparently of typhoid fever. Dr Cross himself signed the death certificate, and she was quickly buried, the doctor marrying his young love a mere fifteen days later. Suspicions were aroused, and when the body was exhumed it was found to contain arsenic. Cross was arrested and stood trial at Munster Assizes before Mr Justice Murphy. The motive was clear enough, and when it was also proved that the doctor had recently purchased arsenic the jury had no difficulty in finding him guilty. He was sentenced to death, the execution date set for Tuesday 10 January 1888. Rejected by his new young wife, who refused to visit him, he continued to protest his innocence of the crime. Three numerously signed memorials in favour of a reprieve were submitted but the sentence was allowed to run its course. Abandoning all hope of salvation, Dr Cross gave his undivided attention to the ministrations of the prison chaplain, the Revd Canon Conolly, who was in constant attendance, but he made no confession.

Berry, who never enjoyed travelling to Ireland, was accompanied by his faithful wife on this trip, she actually being present in the gaol when the execution took place. He records how much her support meant to him:

My wife, who was always anxious for my welfare, offered to accompany me, and I can assure you that I appreciated her goodness of heart. Few women would have made the sacrifice for, as I have often said, my wife had never been the same woman since the day I undertook the duty of hangman.

According to Berry (*The Post*, 29 November 1913), his encounter with Dr Cross caused him to give up hope of ever being able to read murder on a man's face:

Whatever doctors and criminologists may tell you about the signs, don't believe a word, but take the assurance of James Berry that the face gives no indication of the desire to kill, or bears the mark of Cain upon it.

You cannot go by rule or sign, for several of the most notorious men hanged have been handsome and intelligent, and some of the best men the world has seen had the most murderous types of faces you ever beheld.

I was not allowed to lay my hands on Dr. Cross until I was ready to hang him. He was an educated man . . . and belonged to the same class as the officials.

He was, therefore, singularly well treated in prison, and I was only allowed to peep at him through the door of his cell. I did not see him very well, but they told me he was a tall, soldierly old man, and that he was not worrying much over his fate.

The scaffold in the prison at Cork was the only permanent one in Ireland, and was built of iron. Dr Cross could see the grim structure from the window of his cell and it was said that he looked at it every day of his confinement with an attitude of stoical indifference. The governor of the prison, on the other hand, was so grieved over the fate of Dr Cross that he sent his deputy to Berry, indicating that he would not be present at the execution as he did not feel well enough.

On the morning of the execution Dr Cross was up and dressed by the time the Revd Canon Conolly returned to the cell at 6.00 a.m. It was a dull and gloomy morning and a large crowd had assembled outside the prison. At 7.45 a.m. the Sub-Sheriff of the county, Mr John Gale, the prison deputy governor, Dr Moriarty, and the attendant warders entered the cell. On this occasion Berry was not allowed to go in, being informed that the prisoner would be brought to him. Furthermore, members of the press were not admitted to the execution. The procession from the condemned cell commenced, Berry waiting by the west wing, near to the scaffold. He recorded how Dr Cross, whom he described as a handsome, elderly man, with grey side-whiskers and moustache and an unmistakable military air about him, walked towards him as firmly as if he were on the parade ground, his head thrown back and shoulders squared, subsequently submitting to the pinioning without flinching. He continues:

When you hear that a condemned man walked firmly to the scaffold it is generally untrue. But Dr Cross had no fear in him, and his steps never faltered – no, not even when I, James Berry, laid my hands upon him. He was wearing a black frock coat, his collar and cuffs, and these I had to ask him to remove.

For me he had not the slightest respect, and made it clear to me that I was much his social inferior, and only one request did he make.

'Have a little patience with me,' he said, 'I am getting on in years.'

These were the only words he spoke to me, but to someone else who asked him how he felt, he replied that he had no fear.

'Why should I be afraid to face death,' he said, 'I have faced it often enough on the battlefield.'

Under his frock coat he was wearing a cardigan jacket, and this I allowed him to retain.

After I had pinioned his arms, I marched him forward, and, placing him on the scaffold, I prepared to carry out my grim task with a sinking heart.

The clergyman, the Sheriff, the deputy-governor, the doctor, and the others were grouped in front of the scaffold, and, as is the custom, I turned the condemned man with his face to the wall.

Pulling the white cap over his face, I stepped back, and was just about to pull the lever when I saw that he had turned, and was facing the people. I had never seen a dying man do such a thing before, and I was determined that there should be no favours while I was the hangman.

Letting go the lever, I crossed over, and taking him by the arms, I said –

'Dr. Cross, this won't do. You will have to stand in the same way as anyone else.'

Not a word of reply came from his lips, and he allowed me to turn his face to the wall. I put my hand on the lever again, and was about to send him to his doom when I saw that he was again facing the wrong way.

This time I did not speak to him, but merely turned him and sprang back to the lever. He was too much for me, however, and I was just going to turn him a third time when someone touched me on the shoulder. It was one of the officials, the deputy-governor, I think, and he told me not to mind the man.

'Hang him with his face to the crowd. He is an old soldier, and he wants to die with his back to the wall. You will only have an accident if you keep twisting that rope.'

I obeyed orders, and sent him below, the bravest man I have ever yet met on the scaffold.

There was only a thin dividing wall between the yard and the rooms in the gaol in which my wife was waiting for me. She sat there in fear and trembling all the time, and when I pulled the lever she heard the thud of the doors of the drop, and knew that her husband had sent another wretch to face eternity.

After the execution I took my wife away from the prison as quickly as I could.

In Ireland I had to make myself scarce because the jury always wanted me to face them at the inquest, and tell them all the details of the execution. They did not get me, however, but they got the deputy-governor of the prison instead, and they gave him a stiff time of it.

The jury made a fuss because the governor of the jail had not been present at the execution, and they were anxious to know if a confession had been left behind by Dr. Cross. So far as anyone knew, he left no public confession.

Up to the time of a refusal of a reprieve he continued daily to protest his innocence, but after that he never spoke a word about his crime. If he made a confession he made it to the clergyman or the bishop, who gave him the Sacrament before he died, and they naturally would not make it public.

The Sheriff gave me my cheque after I had finished my work, and I decided to take a run into the country to cure my nerves and bring back the colour to my wife's cheeks.

There were only two jaunting cars in the vicinity of the prison, and we took one each and drove out the Coachford Road to have a look at the house in which Dr. Cross and his wife had lived.

I was always interested in the scene of the crime of any man whom I hanged, and we had a good look at the place. After that we drove to Blarney Castle, and had a look at the famous stone which brings eloquence to all who kiss it.

It was in the Irish papers that it was said that I took the opportunity of kissing it, and that the stone immediately fell out of the castle wall. I may as well state, however, that the stone never got the chance.

I was not feeling in the mood to indulge in pleasantries of the nature indulged in by the average tourist, and after a good look at the castle my wife and I returned to Cork and left for Bradford.

The following day *The Times* carried an account of the execution, stating that no sort of confession was left by Cross. At the inquest into the cause of death of the prisoner, before Coroner Horgan, the jury was not satisfied with what they heard, and some journalists among them requested the attendance of Berry. The inquest was adjourned to the following day.

A follow-up account in *The Times* of 12 January 1888 reported that Berry, with his wife and two detectives who had accompanied him from Dublin, had slept in the gaol on the Monday night and then left on the Tuesday morning as the resumed inquest was about to open. They had driven by car to Blarney Railway Station and there boarded the train that left Cork for Dublin at 10.20 a.m. The coroner inquired of Deputy Governor Oxford whether he had the witnesses required the day before, Oxford replying that he had no other witnesses, but that the sheriff had informed him he had no power over the executioner and could not compel him to attend the inquest. The jury insisted on the production of Berry so the coroner further adjourned the inquest to Friday 20 January, issuing a summons for Berry's attendance. The prison physician, Dr Mortimer, reminded the coroner that the interment could not take place until the jury had delivered a verdict, to which the coroner replied, 'I cannot help that. The authorities had a right to look to it before. It is believed that the Lord Lieutenant will issue an order for the interment of the remains, and that no further effort will be made to get Berry back from England to testify to the length of the drop.' That an initial effort was, however, made to get Berry to return for the inquest is evidenced in a letter written by the hangman, now in the collection of distinguished author and crime historian Jonathan Goodman:

London
England
Monday 16/88

Sir,

Having received your letter transferred from B'ford stating that you will issue a summons for my attendance at cork on the 20th inst. I beg to state that the Doctor gave is evidence in a straight forward manner and the dep'ty Governor Oxford and the warders wittnessed the Execution as well and as regards shirking my duty I do not shirk from my duty at all as it is not necessary for me to give evidence in such cases. I never do except when there is an accident occurs. If you like to send me a supeona and the money to pay my First Class Expenses to Cork and Back I will come if it will gratify your curiosity. If I do come I cannot tell you any more than what the Doctor has told you and perhaps not has much. But I am not at all proud if you send me the money to come with I shall be delighted with the second visit to Cork.

Yours Truly
J. Berry

Berry never appeared, but it was recorded in the *Illustrated Police News* of 14 January 1888 that he had given Dr Cross a drop of about 5½ feet. It also commented on the fact that members of the press were not allowed to witness the execution and that:

> . . . very little information was afforded by the officials as to the circumstances attending it; but it was stated that his coat and collar were removed to allow the halter to be properly adjusted, and that the neck of the culprit appeared to have been broken by the shock. Two clergymen accompanied him to the scaffold after he had attended the final service. The culprit partook of the Communion on Monday morning. The announcement of the execution was awaited with great interest in Dublin. He was known to a large number of persons in the Irish metropolis, and special editions of the evening papers were eagerly bought.

Berry alleviates the gravity in his *Experiences* by telling a few humorous tales, one of which he says occurred on the ferry crossing from Ireland in 1887. As he did not travel to Ireland in 1887 he may be referring to his return from the execution of Dr Cross, which was only just into the New Year. One of the passengers was terribly ill with seasickness and a toothache, proving such a nuisance to his fellow passengers and the stewards that, Berry surmised, one of the latter referred the suffering man to Berry for a cure. Begged for advice, Berry admitted that he was 'in the habit of giving drops that would instantaneously cure both the toothache and the sea-sickness, but assured him that he would not be willing to take my remedy'. The man persisted so Berry handed him one of his cards, 'and as he was a sensitive man it gave his nerves a shock that was quite sufficient to relieve him of the toothache, and me of his presence for the rest of the voyage'.

Two months elapsed before Berry's next execution, which took him to Carmarthen. David Rees, aged 25, had robbed and murdered Thomas Davies on 12 November 1887. The latter was carrying his firm's wages from Llanelly to a tin-plate works at Dafen when he was set upon and beaten by Rees and an accomplice, the two assailants subsequently absconding with the money. The accomplice was never found, but Rees was arrested, tried and, on 24 February, sentenced to death, the execution being carried out on Tuesday 13 March 1888.

Berry's next job, scheduled for Tuesday 20 March 1888, was a double execution at Hereford. He arrived at the prison on the preceding afternoon and tested the scaffold. Erected under a shed on the north-western side of the prison buildings, it was the same apparatus he had used in November 1885 for the double execution of Hill and Williams, the convicts this time being Alfred Scandrett and James Jones, both of whom had been sentenced at Herefordshire Assizes for the murder of an aged man, Phillip Ballard, at Tapsley. The two men – each of whom blamed the other during their trial, becoming involved in a tussle in the dock – had broken into their victim's house and assaulted him with an axe. Local press representatives were admitted to witness the execution, and it was noted that both prisoners were 'ghastly pale and agitated'. Neither spoke although their lips moved as though in silent prayer. Berry quickly strapped them and pulled two white caps out of his pocket, placing them over the faces of the doomed men. As the closing words of the service were being repeated he quickly stood aside and pulled the lever. He had allowed a drop of 6 feet and death was instantaneous, although the rope on which Jones was suspended was seen to quiver for about a minute whereas Scandrett's did not move. Despite intense cold a large crowd had gathered outside the gaol to see the black flag hoisted.

The Times of 21 March reported that a letter from the prison chaplain, Mr Leigh Spencer, was read at the inquest on the two men, in which he said:

> It may perhaps be a legitimate opportunity of satisfying remarkable public curiosity if I state that I received very shortly after the trial a confession from both the condemned prisoners of the true circumstances of the crime which they have expiated with their lives. Scandrett struck both blows which caused Mr. Ballard's death with the hatchet, Jones being close to him and an eye-witness.

On 27 March 1888, Berry executed George Clarke, aged 42, an ex-tailor and army pensioner who had been running a pub in Aldershot since retiring from service. He had lived with his wife and children, including an 18-year-old stepdaughter with whom he had a relationship when she was only 16, they having ended this for fear of his wife finding out. However, when the girl then met a man whom she wished to marry, Clarke, presumably in a fit of jealousy, had cut her throat while she was in bed, nearly severing her head. He was tried at Winchester Assizes before Mr Justice Field, sentenced to death, and hanged by Berry at Winchester.

Berry immediately travelled to Shrewsbury to execute William Arrowsmith on the following day. A labourer from Denton, Arrowsmith had murdered his elderly uncle, George Pickerell, aged 80, in a cottage near Whitchurch, beating the old man about the head and then cutting his throat, before stealing some property and money he knew to be in the house.

Two weeks later Berry was travelling back to Ireland for a double execution at Tralee gaol, on Saturday 29 April 1888. Daniel Moriarty and Daniel Hayes had murdered James Fitzmaurice at Lixnaw, Kerry, on 21 January. Armed with revolvers, the two men had shot the victim – an elderly farmer living at Ahabeg – in front of his daughter on a public road. Since their conviction at Wicklow Assizes the prison had been constantly guarded, by police during the day and military at night. Moriarty was a farm labourer who had been married just over a year and Hayes was an itinerant shoemaker from Tralee with several convictions for assault and a serious drink problem. Both men appeared penitent, particularly Hayes. The morning of the execution – to which the visiting justices had refused the press admission – was bright and fine and the condemned men were roused about 6.00 a.m. after a restless night. They declined breakfast and a drink and at 7.00 a.m. joined in mass with Father O'Callaghan and Father Quill. A crowd had gathered outside the gaol and a knot of people was in a field that abutted the area where the scaffold was erected in the capstan millyard inside the walls. This gathering included some of the relatives of the two prisoners, who raised a mournful dirge as the hour of execution approached. At ten minutes to eight the governor and High Sheriff entered the cell and notified the men that their time had come. Berry was in attendance and having been duly authorised immediately pinioned them. They were then led to the scaffold. Halfway up the steps Moriarty stopped as if he wished to say something, but did not do so. However, as the ropes were being adjusted he said, 'I am now going to be hung for what I am innocent of. I know nothing about it.' It was said that Moriarty's confession to the crime had been only partial.

Berry activated the drop and Moriarty died instantly, but 4 minutes elapsed before Dr Falvey, the surgeon, pronounced Hayes dead. The usual inquest was held, at which statements of the two men were read. Hayes declared his innocence and forgave those who swore his life away, whereas Moriarty declared his previous accusation against two other men was false, made only to save his own neck. Both bodies were buried in the scaffold yard (*Illustrated Police News*, 5 May 1888).

Berry conducted another execution at Tralee just a week later, on Monday 7 May, again noting he was 'always afraid to go to Ireland to hang a man, because I believed I was taking my own life in my hands'. This time the prisoner was 35-year-old James Kirby who rejoiced in the nickname 'Fox'. He had murdered Patrick Quirke, nearly 80 years old, at Liscahane, near Ardfert, Kerry, on the morning of 9 November 1887. A young man employed by Kirby, Patrick Cournane, had also been condemned to death for complicity in the crime, but his sentence was commuted to one of penal servitude for life.

Kirby was a married man with two children, and as a tenant farmer he led a comfortable life. His cousin, James William Kirby, who had married Quirke's daughter, had occupied part of an adjacent farm, but after being evicted for failing to pay rent he had moved to America, the farm being left vacant until April 1887. Quirke then took the place, paying the arrears and giving it to his grandchildren. On the day of the murder a party of armed men called Quirke out from his bed and discharged a double-barrelled shotgun into his legs. He died before aid arrived. Patrick Cournane was arrested, and after he asked why 'Fox' Kirby had not been arrested, the latter, together with a 'half-witted' boy named Buckley, was arrested the following Sunday. This was followed by several remands in custody until 10 December when Garrett Kirby, Quirke's grandson, identified Kirby as the person who had fired the shots, Buckley as the man who had called the old man downstairs, and Cournane as having also been present. On 22 February the prisoners were again identified, this time by Quirke's widow and his other grandson, who had previously been afraid to give evidence. The offenders stood trial at Wicklow Assizes, and Kirby and Cournane were found guilty, Buckley's trial being postponed.

Berry arrived at Tralee on the Sunday, having journeyed by train as far as Adfert, where a covered car and police escort awaited him. On his arrival at the prison the warders informed him he was going to hang an innocent man. (Berry wrote that 'the people of Ireland abhored the visits of the hangman and despised his office' and, adding that the Scottish people had similar feelings, observed that if the English thought the same then capital punishment would have been abolished and his offices would not be required.) Kirby received a visit from his wife and an emotional scene took place, only ending when he was dragged away from her and the two broke down. Such scenes always played on the minds of the warders and, of course, Berry himself. It was in his account of this case (*The Post*, 9 May 1914) that Berry noted:

> During the time I was hangman of England it was these last interviews which affected me most, and if possible I always studied to be out of the gaol at the hour fixed for them to take place.
>
> So vivid an impression did the visit of the wives and children of the Edinburgh poachers make on my mind at my

first execution, that years afterwards I used to see their faces in my room at nights. If ever a man was haunted, it was James Berry, but, curiously enough, I ceased to be troubled and slept like an innocent child after I had burned the relics I had left of my victims.

Berry checked the scaffold on the Sunday evening and found it to be in good order. He then went to the cell, where he peeped at Kirby, who was pacing back and forth talking to the warders.

The morning of the execution was dull and, besides the police, only a few women and children were in the vicinity of the gaol. Kirby had spent a restless night but appeared to have cheered up on the Monday morning and was calm as he took part in religious ministrations. Shortly before eight o'clock the High Sheriff went through the formality of taking possession of the condemned man, then handed him to Berry. As he was pinioned, Kirby stated, 'I am going before my God, and as sure as there is a God in heaven I never handled a firearm or shot you, Patrick Quirke.'

The procession formed and wended its way to the scaffold. Kirby ascended the steps calmly and 'almost assisted the hangman in the discharge of his duties', but remained silent. Death was instantaneous. At the inquest that followed the governor gave formal evidence and, in answer to a juror, stated that when being pinioned Kirby had declared his innocence. He left no written statement. Evidence was also given by the sub-sheriff and the prison surgeon, who deposed that death was caused by dislocation of the upper portion of the spine.

Berry described leaving the prison afterwards:

After the execution was over a carriage was brought to the gaol for me, and I was taken across the fields to the station by a mounted escort. A large crowd had assembled to meet me, but the police kept them well in hand until I got into the carriage. They then surged around, and as the train steamed out they booed themselves hoarse, and, shaking their fists, told me what they would do with me if ever I fell into their hands.

They did not need to tell me that to make me miserable. The

fact that an innocent, or a man, leastways, that I believed innocent, had been done to death was sufficient to plunge me into the deepest melancholy, and it was not until many weeks after my visit to Ireland that I began to recover from the nervous breakdown which overtook me. (*The Post*, 9 May 1914)

Cournane, following his reprieve, had been taken to Dublin the previous week, declaring during the journey that he was content to serve a prison sentence for his part in the crime, and adding that Kirby was guilty (*Illustrated Police News*, 12 May 1888).

Despite his claimed 'breakdown', Berry's next execution was in Manchester only a week later, on 15 May 1888. The condemned man, John Alfred Gell, aged 32 and unemployed, was another prisoner to proclaim his innocence. He had been sentenced for the murder of Mrs Mary Miller, aged 46, at Moston, a woman with whom he had been on intimate terms. She was his landlady and, having been separated from her husband for nine years, often allowed Gell to stay without paying rent. Her daughter, Isabella, did not approve, and there were frequent arguments. On one occasion, Gell had struck Isabella, saying that he would 'finish' both her and her mother. Finally Mrs Miller told Gell to find another job or other lodgings. On 1 March Gell left the house at 7 a.m. but returned later, by the rear entrance, and attacked the daughter, striking her twice in the head. She ran out of the house, upon which he then attacked Mrs Miller with an axe, leaving this close to her as she lay dying. A police officer nearby heard the disturbance at the house and arrested Gell as he attempted to flee. The latter admitted that he had intended to kill Isabella Miller as well and then to commit suicide.

At his trial, the defence counsel suggested that some other person was responsible for the murder, despite the strong evidence to the contrary. The state of Gell's mind appeared to be shown in a document found on him. It read:

You have done me no harm with your tongue, but you have hurt me worse. I think that you are a very deep, crafty woman, quite capable of answering the questions the jury may ask. May the Lord forgive you as freely as I do. It is best known to yourself what you have done. I die a broken-hearted lover of Mary Miller. Good-bye, darling; be true to the next.- Alf. (*Thomson's*, 9 April 1927)

Berry recorded that when he left Bradford for the short journey to Manchester, he went over his ropes and selected the one with which he had hanged Dr Cross, this being 'kept for brave men'. He had heard about Gell's exemplary behaviour in prison, he, like so many of Berry's victims, conducting himself throughout in a steadfast manner and unswervingly maintaining his innocence. Struck by the enormous strength of the man when he glanced at Gell through the bars of the cell door, Berry resolved to give him a long drop, and, perhaps with the recent memory of the struggle with Sowery in mind, he decided to have extra warders at the scaffold in case Gell caused trouble. The night before his execution Gell slept well and, on awaking, he ate breakfast of tea and buttered bread, before listening to the ministrations of the Revd Mr Dreaper, who attended him. When Berry arrived in the condemned cell Gell gave a start and his face grew pale, but he pulled himself together and walked over to meet his executioner.

'Good morning, John. It is about time we were going out of here. Keep a stout heart,' said Berry.

'Oh, I am not afraid to die,' replied Gell.

'I am glad to hear it, and I hope you will give me no more trouble than you can help,' advised Berry.

'I won't give you any trouble, if you give me none,' he replied.

'I will be as merciful as I can. Let me put these straps on you now,' said Berry.

As Berry pinioned him, perhaps fully realising the end was near, Gell exclaimed, 'Isabella Miller, I die an innocent man.'

This caused Berry to pause, making him again wonder if he might be about to hang an innocent man. One of the officials motioned him to hurry, so he completed fastening the straps and the procession formed up. The scaffold at Strangeways was only 10 yards from the condemned cell. It was a dull cold morning, but Gell remained resolute, apparently undaunted by the sight of the noose dangling from the beam above him. The chaplain repeated the words of the service while Berry busied himself with the final preparations. It was then, as Berry was adjusting the straps, that Gell made a whispered request to the hangman.

'Wait a minute. I want to speak. Give me a minute Mr. Berry, I have something to say to those gentlemen. It is the last request of a dying man. Do not deny me it.'

Without waiting for assent or denial, he squared his shoulders and looked towards the reporters who were present and made a dying declaration of his innocence, in a solemn voice, 'Isabella Miller, I hope you have now had your revenge. Good-bye! God bless you! I die an innocent man!'

By this time Berry had adjusted the noose and was about to place the white cap over his face, when Gell shouted, 'The Lord have mercy on my soul! I am now about to leave this earth forever.'

Berry drew the lever and the trap opened with a horrible noise, Gell disappearing from view. For a considerable time afterwards Berry worried that he had hanged another innocent man. At the very least, he observed, the condemned man had convinced himself that he hadn't committed the crime (*The Post*, 3 January 1914).

There was an execution a week later, at Leeds, on 22 May 1888. James William Richardson, aged 23, a brick maker from Barnsley, had shot his foreman, William Berridge, after a dispute at the factory on 21 March. The executioner on this occasion was James Billington. Berry's next execution was not until Tuesday 17 July 1888 at Oxford. Robert Upton, a builder's labourer, had beaten his wife Emma to death with an iron bar at Milton-under-Wychwood on 23 May, subsequently being sentenced to death by Mr Justice George Denman at Oxford Assizes on 23 June. Berry arrived in Oxford at 6 p.m. on the Monday, and, in the presence of the prison governor, Lt Col Henry Bevan Isaacson, together with the under-sheriff, chaplain, surgeon, chief and under-warders, and three press reporters, hanged him at Oxford Castle, giving a drop of 5 feet and, as usual, allowing the body to hang for an hour before it was taken down.

After the execution, Berry was seen to take a walk into the town, smoking a cigar and taking refreshment at a well-known hostelry. He afterwards visited the police court, but his presence did not attract much attention, only a few knowing who he was.

At noon, the inquest was held on Upton, the body having been placed in a shell laid over the drop. Members of the jury had heard there had been some mishap and insisted on seeing the body more closely. A sheet that had been thrown over the coffin was pulled back, revealing a gash in the front of the neck, laying open the whole of the soft parts and showing that the spinal column had been cut through. It seemed amazing that decapitation had not resulted. Despite the horrific neck injuries however, Upton's face, we are told,

> . . . wore a singularly pleasing and calm appearance. The wrinkles, which years had worn into it, were all smoothed out; the hands were still clasped as they were when he stood in life, beneath the gallows tree; the eyes were closed; and the lips only slightly apart. His clothes were saturated with blood from the wound opened in the neck in the course of execution, but, beyond this, there was nothing to tell that he had died a violent death. (*The Oxford Times*, 21 July 1888)

Berry must have again suffered discomfort as he waited to see if he would be called at the inquest. At this, the prison governor described the execution, observing that though Upton had been hanged in the usual way, his head had been nearly severed from the body, death apparently having been instantaneous. The Medical Officer, Henry Banks Spencer, declared there to be a very considerable difference between this execution and others he had seen. The rope used had been of the usual texture, but, despite Berry having told him before the execution that the drop was to be 5 feet, having previously said it would be 5 feet 6 inches, in his estimation the drop had been nearer 7 feet, an excess that had surprised him. The skin, windpipe, gullet, and all soft parts of the side and neck were torn through, and the spinal column severed, the body having remained suspended for an hour supported only by the muscles and ligaments behind the spinal cord. Upton, described at the inquest as 61 years of age, 5 feet 10½ inches tall and weighing 147 pounds on his arrival at the prison, was a tall thin man with a small neck. In the opinion of the surgeon a much shorter drop would still have resulted in instant death and would not have caused the same amount of laceration. He stated that at the last execution he had witnessed a drop of about 3 feet had been used, whereas in this case, after the lever was drawn, Upton had disappeared from the scaffold, the top of his head being just visible about a foot and a half beneath the scaffold, the surgeon thus estimating the length of the rope to be about 10 feet. Further describing the awful scene Mr Spencer stated that there had been a great flow of blood, the sound of which had been like water running from a tap.

The jury requested that Berry should be called, and the hangman entered and took the stand. The coroner announced that he understood Berry was desirous of tendering evidence, to which Berry replied, 'I am not desirous of giving evidence, but if you wish it I will, although there is no law in the land to compel me to do so.'

The coroner, somewhat disgruntled at this challenge to his authority, said, 'I have called you; you are here in my presence; and you are bound to answer on oath such questions as I or the Jury may put to you.'

Berry said, 'There is no law.'

The coroner responded, 'I say there is.'

Berry said, 'I don't want to give evidence. I don't offer any, but I will give evidence if you wish me to do so.'

The foreman of the jury, Mr John Bacon, said, 'I asked on my own behalf, and I think several other Jurymen agree with me, that you should give evidence.'

Berry replied, 'Very well, Mr. Coroner, and gentlemen.'

Berry was sworn in and then stated:

I am the person who carried out the sentence of death on Robert Upton this morning. I used the same means as I usually do; exactly. The rope had only been once used before. I measured five feet of rope out with a tape, before the execution, and fixed the rope with that length of drop. My reason for fixing upon five feet was because, where persons are getting into years, I do not give them an extra long drop. I calculated the height, weight, and age of the man. The height given me was five feet ten and a-half, and the weight 147lbs., but I think that has increased since his admission to the prison. I took a rough guess from the case from that of Dr. Cross who was of a similar build, some years older, and a lot heavier. I executed him at Cork, and there was not a drop of blood to be seen. He was not injured in any way. Upton's neck was thinner than that of Dr. Cross. The Chief Warder told me last night that Upton had a thin neck, but I did not examine it. This morning, when fastening the rope, I found that the skin was shrivelled, and the muscles brittle. I knew before I pulled the lever what would happen, but it was too late to alter the rope, or the drop. I have had two or three cases of this kind, where men have been old and infirm. You cannot help it, you know. You find a tree in which the sap has gone, and, of course, it will snap in the wind, and that is just what happened here. I told the doctor that I would give the man a drop of five feet six, and he said five feet would be ample. After the man fell, the rope had stretched a considerable deal, perhaps about eight or ten inches. I have known ropes stretch a foot and a-half. My ropes are all made in Government prisons, and no rope, except it stretches, can be used for purposes of this kind. The rope was a Government regulation one, with a brass thimble at one end. I have examined the rope since, and it is not in the slightest injured. We cannot regulate the drop to the age, weight, condition of a man like this, and the state of his neck. Had I given him three feet six it would have been just the same. A hundred thousand years' experience would not have made any difference to me, unless I had previously seen Upton in the cell, and examined his neck without his knowing it. When the flesh is wrinkled, and there is no nutrition in it, this must happen. If I had given the man two feet six inches drop, and had he fidgeted, the press would have been down upon me. I never saw a jury sit so long on a case as over a bit of a job like this. In other parts of the country it would have been dismissed long before.

Berry had given an aggressive and pseudo-scientific argument. It is unlikely that a previously used rope could have stretched so much if properly attached to the beam. From the foregoing evidence it seems that Berry had allowed too great a drop, certainly well in excess of 6 feet, and that the horrendous wounds were a result of this. Apparently, however, his tirade had the desired effect, at least as far as he was concerned. Berry may have thought that he was above the law, however he was not and in reality coroners had very great powers in their investigations into causes of death. The foreman of the jury declared that the explanation, as far as it went, cleared up some doubts he and the others had, and the coroner, seeing the Yorkshireman's stubborn attitude, quickly brought matters to a close with the following words, 'I do not think we can carry the evidence any further. You have heard the account of the occurrence from the fountain head. There are difficulties in these matters, as Berry has told you. Are you satisfied that the proper man has been hanged, and that the sentence has been properly carried out?' The jury concurred and the usual verdict was entered.

What is interesting in this episode is the fact that Berry was obliged to describe his actions and methods in some detail, and in a public forum. It also reveals his way of reacting to criticism, and the impact of his stubborn and self-important character. Though the coroner was in charge, he obviously realised the futility of arguing with the executioner and so closed the matter before it got out of hand. Berry had again had the last word.

Berry left Oxford by train at shortly after 4 p.m. bound for Worcester, where he was due to conduct an execution on the following day, 18 July. Thomas Wyre, aged 30, was an agricultural labourer who lived with his wife and two children at Wolverly near Kidderminster. Having frequently fallen out with each other, the wife finally told him they should separate, and on 3 March she packed her bags, telling him that she would care for the elder of their two children while he could care for the youngest, James, a 4-year-old boy. Wyre told his wife that he would take the boy to his parents, but instead he murdered him, workmen finding the unrecognisable body in a well at Castle Hill, Wolverly on 2 June. Identification was made by way of the clothing, and Wyre was arrested. He was convicted at Worcester Assizes on 31 June before Mr Justice Denman, and sentence of death was passed, the wretched Wyre subsequently confessing his crime to the prison chaplain. On Wednesday 18 July 1888 he walked, without assistance, to his doom. Berry allowed a drop of 6 feet, and the bolt was drawn as the hour struck. Wyre's neck was broken and death was instantaneous.

On 13 April 1888 the long-awaited Aberdare Report on Capital Punishment was submitted to the Home Office and arrangements made for its printing and circulation. It made mention of the recent near-decapitation of Robert Upton at Oxford, and all aspects of the process of capital punishment were looked at and reported on, including the selection of the executioner, the method of execution and the construction of the gallows. Among other things, it highlighted the dangers of too short a drop resulting in strangulation and too great a drop resulting in decapitation or severe throat injury. However, it clearly indicated that a quick death, even if it resulted in severe injuries to the neck, was preferable to a slow death by asphyxiation. The main recommendations concerned the standardisation of the rope, the scaffold and its costing. It also included a table of drops. Suggested improvements included tying up any slack in the rope, and adopting an adjustable chain on the gallows beam to which the rope with a brass eye could be attached with a 'D' ring. This avoided the less exact method of the hangman tying the rope to the chain or hook on the beam. The Committee had heard of the 'hangman's levees' in pubs and other discreditable conduct including the sale of used ropes and drinking to bolster confidence. This led to the requirement for the hangman to remain in the prison on the eve of the execution and the rationing of alcoholic consumption. Hopefully things would improve, but overall there was little direct criticism of James Berry.

22

The shadow of the Ripper

'There was one large wound over her heart . . .'

Berry's next execution took him to Strangeways Prison in Mancester and was scheduled for 8 a.m. on Tuesday 7 August 1888. At 6 a.m. the condemned man rose and was joined by the chaplain. The culprit was John Jackson, alias Charles Wood Firth, a 33-year-old convict who had been serving a sentence of six months imposed in April for an offence of burglary. As he had some experience as a plumber he was asked to do some work at the prison matron's house. He agreed and on 22 May was taken to the house by assistant warder Ralph Webb, aged 45. Jackson, however, took the opportunity to escape, beating Webb to death in the room, after which he locked the door and made a hole in the ceiling through which he escaped. A large manhunt was started and a few weeks later he was arrested in Bradford after breaking into a house. Found guilty before Mr Justice Grantham at Manchester Assizes, he was sentenced to death. Despite a petition with over 20,000 signatures, the Home Secretary, Henry Matthews, could find no reason to commute the sentence. Jackson made no detailed confession, but admitted his guilt to the chaplain, stating that he had struck the warder when his back was turned to him. The edition of *The Times* that reported this also carried details of Jackson's last moments:

. . . At a quarter before 8 Berry, the executioner, entered the cell and pinioned him. Only 16 paces separated the condemned cell from the scaffold. The culprit took his place in the usual procession with a firm step, and made the response to the prayers on the way to the scaffold. Death appeared to be instantaneous . . . The usual inquest was held.

Berry stated that he had befriended warder Ralph Webb on previous visits to the prison, Webb having been his personal attendant there and having invited him to spend half a day in Manchester when he had last been there, for the execution of Gell, an offer that Berry had declined. Strangely, however, Berry claimed it had grieved him to hang Jackson, since the latter had not intended to kill the warder. Webb's widow was allowed a pension of £15 a year (to which her husband would have been entitled) and £5 a year for her child. Subscription funds raised for her amounted to £145.

Just three days later, on Friday 10 August 1888, a dull and gloomy morning with heavy rain, Berry executed Arthur Thomas Delaney at Derby. Delaney, a fitter aged 21, had murdered his wife in April at Chesterfield. He and his wife had endured an unhappy marriage during which he often assaulted her. On the fatal occasion that he struck her with a poker, she died subsequently in Chesterfield Hospital. According to Berry, Delaney afterwards conducted himself with utter callousness, but *The Times* report of his execution states that he paid great attention to the exhortations of the chaplain and fervently responded to his prayers.

The hanging itself is described by Berry, in an account published in *The Post* of 1 August 1914, as 'one of the few executions I bungled'. He continues:

'When I stood upon the scaffold and looked at my man I knew before I pulled the lever what was going to happen, but it was too late to avert a terrible tragedy. If I had stopped there and then to alter the length of the rope the press and public would have been down upon me, and it is possible that I would never have hanged another man.'

Berry described Delaney's last moments thus:

The tolling of the bell heralded the approach of the Under-Sheriff and his officers, and, according to form, he demanded from the Governor the body of Arthur Delaney for execution.

The procession then proceeded to the condemned cell, which was situated on the left of the large hall, and between two warders Delaney was brought out. Several warders headed the procession, then followed the chief warder and the Governor.

Next came the prisoner, whom I had already pinioned, the gaol chaplain, in his white surplice, being on his right hand a little in advance.

Behind followed the surgeons and the Under-Sheriff, and his clerk with the Under-Sheriff's officer, carrying black wands, brought up the rear.

Slowly the procession moved along past the steps to the entrance hall, where I went on in front to complete my arrangements. The chaplain slowly repeated the solemn Church of England burial service, interrupted here and there by the deep toll of the bell.

A few yards further the prisoner passed his already-dug grave, and beyond it I pinioned his arms and conducted him round the corner in full sight of the covered-over scaffold. Delaney did not flinch, but walked with a firm, quick step, with head erect, muttering as if in prayer.

On arriving at the foot of the scaffold he gave a rapid glance at the crowd assembled to see him die, and several warders stationed on the left of the scaffold then walked up the sloping flags which led to the foot of the scaffold, Delaney walking between them with a jaunty air, apparently unconcerned.

He approached the steps, and in a clear, steady voice he said – 'Lord into Thy hands I commit my spirit.'

On arriving at the top of the steps he said – 'Lord have mercy on my soul,' and he then walked firmly to the drop, where I pinioned his legs.

'Lord Jesus have mercy on my soul,' were the words that came unfaltering and clear.

He took his last look on earth and sun and day. I adjusted the rope, and, stepping back, pulled the lever.

The governor raised his hand. The signal was understood by a warder stationed on the turret of the gaol, and slowly the black flag was fluttered out on the freshening breeze, telling to those waiting outside that Delaney had paid the dread penalty of the law by forfeiting his life for the life he so cruelly took, and had gone from life to death to appear before Him to whom 'all hearts are open, all desires known, and from whom no secrets are hid'.

The man had disappeared, but the rope continued to quiver, and for some moments the doctors and myself stood looking into the pit.

A death-like silence prevailed, and all in the crowd knew that Delaney was slowly dying.

This was yet another unfortunate incident to prey on Berry's mind, but he did console himself with the fact that there was no doubt that the man was a cruel murderer.

The same day a question was raised in the House of Commons over methods of execution. Sir T. Robinson asked the Home Secretary if he was aware of a recent report addressed to the Governor of the State of New York, USA, as to the best mode of conducting an execution in that state. Apparently, methods recommended included electricity or the injection of morphia, 'or by the lethal chamber invented for the painless killing of the lower animals by Dr. B.W. Richardson'. The questioner wished to know if these, '. . . or any other system of executing criminals is more in accordance with the humane feelings of the present day than the barbarous and unscientific method now practiced in this country'. Henry Matthews replied in the negative. He indicated that though he was aware of a recent Act passed in the State of New York concerning the infliction of the death penalty by electricity, the government was not as yet prepared to introduce legislation to alter the method of carrying out executions, although he would give 'careful consideration' to the suggestions of his honourable friend.

Despite the services of the executioner being regularly called upon, reprieves were nonetheless quite frequent. On Tuesday 14 August the governor of Newgate Prison received a communication from the Home Secretary indicating that a reprieve had been granted for Galletly, 'the Regent's Park murderer', who had been entered into Berry's diary for the following Tuesday. For these reprieves Berry received a payment of £5.

At 8 a.m. on Wednesday 15 August 1888 Berry conducted another execution within the walls of Chelmsford Prison. The prisoner was George Sergent, a railway labourer aged 29, who had murdered his wife at Wakes Colne. A dissolute man, Sergent had treated his 20-year-old wife so badly that she returned to her parents, and though he had repeatedly encouraged her to return, his attempts had been to no avail. He finally visited her again on the morning of 17 July, cutting her throat and stabbing her behind the ear in the presence of her mother and sister. Convicted of the cruel murder he became penitent and walked firmly to the scaffold. Despite his neck being broken by the fall, he struggled rather violently on the end of the rope for a few seconds.

Within a week Berry received another £5 for a reprieve when the Home Secretary announced that the Queen was happy to respite the sentence of death passed on a black ship's steward, Charles Arthur, at Liverpool Assizes. This was for the murder of Captain Barlie on the high seas while on board the ship *Daventry Hall*, Arthur having stabbed him in his berth. Petitions raised on this occasion were successful, it being shown that the unfortunate man had been ill-treated by the captain (*The Times*, 20 August 1888).

Berry had another double execution to add to his tally on Tuesday 28 August 1888, this time at Winson Green Prison, Birmingham. The prisoners were George Nathaniel Daniels, aged 29, a stationer's porter, and Harry Benjamin Jones, aged 25, a mechanic.

Daniels, a widower with two children, was a native of Worcester and had been courting Emma Elizabeth Hastings, the daughter of the landlord of the Golden Elephant beerhouse in Castle Street, Birmingham. On the evening of 14 April 1888 he had gone to the hostelry where he spent time with Emma. At eleven o'clock he was in the sitting room on his own and Emma was plaiting her sister's hair in the kitchen. Daniels went to the kitchen and asked her to accompany him to the door. She said she would when she was finished, so he went and stood by the fireplace, but a moment or so later there was a shot and Emma fell to the floor. A second shot was fired, both shots being to the head. There had been no quarrel and Daniels was quite sober. His motive was unclear, but it seems he had been despondent of late and had been drinking and losing money on the horses. He had also been trying to break off his engagement with Emma, though after the shooting he expressed remorse and promised to marry her if she recovered. She was taken to hospital but died several days later, on 20 April. A plea was entered on the grounds of insanity, this running in the family, but it was proved he was of sound mind when he committed the murder and the plea failed. He left the care of his children to his brother in Worcester.

As for Jones, he had for many years been a lodger with a family named Harris at Aston. He became enamoured of Mrs Harris, although she denied giving him any encouragement. On 11 June 1888, Mr Harris, who was frequently away from home, returned unexpectedly, presumably catching his wife in some sort of compromising situation with Jones, upon which Mrs Harris told Jones he would have to live elsewhere. Unable to accept this, he returned three days later and shot both Mr and Mrs Harris, wounding them in the shoulder. He then fired at Florence Mabel Harris, aged 2½, before striking her on the head with his revolver, fracturing her skull (an injury that subsequently led to her death). Not content, he turned next to a baby, just a few months old, lying in bed, striking the child on the head with the end of his revolver, after which he again attacked Mrs Harris and beat her. Finally, some men arrived and detained him. Jones afterwards claimed that he was the father of the murdered infant and the baby.

Both men were convicted and sentenced to death, afterwards paying great attention to the ministrations of the prison chaplain as they awaited their fate and expressing deep sorrow for the crimes they had committed. The inadequate brick shed, initially erected for the execution of Henry Kimberley in March 1885, was so small that the witnessing officials and reporters almost filled it. However, with its ground-level drop it was better than having a raised platform. The representative of *The Birmingham Daily Post* described the proceedings in excruciating detail:

Across the shed stretches a great beam, from which, at a quarter to eight yesterday morning, two ropes were dangling, ready noosed, and each noose with a bone washer to secure the knot from any chance of a slip. The ropes looked new, but Berry – an unpleasantly communicative person, with an ill concealed relish for his job – volunteers the information that each has been used once before . . . On the trap Berry had written the names of the condemned men and their weights, and the length of the drop to be given to each, and had rudely marked the position in which each was to stand. Daniels's weight was put down at 10st. 2lb., and he was to be given a drop of 6ft.; and Jones, whose weight was 9st. 13lb. was to be given a drop of 6ft. 6in. At the last moment, on the advice of the prison surgeon, the positions were reversed, and Jones was given the longer drop. At about seven minutes before eight, Berry, having given a final look to the preparations, left the shed for the condemned cell in order to pinion his men. There was about five minutes of nervous waiting, during which nothing was to be heard but the ceaseless patter of the rain and the sharp sound of the gaol minute – bell, as it slowly counted out the remaining moments of two terribly misused lives – five minutes that seemed like hours to those who stood against the white walls of the place of death, reading over and over again the rough chalk marks on the floor and trying to realise the full meaning of the dread scene they were about to witness. To the onlookers the most terrible feature of the business was the utter commonplaceness of the surroundings and the preparations. One felt keenly that some display of awe-inspiring accessories – even the hushed silence of the multitudes which used to watch the public executions – would have marvellously relieved the tension. But in this whitewashed outhouse, behind innumerable bolts and bars, and in the presence of scarcely a dozen privileged persons, there was an appalling bluntness and plainness about this doing to death in which one had a shuddering sense of personal complicity . . .

It is still a few seconds before eight o'clock when the sound of heavy feet on the pathway blends with the noise of the beating rain, and the next moment the listening ears of those who wait in the place of execution catch the broken strains of the chaplain's voice as he reads to living ears the service for the dead. Nothing can be seen of the procession until it actually reaches the doorway . . . Jones walks unbidden to the trap after a quick glance round the chamber, and he takes his stand in the position allotted to the man who is to die with him, but one of the warders touches his shoulder, and he instantly changes his place. Daniels is placed side by side with him, both men with their backs to the reporters and their faces to the chaplain. It is, perhaps, scarcely a minute before all is over, but how terribly each second lingered. There is no sound save the quick movements of Berry, and the hoarse voice of the chaplain, as, leaning against the wall, his face pale as death, and his dry tongue refusing to do its office, he stumbles almost blindly through scattered passages in the burial service. Berry's preparations are completed with miraculous smoothness and rapidity. The two men stand motionless, to all appearance absolutely incapable of any real sense of what is passing round them – dazed into nerveless torpor. Each, as the white cap is pulled over his face, murmers, 'Lord, receive my spirit. Oh, Lord, receive my soul.' Then the noose is placed round the neck of each, and Berry springs lightly to the lever and knocks away the piece of wood that blocks its working. Then with a great effort one shuts one's eyes. There is a scuffle and a thud, and when one opens one's eyes again all is over, the men have disappeared, and over the cavity stands Berry steadying each rope with his hand with a dreadful air of professional pride. The spectators step up, and look down the trap at the two men hanging in their hideous gravel-coloured garb. Both men have died on the instant. Daniels hangs like a log, without a twitch or a tremor, but at regular intervals muscular contortions run through Jones's frame, giving him a horrible appearance of breathing in deep short gasps. This last horror is too much, and one hastens quickly from the cell into the fresh air. But so swift and precise, with such machine-like dexterity, has been the execution, that those who have witnessed it [struggle] in vain to realise that they have watched two human beings, who five minutes ago were full of lusty life, swing in a moment into the presence of the fearful mysteries of death and eternity.

Both men had showed fortitude when taking their place on the scaffold. The usual inquest was held and it was revealed that Daniels's spinal cord was severed as the result of a broken neck, but in the case of Jones the vertebrae were not broken and death was due to asphyxiation, and therefore not instant. This leaves the question of why the doctor had made the strange decision to change the positions of the culprits on the drop. Surely the blame should not be laid at Berry's door.

Tuesday 7 August 1888 was to be recorded in the annals of crime for reasons other than the execution of John Jackson. While the prisoner spent a restless night in the condemned cell, a brutal murder took place further south, in London. It was a ferocious crime and one that heralded the infamous series of atrocities known as the Whitechapel murders. No known culprit was ever brought to justice and it was never proven that all the murders were committed by the same hand, but nonetheless the name 'Jack the Ripper' would go down in history and mystery in relation to the horrific incidents involved. Whether this unknown killer was responsible for the murder in question will never be known. The initial facts were reported in *The Times* of Wednesday 8 August 1888:

SUPPOSED MURDER. – The dead body of a young woman, aged about 32, and not yet definitely identified, was early yesterday morning found on some stone steps at 37, George-yard-buildings, a block of model dwellings in Whitechapel. There was one large wound over her heart, while several other injuries of the nature of stabs were on her body. Francis Hewitt, the superintendent of the dwellings, stated that it was believed the deceased was seen in the company of some soldiers who frequented a publichouse on Monday evening. The injuries on the deceased are, it is stated, not unlike bayonet wounds, and the police are now making inquiries into the case.

The victim was later identified as Martha Tabram, or Turner, aged 39, a prostitute. An extensive police investigation, led by Inspector Reid of the Whitechapel CID, failed to identify an offender.

On Friday 31 August a further brutal murder occurred in the East End of London when another casual prostitute, Mary Ann Nichols, aged 43, was murdered in Buck's Row, Whitechapel. The body was discovered in the street at 3.40 a.m., her throat having been cut and the abdomen mutilated. The press immediately linked this killing with that of Tabram and another prostitute street murder in Whitechapel in early April 1888, when Emma Elizabeth Smith had been attacked and fatally wounded by a street gang. On 1 September 1888 the papers announced that there was a maniac abroad in the streets of the East End.

On Saturday 8 September 1888 greater sensation and panic was caused by the discovery, at 6 a.m., of the hideously mutilated body of another poverty-stricken streetwalker in the backyard of a shabby tenement at 29 Hanbury Street, Spitalfields in the East End of London. The victim this time was Annie Chapman, aged 47. Her throat had been cut down to the vertebrae, she had been disembowelled and her uterus had been taken away by her killer. The story of the Whitechapel murders was now big news and detectives from Scotland Yard, led by Inspector Frederick Abberline, were engaged in the hunt for the elusive killer.

On Thursday 27 September 1888 the editor of the Central News Agency in the City of London received a letter, written in red ink, purporting to come from the Whitechapel murderer, who claimed he was 'down on whores and I shant quit ripping them till I do get buckled'. He signed himself 'Jack the Ripper'. Details of this letter were published in the press at the beginning of the following week and caused further sensation. In the East End of London the unknown murderer struck again in the early hours of Sunday 30 September, when two more casual prostitutes were savagely killed. The body of Elizabeth Stride, aged 44, was found in the entrance to a yard at the International Working Men's Educational Club in Berner Street, St George's-in-the-East. She was found at about 1 a.m., her throat having been cut, but there was no other mutilation. At 1.45 a.m. the second victim of the night, Catherine Eddowes, aged 43, was found in the south corner of Mitre Square, Aldgate, a short distance away. Her throat had been cut, and there was both facial and abdominal mutilation. The main part of her womb and her left kidney had been taken away by her killer, who had escaped without trace.

In the early hours of Friday 9 November 1888 another prostitute was murdered in the East End of London, at 13 Miller's Court, 26 Dorset Street, Spitalfields. The victim, known as Mary Jane Kelly, aged 25, had been killed in her wooden-framed bed in a single room that she rented. The mutilation this time was on an unprecedented scale in the series, the killer having carried out a virtual autopsy. The throat had been cut to the vertebrae, the face fearfully mutilated,

WHAT YOU GET FOR BREAKING THE LAWS OF THIS COUNTRY

The title slide for Berry's magic lantern
show (see Chapter 32).
(Photo credit: Madame Tussauds)

James Berry at the age of 33 – this is
the 'Cabinet' photograph of himself
given by Berry to publican Dan
Dominic of The Golden Fleece,
Nottingham in August 1885 (see
Chapter Ten). (Photograph from
author's collection)

Quote
No.

Bradford, ... 189
YORKS.

Sir,

I beg leave to state in reply to your letter
of the .... that I
am prepared to undertake the execution you name of
....
at .... on the ....
I also beg leave to state that my terms are as
follows: £10 for the execution, £5 if the condemned
is reprieved, together with all travelling expenses.
Awaiting your reply,
I am, Sir,
Your obedient Servant,
James Berry.

The High Sheriff,
for the County of ....

xample of a page from Berry's Execution
Invoice Book.

James Berry in his police uniform with
a 'young criminal' handcuffed to him.
Unhappy with his lot in the force
Berry resigned. Image from one of
Berry's own lantern slides (see
Chapter Three). (Photo Credit:
Madame Tussaud's)

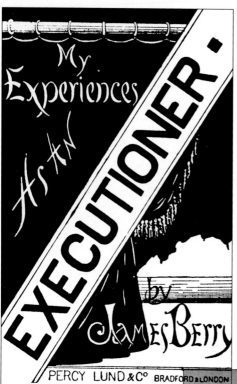

The cover of James Berry's now exceedingly rare book *My Experiences as an Executioner* – Berry claimed that he destroyed half the print run and copies now change hands at a price of £300 plus.

Portrait of James Berry used as a frontispiece in his 1892 book *My Experiences as an Executioner* – this was how he looked at the time he retired as executioner.

William Marwood – public executioner from 1872–1883. The hangman who introduced the 'long drop' to English executions, he was more of a technician than Calcraft. (A rare signed photo in the author's collection)

William Calcraft – public exectioner 1829–1874, the longest serving Victorian hangman. He was generally viewed as a 'bungler' and his victims were usually strangled as he used a short drop.

Moses Shrimpton – poacher turned killer. Convicted for the murder of a police constable he was hanged at Worcester on 25 May 1885. Berry gave him too great a drop resulting in near-decapitation (see Chapter Nine).

John 'Babbacombe' Lee – shown in this rare photograph from Berry's own lantern slide show. This shows Lee as he would have looked at the time of Berry's failure to hang him (see Chapter Eight). (Photo Credit: Madame Tussaud's)

The Glen, Babbacombe, near Torquay, scene of the murder of Miss Emma Keyse on 1[?] November 1884, allegedly by her young employee John Lee. Sentenced to die on 23 February 1885, he became famous as 'the man they could not hang' (see Chapter Eight).

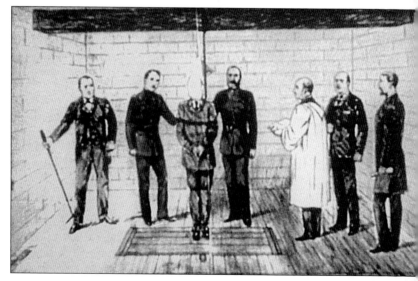

Berry's own lantern slide depicting the failed attempt to hang John 'Babbacombe' Lee. The gallows was constructed in the prison coach-house, the pit being dug into the floo[?] (see Chapter Eight). (Photo Credit: Madame Tussaud's)

Standard letter written by Berry to the Under Sheriff of Norwich offering his services in the pending execution of John Thurston on 9 February 1886.
(Via Richard Spendlove)

The celebrated trial of Mrs Florence Maybrick in August 1889, for poisoning her husband at Liverpool resulted in Berry and Dr Forbes Winslow having 'something to say' in the press. Marked for execution by Berry, she was then reprieved. This cartoon appeared in the satirical *Moonshine* (see Chapter Twenty Six).

1 Bilton Place
City Road
Bradford
Yorks

Sir.

I received your telegram stating that you accepted my services on Wednesday Feb 10th all been well I shall arrive all about the same time I arrived before, I shall go straight to the Prison on my arrival in Norwich. You can depend on me been there

Yours Most Humble
& Obed.t Servant
James Berry
Executioner

Clement Taylor Esq.t
Under Sheriff
Oxford Place
Norwich.

MOONSHINE.   [Aug. 31, 1889.

THE QUESTION OF CAPITAL PUNISHMENT

Mr. Rider Haggard goes to Assyria to collect material for a new novel. Oh, well! This *is* going to work in Assyria's manner.

We are "sick to death" of the Maybrick Case, and of everybody and everything connected with it.

It is gravely stated by the *Echo* that Lord Tennyson walks two or three miles daily. Of course, he goes out to see whether there is any rime on the grass. In his more effusive days there is little doubt but that he has been want out to metre by moonlight alone.

Major Urquhart has formed a camp at Deal, which to give a number of poor boys a short holiday. The lads declare they prefer Deal to birch by day.

The Duke and Duchess of Fife have proceeded to Mar Lodge. It is certainly not within our experience that a newly married couple should be eager to go to the place where Ma(r) Lodge-is.

The sea monster has already appeared. This time it appears to be of French extraction. With a view to its own preservation, the fish judiciously came ashore near Cannes.

Mr. W. H Smith might be styled "The Bland Old Man," were it not that he occasionally varies his general geniality by giving some quibblesome questioner "one from the shoulder."

The height of absurdity.—Attempting to propel a punt with a tadpole.

MR. BERRY (TO DR FORBES WINSLOW): "You've always got something to say."

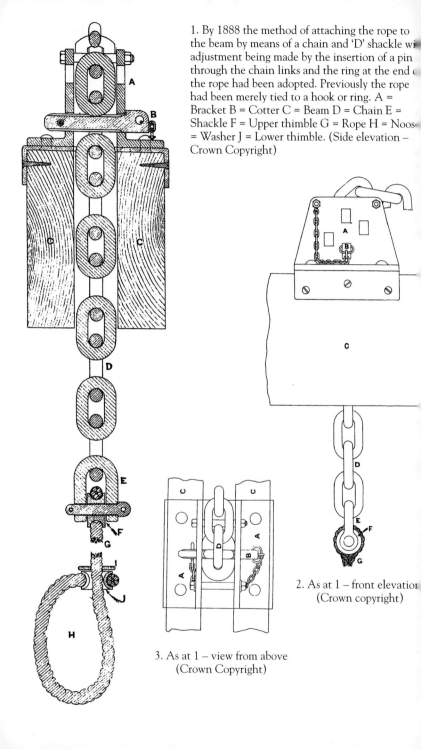

1. By 1888 the method of attaching the rope to the beam by means of a chain and 'D' shackle wi adjustment being made by the insertion of a pin through the chain links and the ring at the end of the rope had been adopted. Previously the rope had been merely tied to a hook or ring. A = Bracket B = Cotter C = Beam D = Chain E = Shackle F = Upper thimble G = Rope H = Noos = Washer J = Lower thimble. (Side elevation – Crown Copyright)

2. As at 1 – front elevation (Crown copyright)

3. As at 1 – view from above (Crown Copyright)

e tableau in Madame
ssaud's Chamber of Horrors
icting the murderess Mrs
ry Eleanor Pearcey
heeler) in a reconstruction
er room in Kentish Town.
e artifacts on display were
ginal items of her property
chased by Madame Tussaud's
I sold to raise money for her
ence. Executed by Berry on
December 1890, she was,
ording to him, the 'Prettiest
nvict I ever hanged' (see
apter Twenty Nine). (Photo
dit: Madame Tussaud's)

The actual
perambulator used
by Mrs Pearcey to
wheel the bodies of
her victims
Mrs Phoebe Hogg
and her baby
through the streets
of North London
on 24 October
1890. Restored and
preserved at
Madame Tussaud's
wax-works
(see Chapter
Twenty Nine)
(Photo credit:
Madame Tussaud's)

The Lipski case – the lock off the door and the bottle that contained the acid (see Chapter Twenty)

'Jack the Ripper' territory, 16 Batty Street, St George's-in-the-East, scene of the murder of Miriam Angel by Israel Lipski on 28 June 1887. He was hanged by Berry at Newgate on 22 August 1887 and his name would become associated with the Ripper case in 1888 (see Chapter Twenty).

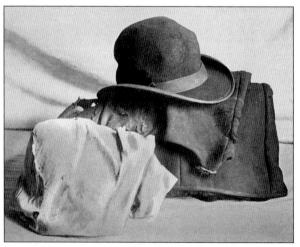

The Lipski case – Israel Lipski's hat and clothes, and Miriam Angel's night-dress (see Chapter Twenty)

huge crowd
gathered outside the
prison at Dundee for
the execution of
William Henry Bury
on 24 April 1889
but was he Jack the
Ripper? (See
Chapter Twenty
Five) (Thomson's
Weekly News)

Greenock Prison,
with Frederick T.
Storey inset. Storey
was executed by
Berry at this prison
on 11 January 1892
(the 'X' marks the
location of the
scaffold in the
prison (see Chapter
Thirty). (Thomson's
Weekly News)

Newspaper montage
showing images of
Mrs Elizabeth Berry and
an older James Berry
superimposed on a view of
the main entrance to
Walton Gaol, Liverpool,
where Berry executed her
on 14 March 1887 (see
Chapter Seventeen).
Thomson's Weekly News)

A photograph of the Newgate gallows showing the long but rather narrow trap and securing chain on the beam for the rope. The lever pulled by the executioner is on the right.

Sir Claude Champion de Crespigny, Baronet – who acted as Berry's assistant using the pseudonym 'Charles Maldon' at the execution of the Netherby Hall burglars at Carlisle on 8 February 1886 (see Chapter Thirteen).

The grim ediface that was Newgate Prison as it looked in Berry's day. The gloomy building was finally demolished in 1902 and was replaced by what is today's Central Criminal Court, the Old Bailey.

Scene in a late Victorian condemned cell – the prisoner is watched over by two warders as he awaits execution.

Illustration of a prisoner sitting in his cell, head in hands, as shown in Berry's own lantern slide show. (Photo Credit: Madame Tussaud's)

An execution being carried out on the Newgate 'drop' in Berry's day. This illustrates how witnesses, such as the press representatives, watched from a distance and would merely see the 'victim' disappear as the drop fell.

Newspaper advertisement for Berry's lantern-slide show, billing Berry a 'Phrenologist and Character Reader – 40 Minutes Eccentri Excruciatingly Continuous Entertainment' (see Chapter Thirty Two

James Billington, executioner for Yorkshire 1884–1891 and public executioner 1891–1901, a 'ready-made' replacement for Berry when he retired in 1891.

The Travellers Rest Inn in Cutler Heights Lane, Bradford today. Berry ran this hostelry for a time and it was here that his daughter died (see Chapter Thirty-Two). (John Adams)

Walnut Tree Farm, Bolton Lane, Bradford as it is today – Berry lived out his final years here. (John Adams)

Bilton Place off the City Road, Bradford as it is today – location of Berry's home during the years he was Public Executioner. The houses on Berry's side of the road have now been demolished but No. 1 was located on the left. (John Adams)

The Travellers Rest Inn in Cutler Heights Lane, Bradford today. Berry ran this hostelry for a time and it was here that his daughter died (see Chapter Thirty-Two). (John Adams)

Berry's lantern slide of Birdcage Walk, Newgate Prison – site of the prison graveyard. The initials of the buried convicts were carved on the wall. (Photo Credit: Madame Tussaud's)

Pinioned, capped and noosed upon the 'drop' – From one of Berry's own lantern slides, it is believed that this is Berry posing on the scaffold to show how a prisoner was executed. (Photo Credit: Madame Tussaud's)

After execution the bodies of executed convicts were carried out for burial within the confines of the prison where they had been executed – scene shown in Berry's lantern slide show.
(Photo Credit: Madame Tussaud's)

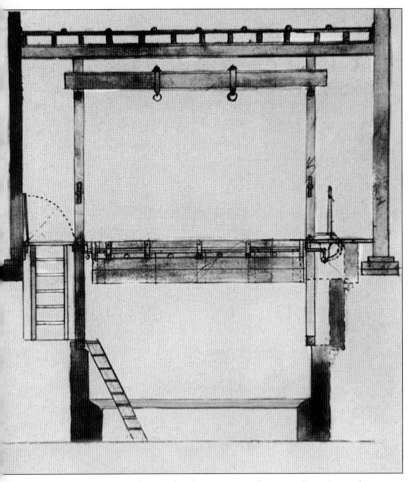

Plan of gallows construction longitudinal section – as shown on Berry's own lantern slides. (Photo Credit: Madame Tussaud's)

James Berry before the pulpit – after his retirement when he became an evangelical preacher. This image is from one of his own lantern slides. (Photo Credit: Madame Tussaud's)

February 1904
Berry at the Midland Station, Bradford intending to commit suicide. An evangelist 'saved' and converted him. This posed photo is from Berry's own lantern slide (see Chapter Thirty Two) (Photo Credit: Madame Tussaud's)

In loving Memory of
JAMES BERRY,
BORN FEB. 8TH 1852, DIED OCT. 21ST 1913.
SARAH ANN BERRY,
BORN OCT. 21ST 1852, DIED MARCH 25TH 1929.

The stone marker on the grave of James Berry and his wife Sarah at Scholemoor Cemetery, Bradford. It is grave no. 781. (John Adams)

and all the bodily organs removed and the heart was apparently taken away by the killer. The name 'Jack the Ripper' was on everyone's lips, but the murderer had again disappeared without trace. Berry, an avid reader of criminal cases in the newspapers, must have dreamt of laying hands on this most notorious of murderers.

On Sunday 20 August 1888 another horrific murder was committed in the East End, at Poplar, but this time the culprit was arrested. It was a domestic case and involved murder and attempted suicide. Levi Richard Bartlett of 248 Manchester Road, Cubitt Town, a general dealer aged 66, had murdered his 56-year-old wife Elizabeth by striking her on the head with a 14lb hammer and cutting her throat as she slept, apparently with a razor. Her left eye had been knocked out by the hammer-blow. She died about an hour after the arrival of the medical men who had been summoned. The couple's marriage had been an unhappy one marked by frequent quarrels and bouts of drinking by Bartlett, and after killing his wife, the latter had told a fellow resident, Thomas Jones, 'Good-bye; I have settled the missus, and I am going to settle myself.' He then went to the bedroom, sat beside his wife's body and cut his own throat with a razor. Despite severing his windpipe he did not die, instead being conveyed in a critical condition to Poplar Hospital. Inspector Michael Crawford, of K Division, was assigned to the case.

On 3 September the inquest resumed on the death of Elizabeth Bartlett, before the Deputy Coroner for the South-Eastern District of Middlesex, Mr George Collier, who had also held the inquest into the death of Martha Tabram. A verdict of 'Wilful Murder' against Levi Richard Bartlett was returned but it would be a few weeks before he would be fit enough to be tried. When he was finally tried at the Central Criminal Court he was found guilty and sentenced to death.

The inquest into the death of Mary Kelly was held in Shoreditch on Monday 12 November, the same day that Berry travelled to London in readiness for the execution of Levi Richard Bartlett at Newgate the following day. Since his conviction Bartlett had expressed contrition for the crime, and efforts had been made to obtain a reprieve, but Henry Matthews, the Home Secretary, could find no grounds for interfering with the course of justice. Present at the execution were the under-sheriffs, Messrs Metcalfe and Halse;

Colonel Milman, governor of Newgate and Holloway prisons; the Revd H.G. Duffield, MA, the Ordinary (chaplain) of Newgate; Dr Gilbert, the surgeon of Holloway; and the usual officials. Bartlett was composed as, supported by warders, he made his way to the scaffold. Berry quickly adjusted the rope around the convict's neck and placed the white cap over his face, and at 8 a.m., as the bell of St Sepulchre's tolled, the signal was given and the trapdoor fell. Death was instantaneous and the body was left to hang for an hour. A small crowd had assembled in the precincts of the prison to watch the hoisting of the black flag. The usual inquest was held.

At the time of the above, Newgate Prison was being used only for the detention and execution of condemned prisoners, so the City Lands Committee of the Corporation of London agreed, subject to the Home Secretary's approval, to the demolition of Newgate and the Central Criminal Court. Demolition would begin in 1902 and what is today's Old Bailey would rise on the site.

Another prisoner awaiting execution at this time was Samuel Crowther, a shoemaker aged 71, who had been found guilty of the murder of John Willis, a gardener, at Dudderhill near Droitwich on 1 August. Caught stealing fruit, Crowther had stabbed him three times and fled. He was convicted at the Worcester Assizes, and though a petition was raised, the Home Secretary declined to advise the Queen to interfere with the due course of the law. Crowther received the news with indifference, and the execution was carried out on Tuesday 11 December 1888 at Worcester County Gaol, the condemned man, described as a cripple, making a full confession to the chaplain just before Berry hanged him and acknowledging the justice of his sentence.

In the House of Commons on Monday 17 December 1888 the question of the behaviour of the public executioner was again raised. Sir E.A.H. Lechmere, MP for West Worcestershire, asked Mr Matthews whether he had ascertained the accuracy of reports that had appeared in the *Daily News* and the *Birmingham Daily Gazette* of 12 December, to which his attention had already been called. These related to activities of Berry at Kidderminster, after the execution of Crowther at Worcester, Berry apparently having visited 'several publichouses, made a speech to a large number of persons, held quite a levee at one of the publichouses, and freely distributed cards bearing his name as public executioner'. Lechmere asked further whether the Home Secretary was aware that 'a strong and general feeling of disgust had been excited at Kidderminster and elsewhere by Berry's conduct'.

Henry Matthews replied that the questioner was no doubt aware that he had answered a question on this subject on the previous Friday. Since then he had received a letter from the High Sheriff, who had called upon Berry for an explanation as to his conduct subsequent to the execution, 'so far as it involved a breach of the conditions upon which his services were engaged. Those conditions were that, prior to the execution he should not go to any place of public entertainment, and that after the execution, as soon as his services were no longer required, he should proceed direct from the gaol to the railway station in a cab accompanied by a warder.' The High Sheriff had promised to send a copy of Berry's reply. Sir E. Lechmere gave notice that he would call attention to the present duties of the executioner at the next session and move that he be placed under the control of the Home Office.

The Kidderminster *Sun* had covered the story on 15 December, stating that Berry had several acquaintances residing in the town. Among these was a barber named Silcox, of Park Butts, who was reported to aspire to becoming Berry's successor and who was alleged to have assisted at Crowther's execution. Berry had arrived at 10.28 a.m., accompanied by 'a crowd of curious-looking individuals'. He first called at The Worcester Cross Inn and then The Anchor, where 'many more or less prominent townsmen had a great "honour" [?] of an introduction to him'. Several town councillors attended his levee, including two who aspired to a post on the County Council, Messrs H.R. Willis and G. Holloway. Berry gave a speech 'which to say the least of it, was not couched in very elegant language'. He related, with apparent pleasure, some of his execution experiences and exhorted his audience not to bear malice, as it led to the gallows. He distributed his 'elaborately got up bevelled-edged visiting cards' freely and they were eagerly taken up as souvenirs:

> He promised to honour the town with another visit when he was again in the locality. Many people remarked that Berry appeared as if he had had a 'drop' himself.

Sir E. Lechmere's investigation of the incident revealed that Berry had visited several public houses including The Anchor Inn in Worcester Street, the Lytteton's Arms in Park Butts and the Plough and Harrow in Bewdley Street. Berry had not left the town until 4.09 p.m. He was reported to be sober and the Chief Constable had given instructions that he was to be watched and arrested if he became intoxicated. He was watched by Inspector Griffiths of the Borough Force, and was heard to speak of Crowther whom he had executed that morning.

In February 1889 G.W. Hastings, the Chairman of the Visiting Justices, wrote a letter of complaint about Berry's conduct to Lord Coleridge, the Lord Chief Justice, Berry's behaviour being described as a scandal. It was stated that the High Sheriff had secured agreement from Berry that, after executing Crowther, he would leave Worcester by train for Bradford, this arrangement prompted by Berry's conduct after the recent double execution at Hereford when he had appeared at Worcester the same day and 'entertained' at public houses, being conducted through the streets by a large crowd to the railway station. Berry had entered into this agreement 'in consideration of a certain sum of money', and, on receiving this after the execution, he had been sent in a cab to the Shrub Hill railway station, accompanied by a warder, from where it had been believed he had gone straight to Bradford. Instead, he had travelled only the 13 miles or so to Kidderminster.

In *Experiences* Berry tells a story obviously relating to the activities that prompted the subsequent complaint by Sir E. Lechmere. However, the two men mentioned in the story, Hill and Williams, were executed in Hereford on 23 November 1885, so it is not certain whether it should relate to the double execution of Jones and Scandrett at Hereford on 20 March 1888.

Another affair which caused me much annoyance at the time arose in Hereford, from the greed for interesting and sensational 'copy' shown by a member of the staff of the *Hereford Times*. He got up some sensational matter to the effect that after the execution of Hill and Williams I retired to a neighbouring hotel where a smoking concert was in progress, and there held a ghastly levee. The worst of this report was that it was based on some foundation of fact, and that a mere colouration of the report made a reasonable and perfectly innocent entertainment appear as if it was something shameful.

The actual facts were that after the execution I was in company with Alderman Barnet, Mayor of Worcester, and a detective sergeant, both of whom were personal friends of mine. With Alderman Barnet I was invited to a social evening held by some of his friends. It was a perfectly private party, and was decorously conducted in every way. When the *Times* representative appeared, as he was known to the gentlemen present, he was invited to join us, simply as a friend. The report of the party was much talked about at the time, and Sir Edwin Lechmere, M.P. for Hereford, made it the subject of a question in the House of Commons.

In September 1888, while tension was building in the East End of London at the thought of an unknown killer at large, the country was shocked to read of another appalling murder in the north, near Durham. The body of Jane Beetmore, aged 27, was found near Birtley at 7 a.m. on the morning of Sunday 23 September 1888. Jane, who had last been seen alive by her friends about 8 p.m. on the Saturday, appeared to have been dead for several hours. It was reported that she had been stabbed in several places about the neck and that the lower parts of the body were also severely injured. The body was taken to her parents' house, about a quarter of a mile distant. There were no clues to indicate the killer, and with news of the unknown Whitechapel murderer in all the recent papers it did not take long for the suggestion to be made that the London killer had moved his operations to a different part of the country. *The Times* of 24 September commented:

A great sensation has been caused in the district, the crime resembling the Whitechapel murders in many particulars.

Another long report on 'The Murder in Durham' appeared in *The Times* of 25 September, and it did nothing to allay the fears of the public. The Victorian press did not pull its punches:

Considerable excitement has been created in North Durham by the discovery of the body of the woman, Jane Beetmoor, at Birtley Fell, near Gateshead, from the circumstances that the wounds inflicted upon her are very similar to those found on the two latest victims in Whitechapel. The immediate cause of Beetmoor's death seems to have been a deep incised wound in the left cheek. The instrument used must have been long and sharp, and it entered the left cheek just below the ear. The wound extended almost right through the neck, and the spinal cord was completely severed. This would have in itself been more than sufficient to cause death. There was a wound also upon the other side of the face. The injury to the lower part of the body had been terribly cruel. The knife, or whatever instrument was used, had evidently been forcibly thrust into the body, and the half-severed bones showed the force that had been used to extend the wound.

The body had been found in a ditch by the side of a wagon track located in the direction the girl had last been seen walking. It was known that a young man named Waddell, who lodged locally and worked at the Birtley Iron Works, had been courting her, and it seemed rather suspicious that he had not been seen since the Saturday, so the police concentrated their efforts on tracing him. Apparently on the Saturday of the murder he had gone to his lodgings the worse for drink, subsequently going out again later that day, despite the protestations of his landlady. It was also known that the murdered girl had recently changed her mind with regard to Waddell and had been trying to free herself from his attentions. Many were convinced of his guilt, and when no trace could be found of his whereabouts a search was made of disused pit shafts in the area in case he had committed suicide.

A newspaper report confirmed that the Scotland Yard authorities had a genuine interest in this murder, believing that it could well be connected with the East London series:

It is stated that Dr. Phillips, who made the post-mortem examination of the body of Annie Chapman, the victim of the last Whitechapel murder, has been sent to Durham. Dr. Phillips, who left London last night [24 Sept.], will examine the body of the murdered woman with the view of ascertaining whether the injuries inflicted on her resemble those inflicted on the Whitechapel victim. Inspector Roots, of the Criminal Investigation Department, also left London last night for Durham, with the object of ascertaining whether any of the facts connected with the Birtley murder are likely to be serviceable in elucidating the Whitechapel crimes. The methods and success of the murderer so closely resemble those of the Whitechapel fiend that the local authorities are strongly inclined to connect the two crimes. As in the last two London cases the murder was effected without any violent struggling on the part of the victim; the actual cause of death was the cutting of the throat, and the same parts of the body were mutilated and in a very similar manner. For the present the police suspend final judgment until the results of Dr. Phillips's examination have been made known.

The following day *The Times* updated the ongoing saga:

The excitement caused by the brutal murder on Saturday of Jane Beetmoor, on Birtley Fell, near Gateshead-on-Tyne, is still considerable. The London police appear to think that there may be some connexion between this and the recent outrages in Whitechapel, and Inspector Roots, of Scotland-yard, with Dr. Phillips, who conducted the *post-mortem* examination on the body of Annie Chapman, yesterday, in company with Colonel White, Chief Constable of the county, drove from Durham to the scene of the tragedy. Dr. Phillips saw the body, but the result of his investigation is not known. It is believed, however, that the examination must have failed to disclose any direct resemblance to the Whitechapel murders, for, although the wounds in each case were somewhat similar, those upon the body of Jane Beetmore had been inflicted by brute force, and did not show any appearance of anatomical skill. Apart from this, the police are inclined to think that the discovery of the deceased's sweetheart, William Waddle or Twaddle [*sic*], who is said to have been seen with her on the night of the murder, and who thereafter disappeared, will lead to a solution of the mystery.

Inspector Roots, however, diligently followed his brief, and on the afternoon of Tuesday 25 September he spent some hours in the company of the local officers taking copious notes and making sketches of the locality of the murder.

Waddell's description was circulated; he was described as about 22 years of age, about 5ft 9in tall, with fresh complexion, small and sunken blue eyes, and brown hair. A distinctive feature was that he had tender feet and walked badly, leaning well forward. The search for his body had proved fruitless, but several sightings of the suspect were reported from Newcastle, Gateshead and other locations, one in particular coming from Robert Lodge, a foreman coke burner from Byers Green, who had spotted a man answering the fugitive's description in a cabin near the coke ovens. This was about 14 miles from the scene of the murder. The search was continued.

The Times of 27 September 1888 made further comment on speculation concerning a possible connection with the Whitechapel murders:

> The action of the London authorities in sending Dr. Phillips and Inspector Roots down to investigate the circumstances of the murder has unquestionably intensified the feeling among the public. The conclusion arrived at by Dr. Phillips after his examination of the body has not yet been divulged, but there seems little doubt that the Birtley Fell murder is the work of a different hand from that of Annie Chapman, the only connexion between the two probably being that the perpetrator of the former had attempted an imitation of the Whitechapel murders after brooding over the cruel details of how the bodies of the women Nichols and Chapman had been mutilated. It seems to be the strong conviction of the police that the murder has been committed by some local man, not by any stranger, and for the present they are practically concentrating their efforts on the discovery of the man Waddle . . .

The funeral of the murdered woman took place on the afternoon of Wednesday 26 September at the parish church of Birtley. A week later, on Tuesday 2 October 1888, *The Times* reported that Waddell had been apprehended at Yetholm in Roxburghshire, Scotland on the previous day. It seems that he had washed his bloodstained clothes and exchanged them for others in a cast-off clothes shop at Berwick on 27 September. The police gave the clothing to an analytical chemist for examination for bloodstains. It was believed that after the crime Waddell had walked to Gateshead and then crossed to Newcastle, going on to Corbridge, near Hexham, where a brother lived. Unable to find him, he had then travelled to Jedburgh, Coldstream and on to Berwick, finally reaching Yetholm, where a civilian named Stenhouse detained him in a semi-starved condition. Described as 5ft 10in tall and possessed of great physical strength, Waddell had sustained himself by begging. Superintendent Harrison went to Yetholm and returned to Gateshead with his prisoner, the latter being charged on 2 October with the murder.

On the 29th of the month Waddell appeared at Durham Assizes before Mr Baron Pollack, charged with the murder of Jane Beetmoore. He was described as being generally of sober habit, but as being drunk on the afternoon of the day of the crime. The jury returned a verdict of 'Guilty' and sentence of death was duly passed.

In the House of Commons on 17 December 1888 a Mr Joicey asked Matthews if any inquiry had taken place as to the sanity of the convict, William Waddell, and if any recommendation to mercy was going to be communicated to Her Majesty. Matthews stated that inquiry had been made and that, having no reason to doubt Waddell's sanity, he was unable to advise any interference with the due course of law.

On Tuesday 18 December 1888 Berry executed Waddell at Durham gaol. The sensational association of this case with the Whitechapel murders had featured widely in the newspapers. Berry's account, which appeared in *The Post* of 10 January 1914, included the following:

. . . William Waddell, whose mysterious crime and strange disappearance thrilled the whole world at a time when the country was in the throes of the horror caused by the ghastly work of the Whitechapel murderer . . . there were many people who at the time believed that the criminal whom I was to hang down in Durham was responsible for the crimson crimes of the East End of London. And so plausible had the theory seemed that Scotland Yard sent one of its cleverest officers and a medical expert to the County of Durham to determine whether or not Jane Beardmore [sic] had died by the hand of the maniac who had plunged London into terror.

After Berry had reported at Durham gaol he had something to eat and went for a walk round the town. He went right round the old cathedral, crossed the bridge, and looked at the reflection of the lights in the river, before going into one of the hotels to hear what was being said of his 'victim'. He records the following encounter:

One man asked me what I thought, and I told him it was a brutal crime.

'It is that and all,' he replied, 'but I don't think the law ought to commit another murder like what's going to happen to-morrow. I'd hang Berry if I had my way.'

'That would be rather a funny way of putting an end to capital punishment,' I said with a laugh.

'How do you make that out?'

'Because if you hanged Berry there would be nobody left to hang you.'

'I'd like to see Berry hang me,' he said.

'So would I! You can bet your life he would make a good job of it.'

Laughing at the incident, I slipped my card into the man's hand, and was out of the place before he had time to read it.

Berry was up early on the morning of the execution and tested the equipment. The trapdoor worked very satisfactorily, and on the way back to his room he prepared his straps. Entering the condemned cell shortly afterwards he found Waddell standing with a look of indifference.

'Time is short,' said Berry, 'Hurry up and I will not give you a moment longer to suffer than I can help.'

Waddell did not reply, so Berry immediately put the straps on him. Still Waddell remained silent, a reaction, Berry claims, that made him nervous. He led the condemned man out into the corridor, wishing he 'was well out of the job'; having taken a dislike to Waddell he was worried that he might bungle the execution. Waddell was unafraid, apparently not seeming to care about anything. He walked with a firm step and held his head erect without uttering a word. The clergyman continued to read the service but no response came from Waddell's lips. Four press representatives were present but at the subsequent inquest they were not allowed to view the body of the executed man with the jury. Berry stated that he gave a drop of 5 feet and that death was instantaneous. Waddell was buried in the prison on the same day.

23

New year, old trade

'I never liked to hang youths . . . '

Berry conducted his first execution of 1889 on New Year's Day at Stafford County Prison. Thomas Clews, a miner aged 23, had murdered Mary Jane Bovell, a widow with whom he had been living at Washerwall near Stoke. He had murdered her when the relationship had soured and, jealous of her seeing someone else, had killed her with a hatchet. He walked firmly and unassisted to the scaffold and appeared to die without a struggle when Berry activated the drop.

Another execution took place at the same time, at Leeds. Charles Bulmer, a groom aged 51, had been convicted on 12 September the previous year of the murder of his wife, Elizabeth, at Lockwood near Huddersfield. The execution took place within Armley gaol and the executioner was James Billington.

Berry immediately travelled down to Maidstone gaol for the execution of William Gower and Charles Joseph Dobell, scheduled for the morning of Wednesday 2 January. Gower, aged 18, and Dobell, aged 17, were charged with the wilful murder of Bensley Cyrus Lawrence, the timekeeper at the Baltic Sawmills at Tunbridge Wells, on 20 July 1888. The two offenders had not been arrested until Friday 12 October, when Superintendent Embery had gone to the Sawmills, where Gower worked, and arrested him. He told Gower that he had information stating that he and Dobell had been concerned together in the murder and had either cast lots or tossed a coin as to which of them would actually shoot the victim. Gower said it was Dobell, and a search of an outhouse where Gower lived revealed the revolver used, in a box, with all six chambers loaded. Dobell was also arrested, and admitted the killing. Both men were remanded in custody.

It appears that Gower nursed some sort of grudge against the murdered man. At the police court hearing on 17 October, a witness, a Salvation Army Captain, stated that when he asked Gower whether the two felt sorry for having murdered their victim, Gower replied, 'Well, no. Sometimes we feel sorry and sometimes we feel that if he were to rise again we would do it again.' The prisoners voluntarily confessed their crime, also admitting to a series of other undetected offences including robbery and incendiarism, for which innocent parties had come under suspicion. They were tried and convicted at the Kent Assizes.

Berry arrived from Stafford on the Tuesday night, and was at once taken to the gaol. In the account of this execution in *The Post* series, he says that the two young men should not have hanged, as:

Neither of the two boys could have been responsible for their crime, inasmuch as they belonged to the degenerate type, and it would have been the more humane course to have sent them to Broadmoor, where there are several murderers who are much more sane than ever were the two lads.

The lads were romantically inclined, and wanted to be bandits, and according to those who investigated the crime privately the murder was the outcome of a boyish adventure. They certainly killed the victim of it, but whether or not they did so intentionally will never be known.

Berry entered Dobell's cell first, and found that the youth had just finished writing a letter to his friends expressing contrition for his crime. Dobell rose and said, 'I suppose you are going to tie me up Mr. Berry.'

'I have got to do it, Charlie,' Berry replied. 'But it will soon be over; don't be afraid now.'

'Oh! I won't be afraid, Mr. Berry. But can you do it in the same cell as Willie is in?'

'I am afraid they would not allow it,' said Berry. 'It is not usual, you know.'

'Oh! Please, Mr. Berry, do let us be pinioned together.'

'Wait a minute then and I will see what I can do for you,' the hangman replied.

Berry spoke with an official outside the cell, stating that such a thing was not possible in the cell but could be done in the corridor, where both would be able to see each other even with one still in his cell. He duly pinioned Dobell in the corridor – the condemned man standing bravely while Berry prepared him – and then went to the other cell and brought out Gower, completing the pinioning while the latter looked across at his friend.

Both prisoners were remarkably self-possessed, despite their youth, and walked firmly to the scaffold. The scaffold was enclosed in matchboard so that the execution could not be seen from the adjoining houses. It had three swivels in the massive crossbeam. Death was stated to have been instantaneous, although in the case of Dobell the rope swayed slightly after the drop.

On 2 October 1888, at Aston in Warwickshire, George Nicholson, a master baker aged 52, was charged on remand with the murder of his wife, Mary Ann Nicholson, at Aston on 22 September. He had killed her with a hatchet, and was committed for trial at Warwick Assizes. On Monday 17 December Nicholson, appeared for trial at Warwick Assizes before Mr. Justice Cave. The couple had married in 1883, she at the time being a widow aged 47 and having a dependent family. Their bakery business failed, and in 1885 they left Birmingham and went to live in Burlington Street, Aston, George finding irregular work as a journeyman baker. The marriage was not a happy one and they frequently quarrelled, usually over money, the little they had largely earned by Mary Ann and her children. In one such quarrel, at about 9.30 p.m. on 22 September, he attacked her as she sat in a rocking chair near the fire, striking her skull in five places and leaving wounds so severe that her brains protruded. He immediately absconded, stopping off at a pawnbroker's in Birmingham and pawning a watch and chain taken from the deceased. On the following evening he was spotted at Walsall, arrested and charged. He denied knowing anything of his wife's death, stating that he had been drunk at the time. Stains were found on his clothes and on the watch he had pawned, the police submitting these for testing to Mr Bostock Hill, the Birmingham Public Analyst. Due to starch contamination on the clothing, however, caused by Nicholson's occupation as a baker, he was unable to confirm that these were bloodstains. Those found on the watch were too slight to be analysed effectively.

The defence attempted to reduce the charge to manslaughter, but Mr Justice Cave directed in favour of the murder charge, saying that the accused was not too drunk to know what he was doing. He was found guilty and the statutory death sentence passed. Berry executed him in Warwick on Tuesday 8 January 1889, the convicted man showing much firmness, fully acknowledging the justice of his punishment and forgiving everyone connected with him. The drop allowed was 6 feet.

On Monday 14 January 1889, Arthur McKeown, aged 32, was scheduled to hang for the murder of his girlfriend, Mary Jane Phillips on 26 August 1888. Despite a reputation for having an affectionate disposition he had a hasty temper and was a jealous man. The two, who had two children, had enjoyed a stormy relationship, and when Mary finally decided to leave him he battered her to death in the house where they lived in Robert Street, Belfast. This meant another trip to Ireland for Berry and in *The Post* account (15 November 1913) he again bemoaned the ordeal of visiting the country:

I picked up my revolver and sent out for cartridges when I knew that Arthur McKeown was to die.

A reprieve for the poor wretch was what I had been wishing for, but the Home Secretary had had no compassion for him, and there was nothing for it but to do my duty.

How I hated these executions in Ireland, and how I trembled sometimes for my own safety.

With the people in Ireland the hangman was not popular. They jeered at me in the streets, and they would even threaten to take my life. The fact that I was journeying to exact the penalty of the law from one who had committed the worst crime against society did not weigh with them in the least. They believed that I was a demon in human form, and so fiercely opposed to me they were at times that I had to have a strong escort to see me out of the country.

Looking back over the events of the past I can see their conduct in a new light, and I have come to the conclusion that had the people of England followed their example the capital sentence might have been abolished by this time. After all, it is the masses who matter, Home Secretaries and Governments merely playing the tune they call.

In either of the two Celtic countries the idea of murdering a man in prison was abhorrent to the public mind, whereas in certain parts of England I found the people not only clamouring for execution, but anxious to fete and make a hero of the hangman.

The best people of the town have invited me upon occasions to sit down with them to dinner on the evening after an execution, and once, I remember, when I consented to do so, I was assailed by The Times for making a public exhibition of myself and my gruesome relics of the condemned cell and the gibbet.

I never went to Ireland without arming myself after a terrible experience I had returning from Galway, and so when I left to hang Arthur M'Keown my pocket bulged with my revolver loaded in every chamber. For company I took my son, Luther, a boy of ten years of age, thinking that if anyone saw us together they would never suspect that I was Berry, the hangman.

Berry claims that the authorities in Belfast were as apprehensive for his safety as he was himself. There was great public sympathy for McKeown and the fear was that Berry would be waylaid to prevent the execution. Two detectives arranged to meet him on his arrival and false reports were inserted in the press to disguise his actual movements. 'Nervous and ill at ease', he travelled to Fleetwood and crossed by steamer to Belfast where the detectives duly met him, advising that if he moved freely in the places where the public would least expect to see him he would be safer from detection. That afternoon he attended a football match at the Cliftonville ground. He was not spotted and enjoyed the match. Afterwards, he went to the prison to check the arrangements for the Monday morning execution, and then, emboldened by his afternoon's experience, he visited several suburban areas that night. On the

Sunday he supervised some alterations he had recommended on the gallows. The steps were done away with, to prevent the culprit stumbling, a pit dug under the beam, and the mechanical arrangements, slightly different to those in other parts of the country, were tested.

On the Monday morning he went to the condemned cell to take a look at the prisoner. McKeown had had no sleep that night, and had risen at 5.00 a.m., tearfully asking for the chaplain. Seeing his waxen face and staring bloodshot eyes, Berry could not help feeling sorry for the man. It was a fine morning with a slight frost in the air and an accompanying haze. As early as 7.00 a.m., as the lamps were being extinguished, a curious crowd was forming outside the gates of the prison.

While Berry was adjusting the rope on the beam, pale-faced and shivering members of the press entered the yard. On seeing Berry they approached to interview him, and being struck by the presence of his 10-year-old son on the scaffold, they asked why he was there. When he failed to satisfy their curiosity, Berry wrote:

> . . . one of them had his revenge by writing afterwards that he found the son of the Bradford celebrity gambolling about the erection with the same freedom and evident enjoyment as if he were awaiting the arrival of some outdoor demonstration. It was a cruel thing to say, and as false as it was cruel.

One has to say that it seems very odd that Berry should allow his young son to witness such grim arrangements.

As the hour approached, Berry chatted with the reporters until the noise of a heavy door announced that he was required. He picked up his pinioning straps and waited, it not being uniform practice in Ireland to complete this procedure in the cell. The approach of the procession was heralded by the sound of the chaplain's voice in prayer. Behind him came the prisoner, repeating the prayers with head bowed and carrying a crucifix in his hand. Berry was very moved, reportedly being transfixed by the sight of the crucifix. He pulled himself together and approached the condemned man, telling him he had to pinion him and asking his forgiveness.

'I have my duty to do and I hope you will not make it more unpleasant than you can help,' said Berry.

The prisoner did not reply, but offered no resistance and stood with downcast eyes as Berry buckled the belts around him. The procession then passed through a door on the right and the scaffold came into view. McKeown did not glance up but bore a haunted dejected look as he moved forward to the instrument of his death, where Berry pointed out the position he should take on the drop. His assistant, a young man from Blackpool, handed him the noose, and Berry then adjusted the white cap, slipped the loop over, steadied his victim with one hand, and finally touched the lever with the other, launching the unfortunate man to his death.

The first to descend to check the body was the doctor. He stood with his watch in his hand waiting for the indications of death in the features and body of the hanged man. A minute and a half passed, then to Berry's horror he saw the eyelids move and the cheek twitch as if the man were still alive. The newspapermen crowded round but Berry assured them that death had been instantaneous and that the execution was one of the most successful he had conducted. He believed that what he had seen was nothing more than a muscular reaction, but, keen to get away in case there should be trouble, he asked the deputy governor if he was satisfied and was given leave to go, though not before being warned that he did so at the risk of offending the coroner. Berry notes that after every execution he conducted in Ireland the jurymen asked to see him. In this instance, however, he was not going to take the risk of answering their questions, and then going out 'to face a murderous crowd, and so I made myself scarce only to escape from death by what was almost a miracle'.

The coroner's jury viewed the body, noting that the face 'bore traces of pain'. Angered that Berry had left the prison immediately after the completion of the execution procedure, they claimed that McKeown had not had a peaceful end and demanded to see the rope if they could not see Berry. They were told, however, that the rope was Berry's property and had left with the hangman. Unknown to them, while the inquest was being held, Berry sat eating his breakfast in a hotel not far from the prison, feeling 'wretched and miserable'. Knowing the feeling that prevailed, he resolved to leave

Belfast as soon as possible, and learning that a train was due to leave for Bangor in 30 minutes, he decided to catch it, fearing that the coroner would call for him. The journey was a tedious one, and Berry noticed a strange jolting sensation all along the line:

Little did I dream that all the time we had been travelling in the face of great danger, and when I left the train and heard that a minute or two afterwards the engine left the rails and turned right over my nerves collapsed completely and those who were with me despaired of ever getting me home.

I felt that I must be going mad, and I swore that if I ever got back to Bradford I would give up the work and settle down to whatever work I could find to do.

In order to get my mind off the scenes I had taken part in my escort suggested that I should go to Groomsport and see the fishing station. I fell in with their wishes and what I saw there helped me to forget things and regain somewhat my usual state of mind.

I dreaded the return to Belfast, for I had to journey thither to catch the steamer for England, but they assured me that nobody would be waiting for me at that late hour in the afternoon, and I allowed myself to be persuaded to return.

After all, if I remained overnight in Bangor, the representatives of the press might get on my track, and I would probably never be allowed to leave Ireland alive.

We journeyed back after tea, and as the train drew into the terminus at Belfast my heart sank within me. The news of my arrival was not long in getting round, having been circulated no doubt by the railwaymen, and before we had left the carriage a large crowd of people had collected.

Those responsible for my safety at once rushed off and brought a car, and, jumping upon it, we were driven away amid the hoots, the jeers, and the groans of all who saw me. When we had left the crowd behind us we dismissed the car, and we were joined by a representative of the press, who had recognised and followed me.

He assured me that the safest course would be to walk openly about among the people, and, taking his advice, I made for the crowded High Street, where I purchased one or two things for my boy, Luther. How to get to the boat safely was now the problem. My protectors sought to buoy me up by telling me that the crowd would not follow me to the steamer, believing that I would endeavour to make for some other port, but I did not believe them, and set out for the pier with the feeling that I would never get on board.

It was no surprise for me to learn before we came in view of the boat that the crowd had preceded me, and when I neared the pier I thought that all Belfast's population was waiting to rend me from limb to limb.

Several thousands of men and women drawn from all classes had collected an hour before the boat was timed to leave, and how I succeeded in getting to the deck of the steamer I am unable to relate.

I am as certain as possible that but for my escort I could never have escaped the fury of the crowd, and even when I stood secure on the boat and listened to the rumblings of rage from that mighty multitude I was fearful lest one of the more desperate should take it into his head to steal up the gangway and avenge the death of Arthur M'Keown.

I reached Bradford safely, but it was many a long day before I was able to shake off the effects of my terrible experiences, and but for the fact that I did not wish to endanger my position as Executioner for England I would never have undertaken the execution of another Irish culprit.

On the morning of Tuesday 8 January 1889, Ebenezer Samuel Weathercroft Jenkins, an artist aged 20, walked into the Punchbowl Inn about 10 miles from Godalming in Surrey and confessed to the murder of his sweetheart and fiancée, Emily Joy, aged 19. At about 7.30 p.m. on the previous evening he had taken her to his studio, a hut situated in a garden surrounded by cottages in Crown Pits, almost in the middle of Godalming, about 200 yards off the main street and within a few yards of a main road. There he had raped and strangled her before, after locking the body in the small hut, making his getaway. The landlord, Augustus Sellers, immediately took Jenkins to Guildford and handed him over to the police. Two constables were sent to the studio with the key, where they discovered the body.

Jenkins was questioned by Superintendent Berry of the borough police and stated that he had committed the murder at about 8 p.m. on the Monday night. Having made his statement he then became excited, expressing the hope that he would be hanged. He was handed over to the county police, who quickly visited the scene of the crime, accompanied by Deputy Chief Constable Barker, who took charge of the case. The doctor was called and he stated that death was due to strangulation. The girl's body was lying on its left side, the face disfigured and the boa she had been wearing twisted twice around her neck and stuffed over her mouth and nose. Among several injuries found, her neck was severely bruised

The girl's mother was a widow and much sympathy was felt for her. The young couple appeared to have been on affectionate terms, but Jenkins, who lived with the Joy family, in Church Street, just outside the town of Farncombe (Emily having a young brother and sister), was found to have been living something of a lie. Always fashionably dressed, he had given the impression of being well connected, frequently speaking of coming into money due to him, and claiming that when he became engaged he would receive a further £500, a similar sum expected when he reached the age of 30. In reality, however, he was very poor. He had dropped his proper surname, Jenkins, and adopted his mother's maiden name of Weathercroft. The family had taken to him, and a wedding date had been set for 15 March, Jenkins talking expansively of having taken a house in Bognor.

It turned out that Jenkins had stolen a jubilee half-crown from a brooch the girl had been wearing and tendered it in The Sun pub to buy six pennyworth of brandy after the murder. He also had blood on the front and sleeves of his shirt, which, he told police, came from his finger, the girl having bitten it in the struggle. A witness testified to having heard screams and the noise of a scuffle in the hut, but since this had stopped after a minute or two and nothing more been heard he had gone on his way and thought no more of it.

With 'Jack the Ripper' still in the news *The Times* of 9 January commented: 'No motive has been assigned for the crime, but it is believed the prisoner's mind has been affected by reading the accounts of the Whitechapel murders.' However, it seems likely that the main motives for the crime were Jenkins's increasingly hopeless financial situation and sheer lust. The papers ascribed jealousy, as his want of means would mean that he could not marry her. Jenkins had lied to the girl that a Mrs Elliott owed him money, whereas, in fact, he owed her money. Jenkins stated that he had told the woman that the money was Miss Emily's and that he wanted the girl to ask the woman for it and she would see them at the studio. A point that told against Jenkins was that the crime appeared to be premeditated, for he had sent a letter to Mrs Joy claiming that Emily and he had agreed to die together and wished to be buried in the same grave. In a written confession, made before Deputy Chief Constable Barker, he stated that, while in the studio, a feeling came over him 'like mad' and he caught the girl by the throat and 'outraged' (raped) her. He held her throat and claimed that before she died she said, 'Goodbye, darling, I am dying!' He was committed for trial for wilful murder.

When the Assizes for the south-eastern circuit opened at Guildford on 14 February, the grand jury, in a presentment made to Mr Justice Hawkins, expressed a wish that the public executioner should be more immediately under the control of the Home Office.

Jenkins was there indicted for the wilful murder of Emily Joy, and the only course left to the defence was to plead insanity. The two doctors called, however, did not consider Jenkins to be insane and the jury soon reached a verdict of guilty. The judge, in passing sentence of death, said that he had never met with so revolting or brutal a crime. 'The prisoner had used the word "seduction" but it was a rape of the worst and most horrible kind. He had in cold-blood murdered the girl, and even taken the trouble to re-arrange her clothes and steal the money from her brooch after he had killed her.'

At 9.00 a.m. on 6 March, Berry waited to execute Jenkins at Wandsworth Prison, a large crowd having assembled in front of the prison to witness the hoisting of the black flag. Although looking very pale, the condemned man walked to the scaffold with a firm step, responding with fervour to the prayers of the chaplain. Allowed a drop of 6 feet 6 inches, he died without a struggle. In his book *The Hangman's Record*, Steve Fielding states that Berry experimented in this instance by strapping 7lb weights to each of

Jenkins's legs to compensate for his small frame and light weight. It was the only time this procedure was adopted.

Another sentence of death was passed on 18 February 1889 at the High Court of Judiciary in Edinburgh, the offender being Jessie King, a 27-year-old mill worker residing in the Stockbridge district of the city. She was charged with having murdered three children by strangulation and suffocation, the first twelve months old, the second six weeks, and the third five months. The children, who were illegitimate, had been 'adopted' by King, she being a so-called 'baby farmer' – a despicable breed of murderess thrown up in Victorian days who, for cash, took unwanted babies into 'care' and subsequently disposed of (i.e. killed) them. Moving about the city, she had repeatedly changed her name while adopting such children, in this case having received sums varying from £2 to £5. By her own admission, she strangled the first of the children and after collecting the second had brought it home and given it whisky to keep it quiet. This had taken the child's breath away, and while it lay gasping she had put her hand on its mouth and choked it. Despite this, and despite no evidence being produced for the defence, she pleaded 'not guilty'. The Solicitor-General withdrew the third charge, presumably through lack of evidence. It took the jury only a few minutes to reach a unanimous verdict of guilty, upon which Lord Justice Clerk passed sentence of death. The woman groaned, shrieked loudly and collapsed in a faint, two policemen finally carrying her from the dock to the cells below.

Described by Berry as a 27-year-old and good-looking little woman, King was to be the fourth woman Berry hanged. Born at Blacksand, Kelvinhaugh, in the Anderston district of Glasgow, she had been mainly occupied in laundry work and ironing as she grew older. In Edinburgh she had fallen deeply in love with a man named Pearson, but he had left her when his old love made life uncomfortable for them. Then, shortly before her arrest, she had given birth to a child, later adopted. After her conviction she reportedly made three attempts to strangle herself; on one occasion a long pin was also found in her possession and on another a piece of rope. She was then watched day and night by a relay of wardresses.

King was suspected of murdering more than the two children for which she was convicted; at least five and probably more. The date for her execution was set for Monday 12 March 1889 at Calton gaol, Edinburgh, the scene of Berry's first execution. The scaffold was erected in an apartment of the condemned cell area, no more than 12 yards for her to walk, and on the Sunday the condemned woman made a full confession. When Berry visited her in her cell she guessed whom he was and asked him not to hurt her. The following exchange, according to Berry, then took place.

'No, I won't hurt you, my dear. Be brave, and you'll never feel a thing. Why did you do it Jessie? You don't look like a woman who would murder anyone.'

She burst into tears, 'Oh, Mr. Berry, I must have been mad. The poor little things had to starve like both of us, and I thought it was the best thing that could happen to them. I couldn't bear to hear their cries, and you know what the world is, Mr. Berry.'

On the eve of her execution she went to bed at eleven o'clock and fell asleep exhausted about half past midnight. She was a little restless and woke a few times during the night, immediately falling asleep again. At five in the morning she was woken and dressed in her own clothes, which included a black cloth mantle, with caps. At six the Roman Catholic priest joined her and, with an assistant, administered the sacrament. Mass was celebrated in the chapel, after which she ate her breakfast.

When Berry entered her cell her composure amazed him and the others present. A group of female warders who had attended her stood at the door, and as Berry approached her they burst into tears and sobbed bitterly. Berry had never seen such a condemned cell before:

In the centre of the room was a table, over which there was a dark cover. On the table was a small vase containing a few faded flowers, a large Bible, one or two prayer-books, and a small portrait of the Master, a syphon of soda water two-thirds empty, and a chemist's glass which had contained wine.

Beside the table was an armchair and two ordinary chairs of a plain pattern, which were almost the only other articles of furniture in the cell. On one of the chairs were two cups and saucers and a plate, on which were several broken slices of bread.

Outside the prison, Calton Hill was crowded. Hearing the wardresses sobbing Jessie asked to say goodbye to them, seeing them one by one. She bore herself bravely, not crying, and took each one by the hands saying, 'The Lord bless you.' Berry then pinioned her, and, taking the white cap from his pocket, put it over her head.

'Now just let me pull it over your face Jessie,' he said. 'It will be better you don't look at these people round you. You'll only break down, you know.'

'No I won't Mr. Berry, I'll be brave,' she replied.

'That's right, be a brave little woman, and it will be all over in a second,' said Berry:

In a way she looked a beautiful girl, a sorry mistake of Nature, and with a sigh I pulled the cap over her face, and once again I told her to be brave.

Immediately the procession started, the clergyman commenced to read the litany in solemn tones. Jessie answered the responses quite distinctly, but there was a sob in her voice and she ran all the way to the scaffold.

A moment had scarcely elapsed from the time she quitted her cell till the poor girl was standing on the drop below the noose. Quickly I stooped down and pinioned her legs, and with the quickness of lightning I put the rope around her neck. Nobody could say that, grief-stricken as I was, my hand was merciless, for the one idea in my mind was to get it all over with alacrity.

When Jessie King felt the rope tighten around her neck she stopped the responses to the litany. Her last words were 'Unto Thy hands, O Lord, I commend my spirit. Lord Jesus receive my soul. Jesus, Son of David, have mercy on me.'

As those last words were uttered I drew the bolt, and Jessie King disappeared from the view of the weeping crowd around the gibbet. I looked down into the pit, and with a sense of glad relief I saw that I had done my work well. The body hung quite still. Neither it nor the rope gave the slightest quiver. The cross was still in her hands, and when I went down I saw that her eyes were closed and a smile upon her face as if she were asleep.

After I had satisfied myself that all was well I looked at the crowd in front of me. The faces of the Magistrates were blanched, the wardresses were in a half-fainting condition, and few in the place could forbear to shed tears.

The procession had progressed with firm step to the execution, but everybody staggered out, longing to get away from the dread sight of doom he and she had beheld.

When I walked out into the yard of the prison the sun was gleaming brightly and a cool breeze was blowing. The first man I saw was Canon Donlevy, the clergyman who had officiated at the execution, and his kind smile helped me to become myself again. I saw that he did not despise me.

'Well father, that sad job is done.'

The Canon, who wore a dejected look, nodded his head, and replied that it was over.

'Don't you think it was really satisfactory, Father?' I said. 'In all my life, I tell you truly, I never saw a woman meet her death so bravely. Such bravery I never in my life witnessed before.'

The Canon nodded again.

'She is a little woman who went to the scaffold with the knowledge of God.'

Berry thanked the canon for his valuable assistance and the latter responded kindly, at which Berry broke down and cried, the clergyman sympathetically striving to comfort him. Subsequently, Berry took the cross from King's hand and carried it reverently to the prison governor, who took possession of it. He recorded that he would have liked to leave it with her, 'but it is not the custom'. A grave was dug on the eastern side of the prison, next to those of Berry's first two victims. King was buried in the afternoon, Canon Donlevy conducting the service.

Berry travelled straight down to Shepton Mallet gaol for the execution of Samuel Reylands, scheduled for the following day. The first man to be hanged at this 200-year-old gaol, Reylands's crime was an appalling one. About 8.00 a.m. on Wednesday 2 January 1889 Emma Jane Davies, aged 9, had set out, as was her habit, to fetch milk for the family from Bridge House at Yeobridge (near South Petherton, Somerset), owned by Major Blake, for whom her father, George, worked. It was a foggy and frosty morning, and when she failed to return home her mother became anxious, finally setting off with her son in search of her. Some time between noon and one o'clock the boy discovered his sister's body lying in a muddy ditch in Gore Field, adjacent to the road. Her clothes were disordered, a blind-cord had been tied around her neck, the body was gashed and cut, and her dress was thrown over her head, which was almost severed from her body. A doctor was sent for and the police called. The milk can that the girl had been carrying was found under her body, heavily battered, this almost certainly having been used to strike her. An old razor was also found nearby, with blood and mud on it. Blood in the field indicated that she had been murdered there before being dumped in the ditch. A man's footprints, discovered in the field, were carefully preserved in the hope that they might lead to the identification of the offender. Dr Walter, of South Petherton, conducted a post-mortem examination of the body and concluded that the child had sustained several heavy blows to the head before her throat was cut.

Emma did not appear to have been sexually assaulted and no motive for the crime could be established. Since several strangers had been noted in the neighbourhood in the weeks preceding the murder it was supposed that one of these had committed the crime, but on the night of Friday 4 January a local labourer named Samuel Reylands, aged 23, was arrested on suspicion of Emma's murder. Rejecting the idea that a stranger was the culprit, the police had swiftly fastened on Reylands as their chief suspect. He had absconded from the district two or three years previously to evade a charge brought against him, returning to his father's house just three months before the murder. Though there was no direct evidence linking him with the crime, there was much circumstantial evidence against Reylands. A woman who had passed the field on the morning of the murder picked him out from a number of other men as being of similar stature to a man she had spotted there. Dr H.J. Alford, the county analyst, examined the prisoner's clothing and, though unable to find bloodstains, identified spots on the back part of his hat as being milk. Reylands had also been seen shortly after the murder perspiring heavily and with wet and muddy boots. Despite all this, he denied killing the girl, but he was nonetheless

271

committed for trial, appearing at the Western Circuit Assizes at Taunton before Mr Justice Wills on 20 February 1889.

There was much interest in the case because of the atrocity of the crime, the age of the murdered girl, and the apparent absence of motive. The only clue to the latter was a threat that the prisoner was said to have uttered, when at Cardiff, that on his return home he would be revenged on the little girl's father, though why he should have said this was not clear. George Davies knew of no quarrel between himself and the prisoner or his family. (According to the under-sheriff there were, in fact, several men named George Davies who either lived or had lived at South Petherton.) The lack of motive led to various lurid press reports. *The Times* of 22 February 1889 stated:

> His Lordship, who summed up at great length, referred to the case as mysterious, very unusual, and exceptional in its circumstances. It was apparently an aimless and motiveless crime by whomsoever committed. It was probably the morbid results of reading the accounts of the horrors which of late have appeared in the newspapers. In this instance, however, there were no traces of any outrage with the view of gratifying the murderer's passions. Whoever committed the crime must have been cool and collected, and able to do what was best to avoid detection afterwards. The crime must have been done with deliberation, and care must have been taken to remove all blood stains and other indications of its commission . . .

The lack of direct evidence was pointed out to the jury and they were warned against convicting on suspicion only, '. . . it was better, if a mistake were made, that a guilty man should be acquitted rather than an innocent one be convicted'. The jurors deliberated for an hour and a half before returning a guilty verdict, upon which the usual sentence of death was passed. Then, on 26 February, *The Times* reported:

> THE YEOBRIDGE MURDER. – Samuel Rylands, who last week, at Taunton Assizes, was convicted of the murder of the little girl Davies, at South Petherton, on January 2, has made a

confession. In a letter written to his parents he confesses that the murder was committed in Cottage-lane. He mentions no details and expresses great contrition for the crime.

No motive was mentioned. The rumour of a grudge against her father still circulated, but it is hard to believe that there was no sexual element to the crime, given the fact that the girl's clothes were disordered and her dress thrown over her head. Perhaps the murderer's initial lust had been dispelled on seeing the awfulness of what he had done.

24

A violent prisoner and a Zulu

'One of the worst jobs I ever tackled was the execution of
Thomas Allen . . . '

April 1889 was to be a memorable month for James Berry. Not only did he conduct a couple of difficult executions but he also claimed to have hanged the infamous 'Jack the Ripper' – and he was the subject of debate in the House of Commons.

The first execution, of four that month, involved another trip to Ireland, and was no doubt viewed with as much apprehension by Berry as his other trips to the Emerald Isle. Peter Stafford had been convicted at Maryborough Assizes on 9 March for the murder of a farmer, Patrick Crawley, at Ballyhoe, County Meath. The condemned man had shot his victim as the result of a long-standing dispute. Stafford maintained his innocence but was sentenced to death, the execution set for Monday 8 April.

Unfortunately for Berry he was to have another unpleasant experience, this time at the hands of his victim rather than abusive crowds. Stafford awaited his fate in Kilmainham gaol, Dublin. His wife, accompanied by her child and her brother, had been allowed to visit him on the Saturday preceding the execution and an emotional meeting had taken place. Despite advice from the chaplain and governor, Mrs Stafford subsequently remained in town in order to be outside the prison at the hour of execution, and on the morning of the fateful day she again tried to see her husband. The governor, Mr Beere, however, refused to allow her into the prison.

Representatives of the press were not allowed to witness the execution, but details of the painful scene were reported. Despite his delicate appearance, Stafford resisted violently when Berry tried to pinion him. The priests in attendance, the Revd Canon Kennedy and the Revd Mr Byrne, succeeded in pacifying the prisoner sufficiently for Berry to pinion his arms, but he subsequently started to struggle again, his desperate situation giving him added strength. It was with great difficulty that Berry, assisted by the warders, carried out the sentence. Stafford had to be forcibly taken to the scaffold and there he cried out, 'Lord have mercy on me! God forgive me my sins!' Those present, witnessing the fraught scene, included the governor, the deputy governor, Mr Lowry the Sub-Sheriff of the County of Meath, the clergymen and the usual warders. Berry gave a drop of 6ft 6in, Stafford's weight being 11 stone, and death appeared to be almost instantaneous, the spinal cord being completely severed and the blood vessels of the neck ruptured.

On Sunday 10 February 1889 Thomas Allen, aged 25, a black seaman said to be a Zulu, murdered Frederick George Kent, the 38-year-old landlord of the Gloucester Hotel at Swansea, situated near to the entrance to the South Dock. Allen, a ship's steward, had recently been discharged from the steamship *Cubana*. Mr and Mrs Kent had closed about 11.00 p.m. and had retired to bed at midnight, placing the day's takings of £30 (in gold and silver) in a cash-box between the mattress and the bed, as was their custom. The murder occurred about 4 a.m. Hearing someone striking a match in the bedroom, and then seeing a man standing near the dressing table, Mrs Kent had roused her husband, who got out of bed and struggled desperately with the intruder. She, meanwhile, had struck a light and, seeing the attack on her husband, seized a revolver that he kept under his pillow. As soon as she saw the chance of taking a shot without injuring her husband, she fired the gun. The bullet lodged in the back of Allen's right thigh, and, dropping to his hands and knees, he crawled under the bed to the dressing table. There, however, he seized the dressing-table mirror and threw it at Mr Kent, before rushing round the bed, blowing out the candle and pushing Mrs Kent away from the door, preventing her from opening it. He renewed the struggle with Mr Kent and by the time Mrs Kent had relit the candle it was to see the intruder – whom she observed to be a black man – rush past her, unlock the door and make good his escape. The only other occupants of the house were two servants and two children, and Mrs Kent shouted for assistance. They found that Mr Kent had been seriously wounded. There was a zig-zag stab under his heart, a deep wound in his throat, and an even deeper wound on the right breast penetrating to the lungs. His thighs and other parts of his body had also been cut in several places. Police Constable Cross was first at the scene and tended the dying man, placing a handkerchief on his wounded throat. Asked who had inflicted the wounds, Mr Kent pointed to the bedroom door and gasped, 'A dark man with thick woolly hair. He stabbed me and cut my throat down there.' Medical aid was summoned but Mr Kent expired three hours later.

The fleeing murderer had left his cap behind, and from this he was identified. He had also left a razor in the bedroom, this being the weapon that had inflicted the various wounds. The police quickly ascertained the story of what had happened and the Chief Constable, Captain Colquhoun, summoned the whole of the force and volunteers to search for the culprit. Footprints leading from the hotel to the docks were found in the snow, and after about six hours Allen was found hiding behind an unused tubular boiler in the Globe Dry Dock nearby. An aggressive crowd assembled as the police took their prisoner to the Guildhall Police Station, Allen being struck on the head amid calls to lynch him. His guilt was clear: he had blood over his cuffs and shirt, and a bullet lodged in the back of his right thigh. He claimed that he had not intended to hurt anyone, saying that he had been in a neighbouring public house on the Saturday night, just before closing time, and had afterwards entered the Gloucester and concealed himself in the bedroom by hiding under the bed, intending to steal the Saturday night's takings. The police believed him to be guilty of previous similar burglaries in the area, and he was remanded in custody.

On 18 March Allen appeared before Mr Justice Grantham at the South Wales Assizes on the charge of murdering Mr Kent. He claimed to have been enticed into the house by a woman of the town, who had suggested that he should go upstairs, conceal himself under the bed and await her arrival, but the woman in question denied this, stating that she had no such conversation on the subject with the accused. The latter's cap and boots had been recovered at the murder scene and under the bed were the marks where his bloody hand had been pressed against the floor. A verdict of guilty was returned, and sentence of death passed.

The execution was set for Wednesday 10 April, at Swansea, and the Home Secretary declined to recommend a reprieve. A few days prior to the execution Allen wrote to the widow of the murdered landlord begging her forgiveness, and on the night before the execution he received, via the prison governor, a letter granting her forgiveness. Berry journeyed to Swansea directly from Dublin, where he had hanged Stafford, and on arriving at the gaol he went to see Allen, afterwards carefully testing the rope in order to avoid any 'accidents'. He was to write later in his account of the execution for *The Post*: 'One of the worst jobs I ever tackled was the execution of Thomas Allan [*sic*] . . . Thomas was a black man, a big, strong fellow, with muscles like iron bands, and it well nigh beat me to hang him.'

The morning of the execution dawned, an overcast day with a layer of snow on the ground. Over 1,500 people had gathered in front of the walls of the building and the police had to clear a way to allow the officials to enter the gaol. Berry looked out of the gateway and saw a boy at the top of a telegraph pole with others on the ground laughing and chaffing him. Allen had slept from midnight until 5 a.m., subsequently seeing the chaplain at seven o'clock and receiving his ministrations with great penitence. Berry visited him early and found him to be in fair spirits considering the gravity of his situation, apparently anxious that the end should come soon. He returned again later, as the hour of execution drew near:

'I am going to take you out now, and I won't give you any trouble if you give me none. If you struggle it will be all the worse for yourself.'

'I will give you no trouble,' was the reply; 'I will die game.'

'That's right Allan,' said I; 'and I hope you will not die without confessing your crime.'

All this I said as I was putting the straps around him.

'I have nothing to say, sir.'

'Surely you are not going to go before your Maker with a lie on your lips?'

But still he was not willing to comply with my request, and so I nodded to the warders. There were four of them, for, as he was such a powerful fellow, we had taken special precautions, and two of them walked on each side of him.

The Under-Sheriff and his deputy, the governor of the gaol, and the governor of another South Wales gaol walked in the procession behind us, and as the cortege wended its way to the scene of the execution the bell was tolled.

The steps of the condemned man were firm and fearless, and he took his place on the trap without exhibiting the slightest signs of nervousness. I placed him with his back to those present, and put the straps round his ankles and the rope round his neck.

As the cap was being fixed, those in the crowd saw the black man move his head slightly and whisper in my ear. They wondered what secret he was imparting to me, but there was no secret about it, and the incident only indicated the fearlessness of my victim.

'May I speak to you?' he asked

'By all means, Allan.'

'May I utter a prayer aloud before you hang me?'

'Certainly. But it must be short; time is nearly up.'

In a devout voice [he] began to pray –

'Lord have mercy upon us. Lord Jesus receive my spirit this day. Lord Jesus look down with pity upon me; take me to Thyself.'

He paused and I sprang aside and took hold of the lever, pulled it sharply, and the poor fellow sank down into the pit. The rope did not quiver.

'Dead, dead!' exclaimed the governor, and so it looked, but the words were scarcely out of his mouth before the man at the end of the rope began to struggle. The doctor assured me afterwards that nearly three minutes elapsed before [he] died, and he thought it would have been better if I had given my victim another six inches. He was probably right.

A great deal of talk was occasioned in the town when it leaked out that on the night before I hanged Allan I went to the Pavilion Music Hall, but nobody seemed to desire to molest me, and I left Swansea without a harsh word being hurled at me.

But I was not free to go home yet a while. Another victim lay in the condemned cell at Bristol awaiting execution, and thither I journeyed to carry out my third execution since leaving Bradford.

On Monday 11 February 1889, John Withey, a butcher living in Cumberland Street, Bristol, was arrested for having stabbed his wife to death. The inquest held on Monday 18 February returned a verdict of wilful murder, ruling that the wound from which she died could not have been self-inflicted. Tried at Bristol Assizes, together with Elizabeth Knutt who was charged with being an accessory, Withey was sentenced to death and remanded to Horfield gaol, Bristol. Knutt receiving a five-year prison sentence.

It was a contentious case. The accused man had been drinking heavily before the murder, which led the jury to conclude that the crime was not premeditated and thus to recommend a merciful sentence. Withey was also of previous good character, so many felt that a verdict of manslaughter would be more appropriate than that of wilful murder. A memorial on his behalf was sent to the Home Secretary, Mr Matthews, outlining these facts and in the House of Commons on Tuesday 2 April, responding to a question raised on the matter by Mr L. Fry, he stated that though he did not agree it was a case of manslaughter he was giving the case his 'most earnest attention', stating further 'I am in communication with the learned Judge with regard to it'. Withey's brother visited him on the Saturday and his children on the Monday.

As late as 11.00 p.m. on the eve of the execution a last effort was made to defer the final penalty of the law. A confession by Frederick Withey, the condemned man's 16-year-old son, claiming that on hearing his mother groaning he had pulled the knife out of the wound, was telegraphed to the Home Secretary, but Mr Matthews was unmoved and decided not to interfere with the sentence. The execution went ahead on the morning of Thursday 11 April, the press being excluded from the execution and afterwards refused all information. Persistent reporters, however, sought what information they could, a report in *The Times* claiming that Withey was self-possessed and walked firmly to the scaffold; death being instantaneous. The chaplain left Bristol after the execution, and immediately afterwards the pressmen learnt from 'an apparently trustworthy source' that Berry had asked Withey if he had anything to say, to which Withey had replied, 'I have confessed to the chaplain that I did it.' *The Post* series of 1914 gives a rather sensational account of the proceedings under the headline: 'The

Truth About John Withey's Confession – Reveals Secret on way to the Scaffold – Remarkable disclosures by James Berry.' Berry claims here that 'Everyone in the gaol believed John Withey to be guiltless. His family cried out for justice, and the people of the place in which he lived said that judicial murder would be done if I hanged him . . .' He dismissed this, however, saying:

> But Withey was unable to hide his guilt from the penetrating eye of the hangman, and when I left the gaol I was secure in the knowledge that he had suffered a just penalty.
>
> He confessed to me in the last moments of his life, and although this has been denied, and no record of the confession has ever been made public, there are those alive to-day who know I am telling the truth.
>
> What made me doubt the innocence of the man at first was the fact that Mr. Justice Hawkins refused to advise the authorities to alter the death sentence.
>
> When the Home Secretary found himself unable to make up his mind he referred the case back to the Judge who had tried Withey. Now Mr. Justice Hawkins was known as the hanging Judge, and to many he appeared to be devoid of all mercy, but I had long been convinced that no man was more careful in coming to a decision, and I felt that if there was the slightest thing in favour of the condemned man, Hawkins would give him the benefit of it.

Contemporary reports in *The Times* back up Berry's assessment. One such report on Monday 15 April 1889 concerning the House of Commons carried the response of the Home Secretary to a question put by Colonel Hill:

> Mr. MATTHEWS said, – I received on Saturday a report from the chaplain of Bristol Gaol which contained the following passage: – 'John Withey never told me that he murdered his wife, neither did he ever deny it. Nor did he ever accuse any one else. More than once he allowed that he might have done it in drunken anger; but he always added that, if he did, he neither knew nor remembered anything about it.' The

governor of the gaol also informs me that although Withey was visited by various relatives and friends, to none of them did he deny the crime. I must leave my hon. friend to put his own construction on these passages.

So what was the 'secret' divulged to Berry by the doomed man? Berry described the execution in some detail:

The gallows had been erected under my supervision for this execution. It was built in the vanhouse, just to the left of the gaol entrance. This was the first occasion on which a man was to be hanged in Horfield Gaol, and naturally everyone was moving about in a nervous and excited manner.

Soon after seven o'clock a crowd began to assemble in the vicinity, and as eight o'clock drew near four or five thousand persons had congregated in the roadway and the fields adjoining the prison, the entrance of which was guarded by a body of police.

Early in the morning the Governor, who was a very humane man, had removed John Withey from the condemned cell, so that his last walk to the scaffold should be a short one.

He had not long been in the new cell before the clergyman arrived at the prison, and the latter went straight to see him, and prepare him for the end. Shortly before eight o'clock, everything being ready, I decided to go and bring my victim out, and when I reached the cell I found him looking very self-possessed in the company of two warders.

'Time is up, John,' I said not unkindly, 'Are you ready?'

'Oh, yes, I am ready, Mr. Berry.'

I proceeded to buckle the straps around him, and while doing so I decided to make sure that I was not hanging an innocent man.

'Are you quite prepared to die, John?'

'I am,' he replied in tones of deep conviction.

'Have you confessed your crime? If not –'

'I have not confessed to a crime I did not commit,' he said firmly. 'I know nothing about it.'

'Look here, John,' I said. 'There is no good in talking like that. This is the last chance you will get, for once I get you out of here I will not give you a second to speak. It will be over in no time.'

But still he remained silent. 'What is the good of being stubborn now. You don't want to go before your Maker with a lie on your lips. You know you murdered your poor wife, and the best thing you can do is to confess.'

He thought over my words, and then he spoke roughly –

'I am not going to confess to you.'

'Will you confess to the chaplain?'

'Yes, I will confess to him.'

'Nothing will please me better,' I said. 'I will go and bring him here at once.'

Outside the door I found a little group of officials waiting and they looked surprised when they saw me coming without my victim.

'The prisoner wishes to confess, sir,' I said, addressing myself to the clergyman.

He stepped back in amazement.

'I don't understand you. Confess to what?'

'To having committed his crime.'

'Impossible! I will not believe it.'

'It is perfectly true, sir.'

'I will never believe it. I have just administered the blessed sacrament to him.'

I went back into the cell, and brought the prisoner out, and one of the officials present asked him if he wished to confess.

The man burst into tears at the question.

'Yes, sir. I want to confess. I was drunk, and I did not know what I was doing.'

'You scoundrel!'

With a look of contempt, the official turned on his heel and walked away, refusing to have anything to do with the execution.

The procession was now formed, and, still weeping bitterly, John Withey took his place in it. He was trembling and heartbroken, and as he walked along the warders had to support him on each side. I think that this was one of the saddest walks I ever took to the gallows, and often since I retired have I looked back with feelings of pity on poor John Withey.

Before he emerged from the cell every man in the prison but myself had been his friend, and believed that he was innocent of the crime of wilful murder, and now everyone's 'hand' was against him. And he seemed to know it – he could not help knowing it; but why, I am not privileged to say.

The walk to the gallows only occupied a few minutes, and once we were there the execution was soon over. John Withey died in tears and without a word.

When the execution was over I left the gaol, and the first person I met was one of my victim's relatives.

'Can I speak to you, Mr. Berry?'

'Certainly. What is it?'

'I have come to get his clothes, and ask you how he died.'

'He died repentant,' said I. 'Before he passed he confessed his crime to the chaplain.'

'It is false, Mr. Berry.'

'If you do not believe me ask the chaplain. He will not tell a lie.'

With a look of despair, the lad walked away.

'I came for his clothes,' he said, 'but now I know the truth I do not want them.'

Efforts made by the townsfolk to obtain the substance of the confession were without result. So deeply grieved was the chaplain that he left the gaol and went on a visit to some friends. The public, however, were determined to get at the bottom of the matter, and a message was sent to Mr. Lewis Fry, M.P. for Bristol.

The latter wired back that no communication had reached the Home Secretary, and later, in response to a communication from Bristol, it was stated that no communication had been received from the gaol to the effect that John Withey had confessed.

That was all the public ever heard about the matter, and not until now have I written the full truth about that grim interview before John Withey walked out to the gallows.

So there still remains an air of mystery surrounding Withey's last-minute confession. That he committed the crime there seems no doubt. That the officials at the gaol were disappointed in him after he confessed, having already convinced them all of his innocence, seems equally apparent. And the words of the chaplain, read by the Home Secretary, really do seem to amount to a confession, albeit guarded. So ended another controversial execution for Berry.

At this time there was serious murmuring against Berry at the highest level. On the various Assize Circuits the Grand Juries had been making presentments to the circuit judges concerning the public executioner, who, it was generally felt, should be brought under the direct control of the Home Secretary. It was an orchestrated campaign, Berry's activities having caused repercussions. A question was raised in the House of Commons on Thursday 11 April 1889, the day of Withey's execution. Sir E. Lechmere, who seems to have been the prime mover against Berry, asked if the Home Secretary had received any copies of these presentments and resolutions of a similar nature adopted by county magistrates at the last Quarter Sessions and if so which ones. Also, could the House be told of any opinions of Her Majesty's Judges received? Henry Matthews confirmed that he had, from the counties of Surrey, Dorset, Westmorland, Leicester, Worcester, Lincoln, Gloucester, Durham, Devon, Nottingham, York, Monmouth, Hereford, Derby, Salop and Glamorgan. He had received no opinions from the judges forwarding them, apart from the Lord Chief Justice, who thought the change 'a very right and rational one', and Mr Justice Denman, who thought that the carrying out of executions had better not be in the hands of the government.

The following day Sir E. Lechmere moved that, in the opinion of the House, the executioner should be placed under the direct control of the Home Office. There was a hint that the campaign to abolish capital punishment was far from over, but, as long as it formed part of the penal process of the law, matters would be improved if the public official administering it were better controlled. Lechmere mentioned 'such scandals as had occurred on recent occasions' and argued that the executioner should be brought under government control to avoid such transgressions. He also pointed out that Berry had 'not been appointed by any body in particular', whereas his predecessors had been appointed by the

Court of Aldermen of the City of London with a view to their carrying out executions at the Old Bailey. From time to time the High Sheriffs of counties and cities, upon whom the responsibility rested, had found it convenient to write to the authorities of the Corporation of London to engage the services of the executioner retained by them, the executioner so appointed receiving a retainer of £20 a year, as well as the additional sum paid for each execution. The object of the retainer had been that the Court of Aldermen were able to secure first claim for the executioner's services when required. In Berry's case, there had been no such appointment; 'he somehow seemed to have slipped into the duties after the dismissal of his predecessor, Binns, for gross misconduct and drunkenness'. (It was not mentioned that Marwood had assumed the job without such an appointment also.) Lechmere further pointed out that there were no actual rules and conditions in force relating to the executioner, with the one exception that he was required by the Home Office to sleep within the precincts of the gaol on the night preceding the execution. He continued:

To show that this was by no means sufficient to ensure the propriety of conduct on the part of the hangman, he might mention that, in May of last year, Berry went down to Hereford to execute two men, and on the night preceding the execution he was *fêted* at a smoking concert, at which he himself was a performer. From Hereford he went to Worcester, and there visited several publichouses and held a kind of levee. The High Sheriff of Worcestershire, anxious to prevent unseemly conduct on the part of the executioner similar to that which had occurred elsewhere, took special pains to speed Berry on his way to his home in Bradford, but instead of proceeding there he alighted at Kidderminster, where a scene occurred which excited a great deal of scandal. He spent five or six hours in the town, visited different publichouses, and delivered two lectures, one on morality and the other on phrenology. He also passed a barber into the gaol under an assumed name. He believed that Berry did this terrible work with all the skill and as much humanity as could be expected, but the great fault of the present arrangement was that the hangman could do as he liked so long as he was not in the actual employment of the High Sheriff of the county.

Thus Berry's transgressions were publicly paraded and the government challenged to bring him under control or find a new official. A ready replacement was still active in Yorkshire, Billington having conducted executions, though not many, throughout Berry's reign, and thus being an experienced hand for the job should he be required.

The presentments and resolutions, and the opinion of the Lord Chief Justice, were in favour of change; namely that the hangman should be properly appointed and should hold a certificate showing that he was qualified by his conduct and in other ways to perform his duties. In France and Germany the executioner was paid or retained by the state, and in the British dependency of Malta the hangman received £30 a year from the British Government.

Voices in support of the motion were heard, Mr Lockwood pointing out that it was not proposed to interfere with the duties of the High Sheriffs as performed through their under-sheriffs, but merely to ask that the Home Office should see that persons were appointed with regard to the way executions were carried out. In June 1888 the Commission had suggested that the High Sheriff should be relieved of all responsibility in connection with the execution of criminals, this being passed to the authority that had charge of all prisoners and that controlled the execution of other penal sentences. This was no longer being proposed, as there were grave objections to such a course, but it was desirable that certificates should be held, thus ensuring that qualified persons would carry out their duties in a proper way. Lockwood continued, '. . . a large number of persons outside that House held strong views on the question of capital punishment. Some were of opinion that it should be abolished altogether; but every one would agree that if capital punishment continued to form a part of the penal code of this country it should be carried out with decency.' Lockwood too, it seems

. . . had heard of scenes such as the hon. baronet had described. Receptions had been held the night before the executions, and the man who was to carry out the sentence of the law was the hero of the hour. The instruments of death were exhibited; and the receptions were renewed the day following.

Lechmere's resolution was seen as a possible means to put a stop to such scandals. Further supporting the resolution, Mr Morrison declared that the hangman should be appointed by and responsible to the Home Office. The greatest scandal of all was that the sheriff engaged the executioner but had no further control over him after the execution was performed. He was supported by Mr Cossham, who observed that the great drawback of the present system was that:

> . . . it had a tendency to make the public executioner a hero. He was horrified the other day, when travelling in a train from the west of England, to find that the same train brought the public executioner, and that at Swindon this man was the centre of attraction for the people assembled in the station.

Against the resolution, Mr Pickersgill said that if adopted it would place the House in an illogical and untenable position. While it would leave the sheriffs responsible for an effectual and decent execution, it would place them under the obligation of employing an executioner whom they had not appointed, and over whom they would not have full authority. It was either a case of leaving responsibility where it was or transferring the entire responsibility and control over to the Home Office. Noting that reporters had been excluded from the recent execution at Bristol, he argued that there was much to be said for this, though he understood there were also reasons against. However, what was indefensible, he stated, was the fact that the practice should vary according to the personal opinions of the sheriff. If the responsibility was turned over, then uniformity one way or the other should be secured.

In reply Henry Matthews made it clear that he did not want responsibility for executions turned over to the Home Office. Taking note of the diversity of views expressed and of one member's speech against capital punishment, he maintained that to remove the responsibility from the sheriff would be a great mistake. It was a 'matter of considerable consequence' that the responsibility for executions should devolve upon local rather than government officers. The presence of such an officer as the sheriff at an execution was an assurance to the public that there would be nothing unfair, and that no undue partiality would be shown to the convict, no matter what his rank, position, political antecedents or status in society might have been. It was important to take care that the right man was executed:

> If the responsibility were transferred to the Home Office he would be bound to send down an official high in rank to be present when the sentence of death was passed, so as to be in a position to take care that the right person was really executed. Every under-sheriff at present was responsible for the performance of that function. You could not leave this and the general responsibility with the sheriff without leaving him also the free choice of the agent for carrying out the execution. One of the persons who most warmly favoured the adoption of the resolution was Berry himself. Berry had written him a letter which would really 'draw iron tears down Pluto's cheek', in which he urged the Home Secretary 'as a Conservative member of Parliament and a gentleman of sound education, to assist Sir E. Lechmere to carry his resolution'. Therefore Berry was one of the persons supporting it.

Matthews was prepared to give a partial undertaking. It would not be easy for the Home Office to select an executioner capable of conducting the terrible function skilfully while at the same time being a man of respectability who might be trusted to abide by the conditions imposed upon him. If such a man could be selected he might be employed by the sheriff if the sheriff thought fit, just as at the present time a scaffold was offered without any insistence that it must be the one used.

> No doubt this plan would give security against such misconduct and painful incidents as attention had been called to. In the Kidderminster case Berry had acted in defiance of the express agreement with the sheriff – that he was not to go to any place

of public entertainment after the execution, but was to proceed direct to the railway station accompanied by a warder. He violated these conditions, and there might be no security that an official from the Home Office would not equally yield to the temptation, which seemed to be offered in a morbid curiosity, except it were the risk of forfeiting his employment. He would consider whether it was possible for the Home Office to select some fit and well-conducted person. It had been pointed out that many persons regarded this as a hateful office, the holder of which, so far from being an object of interest, should be abhorred, and there were few respectable men who would undertake the office unless the temptation was larger than could be offered.

Matthews said that he would undertake to consider the matter but indicated that a suggestion by Mr Justice Denman that a warder in every gaol should be selected for the duty seemed to be quite impracticable. At some gaols there was not an execution in ten years so it would be an extravagant undertaking to appoint an executioner at each of them. It must be understood that if the Home Office tendered the services of a man so selected, it must be left to the sheriffs to decide if he was a fit choice.

Sir E. Lechmere declared himself to a certain extent satisfied with the reply and hoped that the Home Secretary would draw up rules and conditions that would 'secure the object in view'. The amendment was thus withdrawn.

This debate was a warning signal to Berry. He was treading on thin ice and his behaviour was being noted.

25

Was he Jack the Ripper?

'. . . we are quite satisfied that you have hanged "Jack the
Ripper".'

On the night of Sunday 10 February 1889 William Henry Bury, a 29-year-old Londoner, surrendered himself to the Dundee police admitting that he had stabbed his wife. A terrible domestic murder, it was to have greater ramifications when Bury emerged as a suspect for 'Jack the Ripper'. Eventually it would lead James Berry to claim that he had executed the most notorious murderer the world had ever known.

The *Dundee Advertiser* of Tuesday 12 February 1889 carried the sensational story:

TRAGEDY IN DUNDEE
WOMAN SHOCKINGLY STABBED.
MUTILATION OF THE REMAINS.
BODY PACKED IN A BOX
A LONDONER IN CUSTODY.
ANTECEDENTS OF PRISONER.

Particulars of what at present appears to be a tragedy of a most revolting character were made known in Dundee yesterday, and throughout the day created much excitement in the city, and especially in the Eastern district. The remarkable immunity of Dundee from crimes of a serious nature has often been remarked, and the occurrence is surrounded by so unusual circumstances as to arrest more than ordinary attention. The affair is certainly of a most mysterious and sensational class, and the details forcibly bring to recollection some of the worst of the East End of London murders.

About 7.00 p.m. on Sunday 10 February a man called at the Central Police Office in Dundee and asked to see the officer on duty. The only occupants of the Orderly Room were Lieutenant Parr and Constable McKay. Parr took the man – who gave his details as William Henry Bury, aged 29, a sand and sawdust merchant – into an adjoining room and the latter unburdened himself to the officer. He had arrived in Dundee three weeks earlier, having sailed from London with his wife Ellen on Saturday 19 January aboard the steamer *Cambria*, the two having occupied a second-class cabin. Arriving in Dundee late the following night, they had stayed aboard ship overnight and then, after a week in lodgings in Union Street, had taken up residence at 113 Princes Street, Bury having taken a key from the agent to view them and not returned it. On Monday 4 February he and his wife had been drinking heavily and, according to Bury, were so drunk that they did not know the time as they retired to bed. The following morning, upon waking, he had found his wife lying on the floor, dead, upon which he had been 'seized with a mad impulse, and, lifting a large knife near by, he plunged it several times into the abdomen'. Some time after this, afraid at what he had done, he decided to conceal the body, so he dragged a plain white wooden box to the middle of the floor and forced the body into it.

In the course of further questioning Bury made a remark about 'Jack the Ripper', but Parr did not understand what he meant so questioned him no further on the matter. Instead he called out the Chief of the Detective Department, Lieutenant David Lamb, and Bury repeated part of his story to him before handing a key to Lamb and saying, 'There's the key of the door, and you will easily find the box with the body in it. The house can be easily got, and you will know it at once, because there are red curtains on the front window.'

Lieutenant Lamb and Detective Campbell went to the Princes Street address, a 'sunk tenement' and, entering with the key Bury had supplied, began searching the house by candlelight. The front room was devoid of furniture, and on entering the rear room they found the box in the middle of the floor. It was 3ft 3in long, by 2ft 4in across and 2ft 1in deep. Opening it by raising two loose boards on the lid, they pulled back a piece of sheeting underneath to reveal the leg and foot of a female. Proceeding no further they immediately telephoned for aid; the Chief Constable, Mr Dewar, the Procurator Fiscal, Mr Agnew, and the police surgeon were all informed.

Doctors Templeman and Stalker attended the scene and examined the grim contents of the box. The body had been crushed into the box, which was too small to accommodate it easily. On top of the body was a bloodstained woman's ulster, with a hood lined with brown velvet. The head had been forced to one side onto a shoulder, the left leg was broken and twisted to such a degree that the foot rested on the left shoulder, and the right leg had been smashed in order to fit into a corner of the box. The body was lying on its back, on a petticoat and a piece of cloth, while the remainder of the box had been tightly packed with clothing, books, papers etc. Among the books was a small Johnston's dictionary with an inscription on the flyleaf that included the address, 'Emma Perott, 9 Arnold Road, Bow, E.' and a small 'Litany' inscribed 'Miss Ellen Elliot, a gift from her brother George 1868'. The police also found at the property two knives and a piece of rope with hair in it.

The body was lifted from the box and presented a sickening spectacle. There were five or six large wounds in the abdomen, and the entrails protruded from one particularly long and deep cut. There was also a deep red mark round the neck such as would be produced by a rope used in strangulation.

The Chief Constable was updated concerning the examination of the crime scene, and Bury subsequently informed that he was being detained on suspicion of having taken the life of his wife by either strangulation or stabbing, information that he received calmly. He was placed in a cell, a search of his person revealed his wife's bankbook showing several pounds credit, about a pound in silver, some jewellery and a watch.

At about midnight the remains of Mrs Bury were removed from the house and taken to the mortuary, where the doctors conducted an autopsy about an hour later on the instructions of the Procurator Fiscal. They made a careful examination taking three hours. Bury's story had been that his wife had strangled herself and that he had afterwards stabbed her on impulse, but in their opinion the stab wounds had been inflicted with a long-bladed knife prior to strangulation, marks on the body indicating a struggle. A stewardess from the *Cambria* identified the body as that of Mrs Bury.

The police reportedly conjectured that Bury had taken the house in Princes Street, a quiet area, with a definite purpose and distinct plan in mind. The rooms the couple had occupied there were in a basement at the bottom of a four-storey house and were reached by a gate through a railing that bounded the street and down a winding stair. The place had a squalid appearance and there were several broken panes in the windows. To the rear of the premises was another stair leading down to the rooms, at the foot of which was an old wooden door on which was written in chalk 'Jack Ripper is on the back of this door'. Behind this door, and just at the turn of the stair, was another inscription 'Jack Ripper is in this seller'. The writing appeared to be in the hand of a young boy and to have been there for some time, predating the discovery of the murder. This further association with the Whitechapel murders was enough to strike additional fear into the minds of the occupants of neighbouring properties. Those neighbours, living above the basement and in adjoining properties, had no knowledge of the crime.

Bury was described as 5ft 3½in tall, of dark complexion, good-looking with sharp features, and sharp spoken with a definite English accent. He had a full beard with a fair moustache and was well dressed, but had a timid manner about him. He also had a serious drink problem, and on the night of the murder had been seen in a public house, much the worse for drink. His wife was described as about 30 years of age, fair-haired, of middle stature, slim and of genteel appearance.

When Bury appeared before Sheriff Campbell Smith he denied the charge of murder, reiterating his claim that his wife committed suicide by strangulation and that, in an 'insane moment', he had stabbed her after death. He did not wish to enter into his motive for putting the body into the box. The police believed he had stripped and washed the body after the murder, originally intending to dispose of the box with the body in it but subsequently deciding instead upon the suicide story. Apparently he had been spotted in the police court two days after the murder, which suggested he had been contemplating then giving himself up.

The Dundee police contacted the Metropolitan Police in London with a view to learning more of Bury's antecedents. They learnt that he had borrowed some of his wife's money – she having about £240 of her own, part of a legacy she had shared with her sisters – to furnish a house and buy a horse and cart, the latter in support of his business, Bury purchasing sawdust at various mills and selling it on to publicans in the East End and restaurant keepers in the City. As a result of his drink problem he had lost these assets. In August 1888 the couple had occupied lodgings at 11 Blackthorn Street, Bow, and in December they had taken lodgings with a Mr W. Smith, a bricklayer and builder, at 8 Spanby Road, Bow. Mr Smith noticed that the couple were very unhappy, one of the points of disagreement between them being that Bury wanted his wife to draw out all her money and give it to him. Bury, it seems, subsequently spoke to Smith about going to Australia, asking him to make a wooden packing box for the journey and to ensure it was well secured with iron bands at the ends. The box, Bury claimed, was for packing his things in to go to Brisbane, but he had declined to have his name put on the box when Smith suggested this. He left, stating he was going to the docks to board ship for Brisbane, but on making an inquiry with the carman who had taken Bury away, Mr Smith was told that Bury had gone to Dundee. Tellingly the report ended:

> Bury is reported as being of a quarrelsome temper and very easily incited to use his hands rather roughly. Late last night Inspector Abberline with other detectives, who have been engaged in the recent East End murders, were making inquiries among the dead woman's relatives.

News of the murder caused a shock among relatives and friends of the murdered woman at Stratford, Bow and Poplar, where she was well known and respected as a quiet, inoffensive woman who had seemed very happy until she married Bury on Easter Monday, 1888.

The fact that the high-profile Scotland Yard detective and his team of officers, assigned to the Whitechapel murders inquiry, were looking into Bury's antecedents lends credence to the idea that he was treated as a possible suspect for the 'Jack the Ripper' murders. This, of course, was all good copy for the newspapers but a further piece in the *Dundee Advertiser*, from their London correspondent, tended to negate this idea somewhat. It ran:

> The tragedy in Dundee has excited intense interest in London, and the evening papers make it the principal feature in the bill. The newsboys drove a great harvest by crying out 'Another horrible murder and mutilation.' There was some idea at first that the murderer in Dundee might turn out to be Jack the Ripper. His crime seemed to be marked by the same kind of brutal atrocity, but the fuller accounts which came to hand in the afternoon discountenanced the suggestion that the perpetrator of the East End murders had been found in Dundee.

A report on the events in Dundee appeared in *The Times* on the same day as the above, and this contained no mention at all of the Whitechapel murders or of 'Jack the Ripper', merely observing, 'Great excitement prevails in Dundee.'

The following day *The Times* carried more details of the case:

> . . . [the police] in searching Bury's house found a woman's ulster saturated with blood and torn in several places as if ripped with a knife. In the fireplace were found a large number of buttons and parts of a woman's corset. The police are confident that Bury had burned a large quantity of clothing. From this and other evidence in the possession of the authorities, the opinion has been formed that the woman must have met her death while dressed, and that the rope had been first tightly drawn round her neck to prevent her screaming . . .

The report concluded by stating that Bury had lived for some time in Wolverhampton, and latterly at Sunbury Street, London. The woman was stated to be the daughter of a London publican and 'to have been possessed of considerable means'.

There was much speculation as to why the Burys had moved to Dundee and to the motive for the crime. A neighbour in Princes Street, Mrs Smith, stated that Mrs Bury had told her that her husband had fallen into bad company in London and developed a drinking problem, so she had been glad to get him away from

London and such companions. Sadly, of course, it seems that his intemperate habits continued in Dundee. Mrs Smith had also noticed two gold rings – a wedding ring and a keeper – on Mrs Bury, but these were not on her finger when the body was found, instead being found on Bury when he was detained. A spurious document was found in the room, purporting to be from a large Dundee manufacturing firm offering Bury and his wife a job.

On Friday 15 February, Ellen Bury's married sister, Mrs Margaret Corney, of Stanley Road, Stratford-le-Bow, arrived in Dundee from London and identified the body. She then went to the prison where she identified Bury. The latter seemed momentarily taken aback when confronted by his sister-in-law but no conversation was allowed. The funeral was held the same day, before Mrs Corney returned to London in the evening. On Monday 18 February the sheriff signed the warrant and Bury was committed for trial on the capital charge. It was noted in the prison that Bury's demeanour was cool, he took his food and exercise regularly and slept soundly.

At Dundee Judiciary Court on Thursday 28 March 1889 Bury was indicted for the murder of his wife. He pleaded not guilty, sticking to the story that his wife had hanged herself and that he had afterwards mutilated the body. During the trial, however, further facts emerged. Bury had done little or no work for the past year and had constantly demanded money from his wife, striking her if she failed to comply. On one occasion, shortly after their marriage, a landlady in their lodgings in Bow had heard screams in the night, and, entering their room, she had found Bury kneeling over his wife with a large table knife in his hand. They had again been arguing over money. Between two and three in the morning on the night of the murder a neighbour, David Duncan, had heard three loud screams come from the direction of Bury's flat.

There was little to say in his defence, but Bury was sanguine of his eventual release. Mention was made of his wife's morals, the *Dundee Advertiser* remarking:

ELLEN ELLIOT was, it is evident, a woman of frail morals, but yet with something of womanly affection. Seven or eight years ago, when she was 26 years of age, an aunt of hers died, and left her £300 in shares of the Union Bank of London . . . ELLEN

ELLIOT, according to her sister, was a needle-woman, made ladies' waterproof cloaks, and afterwards worked in a jute factory in the East End of London; but in answer to Mr. HAY, who acted as counsel for the prisoner, and made the best possible defence of a very bad case, the sister admitted that ELLEN was a servant in a house which she had heard was a house of bad fame . . .

The Times of March 29 did not mince its words and stated:

Mrs. Corney . . . said deceased was her sister, and before her marriage was in service. Seven years since an aunt left her £300. Prisoner and her sister married in April last. He was often drunk and was always demanding money from deceased. He ill-treated her. Cross-examined, she admitted her sister was servant in a brothel in London, that it was there she first met prisoner, and that she married him after a month's acquaintance . . .

Lord Young summed up against the prisoner and he was found guilty. Sentence of death was passed, the date for execution being set for 24 April. On being led below Bury exhibited signs of breaking down. The trial had lasted about thirteen hours.

He was seen as a callous, greedy and scheming murderer, whose only interest in his wife had been her money. Indeed, the *Dundee Advertiser* of 29 March 1889 described him as 'brainless and heartless'. Harking back to his history in London the paper commented:

Men of BURY'S calibre, we dare say, are not uncommon to the East End of London. He is one of the stunted moral growths which a civilisation that runs all to machinery and monetary speculation is calculated to multiply, and unless we can bring to populations like that of the East End of London fuller and more generous ideas of life we must expect to see frequent outbreaks of hideous and senseless crime.

No mention is made of 'Jack the Ripper', so it looks as if the initial suggestions that Bury may have been the unknown killer had been abandoned.

A petition for a reprieve was raised on Bury's behalf, claiming that there was 'considerable doubt' as to the verdict and suggesting that the peculiarly Scottish verdict of 'not proven' was more appropriate. The Marquis of Lothian, the Secretary for Scotland, rejected the application, his letter of rejection subsequently being read to Bury, who seemed to take the news with resignation, stating he was prepared to meet his fate.

Preparations for the execution were well advanced, a firm of local joiners having constructed the gallows, which were erected on 23 April. Berry and his assistant, a man named Thomas Scott, left Bradford on the morning of 22 April and arrived at Dundee Prison between seven and eight o'clock in the evening. They drove from Caledonian Station to the prison and were accommodated in the lodge formerly occupied by the chief warder, who by this time was living outside the prison.

The execution, at 8.00 a.m. on Wednesday 24 April 1889, was reported at length in the *Dundee Advertiser* of 26 April but warranted only a few lines in *The Times*. The *Advertiser* reported that Bury had retired at 10.00 p.m. on the eve of his execution and was woken and rose at 5.00 a.m. the following morning. He drank tea and said to the warder in charge, 'This is my last morning on earth. I freely forgive all who have given false evidence against me at my trial, as I hope God will forgive me.' He added that he was resigned to his fate. Between six and seven he ate a breakfast of tea, toast and eggs and enjoyed a smoke. He expressed his gratitude to the prison staff for the kindness they had shown. The Revd E.J. Gough entered the cell and remained with him to the end. The Revd D.R. Robertson, the prison chaplain, joined them in the cell at about seven thirty. They ministered to the convict and he received them, showing penitence. About a quarter to the hour the prison governor, Mr Geddes, conducted the attending officials into the corridor opposite the door of the condemned cell, the magistrates and their clerk sitting at a desk that faced the apartment. Six warders were in attendance and formed a guard between the door of the cell and the desk. The door of the cell was shut but those outside could hear the religious ministrations going on within.

At seven minutes to eight the governor knocked on the cell door and entered the cell, explaining to the clergymen and the prisoner that the dreaded hour was upon them. Bury showed no emotion as he stood up to go. A minute later the governor went back into the corridor and spoke with a warder who, in turn, went to the scaffold, where he spoke with the waiting executioner. James Berry went with the warder to the condemned cell, holding his pinioning straps in his right hand. He entered the cell and shook hands with Bury, asking if he had anything to say, but Bury replied that he only wished to thank the prison officials for their very great kindness to him while in their custody, more especially since sentence had been passed. He remarked to Berry that the sentence was a very disagreeable duty to perform, to which Berry replied, with some feeling, that though his duty was very disagreeable it had to be done. He assured the culprit, however, that it would be done in a manner that gave him the least pain possible. Bury submitted quietly to the pinioning and displayed no emotion. He was then taken into the corridor and the governor handed over the warrant for the execution to the magistrates. The prisoner was dressed in his own clothes, consisting of dark trousers, with a vest and smart twill shooting coat, a white linen collar and fashionable blue necktie.

The main, male, wings of Dundee Prison were situated on the western side of the enclosure. The condemned cell was in the north-west corner of the southernmost, or modern, wing, on the ground floor and specially furnished, there being a distance of 30–40 yards to the scaffold, and the whole route being enclosed. A porch connected the two wings and in the westernmost wall of this passage an opening had been made, which led into the shed housing the scaffold. This was enclosed within a rough deal shed, which extended between the two wings, erected to prevent the scaffold being seen from the outside, since this part of the prison was overlooked by a public building on the opposite side of Lochee Road. The scaffold itself was formed by two upright posts, fixed into sockets and fitted with brackets to give strength and solidity. A crossbeam connected them at the top, at the centre of which was a strong iron ring. From the ring dangled a fine manila rope that had been made in Holloway Prison in London. The drop consisted of two doors supported by a bar of T-iron and was operated by a lever on the right-hand side. It was enclosed by a 4ft high railing over which was draped black cloth, so that after the trap was activated no part of the convict's body would be seen.

The procession to the scaffold was formed, Bury flanked by a warder on each side and followed closely by the executioner, upon which it moved slowly forward, the Revd E.J. Gough reading the service. After about a dozen paces the procession halted and Berry smartly undid the prisoner's collar and pulled the white cap from an outside pocket of his coat, slipping it deftly over Bury's head. The procession then moved off again with the warders either side of Bury supporting him. The cap had been put over his face to prevent him seeing the final arrangements for his execution and to give him strength to face the end. When almost the full length of the main corridor had been traversed the procession turned to the left to take the last dozen or so steps to the scaffold. A momentary halt was again made, and the Revd Gough commenced the service in even more solemn tones.

When the scaffold was reached, Berry's assistant, Scott, described as a smart-looking young fellow, was standing on the left side of the structure with the rope in his hand. Bury was immediately placed under the beam, Berry strapping his legs together and taking hold of the rope from Scott. He then placed the noose over the culprit's head and tightened it at the left side. Bury stood with his hands firmly clenched, listening to the words of the service and at the appropriate points uttering 'Amen', and 'Lord Jesus, have mercy on me, Lord Jesus receive my soul.' Punctually, at eight o'clock Berry pulled the lever and Bury fell into the pit below. A drop of 6ft 6in had been allowed and death was instantaneous. The neck was dislocated and the head fell on to the left shoulder. Five minutes later the attending medical men descended into the pit and made a cursory examination of the body. They expressed the opinion that Bury had died without a struggle. After 15–20 minutes the body was drawn up from the pit and onto the platform of the scaffold, where the doctors made a further examination. The whole execution had been conducted without a hitch.

By 8 a.m. a crowd of about 5,000 had gathered outside the front of the prison in Bell Street and Lochee Road, waiting to see the black flag hoisted. As the clock on the Old Steeple was about to strike the hour, they became hushed. The flag fluttered from the top of the pole and 15 minutes later the crowd had dispersed, while the prison bell still tolled. The flag was lowered about 9.00 a.m. A few minutes after the execution, Berry and his assistant ate breakfast, then prepared to leave Dundee. They were conducted through the prison by way of the Police Office and left, unobserved by the public, at ten o'clock. They drove to Tay Bridge Station and departed for Edinburgh on the 10.10 a.m. train. It was the sixth execution to take place at Dundee in the nineteenth century, the previous one having been in 1847. It was also the last.

The usual inquest was held. At sundown the body was placed in a shell, covered with quicklime and buried within the precincts of the prison. Bury had made a confession on the Friday preceding his execution to the Revd Mr Gough, writing a simple statement about the murder that was forwarded to the Secretary for Scotland. But was William Henry Bury in fact Jack the Ripper? The report of the execution in the *Dundee Advertiser* of 26 April 1889 again broached the subject:

When he was apprehended there was a feeling in the community that he might have some connection with the atrocities which had been committed in the Whitechapel district of London, and this feeling was made stronger when it became known that Bury had been long resident in that district of the metropolis. The police immediately took up this point, and wrote full particulars of the tragedy, along with every detail they could learn of Bury, and forwarded them to Scotland Yard, with a request that full inquiries should be made regarding Bury. The London police were somewhat slow to move in the matter, and from this it was inferred that they did not attach much importance to the arrest so far as the Whitechapel murders were concerned. After nearly a week had elapsed they sent down a formal communication to Chief Constable Dewar giving the result of some preliminary inquiries they had made in the district in which Bury had resided. These dealt chiefly with his general habits and character as known to his companions, but no reference was made to the

London murders. They, however, intimated that the investigations would be continued, and subsequent communications received from them went to show that they believed Bury had no connection with the Whitechapel horrors. From the fact, however, that there have been no murders in the East End since Bury migrated to Dundee there are those in the community who still cling to the belief that he had had something to do with these crimes. It may also be pointed out that, while the bodies of the unfortunate victims in Whitechapel were cut and mutilated in a manner which showed that the murderer must have had some surgical skill, this was entirely wanting in the case of Mrs. Bury.

It emerged that Bury's mother had become insane in May 1860, when he was still a baby, and been admitted to the Worcester County and City Lunatic Asylum. His father having already died, a woman had taken pity on the children, raising both Bury and his older brother and sister.

Although it was widely reported, as fact, that the Whitechapel murderer possessed surgical skill, this was a fallacy. At best he possessed some anatomical knowledge but he exhibited no great surgical skill. The idea that Bury was the Ripper was to persist, and has survived to the present day. So what did James Berry think of the idea? His account of Bury's execution appeared in the *Thomson's* series on 12 February 1927. Unfortunately we do not have corroborative evidence to support his story but, in his favour, it appears modest enough and makes no claim that Bury confessed to him. Berry claimed that there were two strangers at the execution of Bury:

There were two strangers in the prison and who they were nobody knew except the men who examined the order for their attendance.

Two quiet-looking men in suits of a London cut, they watched the man die from behind the little crowd at the edge of the scaffold, and then, with their faces strangely marked by excitement, they walked up to me.

'Well, Berry, what do you think?'

'Oh, I think it's the man right enough.'

302

'And so do we. There can be no doubt about it. You'll find there will be no Whitechapel crimes after this. You've put an end to "Jack the Ripper's" games.'

The men who assured me were officers from Scotland Yard sent down to take observation in the prison of Dundee when Bury, the Princes Street murderer, died by my hand, to find out from me if he had made any remarks which could be taken to refer to the sensational London crimes, and to report thereafter to the Crown.

At this stage of the day I am prepared to read a denial of the statements that I am about to make regarding the man to whom I am referring, but, not withstanding, I am frankly convinced that at the headquarters of the Criminal Investigation Department in London the records of the time showed clearly that the view shared by each and all of the officials was that at last the author of the Whitechapel crimes had paid the penalty of his guilt at the hands of the hangman.

When Sir Melville Macnaghten, the assistant commissioner, quitted office a few months ago, he destroyed every evidence which he had to convince him that he knew the identity of the most amazing criminal of modern times, and he has sworn that his lips will remain forever sealed.

The truth or otherwise of what I am about to state must therefore be a matter for the public to judge, but I would just like to point out that were I not quite convinced in my own mind that the conclusions come to by the two detectives are right, I would be the last man to give publicity to them for the sake of earning a little cheap notoriety.

From the bearing of the man, from inquiries I made at the time, and from other reasons, I became firmly convinced in my own mind that Bury was the man who had introduced such a reign of terror into the East End of London, and years of calm reflection in retirement have made me more convinced than ever that I was right.

And so Berry weighed in with his own theory on the world's most puzzling crime mystery – the identity of 'Jack the Ripper'. He made mention in that account of Sir Melville Macnaghten, who had retired from the Metropolitan Police in the rank of Assistant Commissioner (Crime) at the end of May 1913. Berry died, at the age of 61, in October 1913, so these reminiscences made 'a few months' after Macnaghten's retirement must have been recorded only just before Berry's death. Macnaghten's own claims about the Ripper had appeared in an article in the *Daily Mail* of 2 June 1913:

'That remarkable man,' he said, 'was one of the most fascinating criminals. Of course he was a maniac, but I have a very clear idea who he was and how he committed suicide, but that, with other secrets, will never be revealed by me.

'I have destroyed all my documents and there is now no record of the secret information which came into my possession at one time or another . . . '

Macnaghten obviously did not think that Bury was the Ripper, and his own preferred suspect can be identified as Montague John Druitt, a barrister and teacher who had committed suicide by drowning in the Thames in December 1888. Furthermore, the surviving official documents, both Metropolitan Police and Home Office, make no mention of William Henry Bury, showing instead that the identity of the killer was not known.

It would be interesting to know the identity of the two Scotland Yard detectives claimed by Berry to be at the execution. Inspector Abberline's name had been mentioned in the press as making inquiries in London into Bury's antecedents, and it is tempting to speculate that he was one of them. Unfortunately, Berry gives no names, merely stating that they had taken the case up, on Bury's arrest, and that, unknown to the Dundee police, they were 'visiting every haunt of the prisoner, and submitting to a vigorous cross-examination every one who had known him'.

Berry went on to mention the insanity of Bury's mother and his Wolverhampton roots, before continuing:

At last he went to London and settled down in the East End, where he picked up a precarious existence. His home at one time was near the scene of the Whitechapel crimes and his work was that of a butcher of horses.

He opened a shop for the sale of cats' meat, and people who knew him used to see him at work with his long knives. They spoke of the skilful way in which he handled them, and according to the detectives, it was with long weapons similar to those which Bury used in his business that the Whitechapel murders were committed.

Berry claims that on his arrival in Dundee there had been a great deal of excitement, not because the detectives suspected that Bury was the Ripper (this had been kept quiet), but because:

Wherever the hangman goes he feels an atmosphere of repugnance, but the further north you go you feel it more intensified. The people of Scotland don't like the carrying out of the capital sentence.

He went on to describe his first sight of Bury:

When I first caught sight of Bury, and before I knew that he was suspected of committing the Whitechapel crimes, I confess that a strange feeling took possession of me. He was a peculiar-looking man, and undoubtedly he had the air of the uncanny about him.

I saw him at first by accident. He was being exercised in the corridor, and I saw before me a man slightly over five feet in height, with a haunted look in his eyes. He did not appear an ordinary criminal. His face was keen and intelligent, and he was carrying himself with an erect and steady bearing, but, notwithstanding, there was a mysterious something about him which repelled me.

Commenting further on the possibility that Bury was the Ripper, he added for good measure:

The prison library was at his command, and he took advantage of it, but he confined his reading principally to the Bible and other religious works. Here I would just like to remind my readers that Dr. Forbes Winslow, who investigated the

Whitechapel crimes, always held that their author was a religious maniac, who at times believed that he was chosen to carry on a holy crusade.

Perhaps Berry tried a little too hard to prove that Bury was the Ripper. The claim, of course, made good copy and would have boosted the readership of the series (published after his death), and we must not overlook the possibility that whoever ghostwrote the essays may have added various embellishments. The account continued:

The rest of the time he spent in writing, and his handwriting was submitted to the closest scrutiny. The detectives who came from London saw it, and they knew better than anybody else whether or not it was that of the man for whom they and their colleagues had been searching. It settled the matter beyond doubt, for the handwriting of 'Jack the Ripper' was known at Scotland Yard.

The Whitechapel murderer left few clues behind, but twice in his career he had written his name for the detectives to read. Once he had written to Dr. Forbes Winslow, and once a specimen of his penmanship had been found with the body of his victim under the railway arch in the East End of London. The latter was reposing safely in the drawer of the Commissioner at Scotland Yard and he had only to take it out and compare it with the letters written in the condemned cell at Dundee.

I cannot tell you of course that the Commissioner did compare the two, but nevertheless I have put it on record that two of his staff came all the way to Dundee to see the man, to keep their ears open for any confession, and afterwards to submit me to a stiff cross-examination.

Again we see here the account taking on board popular Ripper mythology that had built up over the years. Many letters received by police, press and public were signed 'Jack the Ripper' and there is good reason to believe all were hoaxes and not from the killer. The letter written to Forbes Winslow was dated 7 October 1889, many

306

months after Bury's execution, although Forbes Winslow had himself claimed it was received in 1888. From the content of Berry's account there seems little doubt that Forbes Winslow's 1910 book, *Recollections of Forty Years*, had been used as a source for material. The two Whitechapel murders where victims were found under railway arches were the Pinchin Street torso case of 10 September 1889 and the murder of Frances Coles in the inappropriately named Swallow Gardens on 13 February 1891. Both cases post-dated Bury's execution and were not Ripper killings; furthermore no letters were left by the killer. Forbes Winslow, in his book, did incorrectly mention the police copying a message left 'under the archway' and this appears to be the origin of this confused reference by Berry.

Berry noted that his 'victim' had a smoke before his execution:

> . . . as most of my victims invariably did. One thing I have noticed in the course of my career is that no matter what was their crime, and no matter how they felt, they did not like to go out of the world without a whiff of the pipe or a glass of beer.

Berry's account of the preparations for the execution corresponds to that in the contemporary press. However, unlike the published press reports, he refers to the suspicion that Bury was the Ripper:

> Picking up my pinioning straps, I walked quickly along, but before I went some one touched my arm and reminded me that I had a certain duty to perform before I brought him out into the corridor – I had to find out if he were 'Jack the Ripper'.
>
> When I walked into the cell he looked at me almost defiantly, and then he twisted his face up into a sneer. He was the first to begin the conversation.
>
> 'I suppose you think you are clever to hang me?'
>
> Now, there isn't much in that question when you see it in cold print, but had you heard it spoken you would have thought as I did at the time.
>
> The man about to die laid particular emphasis on the last word he spoke. He talked as if he thought himself to be one who stood head and shoulders above every other criminal who had passed through my hands.

Meanwhile the detectives had drawn near, and were straining their ears to catch any word which might fall from his lips.

I looked at him and waited.

'I suppose you think you are clever because you are going to hang me,' he repeated. 'But because you are to hang me you are not to get anything out of me.'

And he had already admitted the justice of his doom.

Without a word I put him in the corner of the cell and got the pinioning straps ready.

At first he glared at me, and I thought he was going to show fight, but he gave way when he saw that resistance would be futile, and held his arms ready.

He was wearing a smartly-cut suit of ribbed cloth, and looking as spruce as if he were going to a wedding. On his wrists were white linen cuffs with gold sleeve-links, and I told him he would have no further use of them, and might as well discard them. He pulled the cuffs off without a word and threw them in the corner of the cell.

A warder came forward and made to pick them up, but I stopped him, 'Leave them there till I come back,' said I, 'He'd better take his collar off too.'

He did not seem to wish to comply with the request, and I firmly believe that had it been possible to hang him with it on he would have asked me to do it.

To the last, he was vain and anxious to appear at his best before the eyes of those within the prison, so I had to take the collar off for him.

Into the corner of the cell I threw it, and when the execution was over I returned and examined the sleeve-links, which were engraved with the sign of the Masonic craft to which the criminal belonged.

Quickly I pinioned him, and as I did so I began to whisper hurriedly in his ears – 'Now if you have anything to say it will be as well for you to say it. When I get you on the scaffold I will not give you time to unburden yourself. It is your last chance.'

Other men face to face with the last chance have confessed to me after they had assured the chaplain of their innocence, but Bury was to make no confidant of me. He never opened his mouth, and there was nothing left for me to do but to march him out of the condemned cell.

He had not far to walk. When he got into the shed he fixed his eyes upon the beam, and then he turned them on to me, and kept them fixed on my every movement.

Never once did his lips move. There were two warders who had been in constant attendance with him since the sentence had been passed on him, and even to them he did not speak. When, however, I approached to cover his eyes, he glanced in their direction, though there was scarcely the light of recognition.

A second afterwards the trapdoor fell and he died with whatever secrets he may have had locked in his own breast.

I had got nothing out of him, as he had said – nothing but the unshakeable belief that his words conveyed the suggestion that he had a history which he believed put him above – and far above – the level of the ordinary criminal.

After the execution was over the Scotland Yard men came at once to see me.

'Well, Mr. Berry,' they said, 'will you tell us what opinion you have about him?'

'Did you hear him make that statement?' I asked.

'Oh, yes, but unfortunately you could construe it two or three ways. It is nothing definite to go on. What do you think yourself?'

'I think it is him right enough.'

'And we agree with you,' replied one of the detectives. 'We know all about his movements in the past, and we are quite satisfied that you have hanged "Jack the Ripper". There will be no more Whitechapel crimes.'

And there has not been one since!

It will be noted that there are discrepancies between the contemporary press account of the execution and Berry's version. The conversation reported was different, the collar was removed in the cell as opposed to the corridor, and Bury was not hooded until on the scaffold according to Berry. Had a 'sanitised' version been given to the press? And was, as Berry suggests, the presence of the London detectives kept a secret? Certainly Berry's account does not invent a sensational confession whispered only to him. Arguments can be raised for either point of view and the actual truth will never be known.

The question of Bury and 'Jack the Ripper' being one and the same person was again raised in official circles in April 1908 when Mr E.A. Parr, a journalist from Newmarket, wrote to the Secretary for Scotland at Whitehall. Parr stated that he had 'for some time past been gathering matter bearing upon the subject of the "Jack the Ripper" murders', and that he had come across a paper that claimed that Bury had 'made a full confession of the Ripper crimes; which document was forwarded to the Secretary for Scotland'. Also he had been in contact with Berry, the ex-public executioner, who 'told me explicitly that Bury was known to have been Jack the Ripper'. It would seem that Berry was actively propagating the idea that he had indeed hanged Jack the Ripper. Parr asked the Secretary if he could have details of the confession. Of course, no such confession existed. Bury's only confession was made to the Revd Edward John Gough on 22 April 1889, and that was to acknowledge his guilt for the murder of his wife whom he had strangled on 4 February, and for which act he was 'deeply sorry and truly penitent'. There was no mention whatsoever of the 'Ripper' crimes (see file HH 16/69, National Archives of Scotland).

Was 'Jack the Ripper' hanged on that rainy day in Dundee? Well, there remains a slight possibility that he may have been. Do I think that Bury was 'Jack the Ripper'? No, I don't. I think he was a callous, drunken and greedy wife-killer whose plans went badly wrong. The mystery of the identity of 'Jack the Ripper' remains to vex historians, criminologists and true-crime buffs for all time.

26

Murder by poison and axe

'The saddest sight I ever saw on scaffold . . . '

After the excitement of the Bury case, the remainder of 1889 was something of an anti-climax. The year was not without criminological interest, however, among the notable cases followed in the press that summer being 'The Aigburth Poisoning Case', 'The Thames Mystery', and 'The Whitechapel Murder'.

The first case hit the national news on 20 May 1889 when the poisoning of James Maybrick, allegedly by his American wife, Florence, was reported. Maybrick, a Liverpool cotton merchant, had died in his home at Battlecrease House, Cressington Road, Aigburth, on 11 May 1889. By 3 June 1889 Florence Maybrick had been charged with his murder, and, after a seven-day trial at Liverpool, she was found guilty on 7 August and sentenced to death. Berry marked her up for execution but an immediate campaign for a reprieve was instigated. It was the great criminal cause célèbre of 1889 and the trial judge, Mr Justice Stephen, was required to attend the Home Office on 20 August to provide information on the trial. The alienist Dr Forbes Winslow was again prominent in the press, speaking up on behalf of Mrs Maybrick. Two days later the sentence was commuted to life imprisonment and Berry marked his appointments book in red ink 'Reprieved', receiving his £5 fee for the cancellation. The scenario of Forbes Winslow and Berry adopting opposing views was depicted in a satirical cartoon that appeared in *Moonshine*. According to Richard D. Altick, in *Victorian Studies in Scarlet* (London, Dent, 1970), a popular street balled celebrating Mrs Maybrick's reprieve mentioned the celebrated Berry:

> But Mrs. Maybrick will not have to climb the golden stairs;
> The Jury found her guilty so she nearly said her prayers;
> She's at another kind of mashing and at it she must stop,
> Old Berry is took down a peg with his long drop.

Mrs Maybrick would be finally released on Monday 25 January 1904.

The second case involved the finding, between 4 June and the following week, of portions of a dismembered female body (the head was never found) in the River Thames near the Albert Bridge, on the Embankment and in Battersea Park. Police inquiries finally identified the body as that of Elizabeth Jackson, aged 24, who had fallen on hard times and was pregnant. The offender was never traced and the inquest closed on 25 July 1889 with a verdict of 'Wilful murder against some person or persons unknown'.

The third case was, perhaps, the most sensational as far as Londoners were concerned, raising real fears that 'Jack the Ripper' was again at work. Shortly before 1.00 a.m. on Wednesday 17 July 1889 a patrolling police officer discovered the body of Alice McKenzie, aged 39, in Castle Alley, off the Whitechapel Road. She was an 'unfortunate' (a contemporary euphemism for prostitute); her throat had been cut and there were superficial lacerations to the abdomen. The police inquiry failed to reveal the offender but it was quickly decided that it was not the Ripper's work.

On 21 June 1889 the subject of the public executioner was again mentioned in the House of Commons when a Bill was introduced by Sir Edmund Lechmere, MP, proposing that this officer, and any assistants, should be appointed by the Home Secretary, who should assign and regulate their duties. Furthermore, he proposed, they should also be subject to removal by the Home Secretary, if necessary, and should carry certificates of appointment. They should be paid out of money provided by the government and the task of appointing the executioner should be taken from the sheriffs unless such person held the requisite certificate. In the event, the proposal was not adopted.

The summer hiatus ended for Berry on Wednesday 7 August 1889 when he executed Maurice Hickey at Tralee gaol, Dublin. Hickey had been convicted at Maryborough for the murder of his brother-in-law,

Denis Daley, on 22 November 1888 near Castleisland. He made a full confession of his guilt, in writing, before he was executed.

On Wednesday 22 August 1889 Berry executed George Horton, a miner aged 37, at Derby gaol. Horton, a widower, had poisoned his baby daughter at Swanwick in order to obtain £7 insurance money, his dire financial circumstances being the motive.

After his conviction, his children visited him at the prison in what Berry described as 'an affecting scene'. A large crowd gathered outside the prison on the Tuesday night, their numbers swelled by members of the Salvation Army. Berry told the story of the execution:

> I did not see my victim until I brought him out to die. Very early in the morning I was up and about, and my first job was to go and have a final look at the scaffold.
>
> It was erected in the usual spot, against the outer wall of the prison on the right-hand side of the main entrance in Vernon Street. An entirely new structure, it was covered by a shed, and it had been finished according to my instructions. Instead of the usual iron beam, a thick wooden beam was used, at my suggestion, the idea being to obviate the spring which usually accompanies the iron beam.
>
> The scaffold worked well when I tried it, and, satisfied that there was likely to be no hitch, I walked away and had a chat with one of the warders . . .

Berry asked the warder if the prisoner was likely to give any trouble and the warder said that Horton had expressed the hope that he would walk to the scaffold like a man. Berry liked the warder, and the conversation turned to Berry's feelings about his job:

> 'How do you feel yourself, Mr. Berry?' he asked. 'It must be terrible to pull the lever that launches a man into eternity.'
>
> 'You are quite right,' I replied, 'it is awful, and I do not feel at all well, but this man has committed a terrible crime, and someone has to punish him for it.'
>
> 'Yes, I suppose it wouldn't do if everybody was to shrink from the job. There would be no living in the land.'

'You are right,' said I; 'but to hear some people talk about me, you would fancy that I was as bad as that fellow I am going to hang. I wonder what they would feel like if it was their little daughter, poor innocent little thing, that he had poisoned? They wouldn't be talking about a reprieve then.'

'I never thought that they would let that man off, Mr. Berry,' said he. 'A lot of people thought the Home Secretary would give in at the last minute, but I was sure he would not.'

'I never expected it for a moment,' was my reply. 'My experience is that you very rarely get a reprieve in a poisoning case. The Government knows that you can take precautions against a man who uses a knife or a gun, but the poisoner works in the dark and in secret, and that is why the law is always down on them.'

Whilst this conversation was taking place the reporters were ushered into the yard. Berry described them as 'a lot of pale-faced fellows . . . trembling in every limb, yet eager to learn all they could about the poor victim in the condemned cell'. He greeted them with a 'Good morning, gentlemen', and gave a pleasant smile. They nodded in reply, eyeing the ropes and pinioning straps draped over his arm. One of them gave a very cold look so Berry decided to have a 'game' with him. He had, on a previous occasion, frightened a reporter by pretending to put the white cap over his eyes. This time Berry asked the man if he would like to see how the pinioning strap worked, intending, if he consented, to truss him up. At that moment, however, a message came that the sheriff had arrived and was waiting for Berry. He turned to go to the condemned cell, but then stopped, dismayed to see three or four members of the public on a roof overlooking the gaol. Told by an official that nothing could be done to stop the men looking in on the procession, since they were standing on private property, Berry observed that, had he realised, he would have had the walk to the scaffold screened off. However, it was too late to take this measure.

He went to the cell, where he found Horton talking to the parson. Going up to the prisoner, Berry tapped him on the shoulder, pointing to a chair. 'You can sit down if you like,' he said, 'but it might be better for you to stand up. You will keep your nerve if you do.'

'I don't want no chair,' he replied in a low voice. 'I would rather face it like a man.'

'It is much the better way,' said Berry. 'And if you want to be a man you can clear your conscience of any lies you may have told. This is the last chance you will get.'

Horton made no reply, but bent his body a little as Berry finished the pinioning. Berry put his hands on his shoulders and turned him round, whereupon Horton made for the door of his cell with a fixed and glassy stare in his eyes. It had taken only about a minute or so to prepare him, Berry being anxious to get the job over as quickly as he could. The head warder led the way to the scaffold, followed by the chaplain, who walked unsteadily and whose voice broke as he read the service. He was trembling with grief, and Berry felt sorry for him. George Horton walked behind him, a warder on each side, and Berry followed with his hands held at each side of his waist in case he should stumble and fall. However, he did not require any assistance and he walked with a steady step. Berry continued:

I noticed as we went along that he was wearing his hat, so I took it off his head and tossed it across the yard.

The entrance to the scaffold shed was a couple of feet or so above the path, and here for the first time my victim showed a trace of fear. He had been looking fixedly on the ground, but now he looked up in a half dazed manner, and I had to urge him gently on his way.

It was not long before I had him on the drop, and immediately I had pinioned his legs I drew the cap over his eyes and adjusted the rope.

Everybody in the scaffold shed was looking white and haggard, and I saw one man slip a small flask out of his pocket and put it to his lips. At that moment I could have done with a sip myself, but I pulled myself together, and glanced towards my victim to see if he was in position.

In pleading tones he wailed, 'Oh, Lord, receive my soul,' and as the words left his lips I sent him through the trap doors.

He did not die as quickly as I had hoped he would, life remaining for two or three minutes after he had reached the end of the drop; but I do not think he could have suffered any pain, as his neck was broken and the shock must have brought on unconsciousness.

After it was all over, the reporters came flocking around me and asked me how the thing had gone. I told them it had been a very fine execution, and that I was thoroughly satisfied with myself.

Mrs. Maybrick at this time was lying in gaol, having been sentenced to death, and the reporters were all anxious to know if she were to be my next victim. They asked me what I thought about the case.

'Well, I may as well tell you,' said I, 'that I have read all the evidence very carefully, and I have come to the only conclusion.'

'And what is that, Mr. Berry?'

'I am afraid I cannot tell you.'

They pressed me to tell them, but I knew better, for they would have published my views in the papers, and that would never have done.

They next asked whether I thought she would be hanged. I told them that was a question for the Home Secretary to answer, and then I shook hands with them all round and went away with the head warder to have a cup of tea. I was glad it was all over.

The Times reported that the prisoner made a full confession of his crime to the vicar of Swanwick during his incarceration. It also reported that Berry allowed a drop of 6 feet and death was instantaneous.

It was not until Monday 9 December 1889 that Berry conducted his next execution. Benjamin Purcell, aged 50, had murdered his wife, Emily, in their home at Bradford-upon-Avon. Theirs had been an unhappy marriage and in a dispute over some shopping he had seized an axe and split her head open with it; then bludgeoned her head and body with the blunt end and walked to the police station, where he confessed his crime. Baron Pollack sentenced him to death at Wiltshire Assizes.

On Christmas Eve, Tuesday 24 December 1889, surely an inappropriate day for such work, Berry executed William Dukes at

Manchester. Dukes had murdered his employer, George Gordon, at a furniture warehouse at Bury. He had been drinking on the day of the murder, and after being threatened with the sack for not keeping up with his work he had beaten Gordon to death with a hammer. He denied murder, claiming it was an accident, but Mr Justice Charles sentenced him to death at Manchester Assizes.

The last day of the year, Tuesday 31 December 1889, saw Berry at work at Maidstone, executing William Thomas Hook, aged 40, who had beaten his wife, Julia, to death after she had left him with their two sons. Mr Justice Denman sentenced him to death at Kent Assizes. On the same day James Billington conducted a double execution at Leeds. The condemned men were Frederick Brett, aged 39, and Robert West, aged 45, both wife-murderers who had cut their victims' throats. For Berry it was a time of uncertainty and he was well aware of the rival hangman operating in Yorkshire. He did not know it, but he had less than two years of his chosen career left.

27

A period of doubt

'Should I have hanged Richard Davies?'

By 1890 it would seem that Berry was seriously questioning his duties, although, paradoxically, he undoubtedly enjoyed the status and recognition his position accorded him in the public eye. He was also very aware that it would be difficult to earn comparable wages in any other job that might be available to him.

His first execution of the New Year took place at Warwick on Tuesday 7 January 1890. The prisoner under sentence of death was Charles Lister Higgenbotham, a 63-year-old employee of Birmingham Corporation, convicted of the murder of his landlady, Winifred Phillips, aged 76, whose throat he had cut with a knife. It was another messy hanging. Berry gave a drop of only 4ft 6in, but an old wound opened in Higgenbotham's neck and blood gushed out. Although death was instantaneous, the blood was reported to have spurted for several minutes.

Berry's next job was a double execution at Worcester County Prison. It was scheduled for Tuesday 11 March 1890 and the culprits were two brothers, Joseph and Samuel Boswell, aged 29 and 39 respectively, gardeners who had indulged in poaching. A third gardener, Alfred Hill, had accompanied them on their unlawful activities. In the early hours of Sunday 10 November 1889 they had been caught poaching in the grounds of the Duc d'Aumale, at Linehurst, near Evesham, by the under-gamekeeper, Frank (given in *The Times* as William) Stephens, whom they shot dead. Hill was also sentenced to death but was reprieved on the day before the execution.

The two brothers rose at 5.00 a.m. and ate a good breakfast, after which they saw the Revd A. Telfer, the chaplain, who stated subsequently that both men were penitent at the end. At a quarter to eight the bell began tolling and members of the press were conducted to the gallows by a warder, the white caps being drawn over the brothers' heads before they reached the scaffold. Berry's unnamed assistant appeared very nervous, and the work of strapping the men's feet and fixing the nooses round their necks consequently took longer than usual, both men groaning throughout due to their desperate situation. Finally Berry was ready and stood at the lever.

'Now, Sam, good-bye,' said Joseph.

'God bless you, my poor boy,' his brother replied, 'I hope all will be right.'

The prison chaplain repeated the closing words of the service, 'In the midst of life we are in death.' Berry pulled the lever, the drop fell and both men died instantaneously.

On the next day, 12 March 1890, Berry executed William Row, aged 40, at Newcastle. Row was a Manchester shoemaker who had left his wife and run off to Newcastle with his paramour, Lily McClaren Wilson, a woman of ill repute. It was an unhappy partnership and on 3 January they had a dispute, Row suspecting she was supplementing her income with prostitution. He cut her throat with one of his knives, was duly arrested, found guilty of murder and sentenced to death on 21 February by Mr Justice Grantham.

On Wednesday 26 March 1890 Berry executed John Neal, aged 64, at Newgate. Neal had been sentenced to death for the murder of his young wife, whom he had stabbed in a fit of jealousy on 24 January.

Berry's next execution was to prove a very emotional and disturbing experience for him. The date fixed for the execution was Tuesday 8 April 1890 at Knutsford Prison in Cheshire. The condemned was Richard Davies, a frail boy of only 18 who looked much younger. It was a tragic affair, known as 'the Crewe murder', and one in which Berry took a great interest. The father, a tailor aged 50 and also named Richard, was a violent man who had bullied his family, and young Richard had often protected his mother, sometimes coming downstairs in his nightshirt and stepping between the two of them. Together with a younger brother, George, aged 16 – one of several brothers and sisters and a lad described as of 'a lower type of intelligence altogether' than

Richard – he worked for his father in his business at Crewe. On Saturday 25 January Richard and George rushed into the family home claiming that two men had attacked their father in Crewe Lane, Hough, about 4 miles from Crewe. The father's body was found with his head battered in, a bough having been placed across the road to stop the horse and trap he had been riding in. Subsequently interviewed, Richard said a bit too much about the murder, revealing his and his brother's involvement. They were tried before Mr Justice Wills at Chester on 20 March. George appeared the more hardened of the two, bursting into repeated fits of laughter and appearing callously indifferent when a police sergeant held up his father's bloodstained clothes. Richard, conversely, wept bitterly during the trial, especially when his mother gave evidence and, later, during the speech for the defence. Both were found guilty and sentenced to death, despite the jury recommending mercy in view of their youth. A reprieve was granted for George as he was only 16 years old, but the Home Secretary declared himself unable to find sufficient grounds in the case of Richard. The decision caused a great public outcry as there was widespread sympathy for both boys. A great number of people petitioned for their reprieves, one raised in London carrying 35,000 signatures. Richard's mother pleaded her son's excellent character, going as far as, through the defence solicitor, Mr Pedley, sending a telegram to the Queen herself on the night of Sunday 6 April:

> Queen of England, – My boy Richard Davies, whom the jury recommended to mercy, is to be executed on Tuesday. I beseech you to respite him for a week for further inquiry. – MARY DAVIES.

John Davies, another brother, showed a reporter a letter written by young Richard from the prison on the Saturday night. It ran:

> I am glad George has been spared, though he will have a hard life to live. I thank God I have told the truth, although I have not been able to prove it on earth; but God will prove it at our next trial, which will be on the great Judgment Day, if it is not proved

sooner, for George will confess it some day, and then you will see. I hope he will not keep it without confessing it before he dies, for if he does he will both lose peace on earth and in heaven. May God help him to reveal it, when he may be forgiven. It cannot do me any good now, but it will be a good thing for him, for by confessing he will have comfort.

Richard had become extremely penitent and the chaplain, the Revd W.N. Truss, and others who came into contact with him, were convinced that the letters reproduced in the newspapers accurately conveyed the boy's feelings. To the last he firmly protested his innocence of any participation in the actual crime. The Home Secretary came in for great criticism for failing to show mercy but all appeals were to no avail. It was a harrowing situation for Berry to find himself in, and provided yet another example to support those campaigning for the abolition of the death penalty. He arrived at the prison on the Monday evening and began his preparations. At seven o'clock that night the condemned lad partook of the Holy Sacrament and then retired after the departure of the chaplain. He slept well and woke at 5.00 a.m. and dressed, and then ate breakfast before seeing the chaplain at 7.00 a.m. He wrote a statement and handed it to the chaplain at ten minutes to eight. It read:

'I truthfully declare in my last hour that I never struck my father on the night of his death, and that I never had the axe in my hand.'

At the same time he gave the chaplain a letter for his mother that contained similar words.

At four minutes to eight Berry entered the cell with Principal Warder Farrell. Before he could pinion the young lad, who had become extremely thin, he had to fold a sheet and put it against the boy's back, under his waistcoat, so that the belt could be secured. He described the painful proceedings thus:

Outside the prison a huge crowd had collected in the falling rain, and at intervals a howl rent the air, a howl of rage at the crime which was shortly to be committed in the name of the law, for hundreds still believed that Richard Davies had never laid a hand upon his father.

When I got to the door of the condemned cell with the Sheriff I saw the chaplain standing waiting to do his duty. A pale-faced, trembling little man, with a fine face his lips were moving in prayer. Ten minutes before I entered the boy had written a letter to the clergyman, and the ink was not dry when I entered the cell . . .

. . . and I may say that I believed in his innocence. He also wrote a pathetic letter to his mother, in which he said he thanked God he had told her the truth although he had not been able to prove it on earth.

The boy looked up at me with tears in his eyes when I entered, and shrank back. 'Come my little lad, I am not going to hurt you,' said I. 'We have got to put these things on to get it over all the sooner. You won't be frightened, will you?'

He tried to speak, but the words failed to come.

'It will be better than spending all your life in this dreadful place. Try to be brave now, and James Berry will do his best for you.'

He pulled himself up when I went to put the straps on, and I got them quickly round him. To my great grief, however, he was so thin that they would not buckle properly, and I was forced to wind the blankets of his bed round him before he could be properly pinioned.

I brought him out, his hands clasped, his eyes upraised to Heaven, and when the little group in the corridor saw him there was murmurs of pity. 'Poor little chap!' 'It's a shame!'

It was a minute before the hour when the boy emerged from the cell, his arms pinioned, with a pitiful expression and looking as if he were about to cry. However, he walked with a firm step and did not require the assistance of the two warders who accompanied him. Berry claims that his own feet seemed to be 'incapable of motion' and that he staggered along with the arm of a stalwart warder supporting him. The distance from the cell to the scaffold was about 50 yards, along a passage and across an open yard into a low building that had been formerly used as the coach-house. The scaffold was erected in this structure and included a pit in the floor about 7 feet deep to accommodate the drop. The sad procession to the place of execution consisted of the under-sheriff, Mr Walker Greg; the prison surgeon, Dr Fennell; the prison governor, Captain E. Price; the deputy governor, Mr Lewis; and the chaplain, followed by the condemned youth and warders, with Berry behind them.

Rain fell as the procession crossed the yard and a fresh breeze blew. Berry, thinking to prevent the lad from seeing the gallows, placed the white cap over his head. He was positioned over the trapdoor and the noose adjusted about his neck, as the chaplain prayed, 'Into Thy hands we commend his spirit.'

Responding in a feeble and tremulous voice, Davies said, 'My Lord God, I commend my soul to Thee; receive my spirit.'

The next moment Berry pulled the bolt and Davies disappeared from sight. Dr Fennell pronounced that death was instantaneous. The *Illustrated Police News* of 19 April 1890 reported that a momentary vibration of the rope was followed by what was obviously almost instantaneous death, 'the only signs of life for a few seconds being a nervous contraction of the pinioned arms and shoulders'. According to *The Times*:

> The drop was six feet, and the rope, according to certain new regulations, was supplied by the Home Office, and had never been used before.

The usual formal inquest was then held. One can only imagine the profound effect that the execution had on Berry himself. He had carried out his task as mercifully as he was able, but it was a task he would much rather have relinquished.

The MP for the area, Mr W.S.B. McLaren, spoke that night at Crewe and severely criticised the Home Secretary for his failure to reprieve the youth. He could have understood his action, he said, though not agreed with it, had he allowed the law to take its course and let both the condemned hang, but to reprieve one and allow the other to die was 'unwise, wrong and cruel'. The jury's recommendation to mercy was an important part of their verdict and should not have been disregarded. Mr McLaren opposed capital punishment strongly and did not feel that it had any deterrent effect on those who committed murder. It was, he claimed: 'the last remnant of a barbaric age, and should at once be swept away for more just and Christian methods of punishment' (this to loud cheers). He concluded by expressing his deep regret at the sentence being carried out on Richard Davies, and his deep sympathy for the boy's mother, brothers and sisters, because of the hardness of their lot in life.

So what effect did this execution have on Berry? He later wrote:

And now I come to the most sorrowful sight that ever I beheld in my life.

With trembling fingers, with tear-dimmed eyes, I know I shall find the task far beyond me. I would rather not write about the death of young Richard Davies.

He was a child – a child in the eyes of the law – an innocent child in the eyes of many, and the whole country clamoured for his release . . .

Poor little fellow. I hung [sic] him believing him to be innocent. There was not a man in the prison who stood dry-eyed as I sent him to his doom, and for myself I knew no sleep nor any peaceful thoughts for weeks after the dreadful scene.

I can see him still, his tear-stained face, as I went to pinion him. His eyes staring in dumb appeal, his lips moving convulsively.

And it is the bitterest thought of my life that I was not man enough on that occasion to turn to the crowd in front of the scaffold and say – 'I refuse to do the duty you have brought me here to do.'

What would have been the use? As on previous occasions I could not have saved him from his fate, and it would only have been prolonging his agony. Some other hangman would have been called in to do the work.

Berry had concluded that Richard Davies should not have been executed and that there was serious doubt that he had even struck a blow in the murder. The account of this pitiful case surely bolstered the arguments of those against capital punishment.

On Monday 14 April 1890 Berry's York counterpart, James

Billington, 'a barber', appeared before magistrates at Bolton on a charge of assaulting a youth, Alex Halliwell, whom he had struck in the mouth and kicked. Apparently the youth had ducked Billington's son while they were playing on a raft, and the hangman had dealt out his own summary justice. He pleaded provocation and was fined ten shillings plus costs.

Berry's next execution, at Kirkdale gaol, Liverpool, was that of William Chadwick, aged 28, a labourer who had been sentenced to death by Mr Justice Matthews at Liverpool Assizes on 22 March 1890. His crime was the murder of a pawnbroker's assistant, Walter Davies, at Atherton, near Bolton, who had caught him stealing watches from behind the shop counter on 22 July 1889. A scuffle had ensued and Chadwick had knifed the victim.

For this execution a new scaffold had been constructed. The old one was elevated, requiring the prisoner to ascend a ladder to the platform, whereas the new structure adjoined the walls just inside the prison entrance, the use of a pit to accommodate the drop obviating the need for the harrowing climb onto the platform, as in the past. The Russian hemp rope with its coiled noose was suspended from an iron hoop in the ponderous crossbeam. Further iron hoops either side of the suspended noose indicated the facility for a triple execution. Three members of the Liverpool press were present to witness the scene, and, according to the *Liverpool Daily Post*, Berry dealt with the prisoner 'with practiced dexterity, and with all the consideration which this grim officer would allow'. After the white cap was placed over his face the prisoner was heard to say, 'Goodbye, and the Lord bless you.' The chaplain, the Revd Pigot, was deeply affected and replied, 'Goodbye, God bless you, my lad.' Berry then activated the lever and the culprit disappeared below. A look into the pit revealed that death appeared to have been instantaneous as the neck was dislocated, the head hanging to one side and the body exhibiting just a few muscular contortions, but when Dr Barr went into the pit with a warder he found that the man's heart continued to beat for a quarter of an hour after he had fallen. Reportedly Dr Barr observed that there was nothing exceptional or remarkable about this, claiming it to be about the average time the human heart continues to beat after life had become extinct (*Liverpool Daily Post*, 16 April 1890).

The usual inquest was opened just before 9.00 a.m. and the jurors viewed the body of the dead felon, which had been laid out on a stretcher in the old coach-house adjoining the scaffold. There was a placid appearance to the body, and the only indication of violent death suffered was a mark under the ear. Dr Barr gave evidence, stating that the execution had been carried out in 'a very satisfactory indeed' manner, death being caused by dislocation of the neck. Berry had given Chadwick, who was 5ft 5½in tall and weighed 133lb, a drop of 6ft 6in. The *Liverpool Daily Post* reported that, amazingly, 'the rope had stretched from 6ft 6in to 8ft 2½in', which sounds impossible. The full length of the rope should have been 13 feet, and if the length at the drop was found to be 8ft 2½in, as opposed to the calculated 6ft 6in, it would seem to indicate that Berry had adjusted the rope wrongly, giving a greater drop. By this time the rope, which was attached to the chain on the beam by means of an eyelet and shackle, was state-supplied and must surely have been tested and pre-stretched.

Meanwhile, *The Times* of 5 May 1890 carried the following advertisement:

MADAME TUSSAUD and SONS' EXHIBITION.
– CREWE MURDERERS, Richard and George Davies, also Figure of Berry, the Hangman, now added to the CHAMBER of HORRORS.

Berry's appointments book showed John Hindley scheduled to hang at Glasgow on 10 May 1890 but a reprieve was granted. On 10 June 1890, however, he hanged Daniel Stewart Gorrie, aged 30, at Wandsworth. Gorrie had beaten to death and robbed a baker named Thomas Furlonger at Brixton.

On 29 July 1890 Berry was again at Wandsworth, this time executing George Bowling, aged 57, a labourer who had beaten his lover, Elizabeth Nightingale, to death with a hammer at Mitcham, Surrey. Another man, Edward Young, awaited execution at Strangeways on 5 August 1890, but Berry's appointment book is marked 'Reprieved sent to Broadmoor'.

It was a time of much change. Berry, if he is to be believed, was becoming increasingly affected by the disturbing work he performed and the government was beginning to exert more control on the hangman. New ideas to improve the method of executions were also being adopted, the most significant of which was an increased use of the 'new style scaffold' set at floor level with a pit, that obviated the climbing of steps. Berry's career as a hangman, although he did not know it then, had only one more year to run, but there were still sixteen more executions to be performed before it ended.

28

Another bungle

'. . . he was hanged in the real sense of the word.'

On Friday 22 August 1890 Berry executed Felix Spicer at Knutsford gaol, Cheshire. Spicer, a 60-year-old ex-sailor and owner of a guesthouse, had separated from his wife, who kept a seaside café at New Brighton and had been unsuccessfully trying to get her back. On 24 April he cut the throats of two of their three children, then attacked his wife at the café. After a desperate struggle he made off, but was arrested and charged with the murder of the two children and the attempted murder of his wife. Found guilty at Chester Assizes he was sentenced to death, later making an unsuccessful bid to commit suicide while awaiting execution. Berry gave him a drop of 5ft 2in.

On Tuesday 26 August 1890 Berry executed Frederick Davies, a 40-year-old gunsmith who had shot his wife, at Birmingham. The same day, at Leeds, James Billington executed James Harrison, aged 30, a labourer who had beaten his wife to death.

The following day, at Newgate, Berry executed Francois Monteau, a Belgian immigrant and cabinet-maker, aged 51. Monteau had shot another Belgian immigrant, Francois de Grave, after his girlfriend, Marion Du Pond, had left him and become the latter's lover. Despite pleading that it was an accident, he was found guilty and sentenced to death by Mr Justice Grantham.

Another execution was scheduled for 1 September 1890 at Ayr – that of John McDonald – but Berry's appointment book shows him as 'Respited'. His next execution, when it came, was not to be so straightforward as the recent ones he had carried out. The case had been reported as 'The Shotts Murder' and involved a wife murder at

Benhar Row, in the village of Harthill, near Shotts, Scotland. The culprit was Henry Delvin, a 45-year-old miner and father of seven who had beaten his wife to death with a poker in front of their children. Sentenced to death at the High Court he was held in Duke Street Prison, Glasgow to await his fate, the execution being fixed for 23 September 1890. It was the only execution Berry carried out in that city.

Describing Delvin as 'one of the most brutal men I ever sent to eternity', Berry readily admitted an error on his part in this case:

> Devlin [*sic*] did not die a brave man, and his death was a terrible one.
>
> One of the few cases into which miscalculation entered, he was hanged in the real sense of the word. The drop on this occasion was not so great as it should have been, and the poor fellow suffered all the agonies of strangulation before the end came.
>
> The fact was not generally known at the time, the cause of death not being inquired into by the jury at the inquest which followed.

Delvin's murder of his wife was regarded as particularly cruel as he had beaten her persistently over a period of 5 hours, even jumping on her as she lay on the floor, the poor woman dying a week later from her injuries. According to Berry 'the man was looked upon as a fiend in human shape, but, of course, he must have been mad, though at the time of the trial the question of insanity was not considered by most people'. In support of his assessment, Berry went on to note Delvin's fastidious dress sense, the latter rarely having appeared outside work in shabby apparel.

> This to my mind is one of the most important points to consider when you come to analyse the character of the man and to endeavour to find a motive for his crime. Madness takes strange forms, and one of the signs is an overwhelming love for finery and display. People who have been careless in their attire in their youth have been known to become dandies in their decline.
>
> Some of the people I have hanged have been most peculiar

in their behaviour at the last moment, arranging their dress so that they would present a spick and span appearance to the spectators who would never see them in life again.

Another fact that I would like to mention is that never once did I hang a teetotaler. I was not always abstemious myself, the work I was doing forcing me at times to resort to stimulants, and those who knew me well will admit that I was never cranky on the subject of temperance, even after I gave up taking alcohol in any shape or form. It will therefore be all the more convincing when I make the statement that but for the liquor fiend a great proportion of the people I put through my hands would never have been executed.

To return to Devlin [sic], however, he was married to a steady, industrious, well-to-do woman, whom he systematically ill-treated in spite of her great attachment to him. The poor woman was thrashed most unmercifully every Saturday night of the year, but although frequently advised to obtain police protection she would never consent to go against her husband in a police court. She did ask the local constable once or twice to speak to her husband, but beyond that she refused to go, and endeavoured in the face of many difficulties to keep the children tidy and her home comfortable.

People in the neighbouring houses in the rows who could not but see and hear what was going on in the house predicted that Devlin would be hanged for murdering his wife. They looked upon him as a man of a dour, sullen disposition out of doors, who exploded as soon as he gained the interior of his own house.

When Berry arrived at Duke Street Prison he immediately went to inspect the scaffold. He was asked what he thought of it:

I replied that it was the best in the three kingdoms, and that if the occasion ever arose I would be prepared to hang five Scotsmen on it. I never hanged five in my life, but once I was engaged by the authorities to do so. Two of the murderers were afterwards reprieved.

The scaffold was erected exactly opposite the main entrance to the Drygate Wing, against the high wall. A strong hook had been screwed into the crossbeam and from this Berry had suspended a new ¾in Manila rope. First erected in 1883 for the execution by Marwood of the 'Port-Glasgow murderers' Mullen and Scott, the first execution at the prison, Berry considered the scaffold 'perfect' apart from the fact that it was reached by a flight of steps from the corridor. He commented:

> 'Ultimately I was the means of having such steps done away with in many prisons in the country. They were nothing more nor less than a system of torture to the condemned, and few of my victims got up them unassisted.'

He also noted that the route to the scaffold was overlooked by windows of the houses opposite, so he had the sides all the way down covered with canvas to prevent the last walk of the condemned man being seen.

Delvin, who for the three weeks following the passing of the sentence was constantly attended by a warder, was confined in a cell located on the ground floor in the north-east corner of the block of buildings known as the Drygate Wing. There was a small bed at one end of the cell and a grated fireplace at the other. The cell opened onto a corridor that ran the length of the building, about 80 yards long.

Despite the jury recommending mercy no reprieve was forthcoming, much to the prisoner's disappointment. The night before the execution Berry went to have a look at him. He had been allowed to change into his own clothes and was nervously pacing the cell in an excited state. He had a restless night and in the morning appeared emotionally exhausted, being unable to eat his breakfast.

A crowd that was to reach an estimated 10,000 began to congregate in front of the prison. The bell tolled and Berry described the air of 'indescribable gloom' in the prison, most of the officials being suitably attired for the sombre occasion. The prison governor, Mr Alston, wore a frock coat, silk hat and black scarf, and the elderly chaplain wore a black surplice. When Berry entered the cell he was shocked at the sight of the condemned man, who was pale, wore a woeful expression and was shaking like a leaf:

'Now, then, Henry, time is passing, and you will have to get ready,' said I. 'Would you like to make any statement?'

He started up from his seat, and with glazed eyes turned to the governor, saying in a trembling voice – 'I would like to thank you and everyone else for the kind way I have been treated.'

He grasped the hand of the governor firmly, and like the good fellow he was the latter allowed him to hold it while I was doing my duty. When he could no longer allow him to do so he gripped his arm tightly and tried by the only means in his power to give him courage. The priests in the meantime had been chanting the prayers for the dying, and when I was ready I placed the cap on his head and brought him out into the corridor.

When I had a brave man to hang I invariably waited until I was about to draw the lever before I covered his eyes from the world, but in the case of a man like Henry Devlin I never allowed him to catch a glimpse of the beam or the rope that dangled from it. Headed by the chief warder, the procession moved on its way, Devlin being assisted by two of the other officials.

In Scotland they always stuck to their old-time observations, and near the end of the corridor the Magistrates, headed by their halberd bearers, awaited us. The city officers wore their full regalia, and the strange, old-fashioned weapons they carried were draped in black. It was a farce, in my opinion, and I was always against it. If I had had my way I would have pulled the white cap down at once, but the arrangements were not in my hands, and we had to go through the ceremony of having the poor wretch identified.

The Bailies were seated at a table, and on the procession reaching them a halt was made while the governor handed over the prisoner.

The Bailie in charge of the proceedings asked if his name was Henry Devlin, to which he answered 'Yes' in a weak voice. The Bailie then asked him if he had any desire to gratify, and after a slight hesitation Devlin replied in a weary tone that he had none. The Magistrates now handed over the death warrant to me, and I immediately drew the white cap over the eyes of my victim.

'Don't be frightened now, Henry,' I said. 'It will all be over in a second.'

The white cap was the one I had used for Jessie King, and it screened out the sight of the gallows completely from his eyes. Two policemen were stationed on the scaffold to see that no one interfered with it, while a number of others were keeping guard in the immediate vicinity.

The poor fellow stumbled along more dead than alive, and the warders had frequently to put their arms around him to steady his steps. When we reached the scaffold they had to guide him on to the platform. He would have fallen down but for their assistance, and I do not think he could have been conscious of what was taking place.

The Roman Catholic priest was a fine fellow, and he mounted the scaffold and stood beside Devlin while I was getting him ready. Deftly I put the straps around his legs while he continued to tremble like a leaf, and then amid the breathless suspense of the onlookers I put the rope round the poor fellow's neck.

Just as the hour of eight was booming from the steeple I pulled the lever, and he disappeared to his doom.

The dull thud of the trap caused a shudder to run through the crowd in front of the scaffold and in every part of the prison it was distinctly heard.

A long silence followed, for with horror everyone was gazing at the rope which was still vibrating and at the same time a rhythmical murmur was heard by those standing around as if sacred songs were being sung outside the walls of the prison.

From where I stood I could see that everything was not right, but I said nothing to anyone, and it was not until the doctor had examined the body that it began to be whispered about the prison that death was due to asphyxia or strangulation. There was no fracture of the spinal column, and this I put down to the fact that Devlin was a big, powerful chap, and could have done with a longer drop. Strangulation was the old system of execution, and that it was painful to a degree no one knows better than myself.

I was very much upset at the mishap, and would have given

anything not to have been the author of it, but over the past I was powerless, and I had just to try to bear the torture of it.

I tried to console myself with the thought that Devlin had been a brute, but it was a false line of reasoning, and the folly of it was apparent as the years rolled on.

When the black flag was hoisted a man in the crowd outside the prison fainted. Despite Berry's statement that details of the execution were withheld from the press, this does not seem to have entirely been the case. *The Glasgow Herald* of Wednesday 24 September 1890, though having recorded that death was instantaneous, when reporting on the inquest made the following comment:

The cause of death, it may be added, is not stated in the medical certificate. Dr. Sutherland, however, says that death was caused for the most part by asphyxia. There was no laceration of the neck or fracture of the spine – rather an unusual thing with the drop system. The body was placed in quicklime, and buried within the walls of the prison about an hour after the inquest. Immediately after the body had been taken down Berry received his fee, packed up his ropes and straps, and, brown bag in hand, left the prison by the Duke Street doorway. He returned to Bradford by the 10.25 A.M. express from St. Enoch.

Berry's final words on this visit were:

While I was in Glasgow they told me that on one occasion a man hanged by the old method came to life again.

His name was Matthew Clydesdale, and when his body was handed over for dissection he came to life again. The man rose to his feet, to the amazement of the students, some of whom fainted, while others applauded, and the deed that the executioner could not accomplish was finished by the professor of the college, who killed the man by plunging his lancet into the jugular vein.

This case had occurred on 3 October 1818 and was remembered in Glasgow as a remarkable incident. The executioner, 'Tam' Young, had not done his work correctly and Clydesdale had been resuscitated when a galvanic shock had been administered at Glasgow University. Professor Jeffrey had to finish the job as described. It had, naturally, caused a great sensation in the city, and was to prove the last order made for dissection by the Circuit Judges at Glasgow.

29

Mrs Pearcey

'Prettiest Convict I Ever Hanged.'

On Tuesday 23 December 1890 Berry executed Mary Eleanor Pearcey (real name Wheeler) aged 24, a woman he described as the prettiest he ever hanged. She was certainly the most notorious; her effigy was to remain on display in Madame Tussaud's Chamber of Horrors exhibition throughout the twentieth century. The story of her crime is recorded in many books. It was the age-old scenario of a woman's love for a married man, in Mrs Pearcey's case one Frank Hogg, jealousy finally leading to murder. It was also a case that was briefly to bring back fading memories of the 'Jack the Ripper' murders of 1888. Indeed, one Ripper author subsequently made out a case for Mrs Pearcey as the unknown Whitechapel murderer (see *Jack the Ripper: A New Theory*, by William Stewart, London, Quality Press, 1939).

The crime was committed on Friday 24 October 1890 and was discovered when a woman's body was found that evening lying in the pathway opposite a partly erected building in Crossfield Road, South Hampstead, a street under development. The skull was fractured, the body had multiple cuts and bruises, and the throat had been cut so deeply as to nearly sever the head. Dr Augustus Pepper and the noted A Division police surgeon Dr Thomas Bond, who had been involved in the Ripper investigation, examined the body.

At 9.30 p.m. a police officer, PC Roser, then found a perambulator, or bassinet, abandoned outside 34 Hamilton Terrace, St John's Wood. The interior of the pram was bloodstained and there was a piece of butterscotch (toffee) lying in it. The following day the body of an 18-month-old baby girl was found on waste ground in Finchley Road, not far from where the pram had been found.

The story behind the crime is as follows. Frank Samuel Hogg lived with his wife Phoebe (née Styles), aged 31, their baby daughter Phoebe Hanslope, aged 18 months, his sister Clara, and his mother, at 141 Prince of Wales Road, Kentish Town. The couple had married in November 1888 when Phoebe had become pregnant. Mary Pearcey, who lived in a three-room, ground-floor apartment at 2 Priory Street, Kentish Town, had been a family friend of several years. She had assumed the name Pearcey from a former lover, a carpenter-joiner, John Charles Pearcey, of High Street, Camden Town, whom she had met in 1885 and with whom she had lived for three years. She had not married him, and for the past two years, though he had seen her frequently, he had not visited her. Frank Hogg was an unprepossessing man with a large ragged beard, a woebegone appearance and ill-fitting clothing. He held a key for 2 Priory Street and frequently visited Mrs Pearcey, with whom he was conducting a long-term extramarital relationship. Notwithstanding the rather gaunt-featured and prominently toothed effigy later displayed in Madame Tussaud's, Mrs Pearcey was a good-looking woman whose attractions for the opposite sex were patent. She had made a habit of using her feminine wiles to live off men: a 'man of independent means', Charles Crichton of Northfleet near Gravesend, paid for her accommodation and also made regular visits to the young woman. However, it would appear that her heart was reserved for Hogg, though what made him so attractive to her is not clear. This love became an obsession, Pearcey growing hugely jealous of Mrs Hogg; a situation that led to tragedy. The relationship had flourished before Hogg married Phoebe and continued afterwards, both Hogg and Pearcey declaring their love for each other.

Things came to a head that fateful October day when Mrs Pearcey invited Phoebe Hogg, together with her child, to her home for tea. Phoebe Hogg went, taking the child in a wicker pram with her. At some stage during the visit Mrs Pearcey attacked Phoebe in the kitchen with a poker and cut her throat, subsequently putting her body into the pram, on top of the child, and covering it. It is believed that the baby was suffocated by the weight of her mother's body. Mrs

Pearcey then left the house to dispose of the bodies and the pram. On a long circuitous walk she dumped Phoebe's body in Crossfield Road, then disposed of the baby's body in a field near Finchley Road, before finally abandoning the pram in Hamilton Terrace.

With Mrs Hogg missing from home and news of a body found in Crossfield Road appearing in the Saturday morning papers, Clara Hogg went to Mrs Pearcey to ask if she had seen her sister-in-law. The two women went together to Hampstead Police Station, where Miss Hogg gave information on the missing Phoebe and baby. Inspector Sly of S Division sent Detective Sergeants Brown and Nursey with the two women to Hampstead mortuary to see if they could identify the woman's body there. Mrs Pearcey seemed particularly reluctant to do so, suspicious behaviour that the officers noted. Clara identified the body as that of her sister but Pearcey declared, 'That is not her.' Clara and a niece of the murdered woman were kept at the police station to assist with information, and Frank Hogg was called for. He identified his wife's body and was similarly detained at the police station.

The case had attracted high-level attention and Mr Melville Macnaghten, Chief Constable of the Criminal Investigation Department at Scotland Yard, together with the District Chief Constable Colonel Bolton Monsell, attended the station to confer with the senior officers there. Also in attendance were Detective Inspector Bannister, and Inspectors Collis and Wright. Suspicions already aroused concerning Mrs Pearcey were heightened by the discovery that the perambulator had been used to convey the bodies, and it was decided to search her rooms. Detective Sergeant Nursey and Detective Constable Parsons were despatched to 2 Priory Street, with Mrs Pearcey, to make the search. They found signs of a violent struggle in the kitchen, two windowpanes being smashed – concerning which Mrs Pearcey claimed, 'I was trying to catch some mice and broke them' – and various telltale bloodstains.

'I believe you saw her [Mrs. Hogg] yesterday,' said Nursey.

'I know, I should have told you before this,' Pearcey replied, very agitated and her voice trembling. 'She called at 6 o'clock and asked me to take care of the child and asked for money, but she did not come inside. I told Clara about it, and she said I had better not say anything about it as it seemed a disgrace to ask for money.'

At this, Nursey left Parsons in charge of the house and went to send a telegram summoning Superintendent Beard and Inspector Bannister to the scene. The two senior officers attended the premises, a further search was made, and a carving knife with blood on the handle, together with a second carving knife that also seemed to have blood on the handle, were found in a table drawer. There was also a long, heavy poker in the fender. The walls and ceiling of the kitchen were bespattered with blood, and a black skirt in the kitchen likewise appeared to have bloodstains on it, as did a stained apron that had been recently washed. The rug was also much stained with blood, despite what looked like an attempt to clean it. Inspector Bannister took the knives and the poker into the parlour, where Mrs Pearcey was sitting in an armchair, at which she began to whistle, assuming an air of complete indifference. Bannister and Superintendent Beard then interviewed other inmates of the house and took some statements, before Bannister returned to the parlour, where Mrs Pearcey was still whistling.

'Mrs. Pearcey, I am going to arrest you', he said, 'for the wilful murder of Mrs Hogg last night, and also on suspicion of the wilful murder of the female child of Mrs. Hogg.'

She jumped out of the chair and said, 'You can arrest me if you like, I am quite willing to go with you, I think you have made a great mistake.'

She then handed him a latchkey and said, 'This is the key of 141 Prince of Wales Road. Clara gave it to me today.'

Mrs Pearcey was conveyed by cab to Kentish Town Police Station. On the way she said to Bannister, 'Why do you charge me with the crime?'

He replied, 'On account of the evidence.'

She responded, 'Well, I would not do such a dreadful thing, I would not hurt anyone.'

He told her to take off her gloves, which she did. She was wearing two wedding rings, one a brass ring and the other a broad gold one. Her hands were very much cut and scratched about, and all her clothing was considerably bloodstained. The evidence was overwhelming.

She was tried before Mr Justice Denman, at the Central Criminal Court, the Old Bailey, from 1–3 December 1890, and it became clear from her love letters to Hogg that she was infatuated with him. Witnesses were called who had heard screaming from her house on the fatal day and had subsequently seen her wheeling the perambulator along the street. Despite all this, Mrs Pearcey still maintained that she was innocent.

The defence counsel suggested a plea of manslaughter, the killing being the result of a dispute that got out of hand, but Mrs Pearcey would have none of it and maintained, illogically, that she knew nothing of the murder. So adamant was she on this point that some suspected an accomplice was involved, but there was never any evidence of this.

Further details emerged concerning Mary Pearcey. It seems she suffered from a form of epilepsy and had attempted to commit suicide on more than one occasion. A traumatic experience occurred in her formative years, when she was 14. Her father, Thomas Wheeler of Lewisham, with two other family members, had gone at night to Marshall's Wick Farm at Sandridge near St Albans to commit a burglary. The owner, Edward Anstee, thinking he heard someone call his name, went to the bedroom window, whereupon the intruders blasted him to death with a shotgun and then ransacked the house, Mrs Anstee locking herself in the bedroom. The culprits were arrested and Thomas Wheeler was found to have blood on his trousers and boots. The men were found to have been responsible for other burglaries and thefts in the area. Thomas Wheeler was found guilty and hanged by William Marwood on 26 November 1880.

Beyond doubt Mrs Pearcey was a complex character, with flaws in her makeup that led to murder. It is not clear whether the crime was premeditated or the result of an argument that got out of hand. Some suggested that Mrs Hogg had previously feared for her safety where Mrs Pearcey was concerned but exactly what happened will remain a mystery. In the face of damning evidence, however, there could be only one result at the trial. She was found guilty and Mr Justice Denman sentenced her to death.

Her solicitor, Mr Freke Palmer, visited her on the day before her execution. He arrived at nine o'clock and the chief warder and a female warder were present during the interview he had with her. She was in fairly good spirits and, apparently, prepared for her fate. Though pale, and her features somewhat pinched, she was otherwise unremarkable in her appearance. She assured him that she was innocent of the crime and he seemed strongly impressed by her claim. He had, in fact, made strenuous efforts on her behalf to obtain a reprieve, but he had warned her to expect the worst. Pearcey expressed thanks not only to him but also to her counsel, Mr Arthur Hutton, to others involved in her defence, to those who had signed the petition in her favour, and to the prison officials for all the kindness they had shown since her sentence was passed. She informed Mr Palmer of her wishes concerning the disposal of a few trinkets that she possessed, the lawyer remarking that she at no time appeared grief-stricken, even managing to smile at some remarks he made.

He asked, 'Have you anything you wish to say?'

She reiterated, 'I am innocent of the murder.'

'Are you prepared to meet your fate?' he asked.

She answered that she had been ready ever since the judge passed sentence upon her.

Finally he urged her to listen attentively to the ministrations of the prison chaplain, the Revd Mr Duffield, to which she replied that she had done and would continue to do so till the last, but she was innocent of the crime and knew nothing about it. She bade Mr Palmer goodbye in a cheerful manner, having showed little or no emotion at the prospect of death throughout their hour-long interview.

One odd matter worthy of note is the fact that during the interview she had asked Mr Palmer to insert in the Madrid papers the following advertisement:

M.E.C.P. Last wish of M.E.W. Have not betrayed.

She reportedly told Mr Palmer that this message referred to a secret marriage she had pledged never to reveal. If so, she obviously kept her word; he being unable to extract from her either the date of the alleged marriage or the name of the man who, according to her, had first married then deserted her.

At 11.20 her mother, Mrs Wheeler, and sister, Charlotte Amy, visited her, in compliance with wishes she had expressed. Pearcey had requested that this farewell should take place somewhere other than in the apartment railed off for interviews between prisoners and visitors, so she was allowed to see them for 20 minutes in the Revd Mr Duffield's room, attended by only one female warder. Mother and daughter embraced each other emotionally, Pearcey crying bitterly throughout the 20-minute meeting and being much distressed after they left. However, she subsequently became calm and collected. She had been expecting a visit from her lover, Frank Hogg, but he did not come. Her disappointment at this was obvious, and painful, making her subsequent composure seem all the more remarkable. When she was informed of the Home Secretary's decision to refuse to recommend a reprieve she remained calm and said, 'I am innocent of the murder.'

James Berry had arrived at the prison in the afternoon, having been delayed in his journey from the north by a heavy fall of snow. He examined the scaffold and found it to be in perfect order. Told that he had arrived, Pearcey said, 'Oh! He is in good time. Is it usual for him to arrive on the Saturday?' The matron told her that Berry had to make the necessary arrangements.

'Oh! I suppose he will manage. They told me he is a very skilful man.'

Contrary to usual practice, it was announced that the execution was to be private, no press would be admitted. On seeing Mrs Pearcey, Berry fell under the spell that she undoubtedly was capable of casting over men. He described her as 'the most beautiful woman I hanged':

Big blue eyes with a languishing look in them, masses of wavy hair and lips like Cupid's bow, were the attractions that made many a man fall in love with her in the days of her youth.

Her neck was long and shapely, and though there was never anything of the poet or the artist in James Berry, I tell you I was spellbound when I saw her in the condemned cell.

It was a crime to put a rope round it, and surely her Creator never meant her to die with the mark of the hempen strands upon it.

I confess I did not like to kill that beautiful woman, but the law had said she must die, and how could I stand in the way.

It is strange that such a beautiful woman should have been such a fiend in human form, but I suppose that there was something wrong somewhere in her composition.

There was huge public interest in the case and Mr Freke Palmer was receiving nearly 2,000 letters weekly in relation to it. Several people sent him sums of money for the benefit of the prisoner's mother.

Mrs Pearcey went to bed about 10 p.m. on the eve of the execution but did not sleep well. On rising she had very little breakfast. A large crowd assembled outside the gates of Newgate, waiting to see the hoisting of the black flag. At about five minutes to eight, Berry went to the cell in company with the sheriff, the prison governor and the chief warder. He described the scene:

The poor woman was standing there all ready for me, and with her were the wardresses who had remained with her through the night.

'This is Mr. Berry,' said the Governor.

'Good morning, madam,' said I, holding out my hand.

She took it without manifesting the least emotion, and as the death warrant was read she seemed to be the most calm and self-possessed person in the cell.

Indeed, one of the wardresses told me afterwards that on the night before she had answered them that she would give me no trouble but would die like a man.

She was asked if she had anything to urge against carrying out the sentence.

'No, I have not,' she replied. 'It is the law, and it must be carried out. I hope Mr. Berry will be able to manage without any assistance from me.'

'I will manage all right,' said I. 'Is there anything you would like to say about your crime?'

'No one regretted it more than I did,' she answered. 'But some of the evidence given against me at the trial was false.'

'Would you like to enumerate the points?'

'No, I would not. You have not agreed to my last request being granted and I cannot speak.'

Her wish was that her lover should have been brought to see her, but as this could not be fulfilled she elected to go dumb to the scaffold.

'When you are ready, madame, I will get these straps around you,' I said.

'I am quite ready, Mr. Berry,' she replied.

She assisted me by raising her arms, and when I had buckled her up I gave the signal that the procession should start for the scaffold. Two of the warders stepped up to the poor woman as the clergyman began to read the burial service, but she hesitated and drew back.

'Wait a minute,' she said, 'I do not wish any of my nurses to go with me to the scaffold. It will only cause distress. The quieter the better. I do not wish to cause a scene and I can walk by myself.'

'I cannot let you go alone,' replied one of the women, 'I do not mind going with you.'

'Oh, well, if you don't mind going with me I am pleased,' rejoined the beautiful victim of the rope, and she then embraced each of the wardresses in a most affectionate manner. They in turn kissed her fervently and with deep emotion.

Eleanor Pearcey then walked steadily and firmly out of the cell and along the passages. Walking immediately behind her I drew the white cap over her face so that she did not even catch a glimpse of the scaffold, and I was pleased to see that her step never faltered.

When she was standing on the scaffold the wardresses let go her arms and two male warders, who were standing upon the planks, placed across the drop, took hold of her to steady her while I made the final arrangements.

The poor woman never opened her lips, and when I pulled the lever and looked down into the pit I saw that she had had a merciful death.

Present at the execution were Mr L. Kynaston Metcalfe, the deputy under-sheriff for the County of London; Col Milman, the Governor of Newgate and Holloway prisons; Dr Gilbert, the medical officer; the Revd H.G. Duffield, the Chaplain of Newgate and Holloway; and Col Henry Smith, Commissioner of the City Police. As she was being led to the gallows Pearcey had said to Mr Duffield, 'The sentence is just, but the evidence was false.' This was as near to a confession as she got and what exactly she meant by it is not known. She left a letter for Clara Hogg, absolving Frank Hogg from complicity in the murder and stating that he knew nothing about it.

The usual inquest was held after the execution and the jury viewed the body. It was found that the sentence had been carried out satisfactorily and death was instantaneous. A drop of 6ft had been allowed and death was due to a fracture of the vertebrae of the neck, the result of hanging.

Relics of the case still exist, the items belonging to Mrs Pearcey having been sold for £200 to help pay for her defence. Madame Tussaud's purchased the table 'against which Mrs. Hogg was supposed to have been leaning when the blows were struck', the window 'supposed to have been smashed by Mrs. Hogg in her death struggles', together with chairs, oilcloth, cooking utensils, crockery, fireplace, grate and flooring. From the sitting room were couch, chairs, table, mirror, carpet, piano, ornaments, curtains, blind etc. As if all that were not enough, they also purchased Mrs Pearcey's bedstead, other furniture, the perambulator in which the bodies were carried, casts of the head of Mrs Hogg and the baby taken after death, the clothes worn by Mrs Hogg and the baby at the time of death, Mrs Pearcey's receipt in her own handwriting, and the toffee found in the perambulator. All this was displayed in a tableau including the wax effigy of Mrs Pearcey, in the Chamber of Horrors. In the Crime Museum ('Black Museum') at New Scotland Yard are preserved photographs of the murdered Mrs Hogg and Mrs Pearcey, and the execution rope used by Berry.

30

Growing despair – last months as executioner

'The quickest execution that had ever taken place.'

Berry's last execution of 1890 was that of Thomas Macdonald, aged 32, at Kirkdale gaol, Liverpool on Tuesday 30 December. Berry remembered the execution for 'the white cap incident' and as 'the quickest execution I ever performed'.

Macdonald had been convicted for the murder of a schoolteacher, Miss Elizabeth Ann Holt, at Belmont, near Bolton, on Saturday 15 November 1890. It was a callous murder, the young woman, whom Macdonald had known since she was a child in Egerton, having been kicked and stabbed to death and her clothes ripped. She had been missing for a week when her body was found, in a ravine known as Longworth Clough. According to Berry, Macdonald had been besotted with Elizabeth, and when she had refused to marry him he had then stalked her. Already known as a 'bad sort', he had nursed contrasting feelings of love and hate for her, tinged with jealousy. There was much incriminating evidence to link him with the murder, and he was soon arrested, afterwards admitting the crime. He was tried at Liverpool Assizes before Mr Justice Cave on 13 December.

Berry took a 'peep' at him on the eve of the execution, and thought he could detect a look in his eye that suggested madness. He wrote, however,

I did not believe in 'the insanity dodge' then. I used to think the men were feigning so as to escape the gallows, and it was only lately that I changed my mind and began to think that most murderers are mad.

346

Berry returned to his room and smoked a cigar before retiring to bed. He was up early in the morning – '. . . a dark, cold morning in December, with a keen frosty wind blowing' – and went to check the execution shed. The beam was fitted into the roof of a building known as the coach-house. Berry had supervised the erection of the apparatus himself and was satisfied with it.

What he called 'the affair of the white cap' occurred in the precincts of the gaol just before the execution, when he met the press reporters in attendance from Bolton and Liverpool. He tells the following tale:

The reporters and I got on very well as a rule. They were exceedingly courteous to me, and I had very seldom to complain about what they wrote. So far as my personality was concerned, they were generally very flattering, and spoke of me as a humane and a very kind-hearted man.

On this occasion I had no quarrel with the reporters, but seeing them near the scaffold, with white, drawn faces, suggesting terror at the ordeal through which they were about to go, I thought I would have a little passage-at-arms with them.

Just before I got the signal to go and perform the pinioning operation I put my hand in my pocket and said –

'Good gracious me! I have forgotten to bring the white cap.'

Looking at the reporters, I told them I would have to make one, and asked one of them to lend me a handkerchief.

Both hesitated a moment, and then both simultaneously put their hands into their breast pockets and drew out a white handkerchief.

'Yes,' I exclaimed. 'Give me them both; they'll do. Well, I never did such a thing in all my life!'

I then proceeded to tie the handkerchiefs together with knots at the four corners, and when I had completed this I walked up behind one of the reporters with the utmost coolness, and, saying, 'Let's see if this will do,' I slipped it over his head. I thought the fellow was going to drop down with fright, so I pretended the cap would not fit, and said –

'It is too tight, and I shall have to do without it. I have

hanged them without a cap before, and I must do it again. It doesn't make any difference at all to the man.'

I had the real cap in my pocket all the time.

It may be safely assumed that Berry's misplaced humour did not go down too well with the reporter, but it does give an interesting glimpse of his odd idea of fun. This was not the first time that he had played 'games' with the reporters, and it seems strange that he could act in this manner on such a solemn occasion. Perhaps it was his way of relieving the tension.

A large crowd had begun to assemble outside the gaol in the early morning moonlight, the women in their shawls shivering in the cold. When the hour of the execution was reached many of them pressed their ears against the wall of the gaol in an effort to hear the thud of the falling trap.

Macdonald had passed a night in fitful sleep, much of it spent awake with staring eyes and shivering with cold and fear. On this occasion the prisoner was brought to Berry, where he waited away from the cell. On seeing the hangman, Macdonald opened his mouth in silent appeal.

'Come along now, Thomas. Try to pull yourself together, and I will be as merciful as I can,' said Berry.

Macdonald's face went a ghastly white and he trembled.

'There is nothing to be frightened about. It will be over in a few seconds. Fix your thoughts on the Judge you are going to meet, and ask Him to forgive you,' reassured Berry.

An unconvinced Macdonald shivered and shrank back, upon which two of the warders held him while Berry pinioned him. The procession moved off, the prisoner walking with faltering steps, supported by the warders. His lips were moving convulsively. On reaching the place of execution he uttered a gasp of despair and trembled violently. He was half carried onto the scaffold followed by Berry, who quickly strapped his ankles, adjusted the rope, and then slipped the white cap over his head as the condemned man muttered, 'Lord Jesus, receive my soul. Oh, Lord, have mercy upon me.'

The trap quickly opened, and those present congratulated Berry for his humanity. The black flag was hoisted before the hour chimed and the prison doctor assured Berry that it was the 'quickest execution that had ever taken place'. Berry noted that the pressmen were also loud in his praise:

> . . . I was glad that they had been able to see how an execution ought to be carried out. Of late years it has been the custom to exclude the representatives of the press, and I would like to say that this is a step in the wrong direction. The public ought to insist on being represented, as it is the only way to ensure that the last penalty of the law is conducted with decorum and solemnity.
>
> I would even go so far as to say that two or even three members of the public should be admitted, and if this were done I am fairly positive that there would be a diminution in the number of executions in the country.

Obviously Berry did not feel that his antics with the pressmen before the execution formed part of the procedure that should be 'conducted with decorum and solemnity'. As well as expressing the views above, he also felt that the three weeks between sentence and execution system was far too long and inflicted unnecessary suffering on the condemned. He cited the system in France where the condemned man was unaware of the date of his execution and was 'tumbled' out of bed and 'hustled' to his death without knowing what was happening until the last minute.

There was a second execution that same day, at York, James Billington hanging Robert Kitching, who had been convicted for the shooting of a policeman.

At Glasgow Circuit Court on 29 December 1890, Loreto Palambo, an Italian, had been sentenced to death for the murder of a fellow countryman. Berry marked the execution up in his appointment book for 19 January 1891, but a reprieve was granted. It was said that Palambo's sweetheart had walked all the way to London and personally pleaded with Lord Lothian, the Scottish Secretary, for mercy. She had succeeded and Palambo served ten years of his life sentence before being released and returning to Italy (*The Scots Black Kalendar*).

Another trip to Ireland was next on Berry's schedule. Bartholomew Sullivan, a small-time farmer aged 35, awaited sentence of death in Tralee Prison. He had been convicted at the Munster Assizes for the murder of a farmer, Patrick Flahive, aged 21, of Ballyheige, County Kerry, whose body had been found in a field on 30 August 1886. It was alleged that Flahive had been harvesting crops in a disputed field that he had been evicted from, despite being warned not to. That night he was attacked and shot. A lengthy police investigation led to Sullivan, a single man who lived with his sister, being charged but he pleaded his innocence. Evidence suggested that Sullivan, who was said to be a quiet and inoffensive man, had decoyed the victim to the place of his death, two others attacking him there. The execution was set for Monday 2 February 1891.

As usual Berry was apprehensive about travelling to Ireland, to the point that he decided to take his wife with him, recording that, 'I was very nervous when I was ordered to go to Ireland, and I asked my wife to go with me to look after me.' On the way to Tralee a stranger entered the carriage and Berry saw that he was a pressman. The latter engineered the conversation in the carriage to the topic of the execution, eyeing Berry as he did so as if inviting him to join in. Berry, however, had resolved not to respond, and when the reporter subsequently wrote of meeting him he apparently described him as, 'a reserved individual, who was a student of human nature'. He wrote further:

> An ordinary observer would have no means of guessing his favourite pastime. His countenance is a stolid one, with a fixed look of calm determination. Some of his companions were interested in the police hut at Gostatlea, but Berry appeared to be indifferent. For him the centre of attraction was Castleisland, which could be faintly seen in the distance. He gazed long at the surrounding mountains as if they possessed a fascination for him above the average. He was also much interested where moonlight raids took place, and equally so in a certain residence which was partly blown up a few years since.

On arrival at the station a plain-clothed officer met Berry and his wife, and drove them to the gates of the prison. He was told that a couple of hours earlier another officer had been asked to drive the car but had refused saying that he would 'rather give up his position than handle the ribbons for such a person as the hangman of England':

> It vexed me beyond measure to think that anybody would be so inhuman as to try to punish an innocent woman who had never done a soul any harm in her life simply because her husband was a man whose hand was turned against those who had proved themselves unworthy to live in civilised society, but, though I was used to this sort of treatment, I was not going to allow it to conquer me.
>
> When I come to think things over now, however, I am inclined to wish that they had stood out against me. When I took Barth Sullivan to the gallows I had a doubt in my mind as to his guilt, and after the inquest I came to the conclusion that he was one of the many who suffered the most terrible fate of the law for a crime which he did not commit.

In view of the melancholy atmosphere connected with the execution, Berry had no wish for his wife to stay at the gaol. Accordingly he arranged for her to go to private lodgings, but a little later he learned she had been refused admittance to the house. He then told the prison officials that unless his wife was quartered with him he would not carry out the execution, upon which, he tells us, the following exchange took place:

> 'I refuse to hang this man. Get me a car and I'll go home to Bradford.'
>
> The officials looked at me in consternation. My words fell like a bombshell . . .
>
> 'But, Mr. Berry, this is outrageous. You have your duty to do, and you know what the consequences will be if you refuse to do it.'
>
> 'I know my duty as well as any man of you, and I am determined that I won't hang him. You can do it yourself if you like.'
>
> 'What are you making all the fuss about?'
>
> 'You know as well as I do. I have been insulted, and my wife has been slighted.'

'It is not usual to allow a woman to enter the gaol except on a Home Office order.'

'Well, I am the Home Office order in this case, and unless my wife stays in this gaol, I don't, so you can make the most of it.'

'You are quite determined to cause trouble?'

'If that is what you call trouble, I am. Think it over, and let me know. My wife is more to me than any of your Irish murderers, even if I am only the hangman of England.'

And, of course, I won in the end.

Mrs Berry was allowed to share her husband's apartments, occupying the room adjacent to that in which the execution took place. She was later to hear the noise of the trap falling as her husband carried out his deadly work.

The prisoner had never ceased to protest his innocence. As usual, Berry went to see him, and, peeping through the cell door, saw 'a pleasant looking man of the farmer class'. A Roman Catholic priest and two sisters of mercy were in attendance. Berry then checked the gallows and, being satisfied with it, returned to his room, smoked a cigar and retired to bed. Sullivan retired at 11.30, woke at 6.30 and rose. When Berry went to his cell the prisoner appeared unafraid to die. Berry put his hand out and the condemned man shook it heartily:

'I am sorry, Sullivan, but I am only going to do my duty. It is not my fault, but the fault of the law which condemned you,' said Berry.

'And sure, that's all right now. I am not blaming you, but I hope you understand that you are hanging an innocent man.'

'Then I am sorry to hear it. Of course, I can't do anything for you now.'

'I know you can't, but you can tell the authorities that I die an innocent man. Before God, I never had anything to do with the murder of Patrick Flahive.'

'I hope you are not telling me any lie. It would be a terrible thing for you to go before your Judge with a lie on your lips.'

'Sure and you don't need to tell me that. I know that as well as you do, and it is the truth I am telling you, and when this is all over you can tell them outside the walls of Tralee that it is an innocent man you have been hanging this day. It is the words of a dying man I'm telling you, and some day you will know that they are true.'

Berry pinioned his man and the procession moved into the yard, the prisoner walking firmly. He stood steadily on the drop as Berry tightened the straps about his legs and drew the white cap over his face, upon which Berry moved away and pulled the lever, Sullivan dying without a struggle. According to Berry everyone, including the visiting justices, believed him to be innocent. In Berry's view, an innocent man had been sacrificed to satisfy the law. Though he felt no blame could be attached to him personally, this in his view lying solely with those who had secured the conviction, he later often thought of 'Barth' Sullivan and wished that he 'had it in my power to reverse the lever and bring him back to life again'.

Berry carried out another execution in Ireland on Friday 13 March 1891 when he hanged John Purcell, aged 40, at Dublin for the murder of Bridget Smith, aged 60, at Naul, Co. Dublin. Another man, Arthur Leatherhead, awaited execution at Chelmsford on Tuesday 31 March 1891, but Berry's appointment book is marked 'Reprieved'. The next entry shows Arthur Edward Penfold, scheduled for execution at Kirkdale Prison on Wednesday 1 April 1891, but this is again marked 'Reprieved', as was also the case for Bhagwar Sassewokre, scheduled for execution on 7 April, also at Kirkdale, and for Patrick Mahoney, scheduled for Belfast, Co. Down, Ireland on 14 April. Thus Berry had earned £20 in two weeks without having to conduct an execution.

On Tuesday 19 May 1891 he executed Alfred Turner, aged 20, at Strangeways gaol in Manchester, Turner having been condemned at the Manchester Assizes for the murder of his sweetheart, Mary Moran, at Oldham. Apparently motivated by jealousy he had stabbed her in the throat, afterwards reporting to the police that two men had attacked them. However, when he returned with the police to the spot he was horrified to find that the girl was still alive. Asked who had attacked her she pointed at Turner, who fled. He was soon arrested, the poor girl dying the following day. On the day of the execution Turner was described as sorrowful and nervous, and his responses to the chaplain feeble. He was led to the scaffold and exclaimed at the last moment, 'Forgive me, my God.' Only 5ft 3½in tall and weighing 9 stone, he was allowed a drop of 6ft 9in. Death was instantaneous.

Wandsworth Prison was Berry's next venue. The culprit was a German immigrant, Franz Joseph Munch, a 31-year-old baker who had worked for Mrs Bridget Kenrath at Bermondsey, a lady for whom he developed a fondness. A fellow worker, James Hickey, turned out also to be interested in her affections, and on 22 April a drunken Munch had shot his rival. Berry hanged him on Tuesday 21 July 1891.

On Tuesday 28 July 1891 he executed Arthur Spencer, aged 22, at Lincoln Prison. Spencer, an apprenticed pork butcher, had fallen in love with Mary Ann Gardner, a widow ten years his senior, and proposed to her. When she refused him he threatened to shoot her, but she laughed it off. On 31 March he called at her home and proposed once more, but was again rebuffed, upon which he shot her twice in the chest and then tried to shoot himself. The first shot caused a flesh wound in his chest, and the second, fired in his mouth, passed out of the back of his neck without causing serious damage. He pleaded guilty at Lincoln Assizes and was sentenced to death by Mr Justice Vaughan Williams.

It was summer, and things were hotting up for Berry. He would officiate at only a handful of further executions.

31

Berry's last executions

'The executioner seemed in a great hurry . . . '

The next four of Berry's executions were carried out in August 1891, three of them on consecutive days. With his long-standing history of dispute with officialdom, bungled executions, outspokenness, public levees and other transgressions, things were coming to a head.

On Tuesday 18 August 1891 he executed Thomas Sadler, a labourer, at Springfield gaol, Chelmsford, the latter having been convicted at Essex Summer Assizes for the murder of William Wass at Colchester. Sadler had been living with Wass's estranged wife, and when a dispute had arisen over the custody of her children he had stabbed Wass behind the ear with a penknife, the wound proving fatal.

The following day Berry executed Robert Bradshaw, aged 56, at Wandsworth Prison. Bradshaw had cut his wife's throat, almost decapitating her, when she took out a summons against him over threats he had made against her. Increasingly, the press were being excluded from witnessing executions, this being the case here, but one of the inquest jurymen later revealed that the rope that hanged Bradshaw was afterwards covered with blood. On viewing the body, the juror stated, it was not possible to see the condition of the neck as a thick bandage of wadding was wrapped round it, apparently to hide the fact that the long drop had resulted in the neck being torn.

Berry was engaged to conduct an execution the next day, Thursday 20 August 1891, at Kirkdale gaol, Liverpool. He tells an incredible tale of what happened to him before he got there, the story being told in the unpublished *Wages*:

From Wandsworth I had made my way up to London en route for Liverpool. At Waterloo Station I was met by some people whom I took to be real friends. I had been introduced to them some time before. We drove to several places of interest. By and by I became uneasy because of the flight of time. I had to be in Liverpool by six o'clock. But I allowed myself to be persuaded. We had dinner at a Restaurant in the Strand. After that we drove to Chelsea to see some other friends. I noticed a Scotland Yard detective. He said, 'I think you are enjoying yourself but you will be late in arriving at Liverpool. Will they let you into the gaol after ten?' I thought they would. He then told me that there was an express which would land me in Central Station, Liverpool about nine o'clock. I asked him to get into the small waggonette belonging to my friends. He told the driver to make all speed and catch the 5.30. I thought it strange that none of my friends went to the station with me. On arrival at Liverpool I was met by a man who catered for the Gaol. We drove up to the gaol together. Afterwards I went to the small Hotel of which he is the Lessee behind the prison. He asked me to have some supper. I thanked him but was unable to accept. By that time I had become very sick and had been seized with a severe fit of vomiting. The Doctor told me afterwards that but for that sickness I would not have been alive in the morning. I had evidently been drugged by my London 'friends'. I returned to the prison. My sickness continued during the night.

It is an incredible claim and one is left wondering just how much of it is true. Berry was a figure of great public fascination and many enjoyed being a 'friend' of the public executioner. The 'friends' in London could well have fallen into this category, and it is possible that he simply suffered a gastric illness after a rich meal in the restaurant, such an answer being much simpler than his theory of 'drugs' having been administered to him. The latter, though, would more usefully have mitigated his subsequent conduct in Liverpool.

The *Liverpool Daily Post* put a rather different slant on Berry's visit to the 'small Hotel' on the eve of the execution:

Great disgust has been expressed in the city that Berry, instead of proceeding to Kirkdale Gaol on Wednesday night at once on his arrival in Liverpool, decided to go to a public-house near the prison, where there was an exhibition of not a very entertaining kind. Berry was accompanied by several friends, one of whom carried his 'black bag,' without which no executioner travels. The paraphernalia of the hangman was popularly supposed to be contained in this valise, but that is a mistake, as under recent regulations everything is provided by the Prison Commissioners.

The man awaiting execution, John Conway, aged 60 and a bachelor, was a ship's fireman. His crime was an appalling child murder. The body of a boy aged about 10 had been found in a sailor's bag floating in the Sandon Basin at Liverpool on Saturday 16 May 1891. It was removed to the Princes Dock mortuary. The newspapers published a description of the body and he was identified as Nicholas Martin, one of a family of twelve, who lived in Bridgewater Street. He had last been seen playing in the street on the previous Saturday. A suspect was soon identified.

A combination of factors had led to his arrest. The bag and blankets in which the body had been wrapped were identified as having been sold to Conway by a woman who ran a marine store in Park Lane. She knew the man by sight, having often seen him walking in Park Lane in the evenings, and she knew he lived in the South End. Detective Egerton traced a man in Bridgewater Street who also knew Conway and, more importantly, the house in which he lived. The house, at 55 Bridgewater Street, was watched, and when Conway failed to appear the officers entered the house at 11.30 p.m. and found him in bed. He was arrested and taken to the detective office in Dale Street. An identity parade was arranged, and when the woman picked him out he was charged with the murder of the boy, Conway exclaiming 'My God, my God! I am not guilty.'

Also found in the bag with the body had been a piece of brown wrapping paper, a portion of the *Financial News* for 1890, a new tenon-saw and a butcher's slaughtering knife. The evidence however, although strong, was circumstantial. Police then searched the office Conway had used as a branch secretary of the Sailors' and Firemen's Union, situated in a house at 19 Stanhope Street, and discovered that the topmost bedroom, which was unfurnished, had smears of blood on the walls and floor. Attempts had been made to wash parts of the floor. More incriminating evidence was found. A label in his papers had come from the wrapping paper in the bag. The tool dealer who had sold him the knife was located, as was a hansom cab driver who had been hired by Conway to take him to the George's Pierhead at 9.30 on the Monday night. He had been carrying a bag at this time. Witnesses had also seen Conway at 11.30 the same night carrying a pair of shoes, one of which was found afterwards in Corporation Yard, and the other in Greenland Street, these being identified as belonging to the murdered boy. Conway's razor was also found in a backyard in the neighbourhood. It seemed clear that he had lured the boy away from where he was playing and taken him to 19 Stanhope Street, where he had murdered him. Leaving the body until the Monday night, he had then mutilated it, put it into the bag, driven in the cab to the pier, and thrown it into the Sandon Basin.

Conway claimed that he had been paid a sovereign by a foreign sailor to dispose of the bag, having had no knowledge of its contents, but the story was not believed. He was found guilty of murder and sentenced to death, and though a petition was subsequently raised for a reprieve, it was rejected by the Home Secretary.

On the day of the execution he made a statement to the Roman Catholic priest, Father Bonté, admitting his guilt and accepting the justice of the sentence. He protested that his motive was not 'outrage' (i.e. sexual) – he had never entertained such a thought – claiming rather that the crime was down to drink, which had caused 'a fit of murderous mania and a morbid curiosity to observe the process of dying'. He stated that the moment after committing the crime his feelings had been replaced by 'the deepest horror of it, [such that he] would have done anything in the world to undo it'. He also claimed that to dipose of the bag he had boarded a ferryboat and dropped the bag into the water in mid-river, hoping it would be carried out to sea.

For Berry this job, having started badly, was to get worse. In his memoirs he claimed:

In the morning I was upset on finding that the Doctor had sole control of the execution. I had simply to carry out his instructions. They were of such a kind that I feared a dreadful accident. I stated my fears. They were brushed aside. I had to do as I was told.

There are two sides to any story and such is the case here. Berry was already in bad odour with the authorities and clearly they were not going to stand for any more. To add insult to injury the full story was given in *The Liverpool Daily Post* the following day.

Father Bonté joined Conway in his cell a little after 6 a.m. and at 6.45 Mass was celebrated in the prison chapel. Conway made his confession and partook of the Sacrament; then, after prayers, ate a little breakfast. At 7.30 the chief warder joined him and he was taken from the condemned cell, through the prison garden, and into the reception house, where he was put in a cell on the main corridor. Near the cell door a table was placed for Berry's use, hidden from Conway's sight by the closed door.

The members of the press arrived at the gaol at 7.30 and were immediately admitted. In the space between the outer and inner doors they saw Berry standing ready, his pinioning straps dangling from his arm. They noted that he looked 'somewhat scared, and if anything a little nervous'. Through the bars of the gate that overlooked the garden they could see the prison governor, Major Knox, and the prison surgeon, Dr Barr, looking anxious and engaged in close conversation. The doctor was wearing white trousers and the governor was leaning on his customary walking stick. It was a fine day with a chilly breeze sweeping through the enclosure.

The prison bell was tolling dolefully as Berry walked into the reception house at 7.50, his arrival being announced to Conway. 'Good morning,' said Conway; then 'Good bye, Mr. Berry, good bye; God bless you.' He submitted to the pinioning, which Berry effected quickly, and was then led out. As the procession formed the doors of the reception room and the death chamber were simultaneously opened, after which – led by Father Bonté reading the service for the dead, the governor, Dr Barr, Mr F.W. Sharpe (the under-sheriff) and the warders – the procession entered the scaffold area. Conway cast a wild glance at the dangling noose, then lowered his eyes.

It was observed that he already had the white cap perched on his head as he approached the scaffold, whereas it was more usual for the executioner to take this out of his pocket and put it on the prisoner after securing the leg straps. The effect of the wearing of the cap, looking for all the world like a night-cap, resulted in the following evocative press description:

> The horror of the spectacle was increased and almost made grotesque by the singular way the cap was arranged. The murderer at first sight looked like someone walking in his sleep, disturbed by a ghastly dream peopled with horrid spectres.

Within a moment Conway was standing on the drop with the noose about his neck. He looked terribly scared and woeful, like a man in a trance. Berry stood beside him and immediately jerked the white cap over the doomed man's face. The execution should now have been completed with all speed, but it was not to be. Conway, obviously having not expected the cap to be placed over his face, momentarily resisted, then turned sharply on Berry saying, 'I don't want this; don't put this on.'

Berry said, 'Well, what do you want?'

'I want to say something,' replied Conway.

'I have no time,' replied Berry, continuing to pull the cap over the man's head.

At this Father Bonté intervened, remarking that Conway wanted to say something. The priest then looked at the governor, Dr Barr and the other officials in order to gain support for the right of the condemned man to say something. It has to be said that an attempt by the convict to delay the proceedings at this advanced stage should not have been allowed.

Berry stopped his attempt to force the cap down over Conway's face and said, 'Well, then, be quick about it.'

The cap was raised and it was noted that Conway looked scared, exhausted and livid.

'Beware of drink. I want to speak of the officers of the prison, that they were kind to me, and likewise of my father confessor, who was kind to me. I wish that all my prosecutors may be forgiven by God and by me. May the Lord have mercy upon my soul!' uttered

Conway. Many believed Conway had intended to make a lengthy 'scaffold speech' about the evils of drink, only for his nerve to fail him at the last moment.

With a last look upwards he resigned himself to his fate and Berry quickly drew the cap down over his face. The governor gave a signal, Berry pulled the lever and Conway was 'precipitated into eternity'.

It was immediately evident that a mistake had been made. On looking into the pit it was seen that Conway's head had been all but torn from his body, blood gushing from his neck 'in torrents'. His clothes were completely saturated and the noise of blood cascading on the paving of the pit could be heard all over the execution chamber. It continued to 'pour down like a fountain' and those present could hear the sound as long as they remained near the scaffold.

The drop allowed had been 6 feet, this given, says Berry, only after he had protested. The authorities, he claims, especially the doctor, wanted a drop of 6ft 8in, but he would not hear of this, subsequently claiming that if it had been left to him he would have given a drop of only 4ft 6in. Conway weighed 11st 2lb and was 5ft 7in tall.

Immediately after Conway disappeared from sight, Father Bonté turned to the members of the press and others present, and read out Conway's confession.

The press reported:

> The executioner seemed in a great hurry to discharge his ghastly functions, and Conway had less of the courtesy shown him than is usual on such occasions. There was very little of the Burial Service heard in the execution-room. Conway placed his feet together when the executioner knelt down on the flooring to adjust the straps round his legs. He cast a glance down to see that all was right.

The pressmen who looked into the pit from 'the brink of the scaffold' saw that death had been instant owing to the rupture of the blood vessels and the dislocation of the neck. Shocking and detailed descriptions of the execution were published in the Liverpool daily press for all to read:

There was no movement of the rope perceptible after Conway disappeared below. It became taut all at once, and there was not a quiver of a muscle from the senseless corpse. The vengeance taken by the law for the murder of Nicholas Martin was more swift than usual, owing to the immediate bursting of the convict's blood vessels, as well as the fracture of the neck. The rope, looked at from the brink of the scaffold, was imbedded deep into the flesh of Conway's neck, like a saw in a piece of timber through which it has almost cut. It would have been better perhaps had a less drop been given, for Conway was an old man, and some allowance should have been made for the wear and tear of human muscle. His flesh literally gave way as a rotten garment might under a sudden strain. It was worn out, and had very little muscular fibre in it.

These lurid press accounts were to fuel further appeals for the press to be excluded from witnessing executions. In Berry's favour, no speech on the scaffold should have been allowed and the whole proceeding should have been carried out with the greatest speed. Also, it could not be doubted that the convict had died quickly and painlessly.

Needless to say, on seeing the awful mishap the governor hastened the pressmen out of the room, something they obviously did not appreciate since they had hoped to glean more information from the doctor and other officials about the accused and his demeanour prior to execution. They commented:

. . . but yesterday all this was omitted, the object no doubt being to prevent the reporters prying too curiously down into the yawning gulf in which the body of John Conway was hanging at the end of the rope, the weight being sustained only by a few shreds of the muscles of the neck. The sight was one of the most horrifying description that has ever been seen at any execution at Kirkdale. The scene at the scaffold was enough to shock even those who are well-accustomed to those awful legal tragedies. There was a painful interval after Father Bonté had ceased to speak. The outpouring of Conway's blood could be heard distinctly all over the room, and the pit became like a shambles.

The reporters were in the anteroom copying out Conway's statement when Berry entered. He seemed anxious to clear himself of any blame for the bungled execution.

'You have made a mess of it this time, Mr. Berry!' a reporter remarked.

'Not I, I am not to blame for anything that has occurred. All is left to the doctor now, and this comes of not taking my advice. Conway should have had a much shorter drop; but the doctor thought otherwise. Dr. Barr has a preference for the long drop. Don't blame me,' Berry explained.

'Dr. Barr, I suppose, is acting under instructions? The drop is fixed by the new Government regulations, is it not?' said the reporter.

'That is quite true, but this is the result of interfering with me. They would have decapitated him altogether but for me,' said Berry.

Berry otherwise seemed quite unwilling to say much about the execution and it was evident that he was not happy about it:

He spoke with bated breath and whispering humbleness, half apologising, half justifying himself. So far as Conway's actual execution was concerned, there was nothing to complain of. It was done swiftly and effectively, and if the object were to get him out of the world with the least possible delay there was no hitch, looking at the matter from this point of view. The culprit, however, was sentenced to be 'hanged by the neck till he was dead'. He was not executed in this manner, so that strictly speaking the whole affair was bungled terribly. It was a sad spectacle. Berry might have done better if he had been in a cool temper, and if his nerves were steadier.

So the press still held him to blame. Their interpretation of being hanged by the neck until dead seems an exercise in semantics, and one has to wonder if they would have preferred a slower death to the rapid but bloody one they had witnessed. They enlarged on their condemnation of the unfortunate Berry:

That Berry, who hanged John Conway, was thoroughly ashamed of the whole affair appears from his conduct after the execution. Berry has been charged with very rough treatment of his victim yesterday, and those who were spectators at the scaffold could bear this out in particular. He was rough, sharp, and rude to a degree never before witnessed at Kirkdale. What was the cause for this strange procedure is best known to Berry. That he was rude, officious, and cruel to Conway appears to be quite satisfactorily established. He insisted immediately after the pinioning had taken place upon placing the white cap on the murderer's head before he left the corridor of the reception-house, a thing never before heard of. Father Bonté at the time objected to this procedure, as utterly unusual and felt justified in removing the cap, the placing of which on Conway's head at the time was contrary to all precedent. Conway, therefore, left the reception-house, where he was pinioned, without the white cap, but in passing from the first set of rooms to the scaffold-house, Berry took the opportunity of replacing the cap on the prisoner's head, as he had originally put it. Conway was dreadfully inconvenienced and discomforted by this strange conduct, and it is said to be owing to this behaviour that he was only able to collect his thoughts for a few seconds before being launched into eternity. It is said by those who have seen executions at Kirkdale during the last thirty years that they never witnessed such a spectacle as was seen yesterday.

Berry, after the execution was over, went to Father Bonté, and expressed the hope that he felt that everything had been correctly done. He hoped he would forgive him if there had been too much hurry, and wished that nothing might appear in the public Press.

It was a prolonged press assault on Berry's character and conduct. They even stated that he had pinioned the prisoner too tightly, causing him pain and strain on his muscles.

About 2,000 people had assembled outside the prison to witness the hoisting of the black flag, and a hush fell on them as a figure appeared and hoisted it. Several were heard to say, 'He's away now!' – at which the chatter again resumed.

At 9.25 a.m. the members of the inquest jury were admitted to the gaol accompanied by Inspector Hutchinson of the Kirkdale Police Division. They were taken into the old coach-house where they viewed Conway's body. On the governor's orders the press were not allowed, as they had been on previous occasions, to see the remains. The deputy coroner, Mr Husband, and his clerk entered the room allocated for the inquest. The prison governor gave details to prove the sentence and when the jury was asked if they had any questions, one, a Mr James Welding, said, 'Is Berry, the executioner, present? I mean within the precincts of the prison.'

'No; he has gone,' replied the governor.

'I think it is usual to detain the executioner until after the inquest,' said Welding.

'No, never,' replied the governor.

'I beg your pardon. I have been at several inquests of this kind, and I know that Binns was once carpeted,' Welding persisted.

'I have no power to keep him, and if I did I would lay myself open to an action for damages. He is not my servant,' the governor retorted.

'I have been at several executions where the executioner has remained,' responded Welding.

At this point the coroner interjected: 'That has been when everything did not go on as usual. But when everything goes on all right, we do not ask the executioner to stay. The governor tells us that the execution took place in the usual way.'

Turning to Major Knox the coroner said, 'Everything went off all right?'

'Everything,' said the governor, and he signed his deposition.

Dr James Barr, the prison medical officer, then gave his evidence. He stated that he was present at the execution.

'Was it carried out in the usual way?' asked the coroner.

'Yes,' came the reply.

'No hitch at all?'

'No, as far as the execution was concerned.'

The coroner asked the jury if they had any questions, and, none being asked, he presumed they would reach the usual verdict, which they did.

Conway was buried within the precincts of the prison the same day.

The press noted that Berry, contrary to his usual custom, left the gaol before the opening of the inquest and returned immediately to Bradford. A telegram from Bradford informed them that:

He was greatly upset by the shocking spectacle in which he had played so prominent a part, and went to bed almost immediately after his return. An endeavour was made to interview him early in the evening, but his relatives said that he had given instructions that no one was to be allowed to enter his room.

Both in his book and his memoirs Berry put the blame for the accident squarely with the authorities, especially Dr Barr. He notes that Conway was an old man, trembling and terrified at his fate, who apparently pleaded 'Oh, spare my life, spare my life! I am an old man, and would not have long to live, anyway.' The poor man had almost collapsed on the way to the scaffold and had needed the assistance of the warders. Then, says Berry, when he had allowed Conway to speak on the scaffold:

> . . . the priest had stepped excitedly forward and seized my hand, making it appear as if he would loosen the rope from the neck of the condemned man. He did not know what he was doing. I then stood aside for a moment, though keeping my hand on the noose of the knot which I had just adjusted.

Berry knew that the drop he had given was too long, and when he saw what had happened he made up his mind that he would never hang another man. On seeing those present rush forward to look into the pit, he shouted to the warders, 'Take them out! Take them out!' He concluded:

> I was very much upset over what had occurred and what followed was worse still. The way I was treated in the prison was not to my liking, and I should have preferred it if I had been allowed to stay and have a word with the jurymen.
>
> I kicked up a terrible row with the Home Office over their interference, and told them that if they were to fix the drop the Home Secretary could come down and hang the victims. From that day I made up my mind that I would give up the work, and the more I thought about the sad experiences of the day the more I came to see what a terrible crime I had committed against my fellow men.

But it was some time before I was able to hold up my head with other men and say – I am no longer the hangman of England. Would to God I had said it sooner.

Berry's last execution in England was already in his appointment book. He travelled to Winchester to execute Edward Henry Fawcett, convicted of the murder of his estranged wife on 4 April, whom he had shot four times at Portsea, and on Tuesday 25 August 1891 he operated in England for the last time. There were three more executions in 1891; James Billington conducted them all.

Berry wrote further of Conway's execution in his book. He claimed that two days afterwards he received a letter from 'a gentleman in the South of London' who had made his own calculations for the length of drop in this case. He fully agreed with Berry that the drop should have been nearer Berry's calculation of 4ft 6in than that dictated by Dr Barr.

Berry, it would seem, had had enough; but so had the Home Office.

32

The Home Office tightens up

'The employment of Berry as Executioner should no longer be recommended.'

PRISON DEPARTMENT,
HOME OFFICE,
WHITEHALL, S. W.
31st October 1891.

Sir,

I am directed to acquaint you that the Secretary of State has intimated to the Commissioners his desire that the employment of Berry as Executioner should no longer be recommended or suggested to the High Sheriffs <u>by any of his officers</u>, and that, as the Governors may sometimes be consulted in this matter by the High Sheriffs, this decision may be communicated to them for their guidance.

I am to add that a list has been prepared containing the names of three competent candidates for the office of Executioner. Their names & addresses, with particulars are annexed.

Further instructions in regard to the subject of the carrying out of executions will shortly be issued: but, meanwhile, should necessity arise, this list may be brought to the notice of the High Sheriff should you be consulted by him in regard to the choice of an Executioner.

I am,
   Sir,
Your obedient servant,
C.G. Joseph
The Governor, H.M. Prison

The list of competent candidates for the office of Executioner kept at the Home Office gave the following details:

James Billington, age 44, Market Street, Farnworth, near Bolton. He has satisfactorily conducted ten executions, and has been instructed in the duties of Executioner, in accordance with the approved recommendations of the 'Capital Sentences Committee'.

Francis Gardner, age 41, Tubney, Abingdon, Berks. He has not yet carried out an execution, but he has been instructed in the duties of Executioner in accordance with the approved recommendations of the 'Capital Sentences Committee'.

Robert Wade, age 42, 28 Blackburn Road, Church, near Accrington. Ditto.

The Home Office did not employ Berry and so he could not be sacked. The onus was upon the High Sheriffs to secure the services of a competent person to conduct an execution and, theoretically, they could engage whomsoever they pleased. Thus the above letter to the prison governors was deemed the most logical way to prevent Berry's further employment.

The Home Office summed up the situation as follows:

In August '91 at an execution at Kirkdale Berry was reported to have behaved with 'roughness'. (Culprit was nearly decapitated, and Berry stated that he protested against the length of drop).

It was also reported that on the evening before the execution Berry was received at the Court House Hotel by a large crowd, and that he did not arrive at the Prison until 10 p.m. and was followed by a crowd. The Governor stated that it had 'been the custom for executioners to hold levees at the Hotel for years past'.

The above circumstances led to the discontinuance of the employment of Berry as Executioner and to the appointment of the Committee on Executions.

The S of S. in a letter to the Commissioners dated 26.9.91 gave instructions that the employment of Berry as Executioner should no longer be recommended or suggested to the Sheriffs by the S of S or by any of his officers.

A memorandum, on the subject of executions, was issued by the Home Secretary and carried some interesting and revealing details:

1. With a view to assisting the High Sheriffs in the selection and appointment of suitable persons to carry out executions, the Secretary of State has decided that a small list of persons who have acted in, or are believed to be willing and competent to undertake, the office of executioner, shall be kept at the Home Office. Records will be kept of their conduct and efficiency on each occasion of their being employed, and the information thus recorded will be at the disposal of any High Sheriff who may have to engage the executioner. The name of any person who does not give satisfaction, or whose conduct is in any way objectionable, so as to cast discredit on himself, either in connexion with the duties or otherwise, will be removed from the list.

2. When an execution is about to take place the list of names and addresses, and the necessary information from the record kept as above, will be sent to the Governor of the prison for the information of the High Sheriff, and it will be left to the High Sheriff to engage one of them if he thinks fit to do so.

3. The Committee appointed in 1886 to inquire into and to report upon the subject of the carrying out of capital sentences were of opinion that it is very important and desirable that there should be an assistant to the executioner, 'who might gradually acquire experience, might assist where several criminals were simultaneously executed, or might replace the executioner when he was ill, or when his presence was required in different places at the same time'. Sanction has been obtained for the employment of such assistants at the public expense, and the Governor may, if the High Sheriff concurs, engage one or more persons to be present at the execution in order to gain practical

experience and to act as assistants if required under the orders of the High Sheriff. The provisions in regard to accommodating the executioner in the prison, and to his conduct in connexion with the execution and before and after it, will apply also to any assistant who may be so engaged. It must, however, be clearly understood, that the engagements of assistants by the Governor does not take away from the High Sheriff or his deputy or the executioner appointed by him any of the responsibility attaching to the offices they respectively fill.

4. Besides the suggestions contained in the letter from the Home Office, dated 7th October, 1885, the Secretary of State thinks it desirable to express his opinion that executioners should be made clearly to understand that their conduct and general behaviour should be respectable not only at the place and time of execution, but before and subsequently: that they should avoid attracting public attention in going to or from it, and that they should be prohibited from giving interviews for publication to any persons on the subject of their duty. This end would better be secured by their remuneration not being payable till a fortnight after the execution, and the payment of a part of it being made dependent upon their satisfactory behaviour.

5. The Secretary of State suggests that the persons engaged should be required to conform to any instructions they may receive from or on behalf of the High Sheriff as to the day and hour and route for going to and leaving the place of execution.

6. It is suggested that the persons should be required to undertake to report themselves at the prison at which an execution is to take place, and for which they have been engaged, not later than 4 o'clock on the afternoon preceding the day of execution; also that they should remain in the prison from the time of their arrival until they have completed the execution and until permission is given them to leave.

7. With a view to carrying out the objects referred to in paragraphs 1 and 2 as to the record to be kept of the conduct

and efficiency of the person or persons employed as executioner or assistant, High Sheriffs are requested to be good enough to make a report to the Home Office in regard to the manner in which the duty has been performed on each occasion. Reports as to their conduct, character, and efficiency will also be made by the Governor &c. These reports will be recorded at the Home Office, and the information they afford will (as stated in paragraph 1) be placed at the disposal of any High Sheriff who has to appoint an executioner.

8. Straps, pinioning apparatus, &c., and ropes will be put at the disposal of the High Sheriff with and on the same conditions as the rest of the apparatus referred to in the memorandum of 1885. They will be available at the prison.

9. A memorandum of 'Conditions to which any person acting as executioner is required to conform,' having reference to the terms of his engagement and his personal conduct; also a memorandum of 'Instructions for carrying out the details of an execution' have been furnished to the Governors of prisons for the assistance of the High Sheriff if he thinks it desirable to adopt them, when he becomes responsible for the carrying out of an execution.

10. The Secretary of State wishes it to be clearly understood that the suggestions made in this memorandum are not intended in any way to interfere with or diminish the responsibility of the High Sheriff attaching to him by Statute, and in particular that, from the moment when the condemned prisoner is handed over to him, the executioner acts entirely under the Sheriff's orders, and that the Sheriff is alone responsible for his conduct and for his treatment of the prisoner, *e.g.*, in allowing or refusing to allow him to make any statement, or to speak with the Chaplain.

Home Office, Whitehall, December, 1891.
N.B. – As soon as the High Sheriff has fixed a date for an execution he should officially inform the Home Office.

It can be clearly seen that this memorandum was produced as a direct result of the problems experienced with James Berry. He was now part of the history of British capital punishment. The amazing freedom of speech and action he had enjoyed as public executioner would never again be seen in the kingdom.

The new conditions to which the public executioner was required to conform included those described in the foregoing memorandum. A restriction was also placed on the amount of alcohol he would receive while he was lodged at the prison, this being limited to a quart of malt liquor, one pint at dinner and one at supper, or a quarter pint of spirit. It was stressed that the necessary ropes, straps, pinioning apparatus, cap etc. would be provided at the prison and should not be removed from there. The executioner was also required to give such information or make such record of the occurrences as the governor of the prison might require.

Berry did not take his dismissal lightly and continued to be a thorn in the side of the Home Office. He always claimed that he had resigned. Almost immediately his story in book form, *My Experiences as an Executioner* (Bradford and London, Percy Lund & Co., n.d. [1892]), was published. Not up to the task of writing this himself, he entrusted it to an 'editor', H. Snowden Ward. The book is now very rare and commands high prices. Even the 1972 reprint (Newton Abbot, David & Charles Reprints, 1972), with an introduction by the noted crime writer Jonathan Goodman, is very hard to find.

Interestingly, the last entry in Berry's appointment/invoice book, consecutively numbered 290, is for 'James Hearney [*sic*], Longford Gaol', and appears to have been written on 21 December 1891. Heaney had murdered his wife at Longford and was later hanged at Mullingar on 12 January 1892, the executioner being Thomas Henry Scott of Huddersfield, who had previously acted as an assistant to Berry (notably at the execution of William Henry Bury). It was the first execution that Scott appears to have conducted alone and Berry later (1902) refers to him as the man 'who acts as executioner for Ireland'. Does this final entry in Berry's book mean that he had himself applied to conduct the execution at Mullingar but had failed to secure this commission? Scott later acted as assistant to Billington and was still active into the twentieth century.

On Sunday 11 January 1892, Berry went to Greenock for the execution of a circus manager. He had previously been to Greenock to execute John Watson Laurie for the celebrated Arran murder, but when Laurie had been reprieved on the grounds of insanity, the trip had turned into a short holiday, after which he returned to the town, staying in the same hotel and making several friends there.

Frederick Thomas Storey, aged 54, was manager at Cooke's Circus in Greenock. On Friday 14 November 1891 he had stabbed to death Lizzie Pastor, who also worked at the circus, in Argyle Street, Greenock. His motive was jealousy, the result of her refusing his romantic advances. Berry said:

> He did not die as other men. Cool to the last, a man playing a part, he took the curtain with a smiling face.
>
> Frederick Thomas Storey was a wonderful man, and I shall never forget him.

Storey, who had been with the circus all his life, recounted his tale to Berry in a long conversation in the condemned cell on the eve of his execution. Lizzie Pastor, real name Elizabeth Stewart, was a well-known horse-riding artiste hailing from a small town on the east coast of Scotland. She had joined the circus when she met and married a horseback artiste named Harmstone, but the latter died soon afterwards, leaving the young girl a widow. Storey was the business manager of the circus and had fallen in love with the girl. At first she was impressed with his attentions, but she then began to have reservations. He visited hotels and drank a lot, and was clearly on a downhill slope. When she refused to see him after one of his drinking bouts, he became obsessed with the idea that another man was involved with her. Then after a night's particularly heavy drinking, he followed her as she returned to her lodgings in Argyle Street. Sensing she might be in danger, Elizabeth had asked friends to accompany her, but when Storey met her in a passageway and asked to speak with her, they had left, not realising that he was armed with a knife. He was heard alternately pleading with her, raving and threatening her. She tried to calm him but he produced a large clasp knife and stabbed her in the breast, upon which she staggered across the street, bleeding profusely as Storey made off. She was taken into a confectioner's shop and placed in a chair, but she died moments later. Storey was soon arrested and charged with murder. In a trial lasting four hours, he was found guilty and sentenced by Lord Adam to death.

Berry left Bradford on Saturday morning, 10 January, and arrived at Greenock at 7.00 p.m. to find the railway station practically deserted, with no one to meet him. Apparently an official that had arrived earlier in the day had been mistaken for him. Berry drove to the jail and was shown to the governor's office where he saw two detective inspectors and other officials, who informed him of the arrangements that had been made for the execution.

He stayed in quarters at the jail and described the prison as one of the finest designed and best equipped in Scotland. It was loftily roofed, well lit and had a spacious corridor through the centre, running parallel with Nelson Street. The condemned cell was quite large for prison accommodation and had a cheery fire, gas, a table, a comfortable chair in front of the fireplace and a bed. As for Storey, Berry came to look on him as one of the coolest men he had to deal with, perhaps second only to Dr Cross. The only visitor he had received was his son, whom he wanted to grow up into a good man. He refused to see his sister who lived in Nottinghamshire.

Up early on Sunday, the day of the execution, Berry inspected the new scaffold. It was built up against the eastern wall of the prison and a hoarding had been erected to prevent people in the top flat of the nearby Walker's sugar refinery and garrets of the dwelling houses in Upper Nicholson Street from seeing the execution.

It was a short distance from the condemned cell to the scaffold and a door had been knocked out in the eastern side of the prison to avoid a walk in the bitter open air. As early as six in the morning, with the street lamps still burning and only the faintest traces of dawn visible, a crowd had already begun to gather in George Square. By a quarter to eight the largest crowd the prison officials had ever seen had gathered in front of the prison. It was still not daylight but the eastern sky was brightening. Storey had spent a restless night, with the chaplain sitting up with him. Berry entered the cell, and the two men greeted each other, Storey assuring him he would give no trouble. The Baillies then entered and read the death warrant over to Storey, who was subsequently asked if he had any statement to make. He replied:

I have got no statement to make, but I wish to tender my sincere thanks to the governor of the prison and warders for all their kindness to me; also to the Rev. Mr. Frew, my spiritual adviser, whose kindness and attention to me have been very great, and from whose ministrations I have received much benefit. I acknowledge the justice of my sentence, and hope God will have mercy upon me.

It was explained to Storey that his signature would show that the warrant had been read to him and, making a bow, he said, 'I will do so.' He donned his glasses and quickly signed the warrant in a clear and distinct hand, with no tremor, and finished with a dash under his name. Berry stepped forward and placed the main belt around Storey's waist and buckled it tight. After this he put the leather straps over each shoulder. Snow had fallen heavily but the procession was able to move freely to the scaffold along the roofed corridor. As they walked Berry whispered to a warder, 'Look at him. I've forgotten to take off his collar and tie.'

Storey heard Berry and immediately turned and said coolly, 'All right, Mr. Berry. I will take them off myself.' He then removed his collar and tie, handed them to a warder and opened the neck of his shirt. At the scaffold Berry pinioned his hands and feet as the prisoner calmly stood there. He died a brave man to the end.

Whether or not Berry was aware of the Home Office letter of October 1891 directing that his services were no longer to be used, he knew that he was now no longer being required to act as executioner. He claims that he now 'decided to retire' and he sent the following letter to the Home Secretary:

1, Bilton Place, City Road, Bradford, Yorkshire.
March 4, 1892.

To the Rt. Hon. Henry Matthews, Q.C., M.P., Home Secretary, Whitehall, London.

DEAR SIR, – I herewith tender my resignation as executioner for Great Britain. My reason is on account of Dr. Barr interfering with my responsible duty at Kirkdale Gaol, Liverpool, on my last execution there. I shall therefore withdraw my name now as being executioner to England.

Trusting this will be accepted by you on behalf of the Sheriffs of England, I remain, dear sir, your obedient servant,

(signed)   JAMES BERRY,

Late executioner of England.

Berry was making no secret of the fact that the 'accident' at Kirkdale was the fault of the authorities and not himself. He produced a lengthy piece in his book to show how the officials thwarted him and elected for too great a drop, reproducing his tables of drops and a letter written by Dr Barr on the subject. He obviously felt that the public record should show he had resigned, and the following piece appeared in *The Times* of 9 March 1892:

THE PUBLIC EXECUTIONER. – The Home Secretary has received a letter from Berry, the public executioner, resigning his position. The reason he gives for this step is that Dr. Barr interfered 'with his responsible duty at Kirkdale Gaol, Liverpool,' at the last execution there; and he objects to the order issued from the Home Office instructing the medical officers of Her Majesty's prisons to decide the length of the drop required for a condemned prisoner.

Three days later further claims by Berry resulted in a question in the House of Commons being raised by Mr P. O'Brien as to reports in the press. Mr Matthews, the Home Secretary, replied:

I have not seen any Press report containing an allegation of Berry's that he was turned out of Kirkdale Prison to prevent his giving evidence at the inquest. The reports which I have seen of the inquest in the case referred to show that Berry left the prison of his own accord. The Home Office have not given directions that reporters should be excluded from executions. The answer to the second paragraph is in the negative. The admission of visitors, whether reporters or others, to an execution rests with the High Sheriff (31 Vict., c.24, section 3). The Prison Commissioners have not interefered in the matter. I am informed that on the occasion referred to in the question the reporters were made to leave the prison before they had completed their notes in consequence of orders given improperly and without authority by the executioner Berry.

On Wednesday 16 March 1892 Mr O'Brien again broached the subject of the executioner in the House. He asked the Home Secretary if he was aware that the coroner's jury in the case of Dr Cross, executed in Cork about five years previously, failed to record a verdict because Berry had refused his summons to attend and give evidence as to the cause of death. Similarly, in the case at Kirkdale he had avoided giving evidence by leaving the gaol, despite the fact that the jury required it. Therefore would the Home Secretary ensure that Berry's successor would attend all inquests on persons executed to give evidence if so required?

Matthews stated that he had no knowledge of the Dr Cross case, which was the concern of the Irish Government and not the Home Office. It was not the fact that Conway was nearly decapitated that was at issue, but that a juror had asked whether Berry was in attendance and was informed that he was not as it appeared his evidence was not necessary. It was not usual for an executioner to give evidence at the inquest and he could see no reason for giving any directions in the matter. The executioner would, of course, obey the coroner's directions when the occasion arose.

It is most interesting to note a small advertisement that appeared on the front page of *The Times* two days later:

IMPERIAL THEATRE. – England's Prisons and Prisoners. – Tomorrow (Saturday), at 4.30 and 9, in connexion with Mr. JAMES BERRY'S ADVOCACY and ADDRESS in favour of ABOLITION OF CAPITAL PUNISHMENT, a SERIES of ILLUMINATED ILLUSTRATIONS will be given faithfully showing Newgate, its exterior and interior, the condemned cell, old implements of torture, flogging room, &c. Newgate in flames. The Old Bailey Criminal Court, &c. Portland Convict Prison. View of the island, interior of the cells, locking up for the night, parade, searching prisoners, march to the quarries, prisoners at work, &c. Admission 6d., 1s., 2s., and 3s.

Berry was on the offensive. He had lost his job and, despite claiming to be glad to have ceased his grim duties, he missed the financial rewards of the post. Unbelievably he was now, apparently, an abolitionist and a showman, eager to tell the public how wrong the death sentence was. He stuck to his claim that he had resigned and stated that friends who had taken a great interest in his personality and career had urged him to embark upon a lecturing tour to give his views on capital punishment. At length, he claims, he decided upon this course, hiding nothing from his audiences:

> I told them that I had carried out my full share of the terrible work, that I was heartily sorry for doing it, and that I considered I had tarnished my career by undertaking such a life.
>
> For eight and a half years I had never known what it was to have a good solid night's rest. I had always felt a kind of sting in my conscience, a feeling that I had no right to do such a wrong to my fellow men, to men who had never seen me, and who likely would never have seen me if I had not walked into the felon's cell. The conclusion I had come to was that if a man committed a crime he ought to be made to suffer for it, but not by taking away his life.

Berry said that the majority of those he had hanged had committed crime while under the influence of drink and that not one was teetotal. He felt that penal servitude often held greater terrors for these men than the penalty of death. He described the lecture that he delivered:

> My lecture was not such a gruesome business as many people imagined. Those who were running me impressed on me the necessity for being as humorous as possible, and this did not give me a great deal of trouble, as I am naturally of a humorous nature. When I went on to the platform the pianist used to follow my instructions and play the then popular tune, 'Daddy Wouldn't Buy Me a Bow-Wow,' and I also made mistakes in pronunciation and so forth, knowing well that this would give my audience some sense of satisfaction. I always used to get a laugh by referring to Mr. Justice Hawkins as a blood-thirsty old villain.

I had lantern slides to illustrate my lecture, and these were very much enjoyed, especially the one of the prisoners on the treadmill, which was always accompanied on the piano to the tune 'The Man That Broke the Bank at Monte Carlo'. In some places I was well received, in others they would have nothing to do with me, but I always managed to enjoy myself.

Once I met an editor in Ireland who fancied himself a bit of a wit. Informing me that he was a phrenologist, he criticised my bumps and told me something I did not like. But did I take offence when he bared his own neck, and, in order to get some information out of me, asked me, 'If I required your services what drop would you give me?'

I looked at him and laughed, 'A drop of brandy, my boy.'

When I appeared in London at the Aquarium I was told it would be a good thing if I could get a Member of Parliament to preside at my lecture. I went to the House of Commons and saw Mr. Bysam Read, who inquired what my lecture was to be about, and, having informed him, he promptly manifested the strongest objections to the abolition of capital punishment, and accordingly I had to go elsewhere for my chairman.

I opened at the Royal Aquarium, which has now disappeared, and one of my fellow artistes was Captain F. S. Cody and his cowboys. In London everybody who was anybody came to see me, and while the engagement lasted I did very well. It was when I decided to travel the country that I began to see that the people wanted nothing to do with me.

The provincial people knew more than the clever Londoners, and in some places they did not come to hear me at all. In others they came to show their disgust of me. I decided that I would give the whole business up.

The noted journalist, author and playwright George R. Sims met Berry at the Aquarium. Sims tells the story in his book *Glances Back*:

It was in a side room at the Aquarium that I formed one of a very small audience that listened to a lecture by the late Mr. James Berry, the at one time public executioner. Mr. Berry gave us his experiences on the scaffold in lugubrious tones, and he could not have looked more unhappy had he been about to hang himself. I remember that I was introduced to Berry, who put out his hand in greeting. I took it a little nervously. It was the clammiest handshake I have ever had. It was a big hand and a moist hand, and gave one the sensation of grasping a piece of raw beef. One of my abiding memories of the Aquarium is the grasp of the hangman's hand.

In the last week of May 1892 Berry appeared at the Olympia Theatre and Circus in Edgehill, Liverpool. The place had been built only six months when, at about midnight on Saturday 28 May, it was destroyed by fire. In reporting on this incident on Monday 30 May 1892, *The Times* noted the fact that 'During last week the ex-hangman, Berry, was giving lectures' at the Circus, though it suggested no connection between Berry and the fire; he was mentioned merely because he was a figure of public interest.

The fact that Berry could be litigious is beyond doubt. Apropos of his love/hate relationship with the press and his undoubted fondness for publicity, he was involved in legal action with 'Answers' Newspaper Co. Ltd. in early 1890. The case was reported in the press at the time and appeared in *The Bradford Observer* of 17 March 1890. Berry brought a libel action against *Answers*, claiming £500 damages for an article published in the periodical. A man named White had approached Berry in September or October 1889, claiming to be a representative of an American newspaper and asking for Berry's views on execution by electricity, suggesting that the latter's experience of executions was very important. He paid a fee of £3 for the interview, which Berry duly gave after securing verbal and written agreement that whatever he said would not be published in this country. The article, 'A Man of Mystery', appeared, however, in *Answers* on 23 November 1889, and included the following offending extract:

He is a powerful, thick-set man, of about medium stature, and his countenance is not an unpleasant one at a first glance, though upon closer study one discovers that the face reveals the lack of several moral elements in the man's composition, which seems to indicate that the Creator designed him especially for the ends he serves.

A critical observer would probably say that his eyes are too close together, and that their brilliancy is that of the codfish rather than the eagle, while, though the mouth and chin indicate determination, the forehead gives the impression of lack of balance.

A phrenologist would perhaps find that the cranial bumps that indicate sense and shame, pity and sympathy, are not particularly well developed upon the head of Mr. Berry.

The article went on to record the following supposed exchange:

'Have you ever been threatened by the friends of criminals whom you have hanged?'

'Often,' replied Mr. Berry, 'but I don't pay no attention to them. I'm a doin' o' my duty, and I'm protected by th' Government.'

'It was said that if Mrs. Maybrick had not been reprieved a mob would have been formed in Liverpool to prevent your hanging her.'

'They'd never have seen me,' said Mr. Berry. 'I'd 'a been in th' jail and 'anged her before th' mob knew I was about, and I'd been on th' train and on my way back 'ome before they knew she was dead. Why when I 'anged Poole in Dublin, who murdered th' other informer Kenny – O'Donnell, who murdered th' other informer, Carey, having been 'anged at Newgate th' day before – there was a great mob in Dublin to prevent my getting into th' prison, and nobody outside knew Poole was 'anged until I was on th' boat a steaming away for Holyhead.'

'How do you manage that?' I asked again.

'I'll tell you,' said Mr. Berry in a burst of confidence. 'I shaves off my whiskers and I puts on women's clothes. That's th' way I got into Dublin Jail, with my ropes and straps under my clothes, and that's th' way I've done many a job.'

It is interesting to see how the reporter tried to represent Berry's Yorkshire accent and way of speaking in the article. Berry had never dressed in women's clothes and there was no foundation for the claim. It was also pointed out during the proceedings that Berry had not hanged either of the men mentioned. Binns had hanged Patrick O'Donnell at Newgate on 17 December 1883, assisted by Alfred Archer, while a volunteer hangman named Jones had hanged Joseph Poole at Dublin on 18 December 1883.

In mitigation of damages the defendants denied that the words bore the construction Berry had put on them. They withdrew all imputations, admitting that any such meaning was unfounded and apologised. However, this withdrawal and apology had appeared only upon the pleadings, and none was printed in their subsequent papers. The defendants also claimed that the articles in question had been copied from an American paper and that they had been misled, 'just as the proprietors of the *New York Sun* had been misled by the large imagination of Mr. White'.

Berry had been very quick in acting, his writ having been served within a few days of the appearance of the article. By way of placating the plaintiff, counsel for the defence said that:

> They did not for a moment express any doubt that they were dealing with an honest, a decent, and an experienced man, they withdrew all supposed imputations, and had had no intention of making any; and he contended that the highest testimonial possible was one from a person who had said something derogatory to him.

The jury found for the plaintiff and Berry was awarded £100 damages.

In his 1935 book *Life and Death at the Old Bailey*, R. Thurston Hopkins included a chapter entitled 'A Veteran Warder's Experiences', written from information provided to him some years previously by one of the last of Newgate's veteran warders. Included was a tale of Berry the hangman:

> I have an unforgettable picture of Berry, the hangman, in my brain. I went into the 'Old Bell Tavern' near St. Bride's Church one evening to meet my tailor, having arranged to pay him for a suit he was bringing me there, and saw Berry sitting at a small table in a tall hat and an enormous cloak, reading a pile of

manuscript with evident pleasure, a long pipe in one hand, and a pot of beer in the other.

'Hi!' said Berry, 'come over here and join me in a drink'.

He told me he was writing a book.

'What kind of book?' I asked.

He put his large hand to his chin, and winked. He looked very knowing. He had a secret up his sleeve.

'I'm writing a handbook on hanging, and, mark my words, it will make me a famous writer one day.'

That evening Berry drank many pints of ale in less than an hour. He spoke incoherently of many things: of hangmen, actors, kings and criminals; of fishing, otter-hunting and archaeology. He quoted, among other unrecognized sources, his own poems, Shakespeare, and lines from the melodrama, 'Maria Marten, or the Murder at the Red Barn.' He lectured to printers and compositors upon the fine art of hanging. He recited parts of the service for the burial of the dead, mixed up with the judge's words of the death sentence. He offered to fight a pieman and then purchased his stock of mutton pies and distributed them amongst the company. He offered to run me for a five-pound note, but when I accepted his challenge he cooled off, remembering, no doubt, that I was the champion sprinter of the City police at that time. He ended up by kissing the barmaid and the street pieman. Then the tumultuous flow of boisterous fun and battling mirth left him, and his head dropped on the manuscript of his book (afterwards published under the title of 'My Experiences as an Executioner') and he slept like a weary child.

My friend the tailor was late and missed all this fun. He was a little Polish Jew called Lassa, and made clothing for the police at Bridewell Police Station and the warders at Newgate. As soon as Lassa arrived Berry opened his eyes and blinked.

'Bad,' he said, shaking his head. 'I can't stand hanging Jews. They always come back to haunt me. Lipski came back . . .'

Lassa stared at Berry for a minute but evidently he did not hear the mumbled remarks, and Berry soon dozed off again.

After I had retired into a parlour and tried on my new jacket we returned to the bar. Suddenly Berry woke up. He seemed somewhat sobered by his sleep. He heaved himself out of his chair and came over to us, stood swaying, and wagged his finger at Lassa.

'You mush ha' a tankard of beer with me, old fellow. Mush encourage my clients, eh?'

Then he prodded Lassa in the ribs and roared with laughter.

The tankards of ale were brought and paid for by Berry.

He held up his ale, and gave his own curious toast:

'By noose and gallows and St. Sepulchre's Bell
Until we meet – I wish you well.'

'My Got!' exclaimed Lassa shudderingly, and his eyes seemed to start forward by themselves. Not until that moment had the Jew guessed that he was in the company of Berry the hangman.

'I voud not drink with you for a tausand pounds!'

With these words he dashed his pewter on the floor, and with a white, scared face, he turned and fled. Surprising as it may seem, I never saw Lassa again, although I had not paid him for my new suit. He regarded Berry with such loathing that nothing would persuade him to come near Newgate or the Old Bailey after this incident.

Berry was interviewed by a journalist after his 'retirement' and the report appeared in *The Daily Graphic* of 15 March 1892. Berry said:

'It's the things I've seen during the last eight years that make me opposed to capital punishment and it's because I am opposed to it that I am going to start lecturing on the subject.'

'But, Mr. Berry, you never, I think, put forward these objections before you had a dispute with the authorities about the method of executions.'

'No. No, I didn't. but that was because I felt that so long as executions lasted (and I couldn't stop them) I was the best man to undertake a bad business. I believe my way of executing the condemned was the best and most merciful. I used to feel a bit troubled about it at first, and if I had been left to myself I should have given it up after the first one. But my friends, or some of them who would be my friends, said, "Well don't give it up; don't duff it after you've once begun", and so I remained with it. And I maintain that my way is the most merciful way there is. It's all over in three minutes – sometimes in two – from the time the prisoner walks from the gaol door to the end of life for him. I've got drawn up here my table, which is better than any expert knows how to draw up to show how much drop a man ought to have. It's from all weights you see, from nine stone to nineteen, and, men who know something about these things allow that it's the most accurate table ever drawn up. Now, for instance, I should say that you'd want a drop of. . .'.

'Just so, just so; but tell me would you go back to the post if you were left to the exercise of your own judgement?'

'That I would not. Under no circumstances whatever. The man's never comfortable that has it. In some prisons they treat you like a dog. You know [we did not] that it is usual that I should see the condemned the day before the last. Sometimes I see him in the exercise yard. Sometimes I look at him through the grate of the cell (so that he can't see me). Well, in some places they won't even allow that, but just give me a form with the man's name, age, weight and height written on it. Of course, when they only do that I always ask a lot of questions, and make my calculations accordingly. My way, I say again, is the one that takes them out of the world with the least pain, and if the job must be done, surely I'm a better man to judge how than a medical man with no knowledge except his past theories.'

'You think, however, that the job shouldn't be done at all?'

'That I do. And why? Because of what I've seen, and because I'm sure, quite perfectly sure, that the criminal doesn't mind hanging so much as penal servitude. I'm sure of that. I've talked with men who were going to be hung – talked with them in their cells, and they were quite cheerful about it. Glad to be hung and out of the road. Why, look at it. The old offender who knows what penal servitude is – d'ye think he wouldn't prefer to be hung? Why from the time they're condemned they're very comfortable – food sent in to them, every comfort. A good deal better than penal servitude for life they think it, I can tell you. What would I do?'

Berry then went on to explain how he would have three grades of murder for which there would be three varying degrees of punishment. The least serious would get ten to fifteen years' penal servitude, the second would get life with a possible remission as part of the sentence and the worst would get penal servitude for life with a good flogging thrown in at the start of it! In Berry's simplistic view 'I'd guarantee you'd have no more murders very soon. I say to you, I tell you, they don't mind hanging; they hate penal servitude, but the lash . . .'.

33

Post-executioner years

'The crisis of my life.'

When H. Snowden Ward collaborated with Berry on *Experiences*, he acted as editor of the work, stressing that:

The statements are entirely those of the author, though in many cases the words are those of the editor, whose task consisted of re-arranging and very greatly condensing the mass of matter placed in my hands by Mr. Berry. The narrative and descriptive portion of the work is taken from a series of note-books and a news-cuttings book kept by Mr. Berry; who includes the most minute particulars in his diaries . . . In every case, however, the opinions are those of the author, with whom the editor is by no means in entire personal agreement.

Ward began the book with an excellent personal description of Berry, which, to give an idea what it was really like to know Berry, is here quoted in full:

James Berry, though regarded by some people as a monster, and by others as a curiosity, is very much like any other working-man when one comes to know him. He is neither a paragon of perfection, nor an embodiment of all vice – though different classes of people have at times placed him under both these descriptions. His character is a curious study – a mixture of very strong and very weak traits, such as is seldom found in one person. And although one of his weak points is his Yorkshire open-hearted frankness, which he tries to control as much as possible, the man who has only been with him a few days has not by any means got to the depths of his character. His wife has said more than once: – 'I have lived with him for nineteen years, but I don't thoroughly know him yet,' and one can quite understand it, as his character is so many-sided and in some respects contradictory. This partly accounts for the varying and contradictory views of his personality which have been published in different papers.

His strongest point is his tender-heartedness. Perhaps this may be doubted, but I state the fact from ample knowledge. Mr. Berry's occupation was not by any means taken up from a love of the ghastly, or any pleasure in the work. Even in his business as executioner his soft-heartedness has shown itself, for though it has never caused him to flinch on the scaffold, it has led him to study most carefully the science of his subject, and to take great pains to make death painless.

Of this trait I have had many proofs. For instance, I know that on some occasions when he has been due to start for a place of execution, his repugnance to the task has been so great that his wife and her mother have been obliged to use the greatest possible force of persuasion to prevent him shirking his duty . . .

The soft-heartedness of Mr. Berry's nature would quite unfit him for his post if it were not that he possesses a strong resolution, and can control his feelings when he finds duty warring against inclination.

In personal appearance he is a kindly-looking man, thickset and muscular, with a florid complexion and sandy hair. He stands 5ft. 8½in. high, weighs 13 stones, and does not look the sort of man to willingly injure anyone. The appearance of his right cheek is somewhat marred by a long, deep scar, extending downwards from the corner of the eye, which has given rise to one or two sensational stories from the pens of imaginative newspaper men. The scar was caused by the kick of a horse which he attempted to ride when he was a boy about ten years old. The horse was young, unbroken and vicious, and its kick narrowly missed being fatal. Across his forehead is another great scar, the result of a terrible blow received when arresting a desperate character in a Bradford public-house . . .

In conversation Mr. Berry is fluent, apt in anecdote and illustration, and full of subtle Yorkshire humour which he cannot entirely shake off even when talking on serious subjects. He has a very good memory for facts, and is very observant, so that he is always ready with a personal experience or observation on almost any topic. His tastes are simple. His favourite occupations are fishing and otter hunting, of both of which sports he is passionately fond. Frequently when going to an execution in a country town he takes his rod and basket, and gets a half-day's fishing before or after the execution. He seems to like the sport on account of its quiet and contemplative nature, and says that he enjoys the fishing even if he never gets a nibble.

At home Mr. Berry devotes himself largely to mechanical pursuits. At the present time he is working on a patent which he bought recently, and has the topmost room of his house fitted as a mechanic's workshop, with lathe, bench, etc. In spare time he devotes a good deal of attention to his pigeons and rabbits, for he is an ardent fancier, and keeps a large number of live pets.

Ward stated that Berry had had six children, of whom two boys and a girl died young, the remaining two boys and a girl still being alive at the time he wrote. Berry's house was situated at 1 Bilton Place, just off the City Road in Bradford, one of six properties he owned. Apparently when he first took up the office of executioner some of his neighbours were so prejudiced against his work that they refused to 'live next door to a hangman', so he had felt obliged to move. He had bought the above property, together with its neighbouring houses, after which, living down people's prejudice, he had encountered no difficulty in letting the latter to respectable tenants. His own house was furnished in much the same way as similar houses occupied by 'better-class artisans, and it was not at all gloomy'. In his front room Berry had two framed small photographs of murderers he had executed, and in a glass-fronted sideboard were some goblets, cruets and similar items that had been given to him by admirers. In various drawers and cupboards about the house there were a large number of relics and mementos of executions and other 'incidents'. Among these was a 'great knife', or sword, that had been used to behead nine Chinese pirates in Canton. This Berry had obtained in exchange for a rope that he had used to hang several persons. Shortly after this time Berry sold his relics to Madame Tussaud's.

The 1901 census return reveals that Berry, by then aged 49, had moved to 15 North-View Road in the parish of St Augustine's, Bradford North. His occupation was given as 'commission-agent late public executioner, works on own account'. Living with him was his wife Sarah, son Herbert, aged 25, and his mother-in-law Hannah Ackroyd, aged 78. His elder son, Luther, who boarded in a house in the Manningham area of Bradford, was shown as unmarried and working as a tram conductor in Bradford.

Berry's career as a showman on the lecturing tour circuit was not a great success and 'he subsided into private life' (*Famous Crimes Past and Present*, edited by Harold Furniss). On giving up his lecture tours he found himself once again in the position of needing an occupation that would support his family and the better lifestyle to which he had become accustomed, and he subsequently made his living by whatever means he could. Typically he would purchase a line of goods going cheap in Manchester, Oldham or some Midland town, and then sell his wares in small market towns at whatever profit he could make, sometimes playing the part of 'Dutch auctioneer'. It intrigued him that among the crowds there might have been relatives of some of his victims. A favourite resort of his was Barnsley; ironically one of the towns that people had said he would never dare enter after he had hanged the poacher, Murphy. It was a precarious existence, and Berry had not yet

. . . got out of the habit of bracing myself up with stimulants. It was an evil I had learned in prison. When I went to hang a man I was never able to do it until I had had at least a gill of brandy, and after I had had two I would have hanged the governor himself, not to speak of one or two Sheriffs who owed me money.

Despite calling drink an 'evil' it did not stop Berry from taking up a hotel then up for let, The Travellers Rest in Cutler Heights Lane, Bradford. He had heard that it was 'a good paying house', and presumably this was sufficient to overcome any aversion he had to the 'evil' of alcohol. It was while he was here that Berry says he was dealt a tragic blow. It involved his daughter, Emily, described by Berry as so wise above her years that in talking to her 'you forgot she was a child'. Described further as 'a dear child' who 'had known suffering', the unfortunate girl had been afflicted for some time with a spine and hip disease that had caused her to lose the use of her limbs. Her parents had taken her to Seven Oaks Hospital, where she had stayed for twelve months, enjoying the benefit of the best medical help and kind nursing, but the doctors had held out no hope of recovery and Berry had finally taken her home, as he thought, to die. For a time she had been confined to her bed but then Berry was advised to try the effects of a galvanic battery to stimulate her. Willing to try anything that might help, he had tried it, applying the treatment to the soles of her feet and her spine. Gradually she had recovered the use of her limbs until she was 'able to be out and about and was quite herself again'. Converted at the Wesleyan Methodist Chapel and very religious, she was fond of reading and loved by all those who knew her. However, not long after Berry had taken over The Travellers Rest she started 'to pine away like a fading flower'. (She was, in fact, to live for just three years after her apparent recovery.)

The girl, it seems, had often pleaded with Berry to give up drinking:

> I love you when you are sober, but I don't like you when in drink. Why don't you let it alone? You would be happier without it. We all would have more comfort, and people would respect you, and learn to love you. Then mother and I would be able to go out together and enjoy ourselves.

Her entreaties were in vain. Then, on 3 January 1902, she asked for Berry, her mother, brother and 'Granma' to come into her bedroom. Years before, when in his cups, Berry it seems had threatened to turn 'Granma' out of the house. The child had not forgotten, and begged her father to promise not to put 'Granma' out or send her to the workhouse. Berry recounted the moving story:

I gave her the promise. I said, 'No love I'll never put "Granma" out. While I live she shall always have what I have, and be made as comfortable as I can make her.' These words seemed to console her.

She then called her 'Granma' to the bedside and said:– 'I have sometimes said hard things to you. You know I did not mean them. Will you forgive me for saying them?' 'Granma' assured her that she always knew that she was fond of her, so that the hard things had never hurt in any way. 'Granma' also said:– 'I will not be long before I come to you. We will soon be together again in Heaven.'

Our girlie then put my hand into Granma's and asked me to pledge my word that I would look after Granma in her old age. I gave the promise as before God. With that she kissed her Granma and let her go. Then she called her mother to her bedside and said :– 'Mother my time has come and the Lord is calling me away to a better home. I am sorry to die in a public house. I do hope that father will leave it. The sights and wretchedness you see and hear, will kill you.' She then called me to the bedside again and she put my hand into mother's and said:– 'Father I want you to promise me for mother's sake to get out of this house. If you do not, you will not live long. I see it will be your death.'

I said 'Emily it is a good paying house, and I have not been long in it.' She said:– 'Never mind the money it brings. It will be your ruin; what about your soul? What's the good of making money if you are losing your soul? Get out of the public house, father, for your own sake and for mother's.' I saw that she was set on getting that promise. At last I did assure her that I would leave it at the first opportunity.

She then said: – 'I want you to promise also that you will never swear at mother again. Every time you use bad language to her you are making another of her hairs grey; and you will be sorry for it some day. I want you to look after mother and behave right to her.' I gave that promise also. Then she kissed her mother and bade her good bye.

She then called her brother and spoke to him also with the power that only the dying have; and bade him good bye.

As we stood around that bed watching and waiting, she told us that she was seeing the spirits of loved ones who had gone before. They had come, she said, to take her away to Jesus.

She asked her mother if she would place a wreath of evergreen holly with red berries on her grave every Christmas. The promise was given, and has been kept.

By and by she beckoned me to her side; she stretched up her thin wasted arm and placed it around my neck. Then she peacefully fell asleep. There was no struggle. She was sensible to the end. On the face when she had gone was a restful smile.

As Berry said afterwards, in *Wages*, 'It required all that to dig me out of the Public House.' He realised that his being the ex-hangman was a 'draw' to his customers, but that those attracted were not the best class of people:

I knew that it was drink that was the main support of the gallows. It was drink that sent the victims there. What is more, it was drink that goaded the Hangman on to carry out the law. I can imagine no man who has in any way reached even a moderate degree of human development, capable of deliberately hanging his fellow-man before he has executed his own lower nature by drink, and thus nullified his higher faculties, and destroyed the love of his fellow man by taking that which first enchants, and then destroys.

What Berry fails to mention here is that in June 1901 he had applied for re-employment as executioner but been rejected by the Prison Commissioners. It was noted on the file that:

James Berry is an unsuitable person, and the scandal caused by his proceedings in 1887 led to the appointment of the Committee on Executions. The then Secretary of State (Mr. Matthews) intimated that Berry should not be again employed.

C.S.J
26.6.1

Berry wrote a letter to various sheriffs dated Jan 15th 1902:

70 Willow Street Girlington
BRADFORD
Jan 15th, 1902.

Dear Sir,

I beg most respectfully to apply to you for the post of Executioner in any case which you may have to supervise in your county.

From 1883 to 1892 I carried out over 100 executions in different parts of the country, I believe to the entire satisfaction of the Sheriffs. This fact is testified to by Mr Charles B. O. Gepp, Under-Sheriff of Essex, who wrote me on June 26th 1901, as follows:–

'I can testify to the fact that when you were appointed to carry out executions by the Sheriff of Essex, and by his successors, you fulfilled your duties to their and my entire satisfaction, and, had you not thrown up your duties, you would still have been employed by the Sheriff under my direction.'

If you should be good enough to honour me by an appointment, I promise to exert myself to the utmost of my ability to give you every satisfaction.

I remain,
Yours faithfully,
James Berry

On 26 January Berry wrote to Evelyn John Ruggles-Brise, the Prisons Commissioner, applying for the post of executioner in a similar letter to that sent to the sheriffs. It was noted that the then Secretary of State, Henry Matthews, had at the time of Berry's leaving office decided that he should not again be employed.

On 18 February Berry wrote to Lt Col A. Beamish, RE, Surveyor to the Prison Commissioners, telling him that several members of Parliament (whose names he quoted) were supporting his effort to be reinstated by the sheriffs. Beamish was the designer of the new-style gallows and Berry had worked with him on this project. He said that he 'felt confident that you will put in a kind word'. To add a pathetic edge to the request Berry stated:

I have never been able to command a position I held previous and I might state that my aunt died 3 years ago and left my sisters & Bros £1000 each and cut me off without a single penny.

I am pointed out where ever I go no peace of my life and nothing coming in only what my two sons earns. I have two sons 25 & 27 years of age . . .

P.S. I have invented an improvement on the English scaffolds if applied will do away with the long drop and cause sudden death quicker than the present system a very simple affair the flaps of the trap door when the lever has been drawn will fly away like a flash a lightning thus letting the criminal drop with a sudden jerk thus causing dislocation without the uneasyness of an accident to the officials concerned.

On 8 March 1902 Berry again wrote to the Prison Commissioners:

70 Willow Street
Bradford
8th March 1902.

Sir,

I beg most respectfully to ask your kind assistance in obtaining me to regain my position back again. A year last Jan the Home Secretary wrote to our Chief Constable asking him to recommend a person suitable for the position of Executioner one that could be relied on as a fit & proper person. I am glad to state that he recommended my services after making a long & patient enquiries into every detail of my life history so after this most diligent enquiry I was persuaded to destroy the remaining portion of my Books [*Experiences*] which I did over 21,000 out of 40,000 published thinking by taking the advice of my superiors I was taking a step in the right directions.

Now I gave up attending markets and also done nothing since. I think after this I must claim your sympathy in this application.

I will undertake to supervise all executions under the Prison Commissioners to carry out any detail you might order. My eldest son who is drapers Traveller was at a town called Halifax yesterday and called at a Licensed House to bait with his horse, to get his dinner and he came across Tom Scott who acts as executioner for Ireland and he was showing the men who was in the tap room a letter from a Sheriff concerning an Execution which is to take place on the 18th of this month and making use of my name I am sending him a Lawyers letter this morning . . .

I may state he is more or less drunk the greater part of his time and I ordered him away from my premises last time he came to make enquiries about borrowing money; I may also state that I have it from various sheriffs if the Home Secretary will place my name on the list again they will appoint me as in the past. I am trusting you will reconsider this letter. Yours Respectfully, James Berry.

This reference to Scott, who had formerly acted as Berry's assistant, is most interesting. Berry was desperate to regain his old status as executioner but there was no way that the authorities would accede to his requests. Berry's desperation is evidenced by the fact that he claimed to have destroyed over 21,000 copies of his published book.

He eventually moved out of the licensed premises and took up the less lucrative but 'much more cleanly occupation of being a keeper of pigs'. He bred a large herd, but farming did not occupy his thoughts. He was restless and his mind was troubled, as it had been for some time. Apparently he was not getting much sleep and found the nights 'long and weary', being unable to get thoughts of his past life – which he regarded as one of 'sin and wickedness' – out of his mind. He drank in an attempt to drown his thoughts but then he thought of his 'dear mother' and 'dear father' who had tried to lead him into living a good life. 'There was nothing but death and destruction staring me in the face. Often did I wish that I were dead and off the face of the earth,' he recalled. He began to gamble and drank even more.

A Prison Commission file on Berry's appeal for re-engagement carries the following minute:

Mr. Mitford:–
Please see /67T. Mr. Berry makes a piteous appeal, but in spite of all the drawbacks he recapitulates, he has managed to

maintain himself and his wife for 15 years since he ceased to be an Executioner. There are plenty of good men now available and I see no reason why we should engage a man who formerly caused us trouble.

17.12.2

A letter on file, written by Berry to the Prison Commissioners on 5 January 1903, acknowledged receipt of a letter informing him that the Secretary of State would not accept his application. Berry's testimonials were returned to him.

On 25 October 1902 the infamous 'Borough Poisoner', Severin Antoniovich Klosowski, better known as George Chapman, was arrested for poisoning his wife and two common law wives. Landlord of The Crown public house, 213 Borough High Street, he had been arrested by Detective Inspector George Godley, an officer who, as a detective sergeant, had been involved in the hunt for Jack the Ripper. On searching Chapman's premises the police found some medical books referring to poison and a copy of Berry's *Experiences*; a fact which, when published in the newspapers, was spotted by Berry, who immediately wrote to Godley stating that he would like all reference to his book kept out of the case. Declaring his wish to be dissociated from the book, he claimed to have destroyed all the remaining copies that had been in his possession, plus any others he could find. This was obviously part of Berry's endeavour to appease the Home Office in his attempt to get his old post back. In the event the police evidence made no mention of the book (see *Trial of George Chapman*, by H.L. Adam, in the Notable British Trials Series).

Under the constant strain of Berry's behaviour, Sarah Berry's health was giving way. Heartbroken at his conduct, she often prayed to be taken away from her drunken husband, but he drank on and on. The tale of what happened next is revealed in *Wages*. On Saturday 19 December 1903 Berry rose and went out early to drink with some friends at a hostelry near to his home. He had already drunk 'a few bottles of Bass's Beer' by noon, and a friend paid for another bottle for him. There was nothing wrong with the beer, but as Berry lifted his glass to drink it he felt a choking sensation in his throat. He had suddenly become disgusted by alcohol and could not drink it. He told his companions it was high time that he gave it up, at which they laughed, predicting that he would soon come back for another, but he didn't. He hurried home to find his wife washing the dinner pots.

'What have you left your friends so early for, and come home,' she asked, 'when you could have as much drink as you like for nothing?'

He told her that he was disgusted with himself and had resolved never to drink again. Sarah looked at him with wonderment, 'What? You be teetotal! If you keep teetotal for a month something strange will happen.'

Having eaten a good lunch at the hotel he did not want any dinner, so he sat down in his old armchair with his paper, filled his pipe with tobacco and began to smoke. As he sat quietly it seemed that something dropped from his eyes and he could see more clearly. His past life flooded into his mind and he felt ashamed of himself. He took a book out from the library, *The Life of Ned Wright, Converted Burglar*. Sarah came into the room and asked him to sit down, saying that she would do all she could to help if he was going to lead a different life, upon which she made a fire in his room, brought his slippers, took off his boots, and brought a cushion for his feet to rest on. He spent three weeks without going out, reading *Ned Wright* and *Down in Water Street, New York*, as well as other books of a similar kind. He felt disgusted with himself; debased by all the drinking and fighting he had indulged in. To Sarah's consternation, depression took hold, dark thoughts of taking his own life crowding in upon him. He could not keep still and became very nervous, even a knock on the door causing his heart to palpitate with dread. Eventually he did indeed resolve to end his life, but Sarah caught him, he writes, 'at the beginning of my attempt and took away all the weapons and hid them from me'. She was so upset that she told him she would go to the Town Hall and inform the Chief Constable 'what kind of man she had to live with; stating that I was becoming dangerous and she was going to have advice about me'. At that time suicide, and attempted suicide, were criminal offences.

Further attempts to become reinstated as executioner had failed. A note on his Prison Commission file, for February 1904, read:

Berry has several times since appealed to H.O., the Commissioners, and to different persons outside, with a view to being re-employed but his applications have been refused, and to some of his letters no replies have been sent.

The following day, Saturday 13 February 1904, Berry rose after a sleepless night, dressed, and went down into the living room. Sarah had prepared some breakfast but he could not eat. He had no appetite and had eaten little for weeks. All he could think of was that he was unworthy to live and was a disgrace to himself and his family. He had all he needed in life but:

I could not have thought it possible that mortal man could become so low and depraved. I could not sleep at night: I could not rest by day. My burning conscience accused me of having wronged my family: – my innocent, good and virtuous wife, and my sorely suffering children – with my carryings on in sin and wickedness. There was nothing else for it. I must put an end to my life.

At about ten o'clock he shook hands with and kissed Sarah for what he thought was the last time on earth. 'Berry, where are you going?' she said.

'I don't know,' he replied.

Sensing all was not right she pleaded with him to stay, saying, 'You have a good home and plenty to eat. Do try and look up and don't get so low spirited.'

He replied, 'I cannot live in such a state. My own flesh and blood have turned against me and everybody is looking upon me with scorn.'

She said, 'If you turn over a new leaf, and lead a new life, people will soon begin to respect you.'

There was no stopping him however, and he left the house determined to put an end to his life. He could see no other way out of his shame and trouble. He made his way to the Midland Station and, finding that an express was due to leave for London, via Leeds, about noon, he decided to take the train and throw himself out of the window as it passed through the long tunnel between Bradford and Leeds. As he waited, he noticed a placard on Smith's bookstall. It proclaimed that some strange lights had been seen above the church where an Evangelist, Evan Roberts, was to preach. He bought a paper and read further, but again thoughts of his past flooded into his mind such that he wished he had never been born. He was utterly miserable and time seemed to drag interminably as he sat looking at the clock, waiting for the train's arrival. He looked up to the glass roof of the station and asked forgiveness for what he was planning to do.

As the time for the train drew near Berry called out in prayer asking forgiveness. He imagined he saw his mother's face on the glass roof, and it seemed so real he called out, 'Mother I have not a single friend in the world.' He began to weep, but wiped away the tears thinking that he would soon be out of his misery. He cried out again for forgiveness and then fancied he heard a small voice in reply, 'Fear not for I am with thee; thou shalt not be drowned.' At that moment an Evangelist came onto the platform, went to the bookstall and purchased a paper similar to the one bought by Berry. He sat on the same seat as Berry and, after reading for a time, turned to him and commented that they both had a similar paper. Berry replied that he had bought it to read about the strange lights seen above the chapel in Wales, upon which the stranger told Berry he had been led to the platform by the Holy Spirit in order to speak to somebody, observing further that Berry looked in a very bad way. At this Berry spilled out his story; his past sins and wickedness and how he had planned to take his life, declaring that he suddenly felt he should go to Wales and attend Evan Roberts's Revival meetings. The stranger then began to weep also, telling of his own past life and how he had been led to salvation. The man prayed, a small group of people watching by this time, wondering what was happening.

Afterwards, the stranger asked Berry to accompany him to the Bowland Mission Hall, where they would summon a meeting and pray for him, but Berry – explaining his past employment as executioner, which, he feared, put him beyond forgiveness – declared that he would not be converted in Bradford as he was so well known and would be laughed at. The stranger consoled him, assuring him that he could be forgiven, and, finally convinced, Berry agreed to meet him at the Mission Hall at two o'clock.

They parted at the station entrance and Berry went on to the Town Hall, where he caught the Sunbridge Road Car and rode to his home, 2 miles distant. Having wept bitterly all the way home, he found his wife had been weeping also, her eyes swollen and bathed in tears. She asked where he had been and he told her everything, upon which she divulged that she had realised by his look as he left what he was planning to do and had prayed for him. Berry told her of his appointment at Bowland Street Mission Hall and, while he changed his clothes, Sarah prepared a meal for him, but he could not eat. Eventually, he set out for the Mission Hall, praying, arriving as the Town Hall clock struck two to find his new friend, a Mr William Thompson, waiting at the door with a warm welcome. Inside, a large congregation was assembled, Mr Wrigglesworth, the leader of the Mission, and his wife, having made every effort to gather them together after Thompson had informed them of the situation. The congregation began to sing, 'I was lost but Jesus found me . . . ', and then prayers were said and further hymns sung, at which Berry broke down trembling, but he was persuaded to pray. After the meeting, Mr Wrigglesworth arranged for mission workers to take him home and tell his wife of her 'new husband'. They made their way in a procession, singing through the streets, and Berry invited them all to stay for tea. Subsequently he received an invitation to attend a meeting at Bolton Woods, Frizinghall, where a Miss Butterworth was conducting a Mission, and, accompanied by his new friends, he duly attended. Some of the members there were invited to say words to encourage those who were undecided, and then, after a few had done so, Miss Butterworth asked Berry to give his story. He obliged, and the response was immediate, all those assembled starting to sob, seventeen being received into the fold. It was 11 p.m. before Berry returned home:

Arriving at home I at once pulled out my keys and opened the drawer which I had always kept locked. I drew out all the filthy, dirty literature that was there, my dice for gambling, my pipe with figures on it, my cards and many other things that belonged to the Devil's Own, and put them all into the fire. I burnt my cigars, racing calendars, and tips. As far as I know how, I purged out the old leaven of wickedness so that I should have a clean house into which I could invite Jesus to come and dwell. I wanted to be out with the world, the flesh and the devil, and in with Jesus Christ.

Next morning I took my wife up a cup of tea and then I went down and thanked God for preserving my soul and for saving me from the flesh life. I asked Him to keep me from falling. Then I began to read my Bible a book I had never read before. I could think better now. I understood it better. I have kept close to my Bible ever since. I also attended every meeting for months.

Berry had been saved from self-destruction, and was to spend the last years of his life far more at peace with himself and the world. It was perhaps this newfound religious zeal, coupled with the Home Office's refusal to accept his further applications, that resulted in his second book, *Mr. J. Berry's Thoughts Above the Gallows*. More modest than *Experiences*, it was published in 1905 by Parker Bros. & Co., 88 Sunbridge Road, Bradford, and ran to some sixty-three pages. Priced at sixpence the title page stated:

A little work written rather in the interest of truth and justice than to rouse the morbid taste of curiosity.

It makes no boast of literary merit, its mission is:–

> To humbly serve the best;
> This end being reached
> Satisfaction will be obtained

The book carried a portrait of Berry as a frontispiece, and appears to have been Berry's way of purging himself of his 'sins' as a hangman, showing public disdain for capital punishment and pouring forth his religious convictions. His interest in phrenology was evinced in a five-page section at the end of the book giving the 'Phrenological Chart with character of James Berry Late Executioner of Great Britain', together with 'Explanation of the Phrenological Qualities of Mr. James Berry'. This, needless to say, is very complimentary to the author.

34

The final years

'There again they broke down and wept.'

Berry began a new vocation as an evangelical preacher, and his brethren soon realised what a strong draw the ex-hangman was at meetings. Using his own conversion as his central theme he spiced it up with tales of death-cell dramas in which the condemned turned to God in their final hours. Invitations to speak came from far and wide and Berry found himself travelling all over the country, from Scotland to Cornwall. He sold his pigs in order to take up the call and accepted as many invitations as he could.

On one mission, in Motherwell, after relating the story of Gower and Dobell – the two youths whom he had hanged at Maidstone for shooting the foreman – two young men in the hall broke down and had to be assisted out. That evening they came again, once more breaking down in tears. Apparently they had planned to kill one of the pair's sweethearts that night, having been to Glasgow and purchased a knife with which to commit the deed. This they produced: a formidable-looking knife with a ring at one end of the haft. They said, however, that Berry's story had so preyed on their minds that they had decided not to carry out the crime but to turn to God instead. All around were deeply moved as the two declared, 'If it had not been for Mr. Berry being in Motherwell we would have carried out our purpose and committed murder.'

Berry tells of other such incidents. At Taunton one of the worst drunkards in the town was brought to his senses on hearing his testimony and changed his ways for the better. At Blackpool another man was so impressed by the fact that 'Jesus had saved such a big sinner as Berry the hangman' that he began to hope for salvation himself (one can only guess what his sins might have been!). Berry realised that many came to hear him out of mere curiosity, but even of those a number were converted.

Eventually, however, even his life as a travelling evangelist involved some acrimony:

> I had a penitent form, and once I remember a strange dramatic situation that occurred at it. A young man came and knelt down. He was a brother of a man I had hanged, and he had escaped the gallows himself by the skin of the teeth. The jury had found him guilty, and sentenced him to death, but he had been reprieved. I wrestled with him in prayer, but when I asked him a certain question he walked away from me indignantly. I had stirred the leaves of memory which he had rather I had left as they were. [Possibly of George Davies – see chapter 27.]
>
> I believe I could have done good in this line but for two reasons. The one was that my past, while it brought people to the hall, weighed against me, and the other was that many people with whom I was associated in the work had sometimes a difficulty in getting on in a friendly way. I therefore decided to sever my connection, but I did not give up my religion, and I want to put it on record that only through it was I ever able to get a moment's peace in life.

The *Washington Post* of 17 November 1907 carried an article headed 'After Executing 197 Criminals [*sic*] Berry Opposes Death Penalty'. The story told of how Berry had declared he had hanged Jack the Ripper and afterwards kept the culprit's cufflinks as a souvenir. He was referring, of course, to William Henry Bury, who, so the story claimed, had murdered his wife after she had threatened to reveal his identity. Addressing Bury as Jack the Ripper, Berry had supposedly asked what he had to say, to which he replied, 'No. If any one stole anything from me I'd kill the lot to find the right one. I'm not going to give you any big lines, go on with your work, Berry, I'll not say anything.' Whether this gilded tale is actually what Berry said, or inaccurate reporting, we shall never know. The story concluded with the news that Berry was shortly to depart for the United States, where he was booked for an evangelical tour.

It is difficult to date exactly when Berry gave up his preaching, but page seven of *The Illustrated Police News* of 22 October 1910 carried a story that shows he was still very much active within three years of his death. Under the title 'HANGMAN EVANGELIST', the story showed Berry again flexing his legal arm. The piece ran:

JAMES BERRY, formerly the public hangman, is now an evangelist, and a weekend's mission at the Blackburn People's Mission had a sequel on Monday in the county-court, Berry suing the Rev. George Dymock for £4 17s. 4d., money alleged to be due, and costs.

It was said that the parties arranged that the mission should conclude with a Monday evening lecture on 'The Story of My Life,' and that Berry should take the whole of the admission money, without deduction. The hall was packed, but plaintiff received only £6 8s. 9d., whereas he contended he was entitled to £11 5s.

The defence was that the plaintiff received absolutely all the takings.

During plaintiff's evidence defendant's solicitor asked him: 'Do you know you are imputing to the treasurer of the mission an intention to defraud?'

Plaintiff: I don't care.

The Solicitor: Is that what James Berry, evangelist, says? You consider they have conspired to defraud you for their own ends?

Plaintiff: They did it for the sake of getting the building out of debt.

(Laughter.)

The hearing was adjourned.

Over the years relics of the hangman came onto the open market, and drew comment in the press. *The Umpire* of 4 February 1912 carried a piece headed 'Famous Hangsmen's [*sic*] Letters', in which it was noted that the autographs of the hangmen were not 'a valued marketable property'. A collection of letters bearing the signatures of Calcraft, Berry and Billington, together with the 'autograph of the notorious Crippen thrown in' had realised only seventeen shillings at a London sale. Berry's was on a letter to an Ashton editor protesting that an impostor had been attracting attention to himself by declaring in public houses in the district that he was Berry. This collection sounds a fascinating and valuable cache, and today would realise a very high price.

Berry lived out his final years quietly as a farmer, the faithful Sarah still with him. Press photographs show him standing on the steps of his Walnut Tree Farm at 36 Bolton Lane, Bolton, Bradford, a shadow of his former self. He died there, aged 61, on Tuesday 21 October 1913, with Sarah at his side. The cause of death was given as arteriosclerosis/heart failure.

Berry was still a well-known local figure and prominent obituaries appeared in the local press. It was noted that Berry claimed to have executed 'Jack the Ripper', though this had never been proved. The story of William Henry Bury was recapitulated in the report on Berry's death in the *Bradford Daily Argus*. The sensational failure to hang John Lee was also mentioned. The *Bradford Daily Telegraph* of 23 October carried a lengthy report, with a picture of Berry. It noted that:

He first came into prominence in Bradford as a popular busman plying between Bradford and Shipley before the horse cars were introduced. From that he went into the licensed victualling business, and for a time kept a public-house at Low Moor . . .

A native of Bradford, he was widely known in the district, and the writer remembers one occasion when Berry offered to sell him a cigar case which had belonged to a person he had executed. It is well known that several years ago he was involved in litigation regarding the sale of the rope which he claimed had been used for the hanging of Charles Peace, and on that occasion he visited the 'Telegraph' office and, displaying a revolver, vowed that he would take the life of the solicitor whom he imagined had wronged him in this matter.

Deceased had been ailing for some weeks, and his death was not unexpected.

Even *The Times* carried an obituary and noted that Berry had originally been an 'omnibus man' in the Bradford district before horse tramcars were introduced, afterwards keeping a public house.

The piece went on to state that Berry had been appointed assistant to Marwood about 1878, 'and he always claimed that it was he who hanged Charles Peace at Armley Gaol, though the official record at the gaol gives Marwood as the executioner . . .' In 1878 Berry had been a police officer, so this alleged claim is dubious, but he may have been present. An account of John Lee was subsequently given, and the report concluded:

> Berry was always regarded as more or less an eccentric person, and eventually he had difficulties with the authorities and resigned his position. After this he was engaged for a time in lecturing on his experiences, and then he took up mission work in this country and in America. Berry claimed to have executed Jack the Ripper, who, Berry said, was identical with Bury, who was executed for wife murder at Dundee in 1899 [*sic* – actual date 1889].

The mention of Berry's claim about Charles Peace resulted in a letter to *The Times*, and the publication of a small piece on 25 October explaining in detail how Marwood was the executioner of Peace and not Berry. The *News of the World* carried Berry's obituary on 26 October, with a portrait of Berry as he looked at the time of his retirement as executioner. News of his death was also carried in the American press. On 16 November 1913 the *New York Times* carried a large portrait of Berry under the heading 'Hanged Over Five Hundred Persons'!

Berry was buried at Scholemoor Cemetery, Lidget Green, Bradford.

On 25 September 1932 the *Reynolds's Illustrated News* featured an article headed 'MAN HE COULD NOT HANG, Notes From Diary of An Executioner'. It reported that the diary of James Berry had just come to light:

> Hangman Berry held office from 1883 to March 1892. After one execution he wrote in his diary: -
>
> > 'I am sick at heart. I am always like that after an execution. You see, I have had no sleep at all for two nights. I never

closed my eyes in Oxford Gaol (where the execution was to take place) all night. I could not sleep a wink.'

This diary of 180 pages is an extraordinary volume, for in addition to comments by Berry himself, there is a collection of more than 1,000 newspaper cuttings . . .

The location of this material today is not known, although some of it, including the original manuscript of *Wages*, is in the small collection of Berry material at Madame Tussaud's archives.

Over the years, other Berry relics would appear. Charles Duff's best-selling anti-capital punishment work, *A Handbook on Hanging* (EP Publishing Ltd, Rowman & Littlefield, USA, 1974), records the subsequent history of the material Berry supplied to the Nottingham publican, Dan Dominic, in 1885:

Collectors, antiquarians and curators of museums may be interested to know that the actual rope used in the classic failure to hang John Lee, together with holograph letters written by Mr. Hangman Berry, were in 1948 exhibited for sale in a Nottingham junk-shop. Whether or not they have been snapped up by a shrewd investor, I do not know . . .

In 1994 these items appeared in a Cambridge auction house, still in excellent condition. For many years they had been in The Cambridge Museum of Prison, Punishment and Royal Relics &c., principal Mr Edwin Rutter, incorporated in Ye Olde Curiosity Shoppe in Trumpington Street, Cambridge. It would appear that Mr Rutter was probably the purchaser of the items from the 'Nottingham junk-shop'. They were later purchased by Dr Alexander Dale of The Old House, Histon, near Cambridge.

The year 1954 saw publication of the book *Shadow of the Gallows* by Justin Atholl, a well-known crime writer. It was a broad history of judicial hanging and contained many references to James Berry. The success of this book and the amount of research material that Atholl had accumulated led him to write a second volume, *The Reluctant Hangman*, which was published in 1956. This, more or less, was a biography of Berry, and drew upon published and unpublished sources, including many of the press reports. However, it suffered from a lack of chronology and dating, the author not seeming to have had access to Berry's unpublished manuscript, his second published book (which is not even mentioned) or the official files. Nonetheless, it is a very good read and a most interesting work. Atholl refers to Berry's book of press cuttings, his appointments book and notebooks, describing the 'cuttings book' as 'a massive 18in by 14in, quarter leather-bound volume of some hundreds of pages' into which Berry had pasted more than a thousand newspaper cuttings covering all of his executions. He also gives a detailed and colourful description of Berry's collection of murder and victim relics and associated photographs. An unsourced tale tells of Berry selling a rope to an interested party immediately after an execution in 1886. The delighted purchaser was so pleased with his acquisition that, while on the train home, he took it out of his case in front of a carriage full of fellow passengers, explaining that the rope had been used that very morning! One of the fellow travellers was so aghast that he wrote a letter of complaint to the Home Office; another transgression to add to Berry's growing list at the time.

The *Bradford Telegraph and Argus* of 30 January 1957 carried a story by K. Brace headed – 'Executioner who heralded fight against hanging'. It was a topical piece, for the cry in the 1950s to have capital punishment abolished was loud, and, of course, Berry was a true son of Bradford. The story was centred on Mrs Emily Billing of Rendel Street, Bradford. She was Berry's granddaughter and possessed relics of her noted forebear, including a book of printed forms, like an order book with flimsy duplicate pages for carbon copies, with which Berry used to acknowledge requests for his services. It carried entries from 1889 to 1891. There was also a copy of *Experiences* and dusty black boxes containing the lantern slides that Berry had used in his tours after his retirement. Also in the collection, the article states, was a manuscript copy, apparently dictated to a friend, of 'Berry's other and a far less well-known book, *The Hangman's Thoughts Above the Gallows*, a highly-personal confession published in Bradford in 1905' and subtitled 'A little work written rather in the interest of truth and justice than to arouse the morbid taste of curiosity'. It was noted that the work 'can be remembered by few in Bradford today'. There were also some photographs in the collection. *Thoughts Above the Gallows* is not listed in the British Library catalogue but the Central Library at Bradford holds a copy. Berry confesses there that he had a heavy conscience and that he had pursued an ill-considered career as a younger man which had brought him nothing but pain:

> I now hold that the law of capital punishment falls with terrible weight upon the hangman and to allow a man to follow such an occupation is doing him a deadly wrong.

Apparently Mrs Billing had no real interest in the grim profession of her grandfather, but treasured the relics as belonging to a man she remembered as 'a kind-hearted old gentleman'.

John 'Babbacombe' Lee was another man whose name continued to crop up in the press over the years, often in relation to Berry and the failed hanging. The case was discussed in the *Torquay Times* in July 1964 after a television piece on the Babbacombe murder had expounded the theory that the execution failed because of the weight of the chaplain on the planks of the scaffold. This resulted in a reader, a Mr Albert Edward Boardwell of 125 Warbro Road, writing to the columnist of 'Raymond's Roundabout'. Boardwell, who stated that he was aged 65, a native of Yorkshire and the great nephew of James Berry, drew attention to the article in *Thomson's Weekly News* of 19 February 1927 giving Berry's account of the affair, stating that the article had been given to him by one of his aunts forty years previously.

Berry again made news in the summer of 1971 when some of his possessions appeared for sale on 29 June at an auction held by London antique and fine art auctioneers, Phillips, Son and Neale at their monthly book sale. Items listed were 180 slides, a handwritten programme by Berry, and his printed publicity material billing him as a 'phrenologist and character reader', promising 'palmistry explained' and 'heads examined'. Additional items were his record book of executions, his manuscript for a book 'A Hangman's Thoughts', a second manuscript 'An Executioner's Wages', and 'the shirt he used on the scaffold'. It was the collection once owned by Mrs Billing, his granddaughter. News of the auction had first appeared in *The Times* of Wednesday 9 June 1971 in 'The Times

Diary' column under the heading 'Black Berry'! Various newspapers reported on the auction the day after it was held, revealing that Berry's items had sold for £210, being bought by Mr Eric Barton, a book dealer of the Baldur Bookshop, Hill Rise, Richmond. I visited Eric at his Richmond home in the mid-1990s and he informed me that he had sold the Berry collection to Madame Tussaud's.

James Berry died in 1913, but he would be pleased to know that he is not forgotten in the twenty-first century. He was a man of contradictions; an executioner but religious and humane; dour but with a sense of humour; often frightened but at times brave and outspoken; a drinker and an abstainer; above all a loving family man. He was one of the most colourful of the public executioners and has taken a prominent place in the history of British crime and punishment. His methods and refinements of execution did not change very much after his death apart from the positioning of the 'knot' of the rope being changed from the sub-aural position (behind the left ear) to the more effective sub-mental position (under the angle of the left jaw), it being decided that the latter position, used by Marwood, effected a more reliable dislocation of the vertebrae of the neck, and allowed for a shorter drop.

On 26 March 1949, Berry's son, Luther, of 30 Clement Street, Girlington, Bradford, died at the age of 71. His occupation was given as a retired cleaner of the Municipal Passenger Transport, Bradford, and he left a widow, Lydia.

James Berry has appeared in many books, most notably a novel, *Waxwork*, by Peter Lovesey, dramatised for a TV thriller, *Waxwork* (YTV, 23 December 1979), with James Warrier playing Berry and Alan Dobie as Sgt Cribb. His name has now entered the *New Oxford Dictionary of National Biography*, and his place in history is assured.

Appendix I

'The Drop', by James Berry

The matter which requires the greatest attention in connection with an execution is the allowance of a suitable drop for each person executed, and the adjustment of this matter is not nearly so simple as an outsider would imagine.

It is, of course, necessary that the drop should be of sufficient length to cause instantaneous death, that is to say, to cause death by dislocation rather than by strangulation; and on the other hand, the drop must not be so great as to outwardly mutilate the victim. If all murderers who have to be hanged were of precisely the same weight and build it would be very easy to find out the most suitable length of drop, and always to give the same, but as a matter of fact they vary enormously.

In the earliest days of hanging it was the practice for the executioner to place his noose round the victim's neck, and then to haul upon the other end of the rope, which was passed through a ring on the scaffold pole until the culprit was strangled, without any drop at all. After a while the drop system was introduced, but the length of drop given was never more than three feet, so that death was still generally caused by strangulation, and not by dislocation, as it is at present. One after another, all our English executioners followed the same plan without thought of change or improvement, until Mr. Marwood took the appointment. He, as a humane man, carefully considered the subject, and came to the conclusion that the then existing method, though certain, was not so rapid or painless as it ought to be. In consequence he introduced his long-drop system with a fall of from seven to ten feet, which caused instantaneous death by severance of the spinal cord. I was slightly acquainted with Mr. Marwood before his death, and I had gained some particulars of his method from conversation with him; so that when I undertook my first execution, at Edinburgh, I naturally worked upon his lines. This first commission was to execute Robert Vickers and William Innes, two miners who were condemned to death for the murder of two game-keepers. The respective weights were 10 stone 4lb and 9 stone 6lb, and I gave them drops of 8ft 6in, and 10ft respectively. In both cases death was instantaneous, and the prison surgeon gave me a testimonial to the effect that the execution was satisfactory in every respect. Upon this experience I based a table of weights and drops. Taking a man of 14 stones as a basis, and giving him a drop of 8ft., which is what I thought necessary, I calculated that every half-stone lighter weight would require a two inches longer drop, and the full table, as I entered it in my books at the time, stood as follows :–

Weight	Drop
14 stones	8ft 0in
13½ "	8 " 2 "
13 "	8 " 4 "
12½ "	8 " 6 "
12 "	8 " 8 "
11½ "	8 " 10 "
11 "	9 " 0 "
10½ "	9 " 2 "
10 "	9 " 4 "
9½ "	9 " 6 "
9 "	9 " 8 "
8½ "	9 " 10 "
8 "	10 " 0 "

This table I calculated for persons of what I might call 'average' build, but it could not by any means be rigidly adhered to with safety. For instance, I have more than once had to execute persons who had attempted suicide by cutting their throats, or who had been otherwise wounded about the neck, and to prevent re-opening the wounds I have reduced the drop by nearly half. Again, in the case of persons of very fleshy build, who often have weak bones and muscles about the neck, I have reduced the drop by a quarter or half of the distance indicated by the table. If I had not done so, no doubt two or three of those whom I have executed would have had their heads entirely jerked off, – which did occur in one case to which I shall again refer. In the case of persons with scrofulous tendencies it is especially necessary that the fall should be unusually short, and in these cases I have at times received useful hints from the gaol doctors.

Until November 30, 1885, I worked to the scale already given, but on that date I had the awful experience above referred to, which caused me to reconsider the whole subject and to construct a general table on what I believe to be a truly scientific basis . . . The man with whom it occurred was Robert Goodale, whom I executed at Norwich Castle. He weighed 15 stones, and the drop indicated by the first table would therefore be 7ft 8in, but in consequence of his appearance I reduced it to 5ft 9in, because the muscles of his neck did not appear well developed and strong. But even this, as it turned out, was not short enough, and the result was one of the most horrible mishaps that I have ever had. As will be seen from the full report of this case . . . the coroner exonerated me from all blame and testified to the careful way in which I had done my work; but I felt that it was most necessary to take every possible precaution against the recurrence of such an affair. I, therefore, worked out a table of the striking force of falling bodies of various weights falling through different distances [see Appendix VI]. Working with this, I calculate that an 'average' man, of any weight, requires a fall that will finish with a striking force of 24cwt, and if the convict seems to require less, I mentally estimate the striking force that is necessary, and then by referring to the table I can instantly find the length of drop required. To see how this new table works out we may take the case of Robert Goodale again. As he weighed 15 stones his striking force with a drop of 2ft would be 21cwt 21lb, or with a drop of 3ft 26cwt 7lb, so that if he were a man of ordinary build the drop necessary would be 2ft 6in. As I estimated from his appearance that his drop ought to have been about one-sixth less than the standard, I should have given him, working on this new table, about 2ft 1in instead of the 5ft 9in which was actually given. This is an extreme case, with a very heavy man, but all through the table it will be found that the drop works out shorter than in the first table. For instance, Vickers and Innes, the two Edinburgh murderers previously referred to would have had their drops reduced from 8ft 6in and 10ft to 5ft 6in and 7ft respectively if they had been treated according to the present revised table.

On August 20th, 1891, at Kirkdale Gaol, Liverpool, at the execution of John Conway, an attempt was made to dictate to me the length of drop, and a most unfortunate scene ensued. From seeing the convict, Conway, I had decided that the drop ought to be 4ft 6in, a little under the scale rate; and I was surprised and annoyed at being told by Dr. Barr, acting, I believe, under authority, that I was to give a drop of 6ft 9in I said that it would pull the man's head off altogether, and finally refused to go on with the execution if such a long drop were given. Dr. Barr then measured off a shorter drop, some ten or twelve inches shorter, but still much longer than I thought necessary, and I reluctantly agreed to go on. The result, everyone knows. The drop was not so long as to absolutely pull off the victim's head, but it ruptured the principal blood-vessels of the neck.

I do not know who was really responsible for the interference with my calculation, but do not think that the long drop was Dr. Barr's own idea, as the drop which I suggested was on the same system as he had previously commended, and was almost identical with the drop that would have worked out on the basis of his own recommendation in a letter to the Times some years ago. Dr. Barr's letter to me, written in 1884, was as follows :–

1, St. Domingo Grove,
Everton,
Liverpool, Sept. 2nd, 1884.

Sir,

In compliance with your request I have pleasure in giving you a certificate as to the manner in which you conducted the execution of Peter Cassidy in H.M. Prison, Kirkdale. I may now report the statement which I gave in evidence at the Inquest, 'that I had never seen an execution more satisfactorily performed'. This was very gratifying to me.

Your rope was of excellent quality; fine, soft, pliable, and strong. You adjusted the ring, directed forwards in the manner in which I have recommended in my pamphlet, 'Judicial Hanging'. You gave a sufficient length of drop, considering the weight of the culprit, and completely dislocated the cervical vertebrae between the atlas and axis (first and second vertebrae). I have reckoned that the weight of the criminal, multiplied by the length of the drop, might range from 1120 to 1260 foot pounds, and I have calculated that this *vis viva* in the case of Cassidy amounted to 1140 foot pounds.

The pinioning and other details were carried out with due decorum, I hope, whoever be appointed to the post of public Executioner, may be prohibited from also performing the part of a 'showman' to gratify a depraved and morbid public curiosity.

JAMES BARR, M.D.,

Medical Officer, H.M. Prison, Kirkdale.

To Mr. James Berry.

Appendix II

'The Rope', by James Berry

The apparatus for carrying out the extreme penalty of the law is very simple. The most important item is the rope, which must necessarily possess certain properties if the death of the condemned person is to be instantaneous and painless.

For successful working the rope must, of course, be strong, and it must also be pliable in order to tighten freely. It should be as thin as possible, consistent with strength, in order that the noose may be free running, but of course, it must not be so thin as to be liable to outwardly rupture the blood vessels of the neck.

Before undertaking my first execution I gave careful consideration to the question of the most suitable class of rope, and after trying and examining many varieties, I decided upon one which I still use. It is made of the finest Italian hemp, ¾ of an inch in thickness. Before using a rope for an execution, I thoroughly test it with bags of cement of about the weight of the condemned person, and this preliminary testing stretches the cord and at the same time reduces its diameter to ⅝ of an inch. The rope consists of 5 strands, each of which has a breaking strain of one ton dead weight, so that it would seem unnecessary to test it from any fear of its proving too weak, but the stretching and hardening which it undergoes in the testing makes it far more 'fit' and satisfactory for its work than a new, unused rope would be.

It has been said that I use a rope with a wire strand down the centre, but the notion is so ridiculous that I should not refer to it if it were not that many people seem to believe it, and that more than once it has been stated in the newspapers. A rope with a wire strand would possess no possible advantage that I can see, and it would have so many practical disadvantages that I do not think anyone who had studied the matter would dream of using such a thing. At any rate I have not done so, and I know that neither Mr. Binns nor Mr. Marwood ever did. Mr. Marwood used ropes of about the same quality and thickness as my own, while Mr. Binns used a much thicker rope (about 1¼ inch diameter after use), of a rougher and less pliable class of hemp.

Until the commencement of 1890 I supplied my own ropes, some of which, however, were made to order of the Government, and I was able to use the same rope again and again. One I used for no less than sixteen executions, and five others I have used for twelve executions each. These are now in the possession of Madame Tussaud. At the beginning of 1890 a new rule was made under which a new rope is ordered to be supplied and used for most of the executions in England, and to be burned, together with the clothes of the person executed (which were formerly a perquisite of the executioner) by the prison officials immediately after the execution. In Scotland and Ireland I still provide my own ropes.

The rope I use is thirteen feet long and has a one-inch brass ring worked into one end, through which the other end of the rope is passed to form the noose. A leather washer which fits the rope pretty tightly, is used to slip up behind the brass ring in order to prevent the noose slipping or slackening after it has been adjusted.

In using the rope I always adjust it with the ring just behind the left ear. This position I never alter, though of course, if there were any special reason for doing so, for instance, if the convict had attempted suicide and were wounded on the side of the throat, death could be caused by placing the ring under the chin or even behind the head. The position behind the ear, however, has distinct advantages and is the best calculated to cause instantaneous and painless death, because it acts in three different ways towards the same end. In the first place, it will cause death by strangulation, which was really the cause of death in the old method of hanging, before the long drop was introduced. Secondly, it dislocates the vertebrae, which is now the actual cause of death. And thirdly, if a third factor were necessary, it has a tendency to internally rupture the jugular vein, which in itself is sufficient to cause practically instantaneous death.

Appendix III

'Pinioning straps, etc.' by James Berry

The pinioning arrangements, like the rest of the arrangements for an execution, are very simple. A broad leathern body-belt is clasped round the convict's waist, and to this the arm-straps are fastened. Two straps, an inch and a half wide, with strong steel buckles, clasp the elbows and fasten them to the body-belt, while another strap of the same strength goes round the wrists, and is fastened into the body-belt in front. The legs are pinioned by means of a single two-inch strap below the knees. The rest of the apparatus consists of a white cap, shaped somewhat like a bag, which pulls down over the eyes of the criminal to prevent his seeing the final preparations.

Appendix IV

'The Scaffold', by James Berry

U ntil recently, the scaffolds in use in the various gaols differed very much in the details of their construction, as there was no official model, but in each case the local authorities followed their own idea. In 1885, however, a design was drawn, in the Surveyors' Department of the Home Office, by Lieut.-Col. Alten Beamish, R.E. Before being finally adopted, the design was submitted to me; and it seemed a thoroughly good one, as, indeed, it has since proved to be, in actual practice. The design is supplied to the authorities of any gaol where a scaffold is to be erected, from the Engineers' Department at the Home Office; and, with a slight alteration, has been the pattern in general use to the present day [1891]. The alteration of which I speak, is a little one suggested by myself, and consists of the substitution of a slope, or a level gangway, in place of the steps. I had found in some cases, when the criminals were nervous or prostrated, that the steps formed a practical difficulty. The slope, or gangway, was approved by the Home Office, and was first used on April 15th, 1890, at Kirkdale Gaol, for the execution of Wm. Chadwick. It was a simple improvement, but it has turned out to be a very useful one.

At most of the gaols in the country the scaffold is taken to pieces and laid away immediately after use, but in Newgate, Wandsworth, Liverpool, and Strangeways (Manchester), it is kept standing permanently.

The essential parts of the scaffold are few. There is a heavy cross-beam, into which bolts terminating in hooks are usually fastened. In some cases this cross-beam stands on two upright posts, but usually its ends are let into the walls of the scaffold house. Of course, the hooks fastened to it are intended to hold the rope.

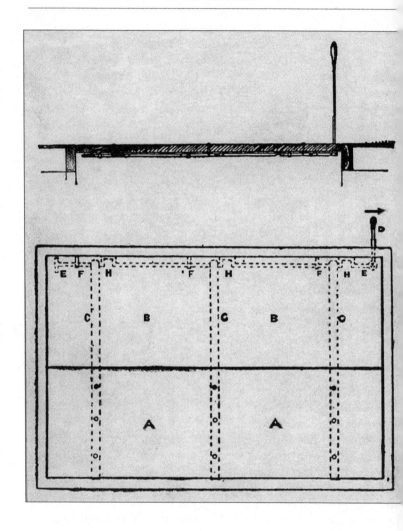

The scaffold proper, or trap, or drop, as it is variously called, is the portion of the structure to which most importance is attached, and of which the Government furnishes a plan. It consists of two massive oaken doors, fixed in an oak frame-work on a level with the floor, and over a deep bricked pit. The plan and section will explain the arrangement. The two doors are marked AA and BB on the plan. The door AA is hung on three strong hinges, marked CCC, which are continued under the door BB. When the trap is set the ends of these long hinges rest on a draw-bar EE, as shown in the plan. The draw-bar is of iron, 1½in square, sliding in strong iron staples, FFF, which fit it exactly. When the lever D is pulled over in the direction of the little arrow, it moves the draw-bar in the opposite direction, so that the ends of the long hinges drop through the openings HHH, and the two doors fall. To set the trap the door BB has to be raised into a perpendicular position, until the other door is raised and its hinges placed on the draw-bar. The arrangement is a very good one; as both doors must necessarily fall at exactly the same moment. Their great weight – for they are of three inch oak – causes them to drop very suddenly, even without the weight of the criminal, and they are caught by spring catches to prevent any possibility of rebound.

Appendix V

'The Proceedings', by James Berry

The hour fixed for executions is 8-0 a.m. in all the prisons, except Wandsworth and Lincoln, where it is 9-0 a.m. Of course, the scaffold and rope are arranged, and the drop decided, beforehand. I calculate for three minutes to be occupied from the time of entering the condemned cell to the finish of life's great tragedy for the doomed man, so I enter the cell punctually at three minutes to eight. In order that my action in hanging a man may be legal, it is necessary that I should have what is known as an 'authority to hang,' which is drawn up and signed by the Sheriff, and handed to me a few minutes before the time set for the execution. Its form varies a good deal. In some cases it is a long, wordy document, full of the 'wherefores' and 'whatsoevers' in which the law delights. But usually it is a simple, official-looking form, engrossed by the gaol clerk, and running somewhat as follows:–

> To JAMES BERRY.
> I, ——, of ——, in the County of ——,
> Esquire, Sheriff of the said County of ——, do hereby
> Authorise you to hang A—— B——, who now lies under Sentence
> of Death in Her Majesty's Prison at ——.
> Dated this —— day of ——, ——.
> —— ——, Sheriff.

This is folded in three, and endorsed outside.

> Re A—— B——.
> Authority to Hang.
> —— ——, Sheriff,
> ——shire.

When we enter the condemned cell, the chaplain is already there, and has been for some time. Two attendants, who have watched through the convict's last nights on earth are also present. At my appearance the convict takes leave of his attendants, to whom he generally gives some little token or keepsake, and I at once proceed to pinion his arms.

As soon as the pinioning is done, a procession is formed, generally in the following order :–

Chief Warder.

Warder.   Warder.

Warder. Chaplain. Warder.

Convict.

Executioner.

Principal Warder. Principal Warder.

Warder. Warder.

Governor and Sheriff.

Wand Bearer. Wand Bearer.

Gaol Surgeon and Attendant.

In some few cases, where the prisoner has not confessed before the time for the execution, I have approached him in the cell in a kindly manner, asking him, as it can make no difference to his fate, to confess the justice of the sentence, in order that I may feel sure that I am not hanging an innocent person. In most cases they have done so, either in the cell, or at the last moment on the scaffold. Of course, the confidences reposed in me at such moments I have never divulged and it would be most improper to do so; but I am at liberty to state, that of all the people I have executed, only two or three have died without fully and freely confessing their guilt.

On the way from the cell to the scaffold the chaplain reads the service for the burial of the dead, and as the procession moves I place the white cap upon the head of the convict. Just as we reach the scaffold I pull the cap over his eyes. Then I place the convict under the beam, pinion the legs just below the knees, with a strap similar to the one used for the elbows, adjust the rope, pull the bolt and the trap falls. Death is instantaneous, but the body is left hanging for an hour, and is then lowered into a coffin, made in the prison, and carried to the mortuary to await the inquest. The inquest usually takes place at ten o'clock, but in some few places it is held at noon. After the inquest the body is surrounded by quick-lime and buried in the prison grounds.

In the carrying out of the last penalty of the law, everything is conducted with decorum and solemnity, and so far as I can see there is no way in which the arrangements at an execution can be improved, unless it is in regard to the admission of reporters. In years gone by a large number of reporters were often admitted, some of them with probably little or no real connection with the papers they professed to represent. Occasionally also there would be one or two feather-brained juniors who seemed to have no proper idea of the solemnity of a death scene, and whose conduct was hardly such as serious persons could approve. The result has been that in many prisons the admission of press representatives has been very rigidly curtailed, and in some cases admission has been absolutely refused. It seems to me that the admittance of a large number of spectators, and the absolute refusal to admit any, are alike mistakes. I speak in this matter as a man whose own work comes under the criticism of the press, and although so far as I am personally concerned, I am perfectly satisfied if I can satisfy the Governor or High Sheriff, I know that there is a large section of the public that thinks the exclusion of the reporters must mean that there is something going on which there is a desire to hush up. I am a servant of the public, as also are the sheriffs, the governor, and the other officials connected with an execution, and the public, through its representatives on the press, ought to have some assurance that the details of each execution are carried out decently and in order. The presence or absence of the press, of course, makes no difference in the conduct of the execution, but it makes a good deal of difference to a certain section of the public. If the Governor of the gaol or the Sheriff were to give three admissions for each execution, with the understanding that any representative suspected of not being *bona fide* would be refused admission even if he presented his ticket, I think that every real objection would be met.

After the execution is over the fact that the sentence of the law has been carried out is announced to the public by a notice fixed to the door of the prison. The form of this notice varies somewhat, but I append one of which I happen to have a copy.

COUNTY OF OXFORD.

EXECUTION of CHARLES SMITH for MURDER.

(The Capital Punishment Act, 1868.)

Copies are subjoined of the official declaration that judgement of death was this day, in our presence, executed on Charles Smith, within the walls of Her Majesty's Prison at Oxford.

Dated this Ninth day of May, One Thousand eight hundred and eighty-seven.

THOMAS M. DAVENPORT, Under-Sheriff of Oxfordshire.
H. B. ISAACSON, Governor of the Prison.
J. K. NEWTON, Chaplain of the Prison.
J. RIORDON, Chief Warder of the Prison.
HENRY IVES, Sheriff's Officer.
Thos. Wm. AUSTIN, Reporter, *Oxford Journal.*
ROBERT BRAZIES, Reporter, *Oxford Chronicle.*
JOSEPH HENRY WARNER, Reporter, *Oxford Times.*
J. LANSBURY, Warder.

SURGICAL CERTIFICATE.

I, HENRY BANKS SPENCER, the Surgeon of Her Majesty's Prison at Oxford, hereby certify that I this day examined the body of Charles Smith, on whom judgement of death was this day executed in the said prison; and that, on such examination, I found that the said Charles Smith was dead.

Dated this Ninth day of May, One thousand eight hundred and eighty-seven.

HENRY BANKS SPENCER,
Surgeon of the Prison.

Appendix VI

Berry's Table of Drops (1885)

SCALE SHOWING THE STRIKING FORCE OF FALLING BODIES AT DIFFERENT DISTANCES.

Distance Falling in Feet Zero	8 Stone	9 Stone	10 Stone	11 Stone	12 Stone	13 Stone	14 Stone	15 Stone	16 Stone	17 Stone	18 Stone	19 Stone
	Cw. Qr. lb.	Cw Qr. lb.	Cw. Qr. lb.	Cw. Qr. lb.	Cw. Qr. lb.	Cw. Qr. lb.	Cw. Qr. lb.	Cw. Qr. lb.	Cw. Qr. lb.	Cw. Qr. lb.	Cw. Qr. lb.	Cw. Qr. lb.
1 Ft.	8 0 0	9 0 0	10 0 0	11 0 0	12 0 0	13 0 0	14 0 0	15 0 0	16 0 0	17 0 0	18 0 0	19 0 0
2 „	11 1 15	12 2 23	14 0 14	15 2 4	16 3 22	18 1 12	19 3 2	21 0 21	22 2 11	24 0 1	25 1 19	26 3 9
3 „	13 3 16	15 2 15	17 1 14	19 0 12	20 3 11	22 2 9	24 1 8	26 0 7	27 3 5	29 2 4	31 1 2	33 0 1
4 „	16 0 0	18 0 0	20 0 0	22 0 0	24 0 0	26 0 0	28 0 0	30 0 0	32 0 0	34 0 0	36 0 0	40 0 0
5 „	17 2 11	19 3 5	22 0 0	24 0 22	26 1 16	28 2 11	30 3 5	33 0 0	35 0 22	37 0 16	39 2 11	41 3 15
6 „	19 2 11	22 0 5	24 2 0	26 3 22	29 1 16	31 3 11	34 1 5	36 3 0	39 0 22	41 2 16	44 0 11	46 2 5
7 „	21 0 22	23 3 11	26 2 0	29 0 16	31 3 5	34 1 22	37 0 11	39 3 0	42 1 16	45 0 5	47 2 22	50 1 11
8 „	22 2 22	25 2 4	28 1 14	31 0 23	34 0 5	36 3 15	39 2 25	42 2 7	45 1 16	48 0 26	51 0 8	53 3 18
9 „	24 0 11	27 0 12	30 0 14	33 0 23	36 0 16	39 0 18	42 0 19	45 0 21	48 0 22	51 0 23	54 0 25	57 0 26
10 „	25 1 5	28 1 23	31 2 14	34 3 4	37 3 22	41 0 12	44 1 2	47 1 21	50 2 11	53 3 1	56 3 19	60 0 9

Appendix VII

The Executions of James Berry 1884–92

1.	31 March 1884	William INNES and	Edinburgh
2.		Robert Flockheart VICKERS	
3.	26 May 1884	Mary LEFLEY	Lincoln
4.	27 May 1884	Joseph LOWSON	Durham
5.	19 August 1884	Peter CASSIDY	Liverpool
6.	24 August 1884	James TOBIN	Wexford
7.	6 October 1884	Thomas Henry ORROCK	Newgate
8.		Thomas HARRIS	
9.	24 November 1884	Kay HOWARTH	Manchester
10.		Harry Hammond SWINDELLS	
11.	8 December 1884	Ernest EWERSTADT	Liverpool
12.		Arthur SHAW	
13.	13 January 1885	Horace Robert JAY	Wandsworth
14.	16 January 1885	Michael DOWNEY	Galway
15.	20 January 1885	Thomas PARRY	Galway
16.	23 February 1885	John LEE (failed execution)	Exeter
17.	17 March 1885	Henry KIMBERLEY	Birmingham
18.	18 May 1885	James LEE	Chelmsford
19.	25 May 1885	Moses SHRIMPTON	Worcester
20.	13 July 1885	Henry ALT	Newgate
21.	3 August 1885	Joseph TUCKER	Nottingham
22.	17 August 1885	Thomas BOULTON	Stafford
23.	5 October 1885	Henry NORMAN	Newgate
24.	23 November 1885	John HILL	Hereford
25.		John WILLIAMS	
26.	30 November 1885	Robert GOODALE (decapitation)	Norwich
27.	7 December 1885	Daniel MINAHAN	Newgate
28.	9 December 1885	George THOMAS	Liverpool
29.	12 January 1886	John CRONIN	Mullingar
30.	20 January 1886	William SHEEHAN	Cork
31.	1 February 1886	John HORTON	Devizes
32.	8 February 1886	Anthony Ben RUDGE	Carlisle
33.		James BAKER	
34.		James MARTIN	

35.	9 February 1886	John BAINS	Lancaster
36.	10 February 1886	John THURSTON	Norwich
37.	16 February 1886	George SAUNDERS	Ipswich
38.	22 February 1886	Owen McGILL	Knutsford
39.	1 March 1886	Thomas NASH	Swansea
40.	2 March 1886	David ROBERTS	Cardiff
41.	31 May 1886	Albert Edward BROWN	Winchester
42.		James WHELAN	
43.	15 June 1886	Edward HEWITT	Gloucester
44.	27 July 1886	William SAMUELS	Shrewsbury
45.	9 August 1886	Mary Ann BRITLAND	Manchester
46.	16 November 1886	Patrick JUDGE	Newcastle
47.	29 November 1886	James MURPHY	York
48.	30 November 1886	James BARTON	Leicester
49.	13 December 1886	George HARMER	Norwich
50.	14 February 1887	Thomas BLOXHAM	Leicester
51.	15 February 1887	Thomas LEATHERBARROW	Manchester
52.	17 February 1887	Edward PRITCHARD	Gloucester
53.	21 February 1887	Richard INSOLE	Lincoln
54.	22 February 1887	Benjamin TERRY	Nottingham
55.	14 March 1887	Elizabeth BERRY	Liverpool
56.	21 March 1887	Joseph KING	Newgate
57.	18 April 1887	Thomas William CURRELL	Newgate
58.	9 May 1887	Charles SMITH	Oxford
59.	16 May 1887	Henry William YOUNG	Dorchester
60.	30 May 1887	Walter WOOD	Manchester
61.	1 August 1887	Alfred SOWERY	Lancaster
62.	16 August 1887	Thomas Henry BEVAN	Knutsford
63.	22 August 1887	Israel LIPSKI	Newgate
64.	29 August 1887	William WILTON	Lewes
65.	14 November 1887	William HUNTER	Carlisle
66.	15 November 1887	Joseph WALKER	Oxford
67.	21 November 1887	Joseph MORLEY	Chelmsford
68.	28 November 1887	Enoch WADELY	Gloucester
69.	6 December 1887	Thomas PAYNE	Warwick
70.	10 January 1888	Phillip Henry CROSS	Cork
71.	13 March 1888	David REES	Carmarthen
72.	20 March 1888	James JONES	Hereford
73.		Alfred SCANDRETT	
74.	27 March 1888	George CLARKE	Winchester
75.	28 March 1888	William ARROWSMITH	Shrewsbury
76.	29 April 1888	Daniel HAYES	Tralee
77.		Daniel MORIARTY	
78.	7 May 1888	James KIRBY	Tralee
79.	15 May 1888	John Alfred GELL	Manchester

80.	17 July 1888	Robert UPTON	Oxford
81.	18 July 1888	Thomas WYRE	Worcester
82.	7 August 1888	John JACKSON	Manchester
83.	10 August 1888	Arthur James DELANEY	Derby
84.	15 August 1888	George SARGENT	Chelmsford
85.	28 August 1888	George Nathaniel DANIELS	Birmingham
86.		Harry Benjamin JONES	
87.	13 November 1888	Levi Richard BARTLETT	Newgate
88.	11 December 1888	Samuel CROWTHER	Worcester
89.	18 December 1888	William WADDELL	Durham
90.	1 January 1889	Thomas CLEWES	Stafford
91.	2 January 1889	Charles DOBELL	Maidstone
92.		William GOWER	
93.	8 January 1889	George NICHOLSON	Warwick
94.	14 January 1889	Arthur McKEOWN	Belfast
95.	6 March 1889	Ebenezer Samuel JENKINS	Wandsworth
96.	11 March 1889	Jessie KING	Edinburgh
97.	13 March 1889	Samuel REYLANDS	Shepton Mallet
98.	8 April 1889	Peter STAFFORD	Dublin
99.	10 April 1889	Thomas ALLEN	Swansea
100.	11 April 1889	John WITHEY	Bristol
101.	24 April 1889	William Henry BURY	Dundee
102.	7 August 1889	Lawrence Maurice HICKEY	Dublin
103.	21 August 1889	George HORTON	Derby
104.	9 December 1889	Benjamin PURCELL	Devizes
105.	24 December 1889	William DUKES	Manchester
106.	31 December 1889	William Thomas HOOK	Maidstone
107.	7 January 1890	Charles Lister HIGGENBOTHAM	Warwick
108.	11 March 1890	Joseph BOSWELL	Worcester
109.		Samuel BOSWELL	
110.	12 March 1890	William ROW	Newcastle
111.	26 March 1890	John NEAL	Newgate
112.	8 April 1890	Richard DAVIES	Knutsford
113.	15 April 1890	William Matthew CHADWICK	Liverpool
114.	10 June 1890	Daniel Stewart GORRIE	Wandsworth
115.	29 July 1890	George BOWLING	Wandsworth
116.	22 August 1890	Felix SPICER	Knutsford
117.	26 August 1890	Frederick DAVIES	Birmingham
118.	27 August 1890	Francois MONTEAU	Newgate
119.	23 September 1890	Henry DELVIN	Glasgow
120.	23 December 1890	Mary Eleanor WHEELER	Newgate
121.	30 December 1890	Thomas McDONALD	Liverpool
122.	2 February 1891	Bartholomew SULLIVAN	Tralee
123.	13 March 1891	John PURCELL	Dublin
124.	19 May 1891	Alfred William TURNER	Manchester

125.	21 July 1891	Franz Joseph MUNCH	Wandsworth
126.	28 July 1891	Arthur SPENCER	Lincoln
127.	18 August 1891	Thomas SADLER	Chelmsford
128.	19 August 1891	Robert BRADSHAW	Wandsworth
129.	20 August 1891	John CONWAY	Liverpool
130.	25 August 1891	Edward Henry FAWCETT	Winchester
131.	11 January 1892	Frederick Thomas STOREY	Greenock

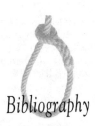

Bibliography

Aberdare, Lord. *Capital Offences Committee Report of the Committee*, London, Eyre and Spottiswoode (for HMSO), 1888

Adam, H.L. *Trial of George Chapman*, Edinburgh and London, William Hodge & Company, April 1930 (Notable British Trials series)

Altick, Richard D. *Victorian Studies in Scarlet*, London, Dent, 1970

Andrews, William. *Bygone Punishments*, London, William Andrews & Co., 1899

Atholl, Justin. *Shadow of the Gallows*, London, John Long, 1954

Atholl, Justin. *The Reluctant Hangman*, London, John Long, 1956

Bailey, Brian. *Hangmen of England*, London, W.H. Allen, 1989

Beadle, William. *Jack the Ripper: Anatomy of a Myth*, Dagenham, Wat Tyler Books, 1995

Berry, James. *My Experiences as an Executioner*, London, Percy Lund & Co., n.d. (1892)

Berry, James. *A Criminal Record Or, Three Centuries of Executions*, Bradford, G.F. Sewell, n.d. (c. 1892)

Berry, James. *Thoughts Above the Gallows*, Bradford, Parker Bros & Co., 1905

Bleackley, Horace. *The Hangmen of England*, London, Chapman and Hall, 1929

de Crespigny, Sir Claude Champion. *Forty Years of a Sportsman's Life*, London, Mills & Boon, 1910

Dernley, Syd, with Newman, David. *The Hangman's Tale*, London, Robert Hale, 1989

Dewar, George A.B. (ed.). *Memoirs of Sir Claude Champion de Crespigny*, London, Lawrence and Bullen, 1896

Doughty, Jack. *The Rochdale Hangman and His Victims*, Oldham, Jade Publishing, 1998

Duff, Charles. *A New Handbook on Hanging*, London, Andrew Melrose, 1954

Ellis, John. *Diary of a Hangman*, London, True Crime Library, Forum Press, 1996

Evans, Stewart P. and Skinner, Keith. *The Ultimate Jack the Ripper Sourcebook*, London, Robinson, 2000

Evans, Stewart P. and Skinner, Keith. *Jack the Ripper: Letters From Hell*, Stroud, Sutton Publishing, 2001

Fielding, Steve. *The Hangman's Record, Vol. One 1868–1899*, Beckenham, Chancery House Press, 1994

Friedland, Martin L. *The Trials of Israel Lipski*, London, Macmillan, 1984

Furniss, Harold. 'James Berry Constable, Bootmaker and Hangman', in *Famous Crimes Past and Present*, vol. IV, no. 44, n.d. (*c.* 1904)

Gatrell, V.A.C. *The Hanging Tree*, Oxford, Oxford University Press, 1994

Goodman, Jonathan and Waddell, Bill. *The Black Museum*, London, Harrap, 1987

Griffiths, Major Arthur. *Fifty Years of Public Service*, London, Cassell and Company, n.d.

Hobhouse, Stephen and Brockway, A. Fenner (eds). *English Prisons To-day*, London, Longmans, Green and Co., 1922

Holgate, Mike. *The Secret of the Babbacombe Murder*, Newton Abbot, Peninsula Press, 1995

Holgate, Mike and Waugh, Ian David. *The Man They Could Not Hang*, Stroud, Sutton, 2005.

Honeycombe, Gordon. *The Murders of the Black Museum 1870–1970*, London, Hutchinson, 1982

Hopkins, R. Thurston. *Life and Death at the Old Bailey*, London, Herbert Jenkins, 1935

Jones, Elwyn. *The Last Two to Hang*, London, Macmillan, 1966

Lambley, Terry. *Nottingham: A Place of Execution*, Nottingham, Terry Lambley, 1981

Laurence, John. *A History of Capital Punishment*, London, Sampson Low, Marston & Co. Ltd, n.d.

Lee, John. *The Man They Could Not Hang*, London, C. Arthur Pearson, 1908

Mackie, Charles (comp. by). *Norfolk Annals, Vol. II. 1851–1900*, Norwich, Norfolk Chronicle, 1901

Pierrepoint, Albert. *Executioner Pierrepoint, An Autobiography*, London, Harrap, 1974

Potter, Harry. *Hanging In Judgment*, London, SCM Press, 1993

Royal Commission on Capital Punishment 1949–1953 Report, London, HMSO, 1953

Rumbelow, Donald. *The Triple Tree: Newgate, Tyburn, and the Old Bailey*, London, Harrap, 1982

Scott, George Ryley. *The History of Capital Punishment*, London, Torchstream Books, 1950

Sims, George R. *Glances Back*, London, Jarrolds, 1917

Smith, Lieut Col Sir Henry. *From Constable to Commissioner*, London, Chatto & Windus, 1910

Stewart, William. *Jack the Ripper: A New Theory*, London, Quality Press, 1939

Stockman, Rocky. *The Hangman's Diary*, London, Headline, 1993

Tod, T.M. *The Scots Black Kalendar*, Perth, Munro & Scott, 1938

Vincent, Benjamin. *Haydn's Dictionary of Dates*, London, Ward, Lock & Co, 1910

White, Bryan. *The Murders of Gloucestershire, Hangings in Gloucester Prison (and others) 1872–1939*, Gloucester, Senior Officer White PRO, 1985

Wilson, Patrick. *Murderess*, London, Michael Joseph, 1971
Winslow, L. Forbes. *Recollections of Forty Years*, London, John Ouseley Ltd,
 1910
Young, Alex F. *The Encyclopaedia of Scottish Executions*, Orpington, Eric Dobby,
 1998

OFFICIAL DOCUMENTS

HO 144/212/A48697 A–F: *Home Office files on James Berry*
PCOM 8/191: *Prison Commissioners' file on James Berry*
PCOM 8/192: *Prison Commissioners' file on James Billington*
HO 144/148/A38492 XC12399: *Home Office files re. failed John Lee execution*
PCOM 8/87 XC12455: *Prison Commissioners' file on failed Lee execution*

NEWSPAPERS

Birmingham Daily Gazette
Birmingham Daily Post
Bradford Daily Argus
Bradford Daily Telegraph
Bradford Observer
Bradford Telegraph and Argus
Daily Graphic
Daily Mail
Daily Mirror
Doncaster Reporter
Dundee Advertiser
Durham Chronicle
Eastern Daily Press
Essex Herald
Glasgow Herald
Gloucester Chronicle
Hereford Journal
Herts Advertiser and St Albans Times
Kent County Standard
Leeds Mercury
Liverpool Daily Post
News of the World
New York Times
Norfolk Chronicle
Nottingham Evening News
Oxford Times
Saturday Evening Post
Saturday Post
Thomson's Weekly News
Times

Torquay Times
Yorkshire Evening Post
Yorkshire Post

PERIODICALS

British Medical Journal
Cassell's Saturday Journal
Hansard
Illustrated Police News
Justice of the Peace
Moonshine
Police and Public
Reynolds's Illustrated News
The Umpire
Yorkshire Life

Acknowledgements

The invaluable help of the staff at the National Archives, Kew; British Newspaper Library, Colindale; National Archives of Scotland; Bradford Central Library; Celtic Research; the Controller of the Stationery Office; Her Majesty's Prison Service Museum; Madame Tussaud's; West Yorkshire Archives, is gratefully acknowledged.

The author would also like to thank the following individuals for their support, assistance and generosity in the compilation of this work: John Adams, Charles Ashton, the late Eric Barton, Jeremy Beadle, Colin Bidwell, Peter Birchwood, the late Ray Cole, Joan Cole, Undine Concannon, Nicholas Culpeper, Rodney Dale, Dr Peter Davies, Steve Fielding, Peter J.R. Goodall, Jonathan Goodman, Mike Holgate, Gareth Jenkins, Andy Jones, Susanna Lamb, Terry Lambley, Peter Lovesey, Joe Mawson, Denis Perriam, Sarah Powell, Donald Rumbelow, the late Edwin Rutter, Keith Skinner, Richard Spendlove, Matthew Spicer, Paul Taylor, Ian Waugh, and last, but certainly not least, my friend and mentor Richard Whittington-Egan.

Special thanks are due to John Adams, another 'son of Bradford', for his excellent photographs of locations at Bradford as they are today. The invaluable advice and guidance of Christopher Feeney and Sarah Bryce at Sutton Publishing is also acknowledged with gratitude.

For assistance above and beyond the call of duty, a special acknowledgement is made to Nick Connell and to my ever-supportive wife Rosemarie.

Index

Index